Alan H. Monroe
Purdue University

Douglas Ehninger
University of Iowa

PRINCIPLES OF SPEECH

5th brief edition

Scott, Foresman and Company

Chicago   Atlanta   Dallas   Palo Alto   Fair Lawn, N.J.

PREFACE

Principles of Speech, Fifth Brief Edition, is designed for use in courses calling for a minimum of textbook work, in short courses, and in courses where training in speech and training in writing are closely related or combined.

Since the effectiveness of the previous editions has been widely proved in practical classroom use, this fifth edition preserves their general approach and concise development. The succinct, straightforward treatment of essential topics has been achieved, however, without sacrificing the inclusion of essential illustrative material. The first eight chapters explain and illustrate the basic principles of speech preparation and delivery. The following six chapters treat, in order, speeches to inform, speeches to persuade, speeches for special occasions, broadcast speeches, discussion, and parliamentary procedure. Assignments accompanying the discussions of these important speaking situations require the student to apply principles explained in the first eight chapters.

For this edition, the text of the entire book has been carefully revised. New oral and written exercises have been added to the assignments found at the end of each chapter, and lists of books and articles for collateral reading have been supplied. Examples and statements have been updated and a new illustration program has been developed to complement the explanation of principles presented in the text. Among the innovations in this edition is the grouping of material on parliamentary procedure so as to comprise a separate chapter (14). The discussion of listening, previously a part of the Supplement, is now a unit in Chapter 3, "The Speech Purpose and the Audience." Chapter 3 of the fourth edition, "How to Stand Up and Be Heard," has been divided into two chapters, "Physical Behavior on the Platform" (4) and "Using the Voice" (5). Moreover, the redevelopment of materials has resulted in two new chapters, "Speech: Nature and Function" (2) and "Beginning and Ending a Speech" (8). Finally, a completely new set of sample speeches has been supplied in the Appendix, and the sample speeches to inform and to persuade have been analyzed in headnotes and marginal comments.

In the preparation of this new edition the authors are particularly indebted to the following persons: Professors James Grissinger of Otterbein College, Harry P. Kerr of Harvard University, Wayne C. Minnick of Florida State University, Thomas M. Scheidel of the University of Illinois, and Donald E. Sikkink of South Dakota State College for suggestions concerning the book as a whole; Professor John W. Black of Ohio State University for his careful reading of Chapter 5 and Professor Wayne E. Brockriede of the University of Oklahoma for checking several technical points in Chapter 14; Professors James Golden of Muskingum College, Ralph Eubanks of the University of Arkansas, and Donovan Ochs and Paul Newman of the University of Iowa for supplying texts of student speeches. In addition, Professors Paul Heinberg of the University of Iowa and George Gunkle of Hunter College made helpful suggestions concerning the voice exercises at the end of Chapter 5 and answered questions concerning other statements in this chapter. Besides the persons here named, the authors wish to acknowledge their debt to the many teachers and students who over the years have made useful suggestions concerning the book, to the authors, speakers, and publishers who have given permission for the use of their textual materials, and to companies and individuals who have supplied photographs.

If the students who use this *Fifth Brief Edition* learn more fully to appreciate the value of good speech and to increase their own skill in speaking and listening to others speak, our purpose will have been fulfilled.

A.H.M.
West Lafayette, Indiana

D.E.
Iowa City, Iowa

CONTENTS

LIST OF ILLUSTRATIONS AND ACKNOWLEDGMENTS

*The authors and the publisher are grateful to those
who contributed materials for the illustration program.
The following list provides information regarding the
subject and the source of illustrative materials.*

SPEECH SITUATIONS: *left,* Herb Comess Photo; *others,* From Max Tharpe Photo Library (3) /**3.**   Linda Crowell, T. Wong Studio /**18.**   SPEAKERS AND LISTENERS: *left to right,* United Press International, Wide World Photos, Inc., United Nations (2) /**25.**   Figure 1, The speech act /**27.**   Figure 2, The communication chain /**28-29.**   AUDIENCE RESPONSE: *left to right,* United Nations, Kalamazoo College, *The New York Times* /**41.**   AUDIENCES: *counterclockwise,* Courtesy of Bethlehem Steel Company, United Press International, Herb Comess Photo /**46.**   AUDIENCES: *left to right,* National Aeronautics and Space Administration, United Press International /**47.**   LISTENING BEHAVIOR: Herb Comess Photos (2) /**55.**   Dwight D. Eisenhower, International News Photos (3) /**61.**   Carl Sandburg, Photo from European; Billy Graham, Wide World Photos, Inc.; Douglas Dillon, *U.S. News & World Report;* Walter Reuther, Nate Fine Photo; J. Roscoe Miller, Herb Comess Photo; Fulton J. Sheen, The Society for the Propagation of the Faith; Martin Luther King, Wide World Photos, Inc.; Enzo Ferrari, *Newsweek* — Curtis G. Pepper /**64-65.**   Drawing, The voice as a wind instrument, Arnold Ryan Chalfant and Associates /**76.**   Drawings, The vocal mechanism (4), Arnold Ryan Chalfant and Associates /**78-79.**   Mouth positions in the formation of sounds, Photos by Jim Ballard (9) /**81.**   VISUAL AIDS: *left to right, top to bottom,* University of Iowa, Photo by Jim Ballard, E. I. du Pont de Nemours & Company, University of Iowa /**126.**   VISUAL AIDS: *upper left,* Courtesy of Bethlehem Steel Company, *upper right,* A.T. & T. Photo; *lower left,* Photo by Jim Ballard /**127.**   Diagram, Arnold Ryan Chalfant and Associates /**129.**   INFORMATIVE SPEECHES: *left to right,* Courtesy of Bethlehem Steel Company, National Aeronautics and Space Administration, Herb Comess Photo /**179.**   PERSUASIVE SPEECH: John F. Kennedy, United Press International /**197.**   MOTIVATED SEQUENCE: Adlai E. Stevenson and UN General Assembly, United Nations (2) /**208-209.**   BROADCAST SITUATIONS: *left to right,* Bradley University, Bradley University, The University of Michigan /**239.**   Lyndon B. Johnson, United Press International /**241.**   "Vistas" program, Donald J. Smetzer Photo, WBBM-TV, CBS Television, Chicago /**247.**   GROUP DISCUSSIONS: *left to right,* From Max Tharpe Photo Library, Kalamazoo College, Bradley University /**253.**   Chart, Parliamentary procedure for handling motions /**280-281.**   Guy Suits, Courtesy of General Electric Research Laboratory /**286.**   Thomas J. Watson, Jr., Courtesy of International Business Machines Corporation /**295.**

CHAPTER 1

BASIC REQUIREMENTS

PRESIDENT SPEAKS TO NATION 8:30 TONIGHT. This announcement heard over radio and television or read in the newspapers at a time of national crisis always arouses strong interest. Why does the President *speak* instead of issuing a written statement? Obviously he feels that by speaking he can make a more personal appeal for unified national support. Because of the great prestige of his office, the President's speech is front-page news. Not as newsworthy, perhaps, but equally significant is the fact that every day one hundred eighty-three million other citizens of this country speak, too. We order groceries, discuss the neighbor's new car, sell life insurance, teach school, address local groups, hold conferences and committee meetings, argue on street corners, or pay compliments to our sweethearts. All of these situations indicate that speech is a necessary part of our daily lives.

Because we use speech constantly, we tend to forget how important it is to us. But if we think for a minute, we will realize how difficult our lives would be if we could not talk. Furthermore, just talking is not in itself sufficient; we also need to talk *well*. Consider the ten or fifteen most influential men or women in your home community. Is it not true that most of them are able speakers? In a democratic society such as ours, the ability to express ideas is almost as essential as the capacity to have ideas. Even in your own circle of friends, the impression you make depends a great deal upon the ease and vigor with which you talk, the

tact with which you advance and defend your convictions, and the attractiveness of your speaking manner.

CHARACTERISTICS OF A GOOD SPEAKER

In speaking, as in most human activities, success depends upon a combination of factors. A good speaker, according to most authorities both ancient and modern, must have integrity, knowledge, self-confidence, and skill.

Integrity

Some nineteen hundred years ago the Roman teacher Quintilian insisted that a good speaker must first of all be a good man. Listeners, Quintilian maintained, cannot separate what is said from the person who says it; they are influenced by their impression of the speaker as well as by the arguments he presents.

If a person is habitually devious or unreliable, speech training may give him skills, but it cannot make him effective. His actions will contradict his words: he cannot convincingly urge honesty in government if he himself cheats in school or business; his appeal for an open mind in others will go unheeded if he himself is bigoted. Even a speaker's choice of words and arguments betrays his character, for he may habitually appear to dodge issues rather than face them or to say what is popular rather than say what is true or just. A speaker of poor character may succeed for a time, but in the long run he will be found out and his appeals will be discounted.

Knowledge

Acquiring the knowledge necessary to become a good speaker is a lifelong and cumulative task. Through thoughtful reading, listening, and observing, you can gain increased intellectual depth and maturity. While the first speeches you deliver may be on relatively simple subjects and may be based in part on personal experiences, they should present worth-while ideas and considered convictions. Soon you will want to reach out beyond immediate and familiar topics — to learn and to speak about subjects in new fields. The more you learn about many subjects, the more effective your speaking will become. Moreover, what you say on any particular topic will reflect the knowledge and understanding of the educated person.

Confidence

A self-confident speaker has an erect but comfortable posture; natural, easy gestures; direct eye contact with his audience; and earnestness and energy in his voice. Moreover, he adapts his information and arguments to the attitudes of his listeners.

Many factors help determine the amount of nervousness a speaker may feel — including the amount of sleep he had the night before his speech.[1] But the experience of many generations of speakers has shown that, in addition to preparing carefully, you can do much to increase your poise and self-control by following three simple rules.

1. *Speak as often as you can.* The first time a person drives a car or flies an airplane alone, he is likely to be tense and unsure of himself, but with each additional experience his confidence grows. In the same way, each successful speech you make will strengthen your self-assurance. Welcome every opportunity to speak, both in your classes and to groups

---

[1] See Theodore Clevenger, Jr., "A Synthesis of Experimental Research in Stage Fright," *Quarterly Journal of Speech*, XLV (April 1959), 134-145.

in the community. Select subjects that you know a good deal about and that you are deeply interested in. Prepare your talks carefully. You will find that after a time speaking becomes a pleasant rather than a painful experience.

2. *Remember that some nervous tension is both natural and good for you.* Even in the deepest sleep our muscles are never completely relaxed. When we are awake our "muscle tonus" is higher, and it increases still more when the mind or body is called upon for some unusual exertion. Naturally, then, when you stand up to talk to a group of people, the tonus of your muscles will rise. But this only means that you are more alert and alive. Much of the sparkle that we admire in good speakers comes from this physical verve and energy. If you are keyed up before you begin to speak, regard this as a good sign; it means that there is small chance of your making a dull or listless speech.

3. *Never allow yourself to give up.* Each time you meet a situation and master it, the more confident you will become; each time you acknowledge yourself beaten or evade an issue, the less confident you will be the next time. Avoid setting yourself too difficult a task in your first speeches — that is, avoid subjects that are detailed or complex — but once you have begun to work on a topic, go through with the job. Confidence, like muscles, develops by overcoming resistance.

Skill

Fluency, poise, control of voice, and coordinated movements of the body mark the skillful speaker. Combined with the qualities of integrity, knowledge, and self-confidence, such skills heighten the speaker's effectiveness by enabling him to communicate his ideas clearly and attractively.

Skill in speaking is gained principally through practice. In practicing, however, take care not to develop artificiality. Good speaking is distinct and lively; it is forceful, but it is also natural and conversational; it commands attention because of the speaker's earnest desire to communicate. Note how speech becomes ineffective when these principles are violated. Doubtless you will recognize some of the following types of speakers:

The Elocutionist — one who talks for display rather than communication. He permits himself to be carried away by the sound of his voice and the graceful manipulation of his body, and forgets that his purpose is not to display his own speaking skills, but to get other people to under-stand or believe.

The Verbal Gymnast — one who makes a parade of language. He never uses a familiar word if he can find an esoteric one; he delights in com-plex sentences and mouth-filling phrases. Disraeli once described the verbal gymnast as a man "intoxicated with the exuberance of his own verbosity."

The Gibberer — one who emits a continuous stream of words with little or no thought behind them. He jumps from one point to another until his listeners are thoroughly confused. He usually concludes his speech with the abrupt remark, "Well, I guess that's all I have to say on the subject."

The Hermit — one who mumbles to himself. He may have a wealth of ideas, well-organized and developed, but he looks at the ceiling or floor, talks in a weak, monotonous voice, and makes no effort to be heard or understood.

The Culprit — one who seems ashamed of what he is saying. He shrinks from his hearers both in voice and manner. Sometimes he apologizes verbally; always he seems self-conscious and tentative. He is never forthright in his statements, and thus gives the impression that he does not believe them himself.

How can you develop the natural, energetic, conversational de-livery which the Elocutionist and his fellow "orators" lack? Your instruc-tor will help you overcome any special difficulties. The course of train-ing you are beginning is designed to develop your abilities steadily and naturally; and Chapters 4 and 5 will suggest many specific ways in which you can improve your use of body and voice. For the present, however, it will help you speak in a lively, conversational way if you always

1. have something you want to say;
2. want someone else to understand or believe it; and
3. say it as simply and directly as you can.

SPEAKING IN THE CLASSROOM

In many classes you are required to participate in informal discussions or to present oral reports. Some practical suggestions concerning these activities may improve your classwork and at the same time help you develop attitudes and skills that are useful in other speaking situations.

Class discussions

Be prepared. In the classroom as on the platform, you must know what you are talking about. Study your assignments daily, relate new facts and ideas to what you already know, think carefully about everything you read, and review materials systematically. Unless you understand the subject, your comments are apt to be trivial or irrelevant.

Be alert. Keep awake, mentally as well as physically. Stand or sit erect even when you are not speaking. Avoid giving the impression that you think the discussion is not worth your attention or that the subject is uninteresting. At least show your interest by your facial expression, and whenever it is appropriate, ask a sensible question or make a useful contribution.

Speak to the point. This is a cardinal rule. If you have nothing to say that bears directly on the point under consideration, then say nothing. Too often a student wanders away from the subject to discuss completely irrelevant matters, and by doing so sidetracks everyone. No matter how important your idea is, wait until the point under discussion is settled before you introduce a new subject. One point must be considered at a time if a discussion is to be profitable.

Talk loudly enough to be heard. Few things are as irritating as inaudible or mumbled speech. When you are asked a question, at least answer "Yes," "No," or even "I don't know" clearly and audibly.

Try not to monopolize the discussion. Keep your comments relatively short except when contributing important new information or developing a significant point of view.

Do not remain silent when you have something worthwhile to say. By all means, speak up whenever you can offer information or ideas which will help the group as a whole. Often it is only by combining the knowledge and thinking of all that the best judgment can be made or the correct answer discovered. If, therefore, you can illuminate a matter by an apt illustration, if you can cite accurate figures bearing upon it, or if you can relay the testimony of someone outside the class, do not fail to do so.

Speak also whenever you can clarify an idea which another person has muddled or when you can correct an error. This, however, must be done tactfully, to avoid giving the impression that you are attacking the person who made the faulty contribution.

Give and accept criticism graciously. If discussion is to be profitable, people must speak their minds freely. Sometimes this means that one of your ideas may be criticized or that you may be called upon to criticize an idea offered by another. When such a situation arises, remember that the purpose of criticism is to promote understanding and not to win a personal victory over an opponent. Frame your criticisms of others' views fairly and objectively; back up what you say with facts and figures; make clear that in criticizing the *idea* you are not criticizing or deriding the *person* who advanced it. When one of your own facts is questioned or one of your own ideas is attacked, accept the criticism graciously. If you think the criticism has merit, adjust your views accordingly; if not, refute it politely or ignore it. One of the hardest things a person must learn is to remain objective and dispassionate when ideas are criticized. Until you do learn this, however, you will never become a valuable member of any discussion or learning group.

Oral reports

Most of the oral reports you are required to present in class fall into one of four categories. They concern (1) some outside reading you have done, (2) a special laboratory experiment you have conducted, (3) a situation, condition, or event you have observed at first hand, or (4) the results of an investigation carried out by a study committee for which you are spokesman.

The purpose and content of reports on outside reading will vary, depending upon the nature of the material to be presented. In a book report for a class in history the author's style may be unimportant, but in a book report for a class in literature it may be a major consideration. Whatever the subject matter, however, it is usually desirable to follow the organization the author himself used in his book or article. Your job is to convey his ideas to the class as clearly and accurately as you can, and ordinarily you can do this best by following his own pattern of presentation. This does not mean that you should reproduce in detail all of the ideas and evidence which the original book or article contains. Your job as a reporter is to condense the material, selecting only the most important of the author's ideas, or to reduce the whole to a convenient summary or précis. You may also need to interpret points which are unclear or difficult and to evaluate the worth of the material. In any event, your report should faithfully reproduce the author's ideas and it should make clear how the book is related to the work of the course.

The report of a laboratory experiment may most conveniently follow the actual sequence of the experiment you conducted. Hence, it would begin by stating the problem you set out to investigate. Then it would review briefly the previous research on this problem, state the hypotheses you selected for testing, outline the testing procedure employed, and discuss the nature and significance of the results. In reports of this sort, visual aids such as diagrams or models may be especially useful, or you may wish to repeat the experiment before the class for purposes of demonstration. (For information on the selection and use of visual aids, see pages 125-127.)

Like a laboratory experiment, the systematic observation of an event or condition follows a well-planned method of investigation. Therefore, in a report of the observation you may reproduce the steps in the inquiry and then state your conclusions. In reporting on the flow of traffic on a city's streets, for example, you might tell when, where, and how certain traffic counts were made, why particular streets or intersections were chosen for study, etc. Then you would offer your conclusions or recommendations. In reporting an event such as a speech or a mass meeting, you might tell in a systematic fashion what you observed about the speaker, the speech, the audience, the room or auditorium, etc. Then you could evaluate the performance in terms of these and similar factors.

A report of the results of a committee investigation should make clear what the committee as a whole decided and not what you as its spokesman may think. Of course, where opinion is split, the minority as well as the majority view should be recognized, and if the committee could not reach a conclusion, this fact should be stated frankly. As in all reports, a systematic order of presentation is important; in many cases this may be a summary of the deliberations by which the committee reached or failed to reach a decision.

Reports, no less than speeches, should be carefully prepared and clearly and attractively presented. In these respects, the advice about the use of the body and voice in speaking (Chapters 4 and 5) and the suggestions for speech preparation in the next section of this chapter will be useful. Finally, in planning reports it is usually a good idea to save time for questions and comments by the listeners. Since your object is to present information and ideas that will be useful to others, you will want to make sure that everyone has an opportunity to understand as fully as possible the material you cover.

THE FIRST CLASSROOM SPEECHES

Having examined some of the principles underlying good classroom discussion and the making of oral reports, let us now consider briefly the talks you will be required to give in your speech course. In all probability, your instructor will ask you to make talks early in the semester—before you have had an opportunity to study in detail the principles contained in later chapters of this book. How should you go about preparing your first speeches? What should you keep in mind when delivering them? The following brief suggestions, which will be developed more fully in later chapters, should help you in your first speech assignments.

Methods of speaking

First, what method of speaking should you use? As your own observation has probably told you, there are four basic methods of speaking: you may present an *impromptu* speech, a *memorized* speech, a *read* speech, or an *extemporaneous* speech.

An *impromptu speech* is a speech delivered on the spur of the moment. No specific preparation is made; the speaker relies entirely on his general knowledge and skill. The ability to speak impromptu is useful in an emergency, but its use should be limited to emergencies. Too often the moment arrives without the spur. Whenever possible, therefore, it is better to plan ahead rather than risk the rambling, incoherent speech which the impromptu method so often produces.

A *memorized speech,* as its name implies, is written out word for word and committed to memory. A few speakers are able to use this method effectively, but usually memorization results in a stilted, inflexible presentation. The speaker either is excessively formal and oratorical or he tends to hurry through his talk, saying words without thinking of their meaning. Besides, with this method it is difficult to make the changes so often needed to adapt a speech to audience reactions.

Like the memorized speech, the *read speech* is written out word for word, but in this case the speaker reads from his manuscript. In speeches where extremely careful wording is required—such as the President's messages to Congress, where a slip of the tongue could undermine domestic or foreign policies, or in the presentation of scientific reports, where exact, concise exposition is required—the read speech is appropriate. Many radio and television speeches are also read from manuscript because of the strict time limits imposed by broadcasting schedules. Viewed as a specialized skill useful in certain kinds of speaking situations, the ability to read a speech effectively is important. But this method should not be resorted to upon occasions when the read speech is neither useful nor necessary. No matter how skilled you may be, in reading you almost inevitably sacrifice some of the freshness and spontaneity that are vital to effective oral communication.

The *extemporaneous speech* takes a middle course between the memorized or read speech and the speech that is delivered impromptu. It is planned and outlined in detail, and sometimes a complete draft is written out, but the words are not committed to memory. Instead, working from his outline, the speaker practices the speech aloud, expressing himself somewhat differently each time he goes through it. He uses the outline to fix the order of ideas in his mind and practices various wordings to develop flexibility of expression. If the extemporaneous method is used carelessly, the result will resemble an impromptu speech—a fact which sometimes leads to a confusion of these two terms. A proper use of the method, however, will produce a speech which is nearly as polished as a memorized one and certainly more vigorous, flexible, and spontaneous. With few exceptions, the talks you deliver in your speech class will probably be extemporaneous.

The essentials of speech preparation

Whether your speech is memorized, read, or extemporaneous, the process of preparation will be much the same. You will need to select and narrow your subject, determine your purpose, analyze the audience and occasion, gather material, make an outline, and practice aloud.

Selecting and narrowing the subject. Sometimes your instructor may assign the subject on which you are to talk. But whether you are given a subject or left free to choose one for yourself, you will have to adapt it to the specified time limits and to the interests and capacity of the classmates who form your audience. (See the discussion "Analyzing the Audience" in Chapter 3.) When you are free to choose your subject, you must also consider your own interests and knowledge. Whenever possible, talk about something you have learned through personal experience or about which you can discover more than your audience already knows. Select subjects in which you are vitally interested and about which you have fresh or original ideas. You will find that you not only speak better on such subjects, but that you will have more poise and self-assurance when discussing them.

The importance of narrowing your subject to fit the time limits cannot be too strongly emphasized. You owe it to your classmates not to intrude on the speaking time which has been allotted to them. Even more importantly, however, you will find that adapting your material to a predetermined time limit generally makes for a more tightly organized and more compelling speech. One of the commonest faults of beginning speakers is selecting a topic too broad to be treated adequately in the time available.

When you have settled upon a general subject, select some particular aspect or segment of it for your speech — no more than you can make clear or convincing within the assigned time limit. For a four- or five-minute speech, instead of discussing "How we can promote highway safety" tell "How seat belts save lives"; instead of explaining "How a big city newspaper operates" tell "How local news is gathered." The narrower your subject, the more fully you can explain or prove the essential points and the more interesting you can make your speech with illustrative facts and stories.

Determining the purpose of the speech. Too often a speaker arises to "say a few words" with no clear idea of his purpose in speaking. When this happens, his own time as well as that of his hearers is usually wasted. It is not enough to center your speech in a definite subject; you must also have clearly in mind the exact reaction or response that you want from your audience. You may wish them to *understand* a term or concept, to *believe* a proposition, to *take some definite action,* or merely to sit back and *enjoy* themselves. Frame your purpose into a clear, concise statement, such as the following: "Specific purpose: to explain the difference between *de jure* and *de facto* recognition." "Specific purpose: to prove that the sales tax is regressive." "Specific purpose: to secure contributions to the campus charity drive." "Specific purpose: to share with the audience some of my misfortunes as a baseball umpire."

Think of each speech as an instrument for winning a definite response from your listeners. Once determined, your purpose should constantly be kept in mind as a guide to the selection and organization of the ideas and facts that compose your speech.

Analyzing the audience and occasion. A good classroom speech, no less than any other, needs to be adapted to the audience and the occasion. Avoid topics which, though they may seem simple and clear to you because of some special experience or study, are too technical for the majority of your classmates. Also guard against imposing your own interests and enthusiasms upon others. The fact that you are an avid student of the social life of the Middle Ages or of Shakespeare's versification does not guarantee that everyone else in the class will automatically share these interests.

Finally, make certain that the speech you are preparing fulfills the assignment you have been given. Each of the speeches your instructor assigns will have a definite goal—to teach you how to organize ideas, to prove a point, to maintain interest, and the like. Always keep this goal in mind. Do not deliver a speech to inform when you are supposed to give a speech to persuade; do not support your argument with explanation and examples when you have been told to use statistics.

The adaptation of speech materials to audiences outside the classroom is considered at some length in Chapter 3. In the classroom and elsewhere, however, the basic principles are the same: Pick a subject that fits your listeners' interests as well as your own; avoid topics which are so specialized or technical that they cannot be understood readily; hold to the stated time limit. These habits which you may begin to practice now will stand you in good stead whenever you speak.

Gathering the material. Having completed your survey of the problem by considering the subject, purpose, audience, and occasion, you are now ready to begin building your talk. Ordinarily you will start by drawing together what you already know about the subject and deciding roughly what ideas you want to include. Nearly always, however, you will find that what you already know is not enough. You will need to gather additional information—facts, illustrations, stories, and examples—with which you can develop your speech. Some of this information may be acquired through interviews and conversations with persons who know something about the subject that you do not know. Other materials will be gathered from newspapers, magazines, books, and government documents, or will come from radio or television programs. In particular, such sources as the "News of the Week in Review" section of *The New York Times,* the *U.S. News and World Report,* the *Wall Street Journal, The Reporter, Harper's Magazine,* and *The Atlantic* should be consulted by a speaker who plans to deal with a current question of public interest. Many other magazines of general interest are indexed in the *Readers' Guide to Periodical Literature,* while numerous encyclopedias, yearbooks, government reports, and other reference materials will be found in your college library.

Making an outline. Early in your preparation you may want to make a rough sketch of the points to be included in your speech. A complete outline, however, cannot be drawn up until all of the necessary material has been gathered. When this material is at hand, you should set down in final order the main points you expect to make, together with such subordinate ideas as are necessary to explain or to prove these points.

In Chapter 7 are described a number of specific patterns by which the ideas in a speech may be arranged. Here, too, you will learn the form which a complete outline should take. For the present, remember two simple but important rules: (1) arrange your ideas in a clear and systematic order; and (2) preserve the unity of your speech by making sure that each point is directly related to your specific purpose.

Notice in the abbreviated outline below how the speaker covers the duties of the various members of a school theater staff. Observe also that instead of wandering off into a vague discussion of the nature of drama or of the value of dramatic training, he holds strictly to his announced purpose of explaining to his audience the job of each staff member. Such clarity of organization and unity of subject matter will make his speech easy to understand and remember.

Specific purpose: To explain the duties of a school theater staff

   I. The staff backstage sees that a play is suitably staged.
      A. The stage manager is responsible for:
         1. Building the set
         2. Painting the set
         3. Setting up the scenes on stage
         4. Shifting scenes between acts
         5. Storing the set after the performance
      B. The chief electrician has charge of:
         1. Arranging the lights
         2. . . . etc.
      C. The property manager . . .
      D. The costume mistress . . .
      E. The make-up chairman . . .

  II. The auditorium staff takes care of things "out front."
      A. The ticket manager . . .
      B. The chief usher . . .
Summary: (important points)

Practicing aloud. With your outline completed you are ready for the final step in preparation: practicing your speech for oral presentation. You probably will find that the best method is to talk the outline through aloud, following the planned sequence of ideas. Do this until you have learned this sequence thoroughly and until you can express each idea clearly and fluently. Then, laying the outline aside, think the speech through silently point by point to make certain that the ideas are fixed in your mind. Next, go through the speech aloud once again, but this time without looking at the outline at all. On your first oral trial you may omit some points and interchange others, but do not let this worry you. Practice until all the ideas are expressed in their proper order and until the words flow easily. The more surely you command your material, the more poise and confidence you will have as you stand before the audience. The self-assurance every speaker desires comes in large measure from always knowing exactly what you are going to say next.

When you can go through the speech several times without forgetting any point or without hesitating unduly in putting your thoughts into words, you may consider your preparation completed. As you practice speaking from your outline, however, preserve a mental image of your classmates and project your speech as though you were actually talking to them. Remember that the good speaker talks *with* people, not *at* them.

To summarize, then, the preparation of a speech requires six steps in three general areas:

	1. Selecting and narrowing the subject
Surveying the problem	2. Determining the purpose
	3. Analyzing the audience and the occasion
Building the speech	4. Gathering material
	5. Making an outline
Practicing the speech	6. Practicing the speech aloud

It may not always be possible, or perhaps even advisable, to arrange your work in the precise order given here. Of course, you will always have to survey the problem before you can start building your speech and you will have to build the speech before you can practice it, but the order in which you take up the steps within each of these general areas should remain flexible. For example, sometimes your analysis of the audience will determine your selection of a subject and, therefore, step 3 will precede rather than follow step 1.

Delivering the speech

Confident of the soundness of your preparation and eager to communicate ideas which are interesting and important, you now stand before the class. How, you ask, should I deliver my talk?

Most of the rules for effective delivery are based upon three cardinal principles: be natural; look at your listeners; communicate with your body as well as your voice. If you begin now to let these principles govern your delivery, you will later find it relatively easy to master the more advanced technics of presentation.

First, then, be natural. Stand and move about in your usual manner —just as you would if engaged in an animated street-corner conversation with a friend. Avoid an excessively rigid posture; above all, do not assume an artificial "oratorical" stance. When you are speaking you want the attention of your listeners to be focused upon the ideas you are expressing, not upon your delivery of them. Anything unnatural or unusual—anything which calls attention from matter to manner—is a distraction and should therefore be avoided.

Second, look at your listeners, not at the floor, the ceiling, nor out the window. People tend to mistrust anyone who does not look them in the eye, and hence they undervalue his ideas. Moreover, they always listen more attentively to a speaker who looks at them while he is talking.

Third, communicate with your body as well as your voice. Realize that as a speaker you are seen as well as heard. Movements of the body, gestures of the arms and head, changes in facial expression and muscle tension all help to clarify and to reinforce your ideas. Keep your hands free; when you feel an impulse to gesture, do so easily and naturally. Let other movements of the body also respond to impulse. Do not force them, but do not hold them back when they seem appropriate and natural. Earnestly attempt to convey your ideas to others, and sooner or later you will be motivated to some sort of bodily response, for such responses are an integral part of face-to-face oral communication.

Developing good speech delivery is essentially a process of habit formation; therefore, it does not happen overnight. Even the three simple principles we have just discussed may be difficult for you to observe at first. Do not be discouraged if your instructor needs to prod you concerning them. Eventually they will become habitual, and you will be able to forget about them. The important thing now is to understand what the principles of good delivery are so as to keep from practicing errors. Time and experience will take care of the rest.

SAMPLE SPEECH

The following speech by Miss Linda Crowell, a junior at the University of Iowa, was prepared to fulfill an assignment similar to Speaking Assignment 5 at the end of this chapter. The students in a beginning public speaking class were asked to present a three- or four-minute talk on a subject of interest to them and their classmates, and to supplement their own knowledge of the subject with information drawn from at least three printed sources.

Miss Crowell chose to talk on poor penmanship not only because she had long been interested in the subject, but also because it met the conditions of the assignment in three other respects: (1) it was simple enough for an inexperienced speaker to handle with ease and confidence; (2) it was potentially interesting and important to her listeners; and (3) it could be covered adequately in the short time she had to speak. This was her specific purpose: "To get my listeners to recognize the value of good handwriting."

In order to fit her remarks within the time limit and to preserve the unity of her speech, Miss Crowell chose to deal with only two aspects of the problem: (1) the results or effects of poor penmanship; and (2) its causes. She developed each of these topics in a clear and orderly fashion, and was careful to complete her remarks on the first before proceeding to the second. Thus, she avoided jumping back and forth between her points or making her talk a stringing together of unrelated ideas. Moreover, by dealing first with the effects of the problem and then with its causes, she followed a logical order which the audience could easily grasp and remember.

Miss Crowell opened her speech by stating the problem with which she was concerned, and aroused interest in her subject by a series of concrete references to "mother's shopping list, . . . sister's homework papers," etc. The use of the word *we* three times in the first paragraph made the audience feel a part of the problem and helped establish a friendly bond between speaker and listener. Through the body of the talk, Miss Crowell presented a number of interesting examples and preserved a natural, conversational style of expression. Her concluding idea made a strong personal appeal to the members of the audience by showing that good handwriting is at times a necessity for everyone and an important part of the etiquette upon which satisfying human relations depend.

On the whole, Miss Crowell's speech is a good example of what an imaginative student can do in developing a simple subject into an interesting talk. Practicing on subjects such as this enables speakers to attempt more difficult and complex topics with confidence.

Poor Penmanship[2]
— *Linda Crowell*

Something has happened to people's longhand lately. Either the art of penmanship is dying or everyone has started using a new language and no one has bothered to tell me about it! We boast the highest literacy rate in history, yet we can't make out our mother's shopping list, our little sister's homework papers, what a waiter scribbles on our dinner check, or our own class notes. We are always in a hurry, so we write in a rapid scrawl to save time. But often it takes more time than we have saved to figure out what we have written!

Mistakes due to poor penmanship are the cause of much lost time and money. The Handwriting Foundation, established by the leading pen and pencil manufacturers, estimates that illegible penmanship

---

[2] Presented January 1963. Supplied through the courtesy of Miss Crowell and Mr. Paul Newman, her instructor.

costs businessmen approximately a million dollars *a week* in scrambled orders, lost time, missent deliveries, clerical mistakes, and inventory foul-up. In a regional office of a large oil company, a card-punch operator misread a poorly written number and fed the wrong figures into her machine. Two thousand incorrect invoices shot out the other end. Illegibility on a national scale piles up astonishing statistics. Each day thousands of carelessly addressed letters end up in the dead-letter bins of our post offices. Each year as many as 400,000 taxpayers wait for refunds because the government is unable to read their tax returns.

The cost of bad handwriting to the college student is also greater than we might imagine. Transport, telephone, and other industries turn down thousands of job applicants because their handwriting is poor. In a survey of several hundred personnel directors, the Handwriting Foundation discovered that 88 per cent regarded legible writing as an important factor in selecting a job applicant. As many as 29 per cent used legibility as one of the criteria for promotion.

We have not always been a nation of scrawlers and scratchers. John Hancock signed the Declaration of Independence in a bold Spencerian hand, underlined with yards of loops and the curlicues of a broken bedspring. Spencerian writing gave way early in this century to the "Palmer method"—a system of endless muscular movements, of dashes, ovals, and "push-pulls." In the 1930's, the age of depression, teachers of penmanship largely disappeared. Good writing was thought to be a frill that could be eliminated from the curriculum. Today most children are taught to print in the first and second grades before being led in the third or fourth into the script form of writing. Most schools give only fifteen to twenty minutes a week to formal instruction in penmanship. The wisdom of shifting from print to script is widely questioned since many people revert to printing in some form in their later years. But whatever form is used, in the modern world writing has become a tool rather than an end product. The result is a handwriting like the trail of a wounded flea—a crazy, rapid scrawl.

The fact that people in a hurry write in a rapid scrawl has led to the belief that the busier and more successful you are, the more illegible your handwriting may become. Suppose young John Hancock was hired by a business firm today. He starts as an office boy. [Speaker writes example of Hancock's signature on board.] After a year he is promoted to mail room superintendent [example of signature]. Then he is promoted to office manager [example of signature]. When he is promoted to vice-president in charge of sales he initials the office memos [example]. But when he becomes president he immediately turns his correspondence over to a secretary to sign for him while he goes out and plays golf.

We all have illusions of grandeur. We can easily imagine ourselves in an executive position, with a secretary to attend to our writing and correspondence. Perhaps we pretend that we *already* have an acceptable "executive scrawl." This attitude makes it easier for us to ignore our bad handwriting. But we can find other excuses too. The trend toward automation reduces the necessity for writing. The click of card-punching, calculating, dictating, and duplicating machines is heard everywhere—doing our work for us. Such sentimental events as birthdays and appendectomies are taken care of—*for* us—by formal greeting cards. We say "Roses are blue, we're thinking of you," or "Here's a little note of cheer to hurry up and get well, dear." Our Christmas cards come with our names already engraved on them. When the old folks have a wedding anniversary we call the telegraph office and send form 31-B or telephone them collect to offer congratulations.

As more and more of our writing is done for us, the automation-bent world asks, "Why do we need better penmanship?" The penman has an answer that cannot be refuted. Perhaps machines will become foolproof; maybe the day will come when nobody who orders "shirts" gets "shorts." But handwriting is still a medium of good manners, and no machine can substitute for that. In a personal exchange the flow of affection, thanks, even of anger, is better conveyed by hand. There are times when we need to talk personally to our friends on paper, in our own handwriting, be it good or bad. There are times when it would be in the worst possible taste to type or to dictate a message. Legible communication—of the hand as well as of the heart and mind—is at these times essential.

Sources

Josef Berger, "The Lost Art of Handwriting," *New York Times Magazine* (February 19, 1961), 43.

Corey Ford, "Excuse This Hasty Scrawl," *Saturday Evening Post* (August 6, 1955), 25.

Robert O'Brien, "Moving Finger Writes—But Who Can Read It?" *Saturday Review* (July 18, 1959), 8-10.

PROBLEMS FOR FURTHER STUDY

1. This chapter has given you suggestions for communicating orally as a participant in discussion, as a maker of oral reports, and as a classroom speaker. Discuss the importance of these skills in classes other than this speech class.

2. In what ways are the speech activities discussed in this chapter employed in the student activity programs at your college?

3. What departments of your college are engaged in trying to learn more about the process of oral communication or increasing its effectiveness? Describe their efforts and achievements.

4. List and describe some of the kinds of speaking that may normally occur in the work of one or more of the following: a commercial airline, a manufacturing plant, an insurance company, a newspaper office, or a government agency.

5. With the aid of your instructor, select for detailed study a speech that has become important historically. Prepare to answer as accurately and completely as possible these questions concerning it:
   a. What had the speaker done prior to the delivery of the speech to establish audience confidence in his integrity, knowledge, and judgment? What did he do during the speech to help establish these qualities?
   b. According to the reports of observers, how did the skills of voice, language, and body help the speaker attain his objective?

6. Attend a speech or lecture given by some prominent person in your community—a minister, teacher, public official, etc.—and in so far as possible attempt to answer the questions asked in Problem 5.

7. Listen to at least two nationally known persons speak on television or in person. Compare the impressions you gain of their integrity, knowledge, self-confidence, and skill.

8. Analyze your own background of knowledge and interests:
   a. List (1) your principal curricular and extracurricular interests, (2) your hobbies and enthusiasms, and (3) the business or profession you intend to enter. Indicate how much you already know about this business or profession first-hand, or as a result of reading or talking with others.
   b. Make a list of subjects connected with your interests or your vocational objective—subjects upon which you think you know enough to give a good speech, or subjects upon which you would like to speak but need more information.
   c. List several social, economic, or political principles which you believe in and would be willing to defend.
   d. Select from the foregoing lists five or six topics upon which you might talk in class during the semester, and narrow each down to where it could be handled in a four- or five-minute speech.

9. Gather as much information as you can concerning the vocational and avocational interests of the other members of the class. Record this data in a systematic fashion and use it as a guide to the selection of the subjects upon which you will speak during the semester and as an aid in adapting these subjects to your hearers.

10. Analyze some situation in which you were highly tense and nervous— your first day in the army or on a new job, before an important final examination, while participating in an athletic contest, etc. What did you do to control your nervousness? How well did it work? Do you think this remedy or a similar one would help combat nervousness when speaking?

11. Take critical notes on any class discussion in which you participate during the next few days. Which student best exemplified the principles of discussion set forth in this chapter? In what ways were these principles violated by various members of the class? As objectively as possible, rate your own performance in the discussion.

SPEAKING ASSIGNMENTS

1. Conduct a class discussion in which you explore how each of the five types of ineffective speakers described on pages 5-6 violates the principles of good oral communication.

2. Following the suggestions on pages 8-9, give a short oral report on one of the following:
   a. Outside reading which you have done on (1) the causes and cures of nervousness while speaking, (2) how to prepare a speech, or (3) why integrity and good character are indispensable to success as a public speaker. (Consult the list of suggested readings below for sources of information on these subjects. Your instructor may recommend additional sources.)
   b. The results of first-hand study or observation—the campus parking situation, the study habits of residents in your dormitory, crowd behavior at an accident scene, significant changes in your college (or home town) during the last two years, etc.
   c. Plans for a coming campus event—homecoming, the junior prom, etc.—as developed by the committee in charge.

3. Following suggestions on pp. 10-17, prepare and deliver a two-minute extemporaneous speech in which you introduce yourself to the class. Cover briefly such topics as the following: where you come from, your major in college, your vocational objective, your extracurricular activities, your hobbies, trips you have taken, jobs you have held, etc.

4. Following the same suggestions for preparation and delivery, present a two-minute speech in which you illustrate from your own experience the truth of some well-known adage or proverb.

5. Again following the same suggestions for preparation and delivery, but supplementing your own knowledge with information gained from at least three printed sources, present a three- or four-minute speech on one of the following topics or a similar topic. Narrow your speech by selecting the one or two aspects of the subject that you think would be most interesting to your classmates.

Foreign sports cars	Highway safety
Today's headline story	The new comedians
Sailing as a hobby	Our city government
Low-budget motion pictures	An unusual new product

SUGGESTIONS FOR FURTHER READING

Aristotle, *Rhetoric,* 1356a, "The Character of the Speaker as a Means of Persuasion;" 1378a, "A Certain Character in the Speaker."

Waldo W. Braden and Mary Louise Gehring, *Speech Practices* (New York: Harper & Brothers, 1958), Chapter II, "How Speakers Prepare Their Speeches."

Theodore Clevenger, Jr., "A Synthesis of Experimental Research in Stage Fright," *Quarterly Journal of Speech,* XLV (April 1959), 134-145.

Paul F. Douglass, *Communication through Reports* (Englewood Cliffs, N.J.: Prentice-Hall, Inc., 1957), Chapter 1, "The Information-Decision Process," Chapter 3, "Case History: Organization of Ideas," Chapter 4, "Clear Statement."

Charles A. McGlon, ed., "How I Prepare My Sermons: A Symposium with Harry Emerson Fosdick, Joseph M. Dawson, Ralph Sockman, Vincent J. Flynn, Joseph Rauch, and Edgar DeWitt Jones," *Quarterly Journal of Speech,* XL (February 1954), 49-62.

Quintilian, *Institutio Oratoria,* xii. i, "The Orator Must Be a Good Man."

Edward R. Robinson, "What Can the Speech Teacher Do about Students' Stagefright?" *Speech Teacher,* VIII (January 1959), 8-14.

Eugene E. White and Clair R. Henderlider, "What Harry Truman Told Us about His Speaking," *Quarterly Journal of Speech,* XL (February 1954), 37-42.

CHAPTER 2

SPEECH:

NATURE AND FUNCTION

In order to understand and apply the detailed principles of public speaking described in later chapters, you first should gain some insight into the rhetorical and psychological foundations upon which these principles rest. What are the nature and function of speech? Of what parts does the act of oral communication consist? How are belief and behavior determined? From what sources do we gain knowledge about speech and its role in society? While comprehensive answers to these questions would fill many books, even a brief consideration should prove helpful.

THE SOCIAL FUNCTION OF SPEECH

One of the best ways to illustrate the nature of speech and its function in society is to consider various theories concerning the origin and development of language. There are many such theories. Some scholars believe that automatic cries of alarm, screams of pain, snarls of rage, and other emotional expressions form the basis of language. As human beings recognized these sounds and made finer distinctions among them, a means of communication evolved which became more and more specific. Gradually language systems developed, employing vocal sounds and written symbols as words to represent thousands of meanings.

A different suggestion is that as men found it necessary to work or fight together in groups for their common good, they discovered the

utility of audible signals in coordinating their effort. Thus, in lifting or pulling heavy objects, the rhythmic grunt which naturally occurred became the signal for all to pull together. A third theory suggests that language began with man's attempt to imitate the sounds of nature (like the child saying "choo-choo" for train) in order to tell about his experiences; and still another holds that meaningful articulation resulted from the movements of the tongue, jaw, and lips which accompanied changes in facial expression. Of course, none of these theories can be proved because we have no records of primitive ages; but a study of the known history of languages and of certain elements common to all language systems lends partial credence to some of them.

While the beginnings of human speech are lost in antiquity, the development of speech in children is well understood. Beginning with simple emotional cries of hunger, pain, and pleasure, the child soon reaches the "babble" stage—that is, he plays with sounds, making all sorts of noises apparently just for the fun of it. He gradually finds that certain of these noises produce reactions; his mother responds to some of his sounds but not to others. When he associates a given sound with the response it secures and begins to use the sound consciously for this purpose, he has discovered a "word." His parents meanwhile talk to him, and he notices similarities between their sounds and his own; through *imitation,* and with encouragement from his parents, he learns additional words and their meanings. Later, words are put together into simple sentences ("Bobby bye-bye," etc.) and gradually this process is extended to more complex phraseology as it keeps pace with the growing complexity of his own thoughts and actions.

Speech, therefore, develops in the child for the same reason that language developed in the race—in order to meet a social need. The child at first cries and gurgles merely to express his own emotions, but as his mastery of vocal sounds improves he discovers how to use these sounds *to get responses from other people*. As he grows older, he uses speech on the playground and in the schoolroom, at home and at the store, in the club and at work. But he always uses it to communicate with someone else, and through this communication he adjusts himself to his environment and his environment to himself.

Because speech is a means of human adjustment, it is a distinctively social tool. Thanks to our speech, we are not isolated individuals, enslaved by the forces of nature. We can join others to make discoveries, impart knowledge, and secure cooperative action; we can develop great industrial enterprises and political organizations, and we can hold these enterprises and organizations together and direct their activities.

Finally, by learning to think, to speak, and to write in language symbols, we can speed up the rate of our own development. In his book *Human Destiny,* Pierre Lecomte du Nouy, the biologist, points out:

> The incomparable gift of the brain, with its truly amazing powers of abstraction, has rendered obsolete the slow and sometimes clumsy mechanisms utilized by evolution so far. Thanks to the brain alone, man, in the course of three generations only, has conquered the realm of air, while it took hundreds of thousands of years for animals to achieve the same result through the processes of evolution. . . . Thousands of young dogs and cats and tens of thousands of chickens and other animals have been run over on the roads since the invention of automobiles. This will continue for a long time, simply because the experience of the parents who have survived by chance cannot be transmitted to the young for lack of speech and tradition. Articulated speech alone has already considerably shortened the time necessary for certain adaptations. What we call the education of young children can be considered as an extraordinarily quick short-cut, replacing the biological process of adaptation, and obtaining in one generation results better than those which required ages amongst the animals at the cost of innumerable deaths.[1]

---

[1] (New York: Longmans, Green and Co., Inc., 1947), pp. 120-22.

Because speech is a social tool designed to communicate ideas from one person to another, we must be careful to distinguish it from mere self-expression. We must not think of speech as a subjective outpouring of ideas and feelings; rather, we must think of it in its functional setting as a means of transmitting thoughts, attitudes, and emotions — as something that goes on *between a speaker and a listener*. If we do this, we shall be less concerned with what speech *is* than with what speech *does;* its form and beauty will be important to us only in so far as they aid in securing the responses we seek from others.

THE NATURE OF THE SPEECH ACT

What chain of events is involved in this process of communication; what happens when a person speaks to another?

Figure 1

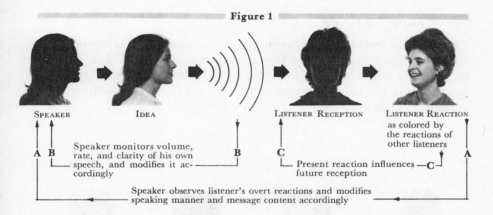

SPEAKER   IDEA   LISTENER RECEPTION   LISTENER REACTION
                                                                               as colored by
                                                                               the reactions of
                                                                               other listeners
A B   Speaker monitors volume,   B   C
         rate, and clarity of his own   A
         speech, and modifies it ac-   Present reaction influences —C
         cordingly   future reception

         Speaker observes listener's overt reactions and modifies
         speaking manner and message content accordingly

Speech as a circular response

First and most important, we must realize that the act of speaking is not a one-way process, but involves a series of interacting elements. The sound of your voice reaches your own ears as well as your listener's and causes you to talk louder, perhaps, or more slowly. Your listener reacts to your message by changes in facial expression or bodily posture, and in so doing not only sends meaningful signals to you as a speaker, but also influences his attitude toward ideas you will express later in your talk. Finally, because of what psychologists call "social facilitation," the reactions of an individual in an audience are influenced by the reactions of those sitting about him. If they seem to be enjoying or believing what you say, he, too, is apt to enjoy or to believe; if, however, they are reacting negatively, the chances are greater that he also will fail to respond as you desire. In Figure 1, the influence which a listener's reactions have on the subsequent behavior of the speaker is indicated by line A. Line B represents the influence the speaker has on himself as he monitors his own speech, and line C suggests that a listener's reaction to an idea, as colored by the reactions of those about him, determines how he will receive ideas presented later in the message.

The interactions described here are most obvious, of course, in the give and take of conversation and group discussion (see Chapter 13). They are equally present in the public speaking situation, however, and unless the speaker adapts to them, his talk can hardly be a success.

The communication chain

Because interaction between speaker and listener is continuous, communication is a circular process which contains no true starting or stopping points. For the sake of simplicity, however, let us break the communication chain into arbitrary segments and describe it as if its various elements always appeared in a regular sequence. (1) We begin

Figure 2

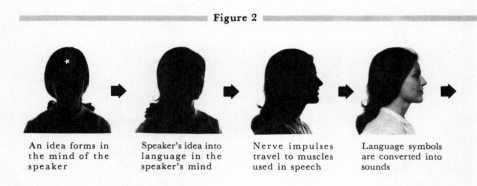

An idea forms in the mind of the speaker

Speaker's idea into language in the speaker's mind

Nerve impulses travel to muscles used in speech

Language symbols are converted into sounds

with a speaker who has an idea which he wishes to communicate to a listener. How he arrived at the idea is itself a complex process which would take many pages to describe.[2] This process, however, is of no concern to us at the moment; nor are we interested in why the speaker wants to transmit his idea to another person. We begin at the point where he has the idea and desires to tell it. (2) In order to communicate, the speaker must translate the idea into language symbols of some kind: words, phrases, sentences — in English or some other language. As yet, however, these language symbols are mental concepts only; they have not emerged from the speaker's mind. To make these symbols audible, (3) nerve impulses from the central nervous system must actuate and control the complex systems of muscles used in speech — the breathing muscles, the muscles of the larynx and jaw, the tongue, the lips, etc. — and (4) these muscles must react in a coordinated movement to produce the proper sounds.

But these sounds are now no longer words and sentences; they are merely disturbances in the molecules of air surrounding the speaker, a wave pattern of compressed and rarefied particles of gas. (5) The

[2] See, for example, John W. Riley, Jr. and Matilda White Riley, "Mass Communication and the Social System," *Sociology Today,* American Sociological Society, R. K. Merton *et al.* (New York: Basic Books, 1959), p. 577, and Bruce H. Westley and Malcolm S. MacLean, Jr., "A Conceptual Model for Communications Research," *Audio-Visual Communication Review,* III (1955),9.

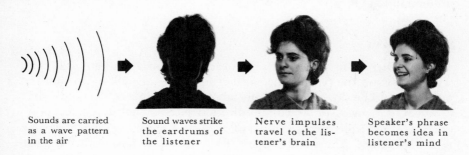

| Sounds are carried as a wave pattern in the air | Sound waves strike the eardrums of the listener | Nerve impulses travel to the listener's brain | Speaker's phrase becomes idea in listener's mind |

Notice that unless each step in the communication chain is present, the process of communication breaks down at some point and the idea cannot be transmitted from the mind of the speaker to the mind of the listener.

outward movement of these wave patterns through the air now transmits the sounds the speaker made until they strike the eardrums of a listener. (The use of telephone or radio, of course, introduces additional steps by changing sound waves to electronic waves and back again to sound waves.) (6) In the ear of the listener, the waves of compressed and rarefied air are again translated into nerve impulses and (7) are carried to the brain by the auditory nerve. When this happens, the listener has "heard" the sounds but he has not yet understood the speaker. As a final step, therefore, (8) he must recognize these nerve impulses as language symbols — words and sentences — and he must attach a meaning to this series of symbols. Thus, what the listener hears arouses thought and feeling in him. These eight steps are illustrated in Figure 2.

From the foregoing description and Figures 1 and 2 it is easy to see why speakers are so often misunderstood by those who hear them. A break or distortion *anywhere* along the chain of events which link the speaker's mind with the listener's will result in an idea different from the one intended. Poor choice of language by the speaker (step 2), poor articulation (steps 3 and 4), interfering external noise (step 5), partial deafness (steps 6 and 7), possession of an inadequate vocabulary or misinterpretation of the meaning by the listener (step 8) — a break at any of these points will result in an incomplete or distorted message. Similarly, a break in the chain of signals which the listener sends back to the speaker or which the speaker sends to himself (see Figure 1) will impair the communication process. In view of these facts, the wonder is not that we sometimes misunderstand one another, but that we ever understand at all.

Speech as habit

If each step in the process of oral communication required conscious effort on the part of the speaker and listener, talking to another person would be slow and painfully laborious. In spite of its complexity, however, for most of us communication is easy, natural, and spontaneous. This is because so much of the act of speaking or of listening to the speech of others is automatic. By practice, we have reduced most of the total process to the level of habit. When we see a certain animal, the word *cat* automatically occurs to us, and if we wish to talk about that animal, habit has established appropriate neuromuscular patterns which cause our speech mechanism to produce the sounds of the word *cat* without conscious effort. Even the sentence structure we use and, to some extent, the arrangement of our larger units of thought are influenced by our established habits of thinking and speaking. As the various steps in the act of speaking become habitual through practice, speaking grows easier for us. By the same token, however, the more our speech becomes fixed by habit, the less conscious we are of it *regardless of whether our habits are good or bad.* Practice makes permanent—but not necessarily perfect. As students of speech, we may profit by examining our speaking habits to see whether they contribute to the clarity with which our ideas are transmitted or whether they distort or impair communication.

THE BASES OF BELIEF AND ACTION

Throughout his history man has inquired with never-failing interest into the causes of his own beliefs and actions. Why do we accept one conclusion and reject another? Why do we choose a first alternative over a second? What forces move us to action, and why do we select the particular course of action that we follow?

As a result of this inquiry, many theories of human behavior have been formulated. But while these theories vary widely in detail and emphasis, on one fundamental they are in essential agreement. Man, they teach us, is *both a thinking and a feeling animal.* Some of his beliefs and actions are based largely, if not entirely, on reasoned judgments; others are almost exclusively the result of feeling or emotion; still others are "mixed" in the sense that reason and emotion each play an important part in their formation.

Man's rational beliefs and actions are perhaps best represented by his work in science and scholarship. Through long training and patient effort, he has learned to exclude desire and feeling from his investigations in these fields and to develop tests which bring his judgments into close accord with the "facts" of his environment. Man's irrational beliefs and actions result from his impulses, drives, and prejudices—those blind motives and desires which may cause him to buy what he cannot afford, to fear what he does not understand, to hate those who are different from him, or even perhaps to engage in mob action and violence.

Most of us, of course, strive to avoid purely irrational beliefs and actions. On the other hand, we find it difficult always to be rational.

Consequently, many of the decisions which direct our daily behavior both as individuals and as members of society are of the "mixed" variety. They have in them some measure of rational judgment, but they are grounded in wants and values.

The relative roles of reason and emotion in determining our "mixed" beliefs or actions have long been disputed. Some philosophers have contended that man is essentially a rational being—that it is this quality which distinguishes him from other animals. Cynics have gone to the opposite extreme and have argued that man's drives and desires exercise almost complete dominance over his beliefs and actions. Today many psychologists adhere to the so-called "field theory" of behavior, which holds that

> instincts, drives, and motives merely supply the going power or energy for most acts and perhaps determine the general direction of action. The specific acts are an outgrowth of the dynamic interplay of environmental factors and such organismic factors as attention, perception, learning, urgency of wants, and so on.[3]

While the welter of theories concerning human behavior may at first prove confusing, from them may be drawn two conclusions of great significance to the public speaker: (1) The speaker who would interest and inform, let alone persuade his hearers, must be mindful that man is both a rational and an irrational animal. Seldom can one achieve his end by appealing to man's rational nature alone or to his irrational nature alone. In the first case the speaker's material will lack the warmth and compulsion upon which interest, and consequently learning, depend; in the second, it will lack the sound explanations and cogent reasonings which are necessary to produce lasting conviction. (2) Whether man's judgments are rational or emotional, they are largely bound up with language. When we objectively reason our way to a conclusion, we manipulate words as the *names* of objects in order to save us the trouble of manipulating the objects themselves. On the side of emotion, civilized man has largely substituted words for deeds, the language symbol for the overt action. We become angry when we are struck by a word just as if we were struck by a fist, and we strike back in the same way; when lovers are separated, words of endearment and affection may take the place of caresses. Indeed, as some present-day

---

[3] Wayne C. Minnick, *The Art of Persuasion* (Boston: Houghton Mifflin Company, 1957), pp. 27-28.

philosophers suggest, language is but an extension of physical behavior, a form of symbolic action.

Because of the close relationship between language and thinking and language and behavior, the speaker who does not think clearly cannot hope to lead his audience to a rational judgment; the speaker who does not use language in a way that will touch his listeners personally cannot hope to appeal to their feelings and sentiments.

SOURCES OF KNOWLEDGE ABOUT SPEECH

Thus far in this chapter we have examined the social function of speech, the nature of the speech act, and the relation which speech and language bear to human behavior. From what sources is our knowledge of these matters and our information about speech in general derived?

For the most part, the body of facts and principles that compose the field of speech come from seven sources: *a priori* assumptions; expert opinion; direct observation; historical evidence; textual analysis, pictures, and recordings; experimental studies; and inferences drawn from other fields of knowledge.

A priori assumptions

To begin with, many important rules and principles of speech are "intentional" or *a priori;* that is, they have been chosen deliberately to represent a certain purpose or point of view. Consider the following statements: (a) "Speech is a tool for transmitting ideas from one person to another"; and (b) "Speech is a means of self-expression." If you accept statement (a), the effectiveness of speech will be determined by how well it communicates; but according to statement (b), effectiveness is to be measured by the beauty and precision with which one speaks. According to (b), you could make an excellent speech all by yourself with no one to listen, but according to (a), the perfectly worded and delivered speech will be useless unless someone else hears it and understands what you mean.

Few *a priori* assumptions will be accepted by everyone, and none can be proved true or false. Acceptance depends upon individual preferences. One must determine the aims and values to which he adheres and then make the assumptions that are consistent with them. As has already been indicated, the authors agree with the first assumption (a) stated above. Therefore, they use it consciously as the basis for many of the principles stated in later chapters. Whether you accept these principles, however, will depend upon whether you agree with the assumption.

Expert opinion

The fact that a great many people say a thing is true does not make it so, and even experts can be wrong in their opinions. Nevertheless, when there is substantial agreement on the truth of a principle among those who have devoted careful study to it, or when those who have used a given method agree on its value, there is at least a presumption that they are right. Many of the principles and methods included in the study of speech rest upon the subjective judgments of experts. Adaptations of statements by Aristotle and Quintilian, for example, are found in many modern textbooks. The successful application of these principles over so long a period is evidence of their essential soundness. Until proof to the contrary is presented, therefore, they may be regarded as reliable and applied with confidence.

Direct observation

A great deal can be learned about speech simply by observing others speak, analyzing the methods they use, and noting the results. Most of us make such observations in a random fashion all the time. By going about it systematically, we can improve the soundness of our judgments. We may select in advance the type of speaking we wish to study and the aspects of speech we intend to concentrate on; we may devise a standard form for recording our observations so that their bearing upon the principle or method we are studying can be summarized and a judgment can be reached.

Two mistakes should be avoided in making observations of this sort. First, one must be careful not to project his preconceived ideas into his observation. It is always easy to see what we *expect* to see. While an observer cannot entirely divorce himself from his observation, he can guard against undue subjectivism. The other mistake consists in jumping to the conclusion that what is observed in one or a few instances is necessarily typical. What is observed to be effective speaking in the United States Senate may not be effective in a business conference, or speech that is appropriate in an informal bull session may not be appropriate in a conversation with the dean. If the mistakes of subjectivism and unwarranted generalization are avoided, however, a great deal can be learned about speech by observing it directly.

Historical evidence

Men and women have been speaking for a long time. Although the speech of past ages cannot be observed directly, careful study of historical and linguistic source material discloses many interesting and important facts. The written reports of contemporary observers give us information about the lives, the manner of speaking, and the influence of great speakers of the past. Biographical material explains the influence of environment and education upon these men and describes the working methods and habits of mind that made them effective. A study of history enables us to understand the economic and social issues (many of them still pertinent today) on which they spoke. Linguistic source material helps us understand the particular meanings they gave to words and to reconstruct the pronunciations they used.

Textual analysis, pictures, and recordings

The texts of important speeches are usually available in written form. In modern times the speaker's voice also is frequently recorded, while newsreels and video tape preserve the visible as well as the audible aspects of delivery. Today such records are available not only for great speakers but for speakers of all kinds, and provide a valuable source of knowledge about speech. Vocabulary, sentence structure, types of logical and emotional appeals, intonation, pronunciation, appearance, movement—all these can be studied from appropriate types of records, and many such studies have been made.

Experimental studies

Certain aspects of speech may be subjected to experimental investigation by an observer who controls not only his observation but also the phenomenon studied. In order to simplify and narrow his inquiry and to rule out complicating influences, the experimenter sets up conditions under which he permits or causes the speech act to occur. Often he uses instruments or apparatus to secure accurate and objective data, or to measure his results. An increasing amount of knowledge about speech is being gathered in this way, including information about such widely different problems as how the vocal folds vibrate, what effect emotion has on the voice, how important humor is in influencing opinion, how to organize a talk most effectively, and what sorts of materials best command a listener's attention.

Experimental evidence may provide us with highly reliable information about many aspects of speech. We must remember, however, that the controls necessary for conducting an experiment tend to destroy the spontaneity with which people usually talk in normal situations. A person may not speak quite the same into a microphone in a laboratory while his thoracic movements are being recorded by a pneumograph as he does before a live audience and without this apparatus around his chest. We must be careful, therefore, not to overextend the conclusions reached in experimental situations.

Inferences drawn from other fields of knowledge

Perhaps no other field of study draws so heavily from related areas of knowledge as does the field of speech. Indeed, it is sometimes suggested that the discipline we call Speech is merely a series of related problems about the communicative act, all of which depend for their solution upon data supplied by neighboring arts and sciences. It is like the hub of a wheel, from which spokes radiate in many directions. The physiologist gives the student of speech information about how the vocal apparatus works. The physicist helps him understand the characteristics of sound waves. The psychologist gives him insight into the nature of memory and emotion. The linguist teaches him about the structure and history of language. The historian, sociologist, and student of literature all provide information which leads to a fuller understanding of human communication. You will find that many of the principles set forth in this book are based upon inferences drawn from these fields.

PROBLEMS FOR FURTHER STUDY

1. It has been said that speech "binds men together" in time as well as space. What do you think this statement means? Do you agree? Can you

think of instances in which speech tends to separate or isolate men rather than bind them together?

2. A man stands in the middle of an open field and loudly expresses his opinions concerning the administration in Washington, although there is no one present to hear him. Would you call this speech? If so, why? If not, why not? If you do not think it is speech, what would you call it?

3. Can you think of cases in which the listener has more control over the speech act than does the speaker? Can you think of other situations in which the listener has little or no control over the speaker's immediate behavior?

4. Construct a model of the communication process which combines the elements of the speech act as pictured in Figure 1 (p. 27) and the parts of the communication chain as pictured in Figure 2 (pp. 28-29). Through appropriate labels and lines make clear the relations among the various parts of your combined model.

5. At what points is the communication chain most apt to break down between normal speaking and normal hearing individuals? What can be done to guard against these breakdowns?

6. Observe your own behavior carefully for a day. Note which of your decisions or actions are based largely upon rational grounds, which are largely irrational, and which are of the "mixed" variety.

7. Estimate the relative influence of reason and emotion in such decisions as your choice of a college, a fraternity, a new car, etc.

8. Is an appeal to man's nonrational nature alone ever justified ethically?

9. Compare historical evidence and experimental studies as sources of knowledge about speech. What kinds of knowledge does each provide? Which seems more valuable to you?

10. Name some faulty speech habits that you have observed. What do you think were the causes of these habits? What can be done to correct them?

11. Find in at least three other courses which you are now taking some principle or some body of knowledge which has been or might be discussed in a textbook on public speaking.

12. May we make any *a priori* assumptions about speech that we wish, or are these assumptions, like other rules and principles, ultimately subject to empirical testing and verification? Explain and illustrate.

SPEAKING ASSIGNMENTS

1. Drawing upon sources suggested in the reading list below or by your instructor, investigate at some length one or more of the following subjects. Report your findings to the class, following suggestions for making reports that are provided in Chapter 1.

How speech and language originated
How a baby learns to talk
Language among animals
Nonverbal communication
Speech as a means of social control

2. Together with several of your classmates, investigate the concept of social facilitation, as developed in H. Kelley and J. Thibaut, "Experimental Studies of Group Problem Solving and Process," *Handbook of Social Psychology* II, Gardner Lindzey, ed. (Cambridge, Mass.: Addison-Wesley Publishing Co., Inc., 1954), pp. 747-752. Read also some of the sources suggested by Kelley and Thibaut. Then hold a discussion before the class in which you consider the ideas you have encountered and apply them to the public speaking situation.

3. Prepare a three-minute speech in which you demonstrate to the class how some simple device or gadget works. You may explain such things as a box camera, an unusual can opener or kitchen tool, an electric light bulb, a flashlight battery, etc. Do not try to sell the device or gadget to the class, but confine yourself to explaining how it works. Demonstrate the object itself and draw on the blackboard such diagrams as may be helpful.

4. Prepare a three-minute speech in which you explain to the class the background and significance of some current news event. Base your discussion on at least three printed sources as well as on any relevant radio or television news broadcasts.

SUGGESTIONS FOR FURTHER READING

David K. Berlo, *The Process of Communication* (New York: Holt, Rinehart & Winston, Inc., 1960), Chapter I, "Communication: Scope and Purpose," and Chapter II, "A Model of the Communication Process."

Jon Eisenson, J. Jeffery Auer, and John V. Irwin, *The Psychology of Communication* (New York: Appleton-Century-Crofts, Inc., 1963), Chapter II, "The Oral Code and Its Origin," Chapter X, "Communication among Animals," Chapter XII, "The Development of Speech in the Child:

First Sounds to First Words," and Chapter XIII, "Language Development in the Child."

Grace Andrus de Laguna, *Speech: Its Function and Development* (New Haven: Yale University Press, 1927). Reissued by Indiana University Press, Bloomington, Indiana, 1963.

Wayne C. Minnick, *The Art of Persuasion* (Boston: Houghton Mifflin Company, 1957), Chapter I, "Persuasion and Society."

Jurgen Ruesch and Weldon Kees, *Nonverbal Communication* (Berkeley: University of California Press, 1956).

Bruce L. Smith, Harold D. Lasswell, and Ralph D. Casey, *Propaganda, Communication, and Public Opinion* (Princeton: Princeton University Press, 1946).

CHAPTER 3

THE SPEECH PURPOSE
AND THE AUDIENCE

If a speech is to be successful, it must have a clear and definite purpose, and the purpose must be related to the interests, abilities, and attitudes of the listeners. Unless the speaker knows in advance the precise response he wishes to win, he is almost certain to wander aimlessly from point to point or to become bogged down in irrelevant details. Unless the response he seeks can be gained from the specific audience he is addressing, his speech will miss the mark.

In this chapter we shall discuss the twin problems of selecting a purpose and adapting it to the audience and occasion. Moreover, we shall consider how the achievement of the speaker's purpose may be materially aided by constructive listening on the part of his audience.

THE GENERAL PURPOSE

The response sought by an after-dinner speaker at a social banquet differs from the response desired by a college professor who lectures to a class, or from that sought by a legislator who urges the adoption or rejection of a bill. Aware of these differences, writers on public speaking have for many years recognized three broad or general types of speech purpose—to entertain, to inform, and to persuade. A speech to entertain, they have taught, seeks a response of "enjoyment"; a speech to inform, a response of "understanding"; and a speech to persuade, a response of "belief or action."

General purpose	Audience response sought
To entertain	Enjoyment
To inform	Clear understanding
To persuade	Belief or action

Although in every speech you will have one and only one general purpose, it does not follow that you will be unconcerned with the others. At times you will need to entertain in order to inform, and usually you must inform in the process of persuading the audience to believe or to act. In every case, however, one of the three general purposes is of primary importance while the others are contributory. You must see to it, of course, that the contributory purposes do not run away with your speech but are used only to help you reach your final goal. The following discussion treats each general purpose in its role as the *primary or ultimate end of a speech.*

To entertain

When your principal concern is to have the members of your audience enjoy themselves, the general purpose of your speech, as we have said, will be to entertain. Although humor is, perhaps, one of the primary means of entertainment, curious or novel bits of information or stories that have a human-interest quality serve the same purpose, particularly if they are striking or unusual; vividness of language and originality of statement also are important. Controversial issues, however, should be avoided; never "grind an ax" in a speech to entertain.

To inform

When your main purpose is to help the members of your audience understand something or when you seek to widen the range of their knowledge, the general purpose of your speech will be to inform. Such is the goal of the scientist who reports the results of his research to a group of his colleagues, of the college lecturer or work supervisor, or of the public figure who addresses community groups on a subject in which he is an acknowledged expert.

In order to convey information successfully, the speaker must relate his ideas to the existing knowledge of his audience, must organize his ideas so that they are easy to follow and remember, and must present enough concrete examples and specific data to maintain interest.

To persuade

The object of a speech to persuade is to influence belief or action. Many speeches have persuasion as their general purpose. Salesmen and publicists attempt to create belief in the superiority of certain products or organizations; lawyers seek to convince juries; ministers exhort their congregations to live better lives; politicians debate issues pro and con.

The essential characteristic of a speech to persuade is that it attempts to prove something; hence, it should be filled with arguments supported by facts, figures, and examples. In order to persuade successfully, however, you not only must show how your listeners should believe or act, but you must make them *want* to believe or act in this way. Therefore, in addition to facts and arguments, you must also introduce strong motive appeals; you must show how the proposal you are advocating is related to your listeners' interests. Your arguments themselves must satisfy certain basic drives that underlie and impel human behavior. So long as the substance of the persuasive speech is essentially logical and the motive appeals are aimed at worth-while ends, such methods for reinforcing and animating arguments are entirely acceptable.

While persuasive speaking often seeks only to influence belief, it sometimes goes a step beyond this and attempts to evoke a definite action from the audience. You may want your listeners to contribute money, to sign a petition, to organize a parade, to engage in a demonstration, or to do any of a hundred other overt acts. Because action is based upon belief, in developing speeches which seek action you should follow the same kind of outline as in speeches which aim only to influence belief. The single distinguishing feature of the actuating speech is that it goes farther; instead of stopping with arguments to secure belief, you ask your listeners to demonstrate their conviction by behaving in a specified way.

To entertain, to inform, and to persuade are, then, the general purposes which a speech may have. To attempt to speak with no more precise objective in mind, however, would be foolhardy. The general purpose of a talk must be narrowed and made more specific before you can hope to communicate successfully.

THE SPECIFIC PURPOSE

We may define the specific purpose of a speech as the *precise response* desired from the audience by the speaker. Formulated into a clear, concise statement, the specific purpose delineates exactly what you want the audience to do, feel, believe, understand, or enjoy. The following examples will illustrate the relationship between the subject of a speech, its general purpose, and its specific purpose.

> *Subject:* Accident insurance for students
> *General purpose:* To persuade — evoke action
> *Specific purpose:* To get members of the student council to approve the group policy offered by the ABC Accident Insurance Company

Or again —

> *Subject:* The effects of weightlessness
> *General purpose:* To inform
> *Specific purpose:* To explain to the audience the effects of weightlessness on the body and the mind of the astronaut

The formation of a clear and concise specific purpose is essential to speaking success because it forces you to clarify in your own mind the exact point which you wish the audience to understand or the exact belief or action which you wish them to endorse as a result of your talk.

Internal and external factors

In choosing the specific purpose of a speech, take account of both internal and external factors. By *internal factors* we mean those considerations which relate only to the speaker himself. What aspect of the subject do you know most about? What part of it interests you most? What are your honest beliefs concerning it? These questions are important because if you are to speak effectively you must center your purpose on those things you know best and in which you are most interested. If you are to speak honestly and sincerely, what you say also must reflect your convictions.

Important as they are, however, internal factors are not the only considerations which must be kept in mind when selecting the specific purpose. Equally essential to a wise choice are a number of *external factors*. These include the occasion on which the speech is to be given, the time limit assigned, and the type, attitude, and authority of the audience to be addressed. Because such external considerations are often overlooked by speakers, they deserve emphasis.

Occasion and time limit

Be sure that your speech purpose fits the spirit of the occasion on which you are to speak. The celebration of a football victory is hardly the place for a serious discussion of nuclear fallout or the necessity for tax reform, and a commemorative or memorial service is not a good place to promote your candidacy for a local office. Do not be humorous when the situation calls for seriousness or serious when it calls for humor. Fit your purpose to the expectancy of your listeners, as that expectancy is determined by the occasion on which they are gathered.

Similarly, fit your purpose to the assigned time limit of your speech. Given an hour to talk, you may be able to lead an audience to understand the working of the Federal Reserve System in expanding and contracting credit; but if you have only five minutes, it may be wiser to choose a less complicated subject.

ANALYZING THE AUDIENCE

As you learned in Chapter 2, the speech act involves a listener as well as a speaker. Talking to hear one's own voice may help to bolster courage on a dark night, but it is not to be confused with the quite different aim of communicating ideas to others. Often speakers forget this important fact. They become so engrossed in their own interests, so impressed by ideas that seem important to them, that they forget they are talking to people whose interests and attitudes may be different from their own. It is a fairly safe assertion that more speeches fail for this reason than for any other. The most important lesson a speaker can learn, therefore, is to see things from the standpoint of his listeners. You must continually ask yourself, "How would I feel about this if I were in their places?" To answer this question accurately requires a thorough analysis of the audience, since it is obvious that an argument which would convince some people would leave others unmoved, and what might be interesting to one audience would be dull to another.

But how are you to find out these things? The best way, of course, is to talk with persons whom you know will be members of your audience. If you do not know any such persons, you can often inquire of others who have had dealings with them. When these methods are impracticable, you will be forced to infer the attitudes and beliefs of your listeners from whatever factual data you can gather concerning them.

General data

Some, if not all, of the following facts should be considered when attempting to estimate the probable interests and attitudes of an audience.

The size of the audience. Will it be a small and highly homogeneous group of fifteen or twenty people, or a large and diversified mass numbering in the hundreds?

The age of those making up the audience. Are your prospective listeners in the same age range, or of widely divergent ages? Age is an important factor in determining people's needs and interests and also suggests the span of their experience with men and events. For a group of young people to understand certain aspects of World War II, lengthy explanations may be necessary; for an older audience, passing references would probably be sufficient.

The sex of members of the audience. Is it to be a mixed audience or are all of the members of the same sex? Men and women differ in their interests, though these interests frequently overlap. Some subjects

suitable for discussion before one sex are unsuitable for the other or for a mixed audience.

The occupation of the members of the audience. Occupation tends to suggest the interests and type of knowledge which people will have. A talk to the members of a county medical association will doubtless differ in purpose and content from one delivered before a local labor union. A fair idea of income level also can be inferred from a knowledge of occupation.

The education of the audience. Both formal education acquired in school and college, and education acquired through experience are important. A Chicago cab driver may not have had broad formal training, but through his work he may have gained a profound knowledge of human nature and of the conditions in his city. Remember to consider both schooling and experience.

Membership in social, professional, and religious groups. Rotary, Knights of Columbus, Sigma Chi, Country Club, Young Republicans, Business and Professional Women, Elks, Chamber of Commerce — what do these organizations mean to you? They suggest, in a general way at least,

How would each of these audiences determine the speaker's choice of topic, materials, and appeals? *Opposite page, counterclockwise,* supervisory employees of Bethlehem Steel Company are briefed on a new safety program, an audience listens to an address at a political dinner, and university students hear a discussion of ethics by Dr. Waldo Beach. *Above, left to right,* Congressmen in joint session are addressed by John H. Glenn, Jr., and men beginning Peace Corps training listen to R. Sargent Shriver.

types of people, points of view, interests, and special abilities. Whenever you learn that a sizable part of your audience is affiliated with some special group, you have gained a valuable clue to their attitudes and concerns.

Audience's knowledge of the subject

The information you gather about the members of your audience should help you make useful inferences about their knowledge in the subject area of your speech. Are they likely to understand technical terms without explanation? Are they likely to have more than an elementary grasp of the subject? Which facts will they consider new and significant, which ones boring and trivial? For a speaker to imply by the tone or content of his remarks that he thinks his listeners ignorant or for him to assume a condescending manner is decidedly tactless, but for him to talk over their heads is an equally bad policy. Your speech should be aimed at a level of knowledge characteristic of the average member of the group.

Audience's fixed beliefs and attitudes

From the time a child first begins to receive impressions of his environment, he starts to form beliefs and to establish attitudes toward aspects of that environment. These beliefs and attitudes are modified by later experience, but by the time we grow up most of us have through conditioning or habit arrived at certain opinions which form the fixed bases for our thinking and conduct. In so far as the experience of everyone is similar, our beliefs and attitudes will be largely the same. Such proverbs as "Honesty is the best policy" and "Spare the rod and spoil the child" are only traditional ways of stating common fixed beliefs. In so far as our experience differs, however, our convictions and attitudes will differ also. Some people, for example, accept only that which can be verified scientifically; others (though they may not admit it openly) believe in hunches, jinxes, and spells. One man may argue the virtues of a vegetarian diet, or of *laissez-faire* economic policies, or of progressive education; another man may think each of these things worthless.

The speaker who knows what beliefs and attitudes have become the fixed bases of his hearers' thinking and conduct can avoid arousing needless hostility and often can frame his proposal in a way that is more readily acceptable. If you can show how your idea accords with a belief already held by the members of your audience, if you can relate your plan or project to one of their existing principles of conduct, your battle is largely won.

Attitude of the audience toward the speaker

Ask yourself what attitude your listeners are apt to have toward you personally and toward your qualifications to address them on your chosen subject. Two things must be considered: (1) the degree of their *friendliness* toward you; and (b) the degree of their *respect* for you or your knowledge of the subject. These two aspects of listener attitude may vary widely. A father's affection for his small son, for instance, may be very strong, but his respect for his son's judgment may not be. On the other hand, the father may have the greatest respect for the judgment of a business associate even though he dislikes him as a person. Respect and friendliness are two different things, but both must be taken into account.

Adaptation to personal hostility. When there is reason to believe that your audience will feel hostile toward you as a person, your first job as a speaker is to attempt to reverse this hostile attitude. You can hardly accomplish the purpose of your speech unless you do so. The method used to attain this end will vary, of course, depending on the cause of the hostility, and the job will be easier if your listeners already respect you. Among other things, however, you will always want to *establish common ground* with your audience. This can often be done by one of the following methods:

1. By showing a friendly attitude toward your audience
2. By displaying fairness, modesty, and good humor
3. By pointing out your own agreement with some of your listeners' cherished attitudes or beliefs
4. By referring to experiences which you and the audience hold in common
5. By tactfully complimenting your hearers' abilities, accomplishments, or friends
6. By demonstrating a genuine concern for the well-being of all
7. By using humor that is in good taste, especially if it is at your own expense

Adaptation to an attitude of condescension. The thing *not* to do when an audience has a condescending attitude toward you is to appear conceited or antagonistic. Of course, you must seem self-confident, but you should temper your confidence with modesty. Gain the respect of your audience by showing sound thinking and a grasp of the pertinent facts. Avoid saying, "I think—"; rather, present the facts and arguments which make your conclusions evident. If it is necessary to mention your own accomplishments, do so in a matter-of-fact, unassuming way.

Attitude of the audience toward the subject

People are either *interested* in a subject or they are *apathetic* toward it. Apathy is usually present if they see no connection between the subject and their own affairs. When your analysis indicates that your listeners will be apathetic, you will need to show them how the problem you are discussing concerns them directly, or you will need to arouse their curiosity about some novel aspect of the subject. Utilize all available means for holding attention. Of course, you cannot neglect doing these things even when members of your audience are already interested because you must be careful not to lose their attention; but you must make a special effort to gain and to hold interest when your listeners are apathetic.

Attitude of the audience toward the speech purpose

If, with no preliminaries at all, you told the members of your audience the specific purpose of your speech, what would be their attitude toward it? This is what is meant by "attitude toward speech purpose." It is not the attitude you hope for at the end of your speech, but the one that exists before you begin. Since an audience is seldom uniform throughout, many different shades of attitude will usually be represented. It is best, therefore, to determine what attitude is predominant and to adapt your speech to that view while making allowances for variations in character or intensity of belief.

When the general end of a speech is *to entertain* or *to inform,* the attitude of members of your audience toward the purpose will be governed largely by their attitude toward the subject; that is, they will either be (a) interested or (b) apathetic. When the general purpose is *to persuade,* their attitude toward the speech purpose will be governed also by their attitude toward the specific belief or action which is urged; hence, their attitude will be one of the following: (a) favorable but not aroused; (b) apathetic to the situation; (c) interested in the situation but undecided what to do or think about it; (d) interested in the situation but hostile to the *proposed* attitude, belief, or action; or (e) hostile to any change from the present situation.

For example, suppose that property taxes in your college community are high and that fraternity property is tax-exempt. Under these conditions, suppose that your purpose were to start a movement for the removal of this exemption so that fraternity houses would be taxed. An audience of local property owners (provided they were not fraternity alumni) would most likely be favorable, but they might need to be aroused before they would take any concerted action. Non-fraternity students would form an apathetic audience since the proposal probably would not affect them one way or the other. The university administration and faculty on the whole would be interested in the situation because of their relationship with both students and community, but they would be undecided whether to support the plan (except those who were influenced either because they owned property themselves or were fraternity alumni). Property owners who were also fraternity alumni or sympathizers would be interested in the situation and desirous of some way to lower the heavy property tax, but they might be opposed to this particular way of doing it because of their fraternity connections. Student fraternity men, on the other hand, would be frankly hostile to any change from the present situation, under which they were enjoying a distinct advantage. Thus, a knowledge of the proportion of each of these groups in the audience would give a good indication of the complexion of their attitude toward your purpose.

Having determined the predominant attitude of your audience toward your subject and purpose, you should be guided by this knowledge in selecting your arguments and determining the structure and content of your speech. If your listeners are apathetic, begin your talk on a point of compelling interest or startling vividness; show them how your subject affects them. If they are hostile to the proposal, you may wish to introduce it more cautiously; emphasize some basic principle with which you know they agree and relate your proposal to it. If they are interested but undecided, provide plenty of proof. If they are favorable but not aroused, try to motivate them by using appeals which touch their needs and interests directly.

No analysis made beforehand is certain to be correct, and even if it is, audience attitudes may change even while you are speaking. Hence, it is important to watch reactions closely when your subject is announced and to continue to do so throughout your entire speech. The way your hearers sit in their seats, the expressions on their faces, their audible reactions—laughter, applause, sharp breathing, shifting about, whispering etc.—all are clues to their attitude toward you, your subject, or your purpose. If you are wise, you will develop a keen sensitivity to these signs of audience reaction and will adapt your remarks accordingly.

SAMPLE ANALYSIS OUTLINE

Keeping in mind the directions for audience analysis which have just been given, study the following analysis outline. Observe how the speaker used the facts at his disposal to draw a picture of the persons making up the audience he would confront, and how he planned to adapt his remarks to their interests and attitudes.

I.   Subject: Representation on the Student Senate

II.   Title: "Neglected Men — And Women"

III. General purpose: To persuade

IV.   Specific purpose: To get the members of the Student Senate to approve a constitutional amendment increasing the number of senators from the Independent Student Association

V.   Specific audience: Student Senate, Purdue University

VI.   Specific occasion: Regular biweekly meeting of the Senate, March 22, 1964, 7:30 P.M., Room 212, Memorial Center. Time: 15 minutes, following the regular order of business.

VII. Audience analysis:
      A. Size: About thirty persons
      B. Sex and age: Men and women, 19-23 years old
      C. Occupation: College students but representing a wide variety of interests and educational objectives
      D. Knowledge of the subject:
         1. A general knowledge of the provisions of the Senate constitution and present system of student representation
         2. A limited knowledge of the dissatisfaction among some independent students toward the present system of representation
         3. In only a few cases, specific knowledge of the problem through talks with the speaker and other students
      E. Primary interests: Their own educational objectives and problems, including membership in campus organizations and participation in campus activities
      F. Fixed attitudes:
         1. Political: Belief in the principle of equal representation for all
         2. Professional: Strong desire for success in their chosen professions; belief that participation in civic affairs will contribute to success and personal prestige
         3. Economic: Attitude not a factor because most of them are economically dependent upon parents or some other outside source of income
         4. Religious: Attitude not likely to enter into consideration of this speech subject
      G. Attitude toward speaker: Personally friendly — a fellow member of the Senate

H. Attitude toward subject: Interest because of their concern about all issues presented to the Senate

I . Attitude toward purpose: In most cases, interest in the situation but hostility toward the proposed change; belief that existing methods are satisfactory and fear of the loss of some influence or prestige

VIII. Proposed adaptation to the audience:

A. Introduce the subject by referring to the Senate's responsibility to treat all student groups fairly

B. Use visual aids to show inequities of the present apportionment of representatives

C. Make the primary appeal to their pride in fulfilling their civic responsibility by giving equal representation to all students

THE RESPONSIBILITY OF THE AUDIENCE: CONSTRUCTIVE LISTENING

In selecting a specific purpose that is adapted both to his listeners and to himself, the speaker increases the effectiveness with which he can communicate ideas. But because communication is a circular rather than a one-way process, it also requires activity on the part of the listener.

In addition to his basic tasks of translating sound waves into nerve impulses, recognizing these nerve impulses as language symbols, and attaching appropriate meanings to them (pp. 28-30), the listener has other important responsibilities. If the ideas communicated are to be of maximum service to himself and to the society of which he is a part, he must make a concerted effort to understand what he hears. He must decide whether the speaker's ideas are pertinent, useful, and true. He must judge whether they are fairly stated and adequately proved or supported. Finally, if he is to enjoy and appreciate the speaker's ideas, he must relate them to his own standards of taste and discrimination. Because of these varied obligations, the ability to listen well is just as important as the ability to speak well.

How can you learn to listen more perceptively and thus improve the accuracy and usefulness of the communication process? While you may make some improvement in listening ability as a matter of course, you will progress more rapidly and make greater improvement if you exert conscious effort. The following paragraphs point out some of the rules for good listening and provide suggestions for acquiring listening skill.

Comprehension

In order to understand the speaker fully and accurately:

1. *Concentrate on each idea as it is expressed.* Just as concentrating on the speaker's words may help you hear them above noise or interference, focusing your thought on his expressed ideas helps you to grasp them clearly. If your mind is occupied with worries about an impending examination or your acceptance into medical school, you may *hear* what the speaker says but fail entirely to grasp his *meaning*.

2. *Recognize the structure or pattern of ideas.* Chapter 7 on outlining presents a thorough discussion of arranging main ideas and subordinate points. Your comprehension of someone else's speech will be increased if you learn to recognize the pattern into which he has arranged his ideas. What is the central thesis? What are the main points, and how are they arranged—in time sequence, or in space, problem-solution, cause-effect, or topical order? What are the minor points, and to which main point do they relate? It is helpful to practice taking notes in a *structured* manner as the speaker proceeds.

3. *Note the supporting details and proof.* As you listen for the idea structure of the speech, note the relationship of the illustrative details to the main points. Listen carefully as the main points are filled in so that you can grasp their full significance and perhaps jot down some of the more important details. Above all, learn not to mistake vivid details for the main ideas they support. (Chapter 6 enlarges on this point.)

4. *Relate the ideas to your own knowledge.* In most instances your comprehension will be increased if you make an active effort to relate what you hear to what you already know. If you know little about the subject, some advance study will help. But whether you know little or much about the subject, avoid letting preconceived opinions close your mind to new ideas. A receptive, objective attitude is necessary for understanding and judgment; listen to *all* the speaker has to say before deciding whether or not you agree with him.

Appreciation

Speakers often attempt to lighten even the most serious speeches with details that are novel or humorous or have a strong human-interest quality. Therefore, appreciation is a characteristic of good listening even when enjoyment is not your—or the speaker's—main concern. If you

Observe the listening behavior of students during an informal discussion led by the late poet, Theodore Roethke. What principles of constructive listening are illustrated by persons in the photographs?

are listening to a speech to inform or to persuade, however, do not permit your appreciation of such details to keep you from the essentially serious task of comprehending or evaluating the ideas presented. If you are listening to a speech to entertain, of course, you do not need to subject it to thoughtful analysis. At such times, you can increase your pleasure with receptive and imaginative listening:

1. *Relax physically and mentally.* Sit in a comfortable, relaxed position. So far as possible, free your mind from other interests and vexing problems and worries.

2. *Cultivate a receptive attitude.* Do not spoil your pleasure by being analytical or hypercritical. This does not mean that you should be completely undiscriminating in your attitude, but that you should be in a frame of mind to react pleasurably to an entertaining speech.

3. *Use imagination and empathy.* Instead of holding back, enter into the situation. Give your imagination free play so that you can join with the speaker in responding to the experiences or images that he describes.

Evaluation

Critical and analytical listening are necessary for evaluation; therefore, appreciative listening, although not ruled out, must be carefully controlled. You must, of course, comprehend the speaker's ideas, but you must do more than merely comprehend. You must analyze the speaker's reasoning and judge the value of his evidence; you must recognize emotional appeal for what it is and accept or reject it knowingly; and you must not let vivid phraseology influence your judgment at the expense of a solid fact. (See the discussion of characteristics of persuasive speeches in Chapter 10.) Consider several factors:

1. *Evaluate the speaker's analysis of the problem.* As you listen, ask yourself whether the speaker has properly analyzed the problem and whether the proposal he advocates is the best way of meeting it.

2. *Evaluate the speaker's reasoning.* Is the speaker's reasoning sound or does it contain flaws in logic?

3. *Evaluate the evidence.* Does the speaker present facts and evidence to prove his points or does he use unsupported assertions reinforced only by vivid phrasing or his own positive manner? Does he present the facts fairly, or does he seem to be biased in presenting facts?

4. *Evaluate the speaker's emotional appeals.* Does the speaker use emotional appeals rather than sound reasoning? Accept or reject such appeals judiciously; avoid being swayed by emotion and prejudice when they are contrary to logic and fact.

5. *Evaluate the way the speaker words his ideas.* Is the speaker's wording accurate or vague? Are false conclusions suggested by loose phraseology? Does the speaker rely on loaded words, name-calling, and generalities instead of on reasoning and evidence?

Listening as a student of speech

In addition to increasing your powers of comprehension, appreciation, and evaluation, as a student of speech you have the special task of studying the speaker's manner and method. By so doing you can develop your ability to judge good speaking and at the same time note ways to improve your own speech.

To analyze a speech thoroughly, you would have to consider many points—in fact, nearly all the topics covered in this book. This would be a long and complex task. Begin by trying something less comprehensive. Each time you hear one of your classmates speak, center your attention on only a few related points, preferably those stressed in the assignment. Later you will be able to judge more points at a time.

A convenient guide to use in criticizing speeches is the chart of common errors printed inside the cover of this book. Remember, however, that your critical analysis of a speech should not be limited merely to pointing out weaknesses. You can help a speaker improve by commenting on his strengths as well as his errors.

If your instructor asks you to evaluate one of the speeches delivered in class, divide your criticism into three steps. First, point out what was good about the speech. (Even the worst speeches usually have something good about them.) Second, tactfully suggest how the speech might have been improved. Third, indicate one or two specific things the speaker should work on the next time.

Do not hesitate to offer thoughtful criticism when it is invited. In a situation where all are trying to learn together, the objective comments of fellow students are seldom offensive. Learn also to accept such comments with good grace. After all, hearing and heeding listeners' criticisms is the best way of learning how to impress an audience.

PROBLEMS FOR FURTHER STUDY

1. Select some subject with which you are familiar. (This subject may be drawn from your major in college, from work experience, from travel, from your hobby, etc.) Assume that during the semester you will be required to present three five-minute speeches on this subject—one to entertain, one to inform, and one to persuade. Select and frame a specific purpose for each speech. Then repeat the experiment, but this time assume that in each case you will be presenting a fifteen-minute speech to a local service club. Let the other members of the class criticize the appropriateness of your choices.

2. Read five printed speeches. (See, for example, such books as *Representative American Speeches,* edited by Lester Thonssen; *The Speaker's Resource Book* by Carroll Arnold, Douglas Ehninger, and John C. Gerber; or recent issues of the magazine *Vital Speeches.*) Try to determine the general and specific purpose of each speech and to evaluate how well the specific purpose was fulfilled.

3. Using as a guide the various factors listed in the sample analysis outline, make a complete audience analysis of the members of your speech class. Get needed information by questioning classmates directly. Use the analysis as an aid in selecting topics for future classroom speeches.

4. Select a speech subject. Frame the specific purpose of a five-minute speech to persuade on this subject to (a) an audience that is favorable but not aroused, (b) an audience that is apathetic, (c) an audience that is interested but undecided, (d) an audience that is hostile toward the

proposition or recommendation, (e) an audience that is opposed to any change from the present situation.

5. Attend a speech or lecture in your community or listen to a speech on radio or television. What were the speaker's general and specific purposes? How would you describe the organization or structure of his speech? How well were his ideas explained or proved? Were there any obvious errors or gaps in his reasoning?

6. During a round of classroom speeches, jot down what you believe to be the specific purpose of each speech. At the close of the round, question the speakers to see if you have interpreted their purposes accurately. In cases where the majority failed to grasp the speaker's purpose, decide who was chiefly at fault—the speaker or the listeners.

7. Make an objective analysis of yourself as a listener. Note both your strong points and your weaknesses. Lay out a specific program for improving your listening ability. In making your analysis and laying out your program for improvement, consult again the suggestions for constructive listening in this chapter and examine such additional sources as your instructor may suggest.

8. List at least five different occasions on which it might be appropriate to give a speech to entertain. (Remember that an entertaining speech is not necessarily a funny one.) Also list five occasions on which a speech to inform might be called for. Do the same for a speech to persuade. During a class discussion, pool your suggestions with those of the other students and construct a master list of at least twelve occasions on which each type of speech is required.

9. Given the facts stated in the audience analysis you prepared for Problem 3, what would be the probable attitude of your classmates toward the following persuasive speakers and their specific purposes?

Speaker	*Specific Purpose*
A professor of English	To urge that intercollegiate athletics be abolished
A football coach	To urge students to study harder
President of senior class	To urge students to participate in campus politics
President of inter-fraternity council	To convince students that fraternities should be abolished

10. Review at least two speeches or lectures which have been given on campus recently and which most of the members of the class attended.

Discuss how well each speaker adapted his remarks to the audience and occasion. If the adaptation was poor, give several suggestions as to how it might have been improved.

SPEAKING ASSIGNMENTS

1. The student of public speaking can learn much about the principles of audience analysis by observing how Dr. George Gallup and the other public opinion "pollsters" break down "the great American audience" to derive the samples upon which they base their predictions. Let several members of the class investigate these methods and report them orally, in individual presentations or in an informal discussion before the class.

2. Select a subject with which you are well acquainted and about which you could say many things. Write out the specific purposes of four or five speeches which you would like to give on this subject in your speech class. Select from these the purpose that seems best adapted to the interests of your classmates, and deliver a five-minute speech on it. At the close of your speech, read aloud the specific purposes which you rejected, and let your classmates and instructor evaluate your choice.

SUGGESTIONS FOR FURTHER READING

Aristotle, *Rhetoric*, 1388b-1391b, "Types of Character; the Young; the Elderly; the Prime of Life; Character as Modified by Fortune; the Influence of Wealth; the Influence of Power."

George Campbell, *The Philosophy of Rhetoric*, Book I, Chapter 1, "Eloquence in the Largest Acceptation Defined, Its More General Forms Exhibited, with Their Different Objects, Ends, and Characters."

George Gallup, *A Guide to Public Opinion Polls* (Princeton: Princeton University Press, 1948).

H. L. Hollingworth, *The Psychology of the Audience* (New York: American Book Company, 1935), Chapter 2, "Preliminary Analysis"; Chapter 3, "Types of Audiences"; Chapter 4, "A Typical Situation."

Daniel Katz, "Psychological Barriers to Communication," *Annals of the American Academy of Political and Social Science*, CCL (March 1947), 17-25.

Ralph G. Nichols and Leonard A. Stevens, *Are You Listening?* (New York: McGraw-Hill Book Company, Inc., 1957).

Elmo C. Wilson, "The Measurement of Public Opinion," *Annals of the American Academy of Political and Social Science*, CCL (March 1947), 121-129.

CHAPTER 4

PHYSICAL BEHAVIOR
ON THE PLATFORM

The effectiveness of your speaking depends both on what you say and on how you say it. Without solid content you will not have anything worth communicating; without effective delivery you cannot convey your thoughts clearly and vividly to others. Just as a pitcher can give a ball direction and power by the way he throws it, so a speaker can give his speech strength and vitality by the manner of his delivery.

The best single assurance of good delivery is straightforward sincerity. Effectiveness does not depend upon applying mechanically a predetermined set of rules; it comes from practice under the direction of a competent instructor who can help you smooth out rough spots and develop points of strength. This chapter and the one that follows provide suggestions to keep you from falling into undesirable habits that later may be difficult to correct; they also explain certain principles to assist you in deriving maximum benefit from your instructor's comments.

Since in the usual speaking situation the audience both sees and hears the speaker, a consideration of delivery involves two basic elements: the speaker's *physical behavior on the platform* (the subject of the present chapter), and his *use of the voice* (the subject of Chapter 5).

The importance of physical or bodily delivery is apparent. People in an audience read meanings into a speaker's facial expression, into the way he stands and walks, and into what he does with his head, arms,

shoulders, and hands. Often a slight shrug of the shoulder or an expressive movement of the hand is more revealing than a hundred words. Moreover, listeners are quick to see any discrepancy between a speaker's actions and his ideas. Vigorous ideas expressed in a languid manner, or trivial ideas propounded with great force or dignity produce an unconvincing if not ludicrous effect. Finally, remember that since the speaker is seen before he is heard, it is through visual rather than auditory impressions that the audience makes its initial estimate of his sincerity, his friendliness, and his energy.

CONTACT WITH THE AUDIENCE

The first thing a speaker must do when he addresses an audience is to make its members feel that he is talking to them personally. Listeners are repelled by a speaker who seems unaware of their identity as individuals. They value a sense of close personal relationship, such as exists in an informal conversation.

Nothing is quite so important a means of establishing personal contact with an audience as the simple device of looking at individuals directly. For this reason, reading a speech or even using notes too closely invariably detracts from a speaker's effectiveness. Since it is impossible to look at each member of the audience at the same time, do as you would in an informal conversation: pick out one person and talk directly to him for a few seconds, looking him in the eye as you do so; then shift to someone else. Be careful that you pick out people in various parts of the audience, however, and that you stay with each one long enough to avoid the appearance of simply wagging your head.

POSTURE

Posture is of prime importance in speech delivery. How do you stand when you talk to people? Are you erect? comfortable? alert? Does your position seem natural or does it call attention to itself because it is awkward or unusual? There is no one best way to stand when delivering a speech, but there are several errors which you should avoid. Do not hide behind a high speaker's stand; stay to one side of it or leave it altogether. Avoid letting the weight of your body fall on your heels; let it fall on the balls of your feet. Avoid bouncing up and down or swaying from side to side. Stand so that you are comfortable without being slouchy, erect without being stiff. Give the impression that you are awake and "on your toes." Show the assurance of one who is in command of the situation and of himself.

MOVEMENT

The eye instinctively follows moving objects and focuses upon them. A sleepy audience often can be awakened by the simple expedient of moving from one part of the platform to another. As long as your movement is natural, easy, and purposeful, it will help you hold attention, maintain interest, and convey your thoughts more clearly.

How much movement about the platform is desirable? How often should you change your position? The answer is to follow your natural impulses. Move about when you feel a desire to do so. Of course, you should avoid continuous and aimless pacing back and forth. But you should also avoid standing glued to a single spot throughout your entire speech. If you are earnestly trying to communicate an important idea to an audience, sooner or later you will feel the desire to move. It will seem natural to change your position as a means of letting your hearers know that you have finished one idea and are ready to start another, or to step forward as a means of stressing an important point.

Remember also that the way you walk to the platform and the way that you leave it are important. Instead of ambling up to the speaker's stand in a slovenly, meandering fashion, walk briskly and purposefully. Let your manner breathe confidence; do not tiptoe timidly, as though you were afraid the audience might see or hear you. Once in position, do not begin your speech immediately. Take time to compose your thoughts and to look at your listeners; *then* begin to talk. When you have finished speaking, do not rush to your seat. Pause at the end of your talk long enough to let your final words take effect; then walk off in a relaxed but dignified way. The total effect of a speech may be ruined by an awkward or poorly timed entrance or exit.

GESTURES

In addition to moving about on the platform, you can use gestures to clarify or to emphasize the ideas in your speech. By gestures we mean *purposeful* movements of some part of the body — head, shoulders, arms, or hands — to reinforce or to demonstrate what you say. Fidgeting with coat buttons or aimlessly rearranging books or papers on the speaker's table are not gestures; they are not purposeful and they do not relate to the ideas you are expressing.

Two simple experiments will show you how important gestures are to communication. (1) Try to give directions for finding a place several blocks distant and notice how necessary it is to point the way and to show turns by movements of the arms or head. (2) Observe two persons in a heated argument and notice how often their hands come into play to emphasize the points they are making.

Besides their usefulness in clarifying and stressing ideas, gestures are also valuable because they help to hold the listeners' attention. Just as we watch the speaker who moves about rather than the one who remains rooted in a single spot, so we listen with greater attention to the speaker who gestures appropriately. Unless the speaker who uses no gestures compensates for the lack in some other way, listeners respond sluggishly and apathetically. On the other hand, a physically active speaker stimulates lively attention and interest.

In emphasizing the importance of gestures, we are not implying that you should simulate a forceful, dynamic delivery if such a manner is uncharacteristic of you. The impulse to make gestures should always come from within and should be a natural response to the ideas you are

communicating. Do not decide in advance that at a certain time in your speech you are going to point your finger at the audience and a moment later shake your fist. If gestures are to be effective, they must arise naturally from an inner state of earnestness, enthusiasm, or emotion. Practice gesturing all you please at home — the more the better — until you can feel the easy swing, the abandon, and the punch of it; but when you stand before an audience, do not force your arms or head to move. If you have practiced sufficiently and are genuinely concerned with communicating important ideas to others, gestures will come naturally as part of your total speaking pattern.

Gestures of the hands and arms

A good speaker should understand the common types of gestures and the purpose for which each type is used. Basically, gestures are

Evaluate the effectiveness of the physical behavior of these speakers — their facial expression, eye contact with the audience, posture, and use of gesture. *Opposite page, clockwise from left:* poet Carl Sandburg, evangelist Billy Graham, Secretary of the Treasury C. Douglas Dillon, and labor leader Walter P. Reuther. *Above, clockwise from lower left:* car manufacturer Enzo Ferrari, Northwestern University president, Dr. J. Roscoe Miller, Bishop Fulton J. Sheen, and Dr. Martin Luther King.

of two sorts, *conventional* and *descriptive*. Let us consider these two types as they are made with the hands and arms, the principal agents used in gesturing.

Conventional gestures. Six basic movements of the hands and arms are used so extensively by speakers that people recognize almost automatically the meanings they are intended to convey. These gestures have become a sort of universal sign language.

1. *Pointing.* When a speaker wishes to indicate a position or show a direction, or when he wishes to call attention to an idea or object, he will often point with the index finger of his right or left hand. He may, for example, point at a map hanging on the wall as he says, "This map you see here is already out of date because the boundaries keep changing so rapidly." Or, as he says, "The argument rests upon this single principle. . . ," he may point in front of him as if the principle were actually there in tangible form. When making an accusation or issuing a chal-

lenge, a speaker will frequently point his finger at the audience or at some imaginary person on the platform beside him.

2. *Giving or receiving.* If you were to hand someone a sheet of paper or to hold out your hand to accept one given to you, the palm would face upward. This same movement is often used by speakers when they are presenting a new idea to the audience or are requesting support for a proposal they are advancing. This gesture indicates, "This is the information I have discovered," or "The ideas I am holding before you deserve your attention," or "I appeal to you to give me your help in this matter." No other conventional gesture is used quite so often as this one because of the wide variety of purposes it may serve. Sometimes it is even combined with the pointing gesture described above — the idea is, as it were, held out in one hand while the other hand directs attention toward it.

3. *Rejecting.* If a dog with dirty paws were to jump up on your clothes, you would push him to one side with your hand. In the same way, speakers often express disapproval or rejection of an idea. They use a sweeping movement of the hand with the palm downward to reinforce such statements as "That proposal is absolutely worthless," "We must put that idea out of our heads," or "It can't be done that way."

4. *Clenching the fist.* This gesture expresses strong feeling, such as anger or determination. It is used to emphasize such statements as "We must fight this to a finish!" or "He's the worst scoundrel in the world!"

5. *Cautioning.* If you wished to calm an angry or excited friend, you might do so by putting your hand lightly on his shoulder. A similar movement of the hand as if on an imaginary shoulder is used by speakers to caution listeners against arriving at too hasty a judgment or against losing their tempers. This gesture is often used with such statements as "Don't take this thing too seriously" or "If you'll just keep quiet a moment, I think I can make the point clear." By using this gesture, speakers attempt to check their hearers' thoughts and get them ready to listen to another idea.

6. *Dividing.* When speakers wish to indicate the separation of facts or ideas into different parts, they will often be observed to move their hands from side to side with the palm held vertical. They use this gesture, for example, when saying, "Part of the great crowd stood on this side of the river, part on the other," or "In these days of national and international tension, we must not, on the one hand, be radical in our ideas, nor, on the other, ultraconservative."

These are six basic movements of conventional gesturing. From what has been said about them, do not infer that they are set and invariable. No two persons will make these movements exactly alike or on exactly the same occasions. Moreover, these movements do not always start from the same positions. Frequently one gesture begins at the point where another stopped, so that an effect of continuity is achieved. And usually it is the movement of the hand and arm rather than the final position they assume that emphasizes the speaker's ideas. Practice alone will make your use of conventional gestures smooth and effective, and this practice will be most valuable when it is guided by the suggestions and criticisms of your instructor.

Descriptive gestures. The movements discussed above carry meaning only by custom or convention, but other movements of the head and body may directly describe or imitate the idea to be communicated. The speaker may describe the size, shape, or action of an object by movements of the hands and arms. He may show how vigorous a punch was by striking the air with his fist, the height of a younger brother by holding out a hand, the speed of an automobile by a quick sweep of the arm, and the details of a complicated movement by performing the movement. Because of their spontaneous and imitative nature, descriptive gestures cannot be cataloged precisely. Useful hints can be obtained, however, by watching other speakers, and your own originality will suggest many possibilities. Merely ask yourself, "How can I best make this idea clear to my audience?" Then use any movements or gestures that occur to you, so long as they are reasonably dignified and in good taste.

Gestures of the head and shoulders

Shrugging the shoulders and shaking the head have the same implications in public speech that they have in conversation, and here as elsewhere are frequently used to gain emphasis.

Facial expression and impersonation

For many years psychologists have been interested in studying how facial expressions convey thoughts and feelings. Everyone's own experience, however, will attest that such expressions often speak as eloquently as words. Of course, you should not attempt to put on a certain expression mechanically. Too often such an attempt results only in an artifical grimace or a fixed smile. Like gestures, facial expressions should be natural and unplanned; they should reveal sincere convictions and deep feelings. If you are well disposed toward your audience, are interested in the subject of your talk, and are enthusiastic about speaking, your face will reflect your attitude and will help emphasize the ideas you express orally.

Sometimes a speaker may want to make an illustration or story more vivid by acting and talking as if he were the person described. In this imitative process the speaker's posture, movements, gestures, and facial expression are combined. His shoulders droop and he develops a slight limp; his hand trembles as it knocks on the door and his face shows surprise at what he sees when the door opens—together, these actions present a character and tell what the character is doing. Such detailed imitation or "acting out" of a point, however, should be done only infrequently and with the greatest caution. Too vivid or dramatic a presentation may center the attention of the audience on the action rather than on the idea being expressed, and thus defeat its own purpose. Moreover, it is essential that audience contact be maintained and that your dignity as a speaker be preserved. Use the method when you think it to be the clearest and surest way of communicating the point you have in mind, but always use it with good judgment and restraint.

CHARACTERISTICS OF GOOD GESTURES

Although you can perfect your gestures only through practice, practice will yield better results if you keep three characteristics of good gestures in mind: relaxation, vigor and definiteness, and proper timing.

Relaxation

When your muscles are strained or tense, you have difficulty expressing yourself naturally, and awkward gestures result. One of the best ways to break your tension is to move about. Warm up by taking a few easy steps or by unobtrusively arranging your notes or papers. To avoid stiffness and awkwardness, make a conscious effort to relax your muscles *before* you start to speak.

Vigor and definiteness

Good gestures are alive and vigorous. Put enough force into them to make them convincing. A languid shaking of the fist is an unconvincing support of a threat or challenge; an aimless or hesitant movement of the arm confuses rather than clarifies. Do not pound the table or saw the air constantly; exaggeration of minor points is ludicrous. Vary the vigor and nature of your gestures, but in the main be vigorous enough to show your conviction and enthusiasm.

Timing

The comedian gets many laughs from his audience by timing his gestures improperly. Try making a gesture after the word or phrase it was intended to reinforce has already been spoken and observe the ridiculous result. The stroke of a gesture—that is, the shake of the fist, the movement of the finger, or the break of the wrist—should fall exactly on, or should slightly precede, the point the gesture is used to emphasize. If you practice making gestures until they have become habitual and then use them spontaneously as the impulse arises, you will have no trouble with this matter. Poor timing is the result of an attempt to use "canned" or pre-planned gestures.

ADAPTING PHYSICAL BEHAVIOR TO THE SUBJECT AND AUDIENCE

Just because a certain type of speech delivery is effective with one subject or with one audience, you must not assume that it will suit all subjects and audiences. As observation will show, good speakers vary their physical behavior according to the size and character of the audience they are addressing and the nature of the ideas they are communicating.

The size of the audience

Generally speaking, the larger the audience, the larger and more pronounced the speaker's gestures will be. What might seem to be a wild swing of the arm to a person close at hand appears quite appropriate to an audience of several hundred. Conversely, small gestures of the arms or slight changes in facial expression, while effective in conversation, seem weak and indefinite to a large group of listeners.

The nature of the subject and the occasion

Subjects on which feelings run strong or which require great and immediate decisions usually motivate speakers to more vigorous bodily action than do subjects which are less moving or crucial. Moreover, occasions such as memorial services or dedications call for dignity of movement as well as of expression, while political meetings or pep rallies require more violent and enthusiastic activity.

All of these considerations must be borne in mind if you are to move and gesture effectively. The immediate task of most student speakers, however, is to learn to move about the platform freely and to make a sufficient number of gestures. Begin by moving several times during each speech you give and by gesturing as often as possible. For the time being, let yourself go. If a classmate tells you that you are pacing aimlessly or using too many gestures, make sure that he does not really mean that your movement or gestures lack sufficient variety. Instead of cutting down on the amount of activity, vary it more. Later, after you have learned to move easily and naturally, you may want to use fewer gestures and to move less often. Until you are completely loosened up and at home in the public speaking situation, however, move and gesture freely and frequently. Bodily activity will not only help reduce nervousness and make your speaking more alive and vigorous, but by freeing you of tensions and restraints may actually help you to think better while you are on your feet.

Finally, remember that learning to move and to gesture effectively is much like learning to comb your hair or to handle a knife and fork. You were not born doing these things, but practice made them habitual. So, too, proper movement and gesture must be practiced until they are habitual and natural. Then they may be forgotten about while you are speaking. They will be automatic in their obedience to impulse and effective in reinforcing your ideas.

PROBLEMS FOR FURTHER STUDY

1. Imagine yourself in the following situations—picture in detail all that has led up to them—and react spontaneously with whatever physical behavior your impulse suggests. Speak out also if you feel impelled to do so.

a. Someone has fired a gun just behind you.
b. A child just in front of you steps into the path of a fast-moving automobile.
c. Someone has just slapped your face.
d. Someone shouts to warn you of a heavy object about to fall on the spot where you are standing.
e. You are marooned on an island and are trying to catch the attention of men on a passing ship.
f. A mob is bent on destruction; as the crowd goes past, you try to turn it in another direction.

2. Getting your elbows well out from your body, keeping your wrists flexible, and using a great deal of energy, do the following exercises in sequence:
a. Shake your arms and hands vigorously as if trying to get something loose from your fingers. Do this with your arms far out at the sides, up over your head, out in front of you; continue until all stiffness is eliminated.
b. While you are shaking your hands and arms, begin repeating the alphabet over and over — not in a monotonous rhythm but as if you were actually talking in highly emotional language. Continue this "talking" while doing the following exercises.
c. Let one hand at a time fall to your side and continue shaking the other.
d. Gradually change from mere shaking of the arm and hand into making varied gestures; that is, point your finger, reject the idea, drive home a point, etc. During this change be sure to preserve the vigor and complete abandon of your arm movements.
e. Get a partner. Harangue each other by repeating the letters of the alphabet loudly and as though you were greatly excited. Keep up a vigorous flow of gestures all the while. Both of you talk and gesticulate at the same time.
f. In a group of four or five, all talking simultaneously, harangue the rest of the class in the same way you did your partner in (e). See which speaker can keep the attention of the class away from the others in the group.

3. Try to communicate the following ideas silently by means of physical action alone. You will need to use descriptive as well as conventional gestures.
a. "Get out of here!"
b. "Why Tom (or Mary)! I haven't seen you for ages!"
c. "You men on that side, sing the first line, and we'll sing the second."

d. "Right in front of me was a big field with a brook running straight through the middle of it."

e. "If we're going to get what we want, we'll have to fight for it, and fight hard!"

f. "Quiet down a little, won't you? Give him a chance to explain."

g. "Come here a minute, Jim, will you?"

h. "Every penny I had is gone."

i. "Now the first thing to remember is this: . . ."

j. "If you think it was easy, you're all wrong."

4. Go to hear some speaker and write a brief report on your observations regarding his platform behavior. Before you go, make a brief outline of the suggestions and warnings contained in this chapter and check the speaker on these points while he is talking. Note both good and bad qualities in the speaker's contact with the audience, as well as his posture, movements, and gestures. Observe particularly what statements he emphasizes with gestures, and what gestures he uses to do this.

5. Attend a motion picture or a play or watch a drama on television and report on the physical behavior of the actors. Comment on such questions as these:

a. What impression of the character was conveyed by the actor's posture and manner of walking?

b. How was movement used to help hold attention?

c. What special meanings were conveyed by facial expression and by movements of the head or shoulders?

d. What conventional and descriptive gestures were especially effective?

e. What relation did you notice between comedy effects and awkward, poorly timed gestures?

SPEAKING ASSIGNMENTS

1. Make a two- or three-minute speech explaining to the class how to do something, such as driving a golf ball, kicking a football, bowling, doing a sleight-of-hand trick, playing a musical instrument, cutting out a dress, etc. Use movement and gestures to help make your ideas clear. Do not use the blackboard or previously prepared diagrams.

2. Make a short speech describing some exciting event you have witnessed —an automobile accident, a rocket launching, a touchdown play, a street-corner brawl. Use movement and gestures to make the details clear and vivid. Try to make your description so colorful that your listeners will tend to project themselves into the situation and to see it as clearly as if

they were actually witnessing it. Remember that to succeed in doing this you will need to imagine yourself in the situation while you describe it; you must feel the excitement in order to communicate it to others.

3. Give a three- or four-minute speech on some subject that arouses your fighting spirit—dishonesty, cruelty, unnecessary red tape, campus injustices, unsympathetic officials or teachers, unfair requirements or restrictions, the denial of civil liberties, biased newspaper reporting, dangerous demagogs. Choose a subject that makes you genuinely angry, excited, or indignant. Let yourself go vocally and physically in denouncing the institution or practice. Be careful, however, to back up what you say with facts; do not merely rant and rave, or merely air a prejudice. You may make a point as strongly as you like, provided you are able to prove it. (Remember to frame a specific purpose and to choose materials suitable to secure the desired response from your listeners.)

SUGGESTIONS FOR FURTHER READING

Marguerite Battye, *Stage Movement* (London: Herbert Jenkins, Ltd., 1954).

William Norwood Brigance, *Speech, Its Techniques and Disciplines in a Free Society,* 2nd ed. (New York: Appleton-Century-Crofts, Inc., 1961), Chapter 16, "Being Seen."

Delwin Dusenbury and Franklin H. Knower, "Experimental Studies of the Symbolism of Action and Voice—I: A Study of the Specificity of Meaning in Facial Expression," *Quarterly Journal of Speech,* XXIV (October 1938), 424-436.

Daniel Katz and R. L. Schanck, *Social Psychology* (New York: John Wiley and Sons, 1938), pp. 348-350.

W. M. Parrish, "The Concept of Naturalness," *Quarterly Journal of Speech,* XXXVII (December 1951), 448-454.

Richard Whately, *Elements of Rhetoric,* Part IV, "Of Elocution, or Delivery."

CHAPTER 5

USING THE VOICE

After long experience in public life, Benjamin Disraeli, the British statesman, declared, "There is no index of character so sure as the voice." It is true that often we tend to judge a person by his voice. A woman whose tones are habitually sharp and nasal may be thought of as a shrew. A man whose voice is harsh or guttural may be judged crude and rough. A thin, breathy voice, dominated by the frequent use of upward inflections, may suggest a lack of conviction or decisiveness.

The conclusions we draw from vocal characteristics, of course, are sometimes incorrect. But whether true or false, such judgments are important to the speaker because they color the listeners' attitudes toward what he says. Sometimes a speaker's voice may be the most important single factor determining the impression his hearers form of him as a person; frequently it is among the major factors.

In addition to the impression the speaker's voice gives of him as a person, there is a second reason why a good voice is important: the speaker can make what he says more interesting and meaningful. Have you ever listened to a child at a church or school program rattle off a piece with so little expression that, even though you heard the words, you could not get their full meaning? On the other hand, can you recall a play-by-play account of some football or baseball game broadcast by a skilled sports announcer? Did not the clarity and vividness of his description depend largely upon the way he used his voice?

How can you as a speaker acquire an effective voice? As in the case of bodily delivery, improvement results chiefly from practice. But unintelligent practice may do more harm than good; repeatedly doing the wrong thing merely fixes a bad habit more firmly. To make practice worth while, you should first understand something about the mechanics of voice production. Also you should be acquainted with the characteristics of a good voice and with certain methods by which these characteristics may be acquired. This chapter provides information about the voice, along with a variety of exercises and practice materials. These exercises, together with the directions and criticisms of your instructor, will help you move toward your goal more purposefully.

THE MECHANICS OF SPEAKING

Strictly speaking, there is no such thing as a *speech* or *vocal mechanism*. We shall use these terms, however, to include those parts of the body which are used in the speaking process.

All the muscles, bones, cartilages, and organs used in speaking have other functions which are biologically more important than producing the voice. The tongue, for example, even though a vital part of the speaking mechanism, is more important in eating. The vocal folds protect our lungs from irritants in the atmosphere and help to regulate the air flow. The very fact that speaking is a secondary function of these organs makes doubly important a program of vocal training, for although we were able at birth to breathe, we had to learn to speak. In the process, many of us did not learn to speak well. We may have established bad habits of articulating; we may have formed the habit of straining our throats as we speak, or of grouping our words into short, jerky units. But even though we may have inadequate speech habits, or bad ones, we all have learned in childhood how to use these organs together in some form of speaking. Let us therefore forget for the present their primary biological functions and consider them together as a single mechanism — the instrument of speech. This instrument may be divided into two major parts: the voice producing mechanism, including the motor, the vibrator, and the resonators; and the articulatory mechanism, including the tongue, teeth, lips, jaw, and the hard and soft palates.

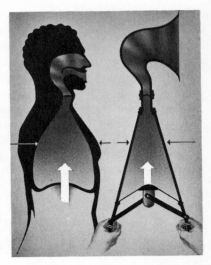

The voice is a wind instrument. This diagram shows how the speaking mechanism functions as a wind instrument. The motor compresses the air in the lungs as shown by the arrows; this compressed air is sent through the vibrator, which first produces the speech sound; the speech tone next enters the resonators of the throat, mouth, and head to be amplified and modified in quality; finally, the tone is affected by the articulatory mechanism, which alters the quality further and serves also to produce the consonant sounds.

The voice producing mechanism

The motor. The motor part of the speech mechanism is essentially a pump for compressing air. It consists of (a) the *lungs,* which contain spaces for the air, (b) the *bronchial tubes,* which converge into the windpipe or *trachea,* out of which the compressed air is released, (c) the *ribs,* and other bones, cartilages, and tissues which serve to hold the motor in place and give leverage for the application of power, and (d) the *muscles,* which alternately expand and contract the area occupied by the lungs, thus first allowing air to enter and then compressing it for expulsion. To detail the large number of muscles used in the breathing process would be beyond the scope of this book. It should, however, be noted that the human air pump works in two ways: Certain muscles draw the ribs down and in when we exhale, so as to squeeze the lungs after the fashion of a bellows, while others—the strong abdominal muscles—squeeze in below to exert pressure up against the bottom of the lungs after the manner of a piston. This double action is also exerted when we inhale: One set of muscles pulls the ribs up and out to expand the horizontal space, while the diaphragm—a layer of muscles and flat tendon tissue—expands the vertical space by lowering the floor of the chest cavity; this two-way expansion creates a suction, so that air rushes into the lungs. Thus, both inhaling and exhaling involve two coordinated actions: moving the ribbed walls of the chest, and raising and lowering its floor.

The vibrator. The air compressed in the lungs during exhalation is directed through the trachea into the *larynx,* which contains the main vibrating unit. The larynx is situated at the upper end of the trachea and is attached above and below by muscles which shift it up and down. The larynx itself consists of a group of small cartilages joined so that they can move as if on joints like the bones of the arm. The position of these cartilages can be changed by a number of small muscles which are delicately intertwined. Within the larynx, stretched between the cartilages, are the *vocal folds.* The *folds* are the tendonous inner or facing edges of two muscles. When sound is to be produced, they come together until there is only a tiny slit between them. The compressed air from the lungs, pushing against and between the vocal folds, causes a vibration which results in sound. The pitch of this sound — its highness or lowness on the scale — depends on the muscles which control the tension and length of the folds. The position of the larynx as a whole is adjusted to a proper relation with the air cavities above by the action of the larger outside muscles which hold it in place. The action of these two sets of muscles, particularly the small internal ones, is largely automatic — they cannot be controlled individually. But we can operate these laryngeal muscles as a group to control pitch.

The resonators. The sound produced in the larynx by the vibration of the vocal folds is thin and weak. It is resonated by a group of air chambers in the head and throat. The principal resonators of the human voice are the upper part (or *vestibule*) of the *larynx,* the throat *(pharynx),* the *nasal cavities,* and the *mouth.* (See the Figures on page 79.) These resonators act much as do the resonating parts of a musical instrument: they amplify the sound, and they modify its quality, making it rich and mellow, or harsh, or whining. Moreover, changes in the size and shape of some of these chambers result in the different tone qualities that constitute the vowel sounds.[1]

The articulatory mechanism

The *tongue, lips, teeth, jaw,* and the *hard* and *soft palates* act as modifying agents in the production of speech sounds. (See page 79.) By

---

[1] By definition, vowels are resonant speech tones produced by the vibration of the vocal folds, amplified in the pharyngeal and oral resonators, and not significantly obstructed by the modifiers.

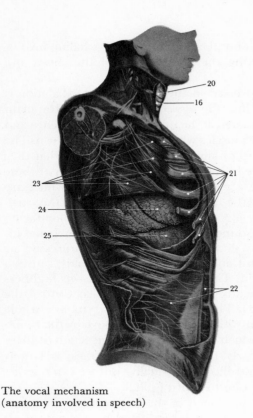

1. Sinuses
2. Nasal cavity
3. Hard palate
4. Upper lip
5. Upper teeth
6. Tongue
7. Lower lip
8. Lower teeth
9. Lower jaw
10. Soft palate
11. Base of the tongue
12. Epiglottis
13. Thyroid cartilage
14. Vocal fold
15. Cricoid cartilage
16. Trachea (windpipe)
17. Esophagus
18. Pharynx (throat)
19. Vertebrae
20. Larynx
21. Rib bones (numbers 6, 7, and 8 cut away)
22. Abdominal muscles
23. Chest muscles
24. Lungs
25. Diaphragm
26. Base of epiglottis
27. Glottis
28. Arytenoid cartilage

The vocal mechanism
(anatomy involved in speech)

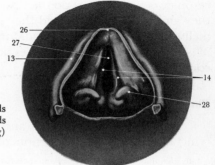

The vocal folds
(laryngoscopic view of the vocal folds
in relaxed position at normal breathing)

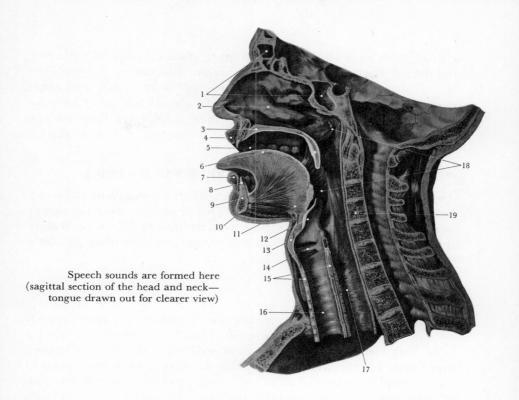

Speech sounds are formed here
(sagittal section of the head and neck—
tongue drawn out for clearer view)

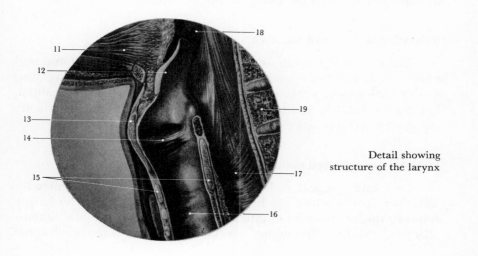

Detail showing
structure of the larynx

moving them we modify the size and shape of the mouth, and, therefore, the quality of the tone. Another important function of the modifiers is the formation of consonant sounds—the stops, hisses, and other interruptions in the steady flow of vowel sounds that serve to make words out of what would otherwise be mere vocal tones. Precision and sharpness of articulation come from the proper use of these modifiers.

PHYSICAL REQUIREMENTS OF A GOOD SPEAKING VOICE

To our description of the speech mechanism, we shall add a few suggestions concerning its effective use. This discussion must necessarily be general. Your speech instructor should be consulted if you need more specific and detailed suggestions concerning any individual problems in the use of your voice.

Control of breathing

Singing tones are often prolonged or sustained, but speech sounds are not. They are short and precise. Therefore, you do not need a large lung capacity in order to speak well; what you need is control over the air you do have. By controlling the amount of pressure exerted on the vocal folds by the air in your lungs, you may vary the strength of your voice and give your utterance power or softness. (See exercises to improve control of breathing on pp. 94–95.)

Relaxation of the throat and neck

Besides causing strain or soreness, tension in the throat and neck causes vocal harshness and a loss of tone flexibility. Pleasing voice quality comes from a relaxed throat coupled with controlled breathing. Letting the head hang limp, yawning, and singing vowel tones softly are good ways to practice relaxation.

Flexible, energetic, and unhurried use of the jaw, tongue, and lips

Four faults appear to be responsible for much of the blurred or indistinct speech which we hear. By avoiding them you can help to improve the intelligibility of utterance. These faults are (a) the "immovable jaw," (b) the "idle tongue," (c) "lazy lips," and (d) too much speed.

 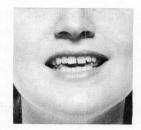 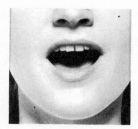

rose   **chee**se   f**a**ther

Contrasting movements, especially of the lips and jaw, produce and distinguish each of these vowel sounds from the others: the *o* in *rose*, *ee* in *cheese*, and *a* in *father*.

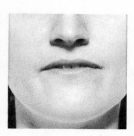 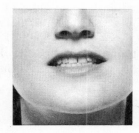 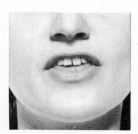

veil   **s**ee   **th**ing

Note characteristic positioning of the articulators, particularly of the lips, tongue, and teeth, for proper formation of these sounds: *v* in *veil*, *s* in *see*, and *th* in *thing*.

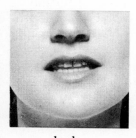 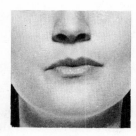 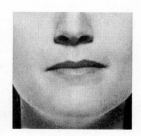

lead   **w**ear   **m**an

Note modifications in the position of the lips and tongue for the formation of sounds represented by the *l* in *lead* and *w* in *wear*.

Prominent use of the articulators is required for formation of *m* in *man*.

Physical requirements of a good speaking voice   81

Some oriental peoples move their jaws very little when they speak; in their languages so much of the meaning is conveyed by variations in tone that scarcely any jaw movement is required. In English, on the other hand, much meaning is conveyed by consonant sounds, and these cannot be made properly unless the tongue is given ample room for movement. Even the vowel sounds are likely to be muffled if the jaws are kept too tightly closed. As you talk, therefore, strive for free and active movement of your jaws. The tongue, more than any other organ, is essential in the formation of sounds such as those represented by the letters *s, l, k,* and *t;* if it is curbed or moves sluggishly, these and similar sounds cannot be sharp. The lips, like the tongue, are made of muscle; if they are allowed to become lazy, the so-called labial sounds, *p, b, m,* and *f,* will be blurred or inaudible.

In working to increase the mobility of articulation, however, remember not to talk too fast. The fourth common cause of indistinctness, as we have said, is excessive speed of utterance. Take time to be distinct; as your jaw, tongue, and lips develop more flexibility and precision, perhaps you can speed up a bit, but for the present avoid rushing.

VOCAL QUALITY

When you describe someone's voice as harsh or mellow or guttural or nasal, you are describing its quality. Quality is often referred to as "timbre" or "tone color." Just as the quality of tone produced by one violin differs from that produced by another, so does the quality of one person's voice differ from another's. In the human voice, quality is determined in part by the conditions under which the initial tone is produced in the larynx and in part by the influence of the resonating chambers. (See Figures on page 79.)

Let us consider a few of the more common types of poor voice quality and see what may be done to remedy them.

Thin, weak voices lack carrying power. More often found in women than in men, this type of voice is faint and lacks body. A number of causes may combine to produce such a voice: the muscles of the tongue and palate may be so inactive that inadequate use is made of the resonating cavities; the pitch level may be too high—even a falsetto—so that the lower resonances are not used (something like this happens when you tune out the lower partials on your radio or hi-fi set); or the power given to the voice by the breathing muscles may be inadequate. Of these causes, the last two are the most common. If your voice is somewhat thin, try lowering your pitch and at the same time talk a little louder. Open your mouth wider, especially on the vowel sounds *ah, oh,* and *aw,* in order to increase the size of the oral cavity and improve its resonating effect. For practice say *bound* as if projecting the word from deep in your chest and bouncing it upon the back wall of the room.

Huskiness and harshness may result either from tension in the throat or from the pressure of too much air against the vocal folds. An irritated or diseased condition of the throat sometimes has the same effect. If a throat examination fails to disclose any pathological condition, the huskiness often can be lessened or eliminated by proper breathing and relaxation. Let the neck muscles become slack; then say a word such as *one, bun, run,* very quietly, prolonging it until it almost becomes a singing tone. Work at this until the tone is clear and free of all breathiness; if you have trouble, use less breath. When the tone seems clear, gradually increase the volume until you can produce a strong tone without tension or huskiness.

Nasality, contrary to popular notion, is more often the result of too little nasal resonance, rather than too much. (Persons with cleft palates usually have too much nasal resonance, but an adequate consideration of their problems cannot be attempted here.)

Say *button* or *mutton.* Notice what happens to your soft palate; did you feel it tighten up just before the production of the *t* sound and then relax to allow the *n* sound to be emitted through the nose? For consonant sounds such as *t* and *p,* the palate has to close tight, but if this tension is continued during the production of vowel sounds, a flat quality is likely to result. To correct this difficulty, begin by working on those sounds which must be produced through the nose—*m-m-m-m* and *n-n-n-n.* Hum these sounds, prolonging them until you can feel the vibration in your nose. At the same time, keeping the lips closed, drop the jaw somewhat and let the sound reverberate in the mouth cavity. When you can feel a "ringing" sensation in both mouth and nose, open your lips and let the *m* become an *ah* thus: *m-m-m-m-m-a-a-ah.* You should still feel some vibration both in the mouth and nose; continue until you do. Once you recognize the sensation of nasal resonance, try the same exercise with other vowel sounds (*m-m-m-m-m-o-o-oh, n-n-n-n-n-ee-ee-ee,* etc.). You will be wise, however, to have your instructor listen to you because, though the chances are slight, it is possible to relax the palate too much so that you give the tone an excess of nasal resonance.

These are by no means the only types of unpleasant quality nor the only causes of poor quality. If you have questions about your voice, ask your instructor for a frank criticism and follow whatever suggestions he may have for improving it. Exercises 1 to 6 at the end of this chapter should also prove helpful.

THE VARIABLE ATTRIBUTES OF VOICE

A flexible voice not only enables you to express your meaning accurately and clearly; it also enables you to transmit to the audience the full depth of feeling behind your ideas. In addition to the quality of the voice, therefore, it is important to consider the different attributes which you can vary as you convey ideas and feelings. These are generally designated by the terms *rate, force,* and *pitch.* That is, you can vary your voice by changing the rate at which you speak, the force with which you speak, or the pitch that you use.

Rate

Most persons speak between 120 and 180 words a minute; however, a uniform rate is not maintained with clocklike regularity. In normal speech the speed of utterance corresponds to the thought or feeling the speaker is attempting to transmit. Weighty, complex, or serious ideas tend to be expressed more slowly; light, humorous, or exciting matters more rapidly. Observe how fast the sports announcer talks when he is describing a completed forward pass or a quick double play; in contrast, observe the slow, dignified rate at which a minister reads the wedding or burial service. An enthusiastic or animated person talks rapidly; a lethargic person talks more slowly. But while an excited person talks fast all the time and a stolid person always talks in a slow drawl, the individual who, though enthusiastic, is yet poised—who, though he believes or feels deeply, is in perfect command of his material and of the speaking situation—varies his rate. He tells a story, lays out facts, or summarizes an argument at a lively pace, but he presents his main ideas and more difficult points slowly and emphatically so that their importance may be fully grasped by the listener.

Besides the number of syllables spoken per minute, two other elements help to determine a speaker's rate. These are *quantity,* or the length of time used in the actual utterance of a sound within a word, and *pause,* or the cessation of sound between words. If one says "ni-i-ine fo-o-o-our three-ee-ee," he is using long quantity; if he says "nine four three" the quantity is short. Similarly, one may say "nine —— four —— three," using long pauses, or "nine, four, three," using short pauses. The longer the quantity or pause, the slower the overall rate; the shorter the quantity or pause or both, the faster the rate.

Quantity. Quantity is usually associated with the mood or sentiment expressed. If you were to say the opening lines of the Gettysburg Address ("Four score and seven years ago, our fathers brought forth on this continent a new nation, . . .") with sharp staccato quantity, the result would be absurd; such serious and dignified sentiments habitually call forth sustained tones. On the other hand, imagine listening to the following play-by-play account of a basketball game delivered in a slow drawl: "Jones passes to Schmidt—he's dribbling down the floor—back to Jones—back again to Schmidt—over to Lee—and it's in! Another basket for. . . ." Like the game itself, such a description needs snap; short quantity provides it.

A good way to develop sensitivity to quantity values is to practice reading aloud selections in which some particular sentiment prevails or in which there is a definite shift from one sentiment to another. A number of the passages of poetry and prose at the end of the chapter are of this type. Notice when studying them that vowel sounds are usually longer than consonant sounds, and that some consonant and vowel sounds are longer than others. The word *roll,* for example, contains sounds that are intrinsically longer than those in *hit.* Many words suggest their meaning by the duration of the sounds they contain. Writers know this and use such words, either consciously or because of an unconscious sensitivity to these values, to help convey their feelings. By absorbing the sentiments or emotions expressed in the practice selections and then reading them aloud, you will develop a sensitivity to quantity values, and the expressiveness of your voice will be increased.

Pause. Pauses punctuate thought. Just as commas, semicolons, and periods separate written words into thought groups, so pauses of different lengths separate spoken words into meaningful units. Haphazard use of pauses in oral reading, therefore, is as confusing to the listener as the haphazard use of punctuation is in silent reading. Be sure when you read aloud that your pauses come between thought groups and not in the middle of them. Moreover, in reading aloud remember that written and oral punctuation differ; not every comma calls for a pause, nor does the absence of punctuation always mean that no pause is required.

Often a pause may be used for emphasis. Placed immediately after an important statement, it suggests to your audience, "Let this idea sink in." A pause before the climax of a story sometimes helps to increase suspense; a dramatic pause at the right moment may express the depth of your feeling more forcefully than any words could.

Many speakers are afraid to pause. Fearing that silence will focus attention on them personally, they rush on with a stream of words, or, failing to find words readily, they substitute such sighs and grunts as *and-er-ah.* These random syllables not only draw attention away from the ideas being expressed, but also are extremely annoying to the listener. Remember that a pause seldom seems as long to the audience as it does to the speaker and that the ability to pause for emphasis or clarity is an indication of poise and self-control. Do not be afraid to pause whenever a break in utterance will help clarify an idea or emphasize an important point more strongly. Concentrate on the thought or emotion you are trying to convey and let your voice respond accordingly. But above all, when you do stop, stop completely; do not fill in the gap with *er, ah,* or *um.* Such meaningless vocalizations defeat entirely the purpose of a pause.

Force

The first requirement any audience places on a speaker is that he have adequate vocal force—that he talk loudly enough to be heard easily. A certain amount of force also is needed if the speaker is to give an impression of confidence and vigor. Talking too softly suggests that you are not sure of yourself or that you do not care whether your audience hears you. On the other hand, continuous shouting wears out an audience and dissipates attention. People become quite as bored by a continuous loud noise as by a continuous soft one. With force, as with rate, variety should be your objective.

Force is varied primarily for emphasis. Either by increasing the loudness of a word or phrase or by pointedly reducing its loudness, you can make that word or phrase stand out. Moreover, by changing the degree of force, you can reawaken lagging interest. A drowsy audience will sit up quickly if you suddenly project an important word or phrase with sharply increased force. Remember, however, that the effect is not produced primarily by the stepped-up force, but rather by the *change:* a sharp reduction may be quite as effective as a sharp increase. Silence can awaken a man sleeping in a noisy room.

While you are practicing to develop flexibility of force, observe what happens to the pitch and quality of your voice as the force varies. The natural tendency of most speakers is to raise their pitch whenever they try to speak louder. You probably have noticed that when you shout, your voice is keyed much higher than when you speak in a conversational tone. This is because the effort required to produce a loud tone tends to increase muscle tension throughout the speaking mechanism, and the greater tension produces higher pitch as well as more force. Sometimes the tension in the throat is so great that the voice becomes harsh as well. A little practice, however, will help you to overcome this tendency. Just as you have learned to wiggle one finger without moving the others or to wink one eye without the other, so you can learn to apply force by contracting the breathing muscles without tightening the muscles of the throat or unnecessarily raising the pitch of your voice. A good way to begin is by repeating a sentence such as "That is absolutely *true!*" Hit the last word in the sentence with a greater degree of force *and at the same time lower your pitch.* When you are able to do this, say the entire sentence louder, and louder, and louder, until you can shout it without raising your pitch. Keep a fairly sustained tone and try to maintain a full, resonant quality. By controlling the force of your voice, you will make your speaking more emphatic and convey to your audience an impression of reserve power. Remember, however, that in actual speech force always should be applied in response to inner feeling; conscious vocal manipulation to secure one form of force rather than another is bound to sound artificial and hollow. Only in practice drills should you pay direct attention to your voice. When speaking or reading to others, concentrate on the ideas being expressed, not on how you are saying them.

Pitch

Just as singers' voices differ, some being soprano or tenor and some contralto or bass, so do speakers' voices vary in their normal pitch level and range. Unless you talk in your normal pitch range, there is danger of straining your voice. You will find, however, that there is considerable leeway within your normal range. Few beginning speakers use enough variation; they tend to hit one level and stay there. We shall, therefore, discuss not only the *key*, or general level of pitch, but also changes within pitch range—both abrupt changes called *steps*, and gradual changes called *slides*, together with the *melody pattern* thus produced. Nothing improves the vivacity of speech so much as effective variation in pitch.

Key. Most of us have a wider range of pitch than we suspect. Nearly everyone can easily span an octave, and many people have voices flexible enough to vary more than two octaves without strain. We normally speak at a general key-level, taking excursions above and below this key-level, and within it, to vary our expression. The key-level at which we speak creates a definite impression; ordinarily, a pitch that is continuously high suggests weakness, excitement, irritation, or extreme youth, while a lower key-level suggests assurance, poise, and strength. For that reason, your customary pitch should normally be in the lower half of your pitch range, but your voice must not remain there all the time or it will soon prove monotonous to the listener.

Sometimes when you are increasing force, you will find that your voice is getting out of control and going to a higher and higher key until it cracks under the strain. If you notice tension in your throat, pause for a moment and lower your pitch back to your normal key.

Steps and slides. There are two ways in which pitch is changed in connected speech—by steps and slides. For example, suppose that someone makes a statement with which you agree completely and you say, "You're exactly right!" The chances are that you would say it something like this:

Notice that a complete break in pitch level occurs between the first and second syllables of the word *exactly*. This sort of abrupt change in pitch is called a *step;* on the word *right,* however, a more gradual pitch inflection takes place during the actual production of the sound—such a continuous change of pitch within a syllable is called a *slide*. Both steps and slides may go upward or downward depending on the meaning intended; slides are sometimes double, the pitch going up and then down or vice versa, as when one says,

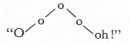

"O⌒o⌒o⌒o⌒oh!"

to express the meaning, "I didn't realize that!" In general, an upward step or slide implies interrogation, indecision, uncertainty, doubt, or suspense, while a downward inflection expresses firmness, determination, certainty, finality, or confidence. If you were to say, "What shall we do about it? Just this. . . ," a rising inflection on the question would create suspense in your listeners, while a downward inflection on the last phrase would assure them that you were presenting an answer. A double inflection, as indicated by the example above, often suggests surprise, doubt, or contradiction of meaning; it also frequently expresses irony or sarcasm, and conveys all sorts of nuances.

When you are speaking, do not, of course, say to yourself, "This sentence requires a double inflection; I shall raise my pitch on these two words and come down on that one." Such concentration on the mechanics of utterance would destroy all communicative contact with your audience. Rather, in private and in class exercises, read aloud selected passages whose meanings call for various pitch inflections. This practice will help you develop the flexibility upon which varied and expressive utterance depends.

Melody patterns. In all kinds of speech, the rhythm and swing of phrase and sentence weave themselves into a pattern of continuously changing pitch. As the thought or mood changes, this melodic pattern also changes. If you develop flexibility of pitch inflection, your melody pattern will adjust itself automatically to the thought or mood you intend to express, but be on the watch not to fall into a vocal rut, unconsciously using the same melody for everything you say. A monotonous melody pattern is just as ineffective as staying in the same key all the time. Beware particularly of see-sawing back and forth between the same notes in a sing-song voice. Avoid also the tendency of many beginning speakers to end every sentence with an upward slide so that assertions sound like questions rather than statements of fact or opinion. A monotonous downward cadence, on the other hand, is equally undesirable, since it robs you of the power of expressing inquiry or uncertainty when you wish to do so.

EMPHASIS AND CLIMAX

By constantly altering the rate, pitch, and force of your voice, you can introduce variety into your speech and make it easier and more enjoyable to listen to. As we have suggested, however, such variation also helps you express meanings more clearly. This is because vocal variation enables you to discriminate between ideas of primary and secondary importance, and to emphasize the primary ones while holding the secondary ones in the background.

Emphasis

As we have already suggested, any change of rate, force, or pitch emphasizes an idea by making it stand out from those that precede or follow it. This is true regardless of the direction of the change. Whether the rate or force is increased or decreased, whether the pitch is raised or lowered, emphasis will result. And the greater the amount of change or the more suddenly applied, the more emphatic the statement will be.

Take a simple sentence such as "John stole my watch." Notice the different shades of meaning that result when you say the sentence over four times, first emphasizing *John,* then *stole,* then *my,* and then *watch.* The first way points out the thief, the second tells what he did, the third calls attention to the rightful owner, and the fourth names the article stolen. All of these ideas are implicit in the sentence, but the way you say it conveys to your listener the meaning which is uppermost in your mind. Often, through the use of varying inflections, a single word can be made to mean several different things. You can speak the name *Tom* as a question ("You are Tom, aren't you?"), as a command ("Stop that!"), as a request for attention ("Listen a minute."), as a cry for help ("Come here quickly!"), and so on.

Speaking that lacks appropriate emphasis is not only dull and monotonous but is also difficult to understand or evaluate. Avoid under-emphasis—jumbling your ideas together without regard for their relative importance—or your crucial points will be lost in a mass of details. On the other hand, however, avoid overemphasis or continuous emphasis. If you emphasize a point beyond its evident value or impor-tance, your audience will lose faith in your judgment. If you attempt to emphasize everything, the effect will be the same as if you emphasize nothing because no one idea will stand out from any other. Pick out the ideas that are important and give them the significance they deserve. Be judicious in your use of emphasis.

Particularly when the purpose of your speech is to entertain rather than to inform or persuade, you should avoid a heavy or overemphatic manner of delivery. Unless your own manner suggests that you are enjoying yourself, you cannot encourage enjoyment in others. Be genial and good-natured and let your speaking be alert and lively. Keep your rate relatively fast and use pauses and inflections to bring out the humorous or novel qualities in your ideas. In no other type of speaking is vocal flexibility and responsiveness quite so important.

Climax

Frequently a speaker gives expression to a thought or feeling that rises steadily in power until it reaches a point where the strongest appeal is made. Such peaks of thought or feeling require climactic vocal expression. Each successive thought unit, whether it is a word, phrase, or sentence, is uttered with a successive increase of force, with more rapid rate, with a higher level of pitch, or with any combination of these changes.

Some immature speakers try for too many climaxes in a speech, and as a result the effect they desire is lost by repetition; climaxes become commonplace and by the end of the speech are no longer climactic. One good climax has more power to move an audience than five mediocre ones, frequently even more than five good ones. Save your climaxes for the places where they will be most effective, usually near the end of the speech or at the ends of major thought units.

Beware also of anticlimax. When successive stages of climactic power begin to follow one another, the audience expects them to continue until the peak of interest or of emotional power has been reached. If before this peak has been attained the increases of power begin to lessen or the climactic movement stops, the audience feels let down. Start slowly enough or quietly enough or at a low enough pitch so that you can keep on building until the natural culmination of the movement has been reached. Furthermore, once you complete a vigorous, moving climax, pause and shift your mood and manner of speaking completely, or stop altogether. Do not extend the climax unduly or dissipate its effect by saying the same thing over in colorless, ordinary language.

ACCEPTABLE PRONUNCIATION

Spoken words are the sound symbols of meaning. If you fail to pronounce them correctly, your listeners may not understand what you are saying. Even if your words are recognized, any peculiarity of pronunciation is quickly noticed by the audience and may distract attention from your thought or even reflect unfavorably on you.

Because standards differ, it is sometimes difficult to know which pronunciation is acceptable. For most words, a good dictionary provides a reliable guide to usage. But with respect to a few words, even the newest dictionary is likely to be out of date. Moreover, few dictionaries take sufficient notice of regional differences in pronunciation. An educated native of Louisiana pronounces words differently from a man who lives in Montana. A Chicagoan is easily distinguished from a Bostonian by his speech. The pronunciation recorded in the dictionary should, therefore, be modified to agree with the usage of educated people in your community.

A common error of pronunciation is to accent the wrong syllable. Thus, we hear persons say *genu-íne, dé-vice, the-aý-ter, pre-fér-able,* instead of the more generally accepted *gén-uine, de-více, the-ater,* and *préf-erable.* In some cases, an improperly placed accent or stress actually changes the meaning of a word. Consider, for example, the change produced by shifting the stress from one syllable to the other in the word *content.* Yet the rules of stress are by no means inflexible when words are used in connected speech. Emphasis and contrast often require the shifting of stress. Notice what you do to the accent in the word *proceed* when you use it in this sentence: "I said to proceed, not to recede." Moreover, many words change in sound when they are stressed; this is especially true of short words such as pronouns, articles, and prepositions. Ordinarily you do not stress such words. For example, you ordinarily say, "I gave 'im th' book." Circumstances, however, may cause you to stress the third word or the fourth one, saying, "I gave *him* th' book," or "I gave 'im *the* book." Thus, both conventional accent and the requirements of contrast and emphasis influence the placing of stress in words. Effective use of stress is essential for intelligible utterance and for vigorous, animated expression.

Errors in pronunciation sometimes arise from the omission of sounds (such as *guh'mnt* for *government*), from the addition of sounds (such as *athalete* for *athlete*), and from the substitution of sounds (such as *arful* for *awful*). The way words are spelled is not always a safe guide to pronunciation, for English words contain many silent letters (of*t*en, i*s*land, mor*t*gage), and many words containing the same combinations of letters require different pronunciations (b*ough*, r*ough*, thr*ough*; call*ed*, shout*ed*, gasp*ed*). In determining acceptable pronunciation, you also should consider the formality of the occasion; many omissions acceptable in conversation become objectionable in a formal address. In radio and television broadcasting, careful pronunciation is particularly important. Because many programs are heard throughout the nation, broadcasting is tending to minimize regional differences in pronunciation and to develop a common standard across the country. In general, however, what is good pronunciation elsewhere is also good "on the air."

Do not be so labored and precise as to call attention to your pronunciation rather than to your ideas; but do not take this warning as an excuse for careless speech. Avoid equally pronunciation that is too pedantic or too provincial. Use your ears; listen to your own pronunciation and compare it with that of educated people in your community. If your pronunciation is faulty, keep a notebook in which you list the words you miss, and practice them frequently.

AUDITORY ASPECTS OF WORD CHOICE

The English language contains many words that have different meanings but have the same, or very similar, sounds: words such as *one* and *won*, *for* and *four*, *sick* and *six*, and the like.[2] Moreover, the acoustic difference between certain individual sounds is often too small for clear differentiation if all the other sounds in the word are the same. Thus, it may be difficult to understand the rapid utterance of a phrase such as *fine Rhine wine*.

Articulating carefully and lengthening the duration of syllables will help reduce misunderstandings of this sort. When you talk on subjects requiring the use of terms—particularly technical terms—which are unfamiliar to your listeners, talk more slowly, prolong your syllables, and articulate more carefully. Wherever possible, try to use words which cannot be mistaken in context. In particular, be careful about using similar sounding words close together in sentences where the meaning of the first word may carry over to the second.

---

[2] See Exercise 15, p. 102, for lists of words that are easily mistaken for one another.

The story is told of a reporter who interviewed a farmer by telephone and reported in his newspaper that the farmer had just purchased 2008 pigs. The farmer had actually told him that he had bought "two sows and eight pigs." A difference of only one sound resulted in an error of 1998 hogs. Although errors of this magnitude do not often occur, a listener is frequently confused by what he thinks he hears until something is said later in the discussion to clarify the point; in the meantime the effectiveness of the intervening remarks is usually reduced. Be careful, therefore, to think of words in terms of the way they *sound* and not the way they look in print. Remember, it is what the listener *thinks* he hears that determines his response.

In this chapter we have covered a great deal of ground. We have described the major parts of the human speech mechanism. We have discussed vocal quality and explained how it may be improved. We have talked about variety of rate, force, and pitch, and have examined the relation between these variables and the meaning and emotional intent of the speaker's words. We have considered means of gaining vocal emphasis and have reviewed certain basic problems of pronunciation and intelligibility. Do not assume that you will be able to master in a day or a week all of the vocal skills that have been described. Take time to digest the ideas we have presented; above all, practice the exercises below. Return to these exercises again and again, even after you have mastered them, so that your skill will not become rusty through disuse. Remember that any speech skill, before it can be natural and effective with an audience, must become so much a habit that you are able to forget about it completely when you get up to speak.

EXERCISES

To improve control of breathing

1. Practice expelling the air from your lungs in short, sharp gasps; place your hand on your abdomen to see that there is a sharp inward contraction of the muscle wall synchronous with the chest contraction on each outgoing puff.
   a. Then vocalize the puffs, saying "Hep! — Hep! — Hep!" with a good deal of force.
   b. In the same way, say "bah, bay, bee, bo, boo," with staccato accents and considerable vigor.

2. Fill your lungs; then exhale *as slowly as possible* until the lungs are empty. Time yourself to see how long you can keep exhaling without a break. (Note that the object here is not to see how much air you can get into the lungs but how slowly you can let it out.)

   a. Filling your lungs each time, vocalize the outgoing breath stream first with a long continuous hum, second with an *oo* sound, and then with other vowel sounds. Be careful not to let the sound become "breathy"; keep the tone clear.

   b. Place a lighted candle just in front of your mouth and repeat the series outlined above. The flame should just barely flicker.

3. On the same breath alternate the explosive and the slow, deliberate exhalations outlined in the two preceding problems. Practice until you can shift from one to the other easily both in silent breathing and in vocalized tones.

To induce relaxation of the throat

4. Repeat the following sequence several times in succession:

   a. Keeping your eyes closed and your neck and jaw muscles as relaxed as possible, raise your head easily to an upright position and then yawn with your mouth open as wide as possible.

   b. While your mouth is thus open, inhale deeply and exhale quietly two or three times; then intone "a-a-a-ah" very quietly.

   c. Say "m-m-a-a-ah" several times slowly, each time nodding the head forward quietly and without tension.

To improve the quality of tone

5. Intone the following words quietly at first, then louder, and louder; try to give them a ringing quality; put your fingertips on the nose and cheekbones to see if you can feel a vibration there. Avoid breathiness.

one	home	tone	alone	moan
rain	plain	mine	lean	soon
ring	nine	dong	moon	fine

6. Read aloud the following passages in as clear and resonant tones as you can produce. Be sure that you open your mouth wide enough and that you use only enough air to make the tones vibrate. Do not force the tone. If you notice any tension in your throat or harshness in your voice, go back to the preceding exercises until the tension and harshness disappear.

from THE ANCIENT MARINER

Alone, alone, all, all alone,
Alone on a wide, wide sea!
And never a saint took pity on
My soul in agony.

Samuel T. Coleridge

from THE RAINY DAY

The day is cold, and dark, and dreary;
It rains, and the wind is never weary;
The vine still clings to the mouldering wall,
But at every gust the dead leaves fall,
And the day is dark and dreary.

Henry W. Longfellow

from RECESSIONAL

God of our fathers, known of old,
  Lord of our far-flung battle-line,
Beneath whose awful Hand we hold
  Dominion over palm and pine—
Lord God of Hosts, be with us yet,
Lest we forget—lest we forget!

Rudyard Kipling

Selected passages for further practice in improving quality

Some of these selections are included because of the emotional tone they portray; others because of the vocal control they require. All of them, however, call for a clear, resonant quality. Study them first for their meaning; try to understand fully what the author is saying. Then absorb the feeling; allow yourself to follow the author's mood. Finally, read the passages aloud, putting as much meaning and feeling into your reading as you can.

from THE CONGO[3]

Fat black bucks in a wine-barrel room,
Barrel-house kings, with feet unstable,

---

[3] From Vachel Lindsay, *The Congo and Other Poems.* Copyright 1914 by The Macmillan Company and used with their permission.

Sagged and reeled and pounded on the table,
Pounded on the table,
Beat an empty barrel with the handle of a broom,
Hard as they were able,
Boom, boom, BOOM,
With a silk umbrella and the handle of a broom,
Boomlay, boomlay, boomlay, BOOM.

Vachel Lindsay

from THE MAN WITH THE HOE[4]

Bowed by the weight of centuries he leans
Upon his hoe and gazes on the ground,
The emptiness of ages in his face,
And on his back the burden of the world.
Who made him dead to rapture and despair,
A thing that grieves not and that never hopes,
Stolid and stunned, a brother to the ox?
Who loosened and let down this brutal jaw?
Whose was the hand that slanted back this brow?
Whose breath blew out the light within this brain?

Edwin Markham

WIND IN THE PINE[5]

Oh, I can hear you, God, above the cry
    Of the tossing trees —
Rolling your windy tides across the sky,
    And splashing your silver seas
        Over the pine,
        To the water-line
    Of the moon.
Oh, I can hear you, God,
    Above the wail of the lonely loon —
When the pine-tops pitch and nod —
    Chanting your melodies
Of ghostly waterfalls and avalanches,
Swashing your wind among the branches
    To make them pure and white.

---

[4] Copyright by the author and used with permission.
[5] From *Covenant with Earth* by Lew Sarett. Edited and copyrighted 1956 by Alma Johnson Sarett (Gainesville: University of Florida Press).

Wash over me, God, with your piney breeze,
   And your moon's wet-silver pool;
Wash over me, God, with your wind and night,
   And leave me clean and cool.

Lew Sarett

GOD'S GRANDEUR

The world is charged with the grandeur of God.
   It will flame out, like shining from shook foil;
   It gathers to a greatness, like the ooze of oil
Crushed. Why do men then now not reck his rod?
Generations have trod, have trod, have trod;
   And all is seared with trade; bleared, smeared with toil;
   And wears man's smudge and shares man's smell: the soil
Is bare now, nor can foot feel, being shod.

And for all this, nature is never spent;
   There lives the dearest freshness deep down things;
And though the last lights off the black West went
   Oh, morning, at the brown brink eastward, springs—
Because the Holy Ghost over the bent
   World broods with warm breast and with ah! bright wings.

Gerard Manley Hopkins

DOOM IS DARK AND DEEPER THAN ANY SEA-DINGLE[6]

Doom is dark and deeper than any sea-dingle.
Upon what man it fall
In spring, day-wishing flowers appearing,
Avalanche sliding, white snow from rock-face,
That he should leave his house,
No cloud-soft hand can hold him, restraint by women;
But ever that man goes
Through place-keepers, through forest trees,
A stranger to strangers over undried sea,
Houses for fishes, suffocating water,
Or lonely on fell as chat,
By pot-holed becks
A bird stone-haunting, an unquiet bird.

There head falls forward, fatigued at evening,
And dreams of home,
Waving from window, spread of welcome,
Kissing of wife under single sheet;
But waking sees
Bird-flocks nameless to him, through doorway voices
Of new men making another love.

Save him from hostile capture,
From sudden tiger's spring at corner;
Protect his house,
His anxious house where days are counted
From thunderbolt protect,
From gradual ruin spreading like a stain;
Converting number from vague to certain,
Bring joy, bring day of his returning,
Lucky with day approaching, with leaning dawn.

W. H. Auden

To develop flexibility in vocal manipulation

7. While repeating the alphabet or counting from one to twenty, perform the following vocal exercises (trying throughout to maintain good vocal quality and distinctness of utterance):

a. Beginning very slowly, steadily increase the speed until you are speaking as rapidly as possible; then, beginning rapidly, reverse the process.

b. Stretch out the quantity of the vowel sounds, speaking at a slow rate but allowing no pauses between letters or numbers; then shift to short quantity with long pauses. Shift back and forth between these two methods with every five or six letters or numbers you say.

c. Begin very softly and increase the force until you are nearly shouting; reverse the process. Then practice shifting from one extreme to the other, occasionally changing to a moderate degree of force.

d. Keeping the loudness constant, shift from an explosive application of force combined with a staccato utterance to a firm, smooth application of force.

e. Stress alternate letters (or numbers); then change by stressing every third letter, every fourth, etc.; then change back to alternate letters again.

f. Begin at the lowest pitch you can comfortably reach and raise the pitch steadily until you reach the highest comfortable pitch; reverse the process. Shift back and forth suddenly from high to low to middle, etc.

g. Practice slides with the vowel sound *oh*. Try upward slides, downward slides, and those which are double—going up and down or down and up.

h. Using a half dozen letters or numbers, practice similar pitch changes in steps; then alternate steps and slides.

i . Combine the above pitch variations into as many different complex patterns as your ingenuity and patience will permit. (Mathematically, there are several hundred different permutations and combinations.)

8. Vary the *rate* with which you say the following sentences in the manner indicated:

a . "There goes the last one."
   (1) Use long quantity, expressing regret.
   (2) Use short quantity, expressing excitement.
   (3) Use moderate quantity, merely stating a fact.

b. "The winners are John, Henry, and Bill."
   (1) Insert a long pause after *are* for suspense; then give the names rapidly.
   (2) Insert pauses before each name as if picking them out.
   (3) Say the whole sentence rapidly in a matter-of-fact way.

9. In the manner suggested, vary the *force* with which you say the following sentences:

a . "I hate you! I hate you! I hate you!"
   (1) Increase the degree of force with each repetition, making the last almost a shout.
   (2) Say the second *hate* louder than the first, and the last one *sotto voce*.
   (3) Shout the first statement; then let the force diminish as if echoing the mood.

b. "What kind of a thing is this?"
   Repeat the question, stressing a different word each time. Try not to raise the pitch, but to emphasize by force alone.

c . "I have told you a hundred times, and the answer is still the same."
   (1) Make the statement a straightforward assertion, using sustained force.
   (2) Speak the sentence with a sudden explosion of force as though you were uncontrollably angry.
   (3) Speak the sentence with deep but controlled emotion, applying force gradually and firmly.

10. Practice varying the *pitch* with which you say the sentences below, following the directions given:
   a. "I certainly feel fine today—that is, except for my sunburn. Now don't slap me on the back! Ouch! Stop it! Please!"
      Begin confidently in a low key, successively raising the pitch level until the *please* is said near the top of your range. Repeat several times, trying to begin lower each time.
   b. "Oh, yes. Is that so."
      Say this sentence as indicated in the following notations. Diagonal lines indicate slides; horizontal ones indicate a level pitch; and differences in height between the end of one line and the beginning of the next indicate steps. Each line represents one word.

   (1) ＿ ⎺ ＿ ⎺ ＿

   (2) ＿ ／ ＿ ⎺ ＼

   (3) ⎺ ＼ ＿ ＿ ／

   (4) ＿ ∧ ＿ ＿ ∧

   (5) ⎺ ⎺ ＿ ＿ ⎺ ＼

   What are the different meanings conveyed?
   c. Say the sentence with varied pitch inflections so that it will mean as many different things as possible.

11. Practice reading aloud sentences from prose and poetry that require emphasis and contrast to make the meaning clear. Vary the pitch, rate, and force in different ways until you feel you have the best possible interpretation of the meaning. Here are some examples for practice:
   a. One of the most striking differences between a cat and a lie is that a cat has only nine lives. —*Mark Twain*
   b. So, Naturalists observe, a flea
      Has smaller fleas that on him prey;
      And these have smaller still to bite 'em;
      And so proceed ad infinitum. —*Jonathan Swift*
   c. I have waited with patience to hear what arguments might be urged against the bill; but I have waited in vain: The truth is, there is no argument that can weigh against it. —*Lord Mansfield*
   d. Gentlemen may cry, peace, peace!—but there is no peace. The war has actually begun! I know not what course others may take; but, as for me, give me liberty, or give me death! —*Patrick Henry*

e. Some books are to be tasted; others to be swallowed, and some few to be chewed and digested; that is, some books are to be read only in parts; others to be read but not curiously, and some few to be read wholly, and with diligence and attention. — *Francis Bacon*

f. "Beauty is truth, truth beauty," — that is all
Ye know on earth, and all ye need to know. — *John Keats*

12. Read the following passages so as to give the effect of climax: first practice the climax of increasing force, and then that of increasing intensity of feeling with diminishing force.

a. There is no mistake; there has been no mistake; and there shall be no mistake. — *Duke of Wellington*

b. Let us cultivate a true spirit of union and harmony. . .let us act under a settled conviction, and an habitual feeling, that these twenty-four States are one country. . . .Let our object be, OUR COUNTRY, OUR WHOLE COUNTRY, AND NOTHING BUT OUR COUNTRY. — *Daniel Webster*

To increase distinctness of articulation

13. Stretch the muscles of articulation:

a. Stretch the mouth in as wide a grin as possible; open the mouth as wide as possible; pucker the lips and protrude them as far as possible.

b. Stretch out the tongue as far as possible; try to touch the tip of the nose and the chin with the tongue tip; beginning at the front teeth, run the tip of the tongue back, touching the palate as far back as the tongue will go.

14. With vigorous accent on the consonant sounds, repeat "pah, tah, kah" several times. Then vary the order, emphasizing first *pah,* then *tah,* then *kah.* In the same way practice the series "ap, at, ak" and "apa, ata, aka." Work out additional combinations of this sort, using different combinations of consonants and vowels.

15. Experiments have shown that the words grouped in fours below are easily mistaken for one another under conditions of noise interference.[7] Practice articulating them distinctly and precisely. Then with your back to the rest of the class and with another student creating a noise by reading aloud from the textbook at the same time, read down one column or across one row, choosing one word at random out of each four. Announce before you start which column or row you are going to read from, pause

---

[7] Taken from answer sheets for standardized tests developed by C. Hess Haagen, printed in *Intelligibility Measurement: Twenty Four-Word Multiple Choice Tests,* OSRD Report No. 5567 (P.B. 12050), issued by the Office of Technical Services, Department of Commerce, p. 21.

briefly after each word, and have other members of the class put a check by the word they understood you to say. (This is not an accurate *test* of intelligibility but should provide interesting practice.)

	A	B	C	D	E	F
(1)	system	firm	banner	puddle	carve	offer
	pistol	foam	manner	muddle	car	author
	distant	burn	mother	muzzle	tarred	often
	piston	term	batter	puzzle	tired	office
(2)	heave	detain	scream	porch	fable	cross
	heed	obtain	screen	torch	stable	cough
	ease	attain	green	scorch	table	cloth
	eve	maintain	stream	court	able	claw
(3)	roger	pure	petal	vision	bubble	thrown
	rupture	poor	battle	bishop	tumble	drone
	rapture	tour	meadow	vicious	stumble	prone
	obscure	two	medal	season	fumble	groan
(4)	art	sponsor	game	cape	texture	eye
	heart	spotter	gain	hate	lecture	high
	arch	ponder	gage	take	mixture	tie
	ark	plunder	gang	tape	rupture	hide
(5)	comment	exact	made	process	glow	single
	comic	retract	fade	protest	blow	jingle
	cannon	detract	vague	profess	below	cycle
	carbon	attack	may	possess	low	sprinkle
(6)	bumper	cave	pier	divide	kitchen	baker
	number	cake	pierce	devise	mission	major
	lumber	cage	fierce	define	friction	maker
	lover	case	spear	divine	fiction	banker
(7)	gale	glamour	ward	leap	second	rich
	jail	slimmer	wart	leaf	suction	ridge
	dale	swimmer	wash	lease	section	bridge
	bail	glimmer	war	leave	sexton	grip
(8)	danger	enact	hold	crater	seaport	joy
	feature	impact	old	traitor	keyboard	going
	nature	relax	ode	trainer	piecework	join
	major	intact	hoed	treasure	eastward	dawn

16. Make a list of as many tongue twisters as you can find and practice saying them rapidly and precisely. Here are a few short examples to start on:

a. She sells sea shells on the seashore.
b. National Shropshire Sheep Association.
c. "Are you copper-bottoming them, my man?" "No, I'm aluminuming 'em, mum."
d. He sawed six long, slim, sleek, slender saplings.
e. Dick twirled the stick athwart the path.
f. Rubber baby-buggy bumpers.
g. B — A, Ba; B — E, Be;
   B — I, Bi; Ba Be Bi;
   B — O, Bo; Ba Be Bi Bo;
   B — U, Bu; Ba Be Bi Bo Bu!
h. Twenty Scots in assorted tartans went to Trenton.
i. Winds were eastward for the Easter weekend.

17. Read the following passages in a distinct and lively fashion; move the tongue, jaw, and lips with energy:

from ALICE IN WONDERLAND

"You are old," said the youth, "and your jaws are too weak
   For anything tougher than suet;
Yet you finished the goose, with the bones and the beak —
   Pray, how did you manage to do it?"
"In my youth," said his father, "I took to the law,
   And argued each case with my wife;
And the muscular strength which it gave to my jaw
   Has lasted the rest of my life."

Lewis Carroll

from THE PIRATES OF PENZANCE

I am the very model of a modern Major-General,
I've information vegetable, animal, and mineral,
I know the kings of England, and I quote the fights historical,
From Marathon to Waterloo, in order categorical;
I'm very well acquainted too with matters mathematical,
I understand equations, both the simple and quadratical,
About binomial theorem I'm teeming with a lot o' news —
With many cheerful facts about the square of the hypotenuse.

I'm very good at integral and differential calculus,
I know the scientific names of beings animalculous;
In short, in matters vegetable, animal, and mineral,
I am the very model of a modern Major-General.

I know our mythic history, King Arthur's and Sir Caradoc's,
I answer hard acrostics, I've a pretty taste for paradox,
I quote in elegiacs all the crimes of Heliogabalus,
In conics I can floor peculiarities parabolous.
I can tell undoubted Raphaels from Gerard Dows and Zoffanies,
I know the croaking chorus from the *Frogs* of Aristophanes,
Then I can hum a fugue of which I've heard the music's din afore,
And whistle all the airs from that infernal nonsense *Pinafore*.

Then I can write a washing bill in Babylonic cuneiform,
And tell you every detail of Caractacus's uniform;
In short, in matters vegetable, animal, and mineral,
I am the very model of a modern Major-General.

Gilbert and Sullivan

To encourage acceptable pronunciation

18. Make a list of words which you have heard pronounced in more than one way. Look them up in a dictionary and come to class prepared to defend your agreement or disagreement with the dictionary pronunciation. Here are a few words on which to start:

abdomen	creek	gauge	indict	route
acclimated	data	gesture	inquiry	theater
advertisement	deficit	grievous	recess	thresh
alias	drowned	humble	research	vagary
bona fide	forehead	idea	roof	yacht

To improve intelligibility

19. Try to understand the significance of the following passages before you begin practicing them. Then begin by reading them as you would before a small, quiet audience; next as you would need to do if the audience were large or there were considerable noise interference. Remember, however, that exaggerated precision, loudness, syllable duration, etc., beyond the amount clearly required for easy intelligibility in the actual situation will sound artificial to your listeners and is not good speech.

from ESSAY ON SELF-RELIANCE

A foolish consistency is the hobgoblin of little minds, adored by little statesmen and philosophers and divines. With consistency a great soul has simply nothing to do. He may as well concern himself with his shadow on the wall. Speak what you think now in hard words and tomorrow speak what tomorrow thinks in hard words again, though it contradict everything you said today—"Ah, so you shall be sure to be misunderstood."—Is it so bad, then, to be misunderstood? Pythagoras was misunderstood, and Socrates, and Jesus, and Luther, and Copernicus, and Galileo, and Newton, and every pure and wise spirit that ever took flesh. To be great is to be misunderstood.—*Ralph Waldo Emerson*

from THE SEA AROUND US[8]

For the sea as a whole, the alternation of day and night, the passage of the seasons, the procession of the years, are lost in its vastness, obliterated in its own changeless eternity. But the surface waters are different. The face of the sea is always changing. Crossed by colors, lights, and moving shadows, sparkling in the sun, mysterious in the twilight, its aspects and its moods vary hour by hour. The surface waters move with the tides, stir to the breath of the winds, and rise and fall to the endless, hurrying forms of the waves. Most of all, they change with the advance of the seasons. Spring moves over the temperate lands of our Northern Hemisphere in a tide of new life, of pushing green shoots and unfolding buds, all its mysteries and meanings symbolized in the northward migration of the birds, the awakening of sluggish amphibian life as the chorus of frogs rises again from the wet lands, the different sound of the wind which stirs the young leaves where a month ago it rattled the bare branches. These things we associate with the land, and it is easy to suppose that at sea there could be no such feeling of advancing spring. But the signs are there, and seen with understanding eye, they bring the same magical sense of awakening.—*Rachel L. Carson*

To increase vocal variety and emphasis

20. Clip a paragraph from a newspaper story describing some exciting incident and read it with appropriate vocal variety.

21. Memorize a section of one of the speeches printed in this book, as assigned by your instructor, and present it in such a way as to make the meaning clear and the feeling behind it dynamic.

---

[8] *The Sea Around Us,* rev. ed. (New York: Oxford University Press, 1961), pp. 28-29.

22. Find an argumentative editorial or magazine article with which you agree or disagree. In your own words attack or defend the point of view presented, and do so with all the emphasis, contrast, and vocal variety of which you are capable.

Selected passages for practice

Before you begin to practice a passage, study it carefully to understand its full meaning and determine its dominant mood. Some of the selections are light and fast moving; others are thoughtful and serious; at least one contains a marked climax. Avoid superficial or mechanical manipulation of the voice; read so as to make the meaning clear and the feeling contagious to your listeners. Effective reading requires that you practice enough in private so that before an audience you will not have to keep thinking of your voice but will be able to concentrate on communicating ideas and feelings.

THE DISAGREEABLE MAN

If you give me your attention, I will tell you what I am:
I'm a genuine philanthropist—all other kinds are sham.
Each little fault of temper and each social defect
In my erring fellow-creatures, I endeavor to correct.
To all their little weaknesses I open peoples' eyes,
And little plans to snub the self-sufficient I devise;
I love my fellow-creatures—I do all the good I can—
Yet everybody says I'm such a disagreeable man!
    And I can't think why!

To compliments inflated I've a withering reply,
And vanity I always do my best to mortify;
A charitable action I can skillfully dissect;
And interested motives I'm delighted to detect.
I know everybody's income and what everybody earns,
And I carefully compare it with the income-tax returns;
But to benefit humanity, however much I plan,
Yet everybody says I'm such a disagreeable man!
    And I can't think why!

I'm sure I'm no ascetic; I'm as pleasant as can be;
You'll always find me ready with a crushing repartee;
I've an irritating chuckle, I've a celebrated sneer,
I've an entertaining snigger, I've a fascinating leer;
To everybody's prejudice I know a thing or two;
I can tell a woman's age in half a minute—and I do—

But although I try to make myself as pleasant as I can,
Yet everybody says I'm such a disagreeable man!
    And I can't think why!

William S. Gilbert

STORM FEAR[9]

When the wind works against us in the dark,
And pelts with snow
The lower chamber window on the east,
And whispers with a sort of stifled bark,
The beast,
    "Come out! Come out!" —
It costs no inward struggle not to go,
Ah, no!
I count our strength,
Two and a child,
Those of us not asleep subdued to mark
How the cold creeps as the fire dies at length, —
How drifts are piled,
Dooryard and road ungraded,
Till even the comforting barn grows far away,
And my heart owns a doubt
Whether 'tis in us to arise with day
And save ourselves unaided.

Robert Frost

RICHARD CORY[10]

Whenever Richard Cory went down town,
We people on the pavement looked at him:
He was a gentleman from sole to crown,
Clean favored, and imperially slim.

And he was always quietly arrayed,
And he was always human when he talked;
But still he fluttered pulses when he said,
"Good morning," and he glittered when he walked.

---

[9] From *Complete Poems of Robert Frost.* Copyright 1935 by Holt, Rinehart & Winston, Inc. Reprinted with permission of Holt, Rinehart & Winston, Inc., New York, and Laurence Pollinger, Ltd., London.
[10] From Edwin Arlington Robinson: *Collected Poems.* Reprinted with special permission of Charles Scribner's Sons and Macmillan & Co., Ltd.

And he was rich — yes, richer than a king —
And admirably schooled in every grace:
In fine, we thought that he was everything
To make us wish that we were in his place.

So on we worked, and waited for the light,
And went without the meat, and cursed the bread;
And Richard Cory, one calm summer night,
Went home and put a bullet through his head.

Edwin Arlington Robinson

from A LETTER TO THE CORINTHIANS (1 CORINTHIANS, 13)

Though I speak with the tongues of men and of angels, and have not
charity, I am become as sounding brass, or a tinkling cymbal. And
though I have the gift of prophecy, and understand all mysteries,
and all knowledge; and though I have all faith, so that I could remove
mountains, and have not charity, I am nothing. And though I bestow
all my goods to feed the poor, and though I give my body to be burned,
and have not charity, it profiteth me nothing. Charity suffereth long,
and is kind; charity envieth not; charity vaunteth not itself, is not
puffed up, doth not behave itself unseemly, seeketh not her own, is
not easily provoked, thinketh no evil; rejoiceth not in iniquity, but
rejoiceth in truth; beareth all things, believeth all things, hopeth all
things, endureth all things. Charity never faileth: but whether there
be prophecies, they shall fail; whether there be tongues, they shall
cease; whether there be knowledge, it shall vanish away. For we know in
part, and we prophesy in part. But when that which is perfect is come,
then that which is in part shall be done away. . . . And now abideth
faith, hope, and charity, these three; but the greatest of these is charity.
— *Paul, the Apostle*

I WILL BE HEARD

I am aware that many object to the severity of my language; but is
there not cause for severity? I will be as harsh as Truth and as uncom-
promising as Justice. On this subject I do not wish to think, or speak,
or write with moderation. No! No! Tell a man whose house is on fire
to give a moderate alarm; tell him to moderately rescue his wife from
the hands of the ravisher; tell the mother to gradually extricate her
babe from the fire into which it has fallen — but urge me not to use
moderation in a cause like the present. I am in earnest — I will not

equivocate — I will not excuse — I will not retreat a single inch — and I will be heard. — *William Lloyd Garrison*

THE MOTH AND THE STAR[11]

A young and impressionable moth once set his heart on a certain star. He told his mother about this and she counseled him to set his heart on a bridge lamp instead. "Stars aren't the thing to hang around," she said; "lamps are the thing to hang around." "You get somewhere that way," said the moth's father. "You don't get anywhere chasing stars." But the moth would not heed the words of either parent. Every evening at dusk when the star came out he would start flying toward it and every morning at dawn he would crawl back home worn out with his vain endeavor. One day his father said to him, "You haven't burned a wing in months, boy, and it looks to me as if you were never going to. All your brothers have been badly burned flying around street lamps and all your sisters have been terribly singed flying around house lamps. Come on, now, get out of here and get yourself scorched! A big strapping moth like you without a mark on him."

The moth left his father's house, but he would not fly around street lamps and he would not fly around house lamps. He went right on trying to reach the star, which was four and one-third light years, or twenty-five trillion miles, away. The moth thought it was just caught in the top branches of an elm. He never did reach the star, but he went right on trying, night after night, and when he was a very, very old moth he began to think that he really had reached the star and he went around saying so. This gave him a deep and lasting pleasure, and he lived to a great old age. His parents and his brothers and his sisters had all been burned to death when they were quite young.

Moral: Who flies afar from the sphere of our sorrow is here today and here tomorrow. — *James Thurber*

SUGGESTIONS FOR FURTHER READING

Virgil A. Anderson, "A Modern View of Voice and Diction," *Quarterly Journal of Speech,* XXXIX (February 1953), 25-32.

Donald H. Ecroyd, "A Rationale for the Teaching of Voice and Diction," *Speech Teacher,* VIII (September 1959), 256-259.

---

[11] Reprinted with permission from *The New Yorker,* February 18, 1939. Copyright 1939 by The New Yorker Magazine, Inc.

Ray Ehrensberger, "An Experimental Study of the Relative Effectiveness of Certain Forms of Emphasis in Public Speaking," *Speech Monographs,* XII (1945), 94-111.

Grant Fairbanks, *Voice and Articulation Drillbook,* 2nd ed. (New York: Harper & Brothers, 1960).

Harvey Fletcher, *Speech and Hearing in Communication* (New York: D. Van Nostrand Company, Inc., 1953).

Giles W. Gray and C. M. Wise, *The Bases of Speech,* 3rd ed. (New York: Harper & Brothers, 1959), Chapter 3, "The Physiological Basis of Speech"; Chapter 4, "The Neurological Basis of Speech."

Ralph R. Leutenegger, *The Sounds of American English: An Introduction to Phonetics* (Chicago: Scott, Foresman and Company, 1963).

C. K. Thomas, *Handbook of Speech Improvement* (New York: The Ronald Press Company, 1956).

CHAPTER 6

SUPPORTING ONE POINT

There are many speaking situations in which, instead of presenting a long and complex talk, you wish only to explain or to prove a single point. The need for such "one-point" speeches arises in class discussions and informal arguments, or on occasions requiring reports or instructions. Moreover, speeches to entertain customarily consist of a series of stories or anecdotes unified around one humorous thought.

Besides being useful in actual speaking situations, the one-point speech is valuable as a learning device. Attempt to explain or prove just one idea at first, and leave until later the longer and more complex types of speaking. If while you talk you are able to keep your eye on one point rather than several, you will be less apt to ramble over a number of unrelated thoughts or to propound vague abstractions and generalities. Then, too, most long and complex speeches are actually a series of one-point talks tied together into a more comprehensive line of explanation or argument. Hence, in learning how to develop one-point talks, you are mastering a skill required in longer speeches.

THE NEED FOR SUPPORTING MATERIAL

In a one-point speech, as in any other, ideas must be developed and supported if they are to be grasped by the audience. Listeners find it difficult to understand abstract statements; nor will they usually believe a proposition or act upon a proposal without proof or stimulation. In giving a speech, therefore, you not only must state the point you wish to communicate; you also must amplify and support it.

Suppose that the purpose of your speech is to explain to an audience why "'Bad' money drives out 'good' money," or to prove that "Speed is the principal cause of automobile accidents on our highways." How would the average listener react to each of these statements upon first hearing it? In the first case, he would be almost certain to think, "I do not understand this assertion; please explain it." In the second, he would probably think, "I doubt or disbelieve this statement; prove it." These reactions would not arise because the hearer was dull or obstinate, but out of a natural inability to comprehend an abstract and rather ambiguous statement and an honest reluctance to accept any proposition without some notion of the evidence and reasoning which underlie it. Materials which provide explanation or proof are *supporting materials* and are of two principal types, verbal and visual. In this chapter we shall consider these types and then illustrate how they may be used to develop a one-point talk.

THE FORMS OF VERBAL SUPPORTING MATERIAL

Several forms of verbal support may be used to develop or prove the ideas in speech:
1. Explanation
2. Analogy or comparison
   a. Figurative analogy
   b. Literal analogy
3. Illustration (detailed example)
   a. Hypothetical illustration
   b. Factual illustration
4. Specific instance (undeveloped example)
5. Statistics
6. Testimony
7. Restatement

Sometimes two or more of these forms are combined, as when statistics are used to develop an illustration, or when the testimony of an authority is given to add weight to an explanation. At other times the forms are used singly, the speaker's choice of materials depending upon the type of support he needs. Comparison, figurative analogy, and hypothetical illustration, for example, are helpful primarily in making ideas clear and vivid, while specific instances, statistics, and testimony serve better as proof. Literal analogy, factual illustration, and restatement serve both purposes.

Explanation

A complete explanation of an operation or concept often involves the use of several forms of support. In fact, Chapter 9 is devoted to speeches the entire purpose of which may be to clarify or explain. But the term *explanation* is used more narrowly here to refer to a paragraph or unit within a speech. By it we mean *a simple, concise, expository passage which clarifies an obscure term or sets forth the relation between a whole and its parts.*

This is how Leonard Bernstein explained the term *Blues* in a lecture to a television audience October 16, 1955. Observe that before he told what he meant by *Blues,* he was careful to tell what he did not mean. In this way he narrowed the area of reference and prepared his listeners to understand the term more readily.

> Most people use the word *Blues* to mean any song that is "blue" or torchy or lowdown or breast-beating—like "Stormy Weather," for example. But "Stormy Weather" is not a Blues, and neither is "Moanin' Low," nor "The Man I Love," or even "The Birth of the Blues." They are all popular songs.
>
> The Blues is basically a strict poetic form combined with music. It is based on a rhymed couplet, with the first line repeated. For example, Billie Holiday sings:
>
> *"My man don't love me, treats me awful mean;*
> *Oh, he's the lowest man I've ever seen."*
>
> But when she sings it, she repeats the first line—so it goes:
>
> *"My man don't love me, treats me awful mean;*
> *I said, my man don't love me, treats me awful mean;*
> *Oh, he's the lowest man I've ever seen."*
>
> That is one stanza of Blues. A full Blues is nothing more than a succession of such stanzas for as long as the singer wishes.[1]

In a speech at the University of Portland, Mortimer J. Adler ex-

---

[1] "The World of Jazz," in *The Joy of Music* (New York: Simon and Schuster, 1959), p. 109. Stanza from "Fine and Mellow" by Billie Holiday.

plained his conception of a liberal education, first by breaking it down into its parts, and then by giving examples of liberal studies:

> Liberal education means two things essentially. On the side of the liberal arts, it means all the basic skills of the mind — the skills of reading and writing and speaking and listening, observing, measuring, and calculating; the skills essential to all forms of learning; the skills required for all forms of communication. And on the side of substance, liberal education means the humanities, which centuries ago would have been called "humane letters." By that one does not just mean poetry or history, but even more philosophy and theology, and even the natural and social sciences when these are studied with a humane rather than a technical interest.
>
> Let me explain this one step further. The humanities, as the word itself should suggest, represent the permanent and universal features of human life and society, which stem from the constancy of human nature itself — the powers and aspirations of man. Hence philosophy and theology are central and must be central in any humanistic education. As Cardinal Newman has taught us all, to be basically liberal, education must be through and through philosophical and theological.[2]

Although explanation is a good way to begin to make an idea clear, it may not in itself be adequate. Therefore, you must always stand ready to bolster it with comparisons, illustrations, or restatement. Be careful, too, not to make explanations too long or involved. Many an audience has been put to sleep by a long-winded explanation full of abstract details. Keep your explanations simple, brief, and accurate; combine them with other forms of support as necessary. This is a good rule to follow in all forms of oral or written communication.

Analogy or comparison

An analogy or comparison points out the similarities between something which is already known, understood, or believed and something which is not. It explains or proves the unknown by relating it to the known. Analogies are of two kinds: figurative and literal. A figurative analogy draws a comparison between things belonging to different classes or orders of being; it compares airplanes with birds, the heads of states with the captains of ships, the human heart with a power

---

[2] Mr. Adler's address, delivered on January 13, 1963, is reprinted in *Town and Gown,* Alumni Magazine of the University of Portland (January 1963).

plant, etc. A literal analogy, on the other hand, compares members of the same class—cities with cities, colleges with colleges, and the like.

Dr. Louis Hadley Evans, Minister-at-Large for the Presbyterian Church, used brief figurative analogies to explain what he meant by the terms *deist* and *theist*.

> To you this world is what: a clock or a car? Is it a huge clock, that God once made, that He wound up at the beginning and left to run of itself? Then you are a *deist*.
>
> Do you believe that it is rather a car, that God once made, but that does not run without His hand on the wheel, without His ultimate and personal control? Then you are a *theist*.[3]

And General H. F. Harding, in a speech before the Creative Problem Solving Institute on September 6, 1963, drew this analogy between the nurturing of plants and the nurturing of ideas:

> Farmers learned long ago that Seed Beds are vital for growing plants and flowers. The gardener must provide good soil, fertilizer, water, sunshine, insecticides, and loving care—all in the right proportion at the right time if he wants tender flowers to grow. So it is in the world of new ideas. They too need protection and nourishment in the early stages. The men who nurture new ideas need a special kind of approval.[4]

Although figurative analogies may occasionally be used as proof, their principal function is to make ideas clear or vivid. Literal analogies, on the other hand, are common and useful means of proving points. A speaker, for example, may advocate the adoption of a certain system of registration at his college because that system has worked well at a neighboring institution. Similarly, one could argue by analogy that stricter driver's license examinations would reduce traffic accidents in his state because they have done so in a neighboring state, or urge the rejection of proposed legislation because it closely resembles legislation that has proved unworkable in the past.

Because it attempts to base a conclusion on a single parallel instance, a literal analogy used as proof must meet a rigid test. Unless the in-

---

[3] "Can You Trust God?" A television sermon in the *Man to Man* series. Pamphlet No. 10 (National Council of Churches of Christ in the U.S.A.), p. 4.

[4] "What Are Your Ultimate Objectives?" *Vital Speeches*, XXIX (October 1, 1963), 759.

stances compared are *closely parallel in all essential respects,* the analogy is inconclusive. Although a certain system of registration has worked well in a small college, we cannot conclude that it would also work well in a large university, nor does the experience of a lowland or "plains" state in reducing highway accidents provide good evidence that the same result would follow in a mountainous state. Do the similarities between the items compared outweigh any differences that may be relevant to the conclusion you are drawing? This is the question you must always ask when you use a literal analogy.

Illustration

A *detailed narrative* example of the idea or statement to be supported is called an illustration. Sometimes an illustration describes a condition or turn of events which the speaker wishes to emphasize; sometimes it relates the results which have been obtained from the adoption of a plan or proposal. Always, however, an illustration is an expanded example, presented in narrative form, and having about it some striking or memorable quality.

There are two principal types of illustrations: the hypothetical and the factual. The first tells a story which *could have* happened or *probably will* happen; the second tells what *actually has* happened.

The *hypothetical illustration* is an imaginary narrative. It must, however, be consistent with the known facts. It must be reasonable. The following hypothetical illustration is taken from a speech delivered in 1947 by Charles J. Stilwell:

> Let's put ourselves in the other fellow's place. If you got no satisfaction out of your job as employer, if you had no pride in the sense of accomplishment, if you didn't feel yourself a vital part of a dynamic organization, all the pay you would get would be money. Take away all those things that make up your compensation, and every one of you would demand that your pay be doubled, because money would be all that was left.
>
> Out in your shop a man comes to work at 7 A.M. He doesn't know too much about his job and almost nothing about his company or how his work fits into it. He works 8 hours and goes home — with what? His pay and nothing more. Nobody (except the union steward!) took much if any notice of him. Nobody complimented him if he did do well because nobody except a foreman *knows* whether or not he did

well, and he realizes *that* fact. Nobody ever flattered him by asking his opinion about something. In millions of cases nobody ever told him the importance of his work.

At night he goes home to his family and neighbors—unimportant, with nothing to boast about or even talk about. And the union calls a meeting to discuss a grievance—that workman can get up on his feet and sound off while people listen, he can be an officer with a title, he can boast to his family and friends how he "gave those big shots of the company what-for!" A strike vote is exciting!—Being a picket is important!—He gets looked at and talked about; he wears a badge!

Again, let's be honest. If you and I were in that worker's situation, wouldn't we do pretty much what he's doing?[5]

Because aspects of the narrative can be manipulated at will, a hypothetical illustration is an especially valuable means of clarifying an idea and making it vivid. Also, it provides a good way to explain a complicated situation or plan. Instead of talking in general terms, the speaker may take a person, perhaps himself or a member of the audience, and picture that person going through the various processes which the plan entails. As proof, however, the hypothetical illustration, like the figurative analogy, is at best of doubtful value. The very fact that the details can be manipulated by the speaker may cause the audience to withhold credence.

Factual illustration. As a description of an actual experience or event, a factual illustration not only clarifies, but also may serve as proof. The following remarks from a speech by General Lauris Norstad, former Supreme Allied Commander in Europe, contain a factual illustration. Speaking at the annual Printing Week Dinner in New York City on January 17, 1963, General Norstad was here describing the mental state of Europeans in the years immediately following World War II:

We can only move forward by looking in that direction but sometimes we may be excused for a backward glance to note the course we have run, to measure the extent and the significance of the changes that have taken place. . . .

It will be just twelve years ago next Monday that I landed in Wiesbaden, Germany, to assume my first command in Europe. I was very warmly welcomed by the Germans of that community as well

---

[5] "Effective Leadership for Better Employee Relations," presented December 4, 1947 before the Labor Relations Session of the Congress of American Industry. *Vital Speeches,* XIV (December 15, 1947), 157.

as by the Americans, and for a moment I mistook this as a tribute to me. But on second thought, I realized that I had no fame or reputation which could possibly have preceded me, so I was compelled to look for another answer. Failing to find it by my own efforts, I asked some friends and they were kind enough, perhaps cruel enough, to set me straight. The warmth of my reception came from the fact that, as I left the aircraft that had brought me from Washington, I was accompanied by my wife and twelve-year-old daughter. People who had been conditioned to feel that war was not a question of *whether* but of *when* felt that I would not unnecessarily expose my family had the threat been imminent, the danger near. This incident, this personal experience, seemed to me to be typical of the time, to reflect the mood of that bleak hour.[6]

Three considerations should be kept in mind when choosing a factual illustration to support or prove an idea. First, is it clearly related to the idea? Is the point of the illustration obvious? Second, is it a fair example? If you are citing an event or experience as an illustration of a general principle, you must be sure that the event or experience is typical. An audience is quick to notice unusual circumstances in an illustration, and if you seem to have picked an exceptional case, your narrative will not be convincing. Third, is the illustration vivid and impressive? One of the chief values of an illustration is the sense of reality it creates. If this quality is absent, the advantage of using the illustration often is lost. Be sure that your illustrations are *pointed, fair,* and *vivid.*

Specific instance

A specific instance is an undeveloped illustration or example. Instead of describing a situation in detail, you merely refer to it in passing. When time prevents the development of an illustration to clarify an idea or to show the seriousness of a problem, you may sometimes achieve the same result by mentioning a number of instances which are already more or less known to the audience. In a speech delivered August 16, 1963, before the Inter-American Defense College, C. Langdon White, Professor of Geography at Stanford University, used specific instances to remind his listeners of some of the difficulties in our relations with Latin America:

---

[6] "Authority over Nuclear Weapons," *Vital Speeches,* XXIX (February 15, 1963), 259.

The road to good neighborliness [with Latin America] is strewn with a number of obstacles, obstacles that are partly geographic and partly human. I submit here a few of the more obvious and significant differences between us:

1. Difference in language
2. Difference in race
3. Difference in religion
4. Differences in stage of economic development
5. Differences in our legal systems
6. Differences in our ideas of democracy (except perhaps on paper)
7. Differences in our attitude toward manual work
8. Differences in standard of living . . .
9. Differences in per capita annual wage: $400 average for Latin America, $2,450 for U.S. (1963)
10. Differences in rate of literacy

These differences form a chasm, a *cultural chasm*, that is not easy to bridge. As a result of the differences listed, we tend to irritate each other; in a slangy sense, we just do not see eye-to-eye.[7]

If the names, events, or situations cited by the speaker are well known to the listeners, specific instances may serve as proof of a contention. To an American audience, for example, the assertion that a poor boy may become President can be supported merely by mentioning the names of Andrew Jackson, Abraham Lincoln, and Herbert Hoover. On subjects with which the audience is not familiar, however, or on subjects concerning which people have marked differences of opinion, it is well to use more fully developed examples or illustrations.

Statistics

Statistics are figures which indicate relationships among phenomena or which summarize and interpret bodies of data; they express in numerical form facts which have been carefully selected and analyzed. Statistics not only enable a speaker to summarize a great deal of data quickly, but they are indispensable when attempting to isolate trends or to predict future developments.

Dr. Juanita M. Kreps of the Department of Economics at Duke University used statistics effectively to point out recent changes in the

---

[7] "Anglo-America and Latin America: Can They Become Better Neighbors?" *Vital Speeches*, XXIX (October 1, 1963), 746.

income level of the American family. She was speaking on "The Status of Women" July 19, 1962, at a leadership training workshop of the North Carolina Council of Women's Organizations.

> You are aware, of course, that the postwar era has been one of rapidly rising incomes. These incomes, although partly reflecting the inflationary bias of the economy, have nevertheless risen a good bit more, in fact, than prices. The result has been rising standards of living for most people.
>
> How much have incomes risen?
>
> Between 1947 and 1960 average family income (in current dollars) rose from $3,000 to $5,600 — an increase of about 85 per cent. In the same period, consumer prices rose substantially, however; only about one-half of the increase in current dollar incomes represented an increase in purchasing power. In terms of constant (1960) dollars, the median family income rose from $4,000 in 1947 to $5,600 in 1960, or about 40 per cent. The rate of growth was thus about $2\frac{1}{2}$ per cent per year for the period.
>
> If one wants to view income change for a slightly longer period, the median real wage and salary income of primary families in the United States doubled between 1939 and 1960 — rising from $2,700 to $5,400 (income in both years expressed in 1960 dollars). Thus, for the 21-year period the growth rate was about $3\frac{1}{2}$ per cent, the higher rate reflecting the increased employment and higher productivity which accompanied our preparation for and entrance into World War II.[8]

Notice that Professor Kreps did not merely cite figures, but that she also indicated their significance by comparing them one to another. Figures by themselves tell little; you must establish trends — increases, decreases, concomitant variations, etc. — in order to secure understanding or affect belief. Remember, too, that masses of figures or unusually large or small figures are often difficult for an audience to comprehend and therefore should be translated into more immediately understandable terms. In the following passage, Hugh L. Dryden, Deputy Administrator of the National Aeronautics and Space Administration, used a number of comparisons to show how large a building would be required to house the Saturn V manned lunar rocket:

> The Vertical Assembly Building will be one of the largest structures on earth. According to present plans, the high-bay area will be 524

---

[8] *Vital Speeches,* XXVIII (September 1, 1962), 698.

feet tall, about as tall as the Washington Monument, or only 58 feet less than the Gulf Building in Pittsburgh. It will be almost as wide and long as it is tall, 448 by 513 feet. The height of the door is 456 feet, tall enough to permit a 41-story building to slide through. Its total volume will be about 128 million cubic feet, more than twice that of the Merchandise Mart in Chicago and $1\frac{2}{3}$ times the volume of the Pentagon Building in Washington. Four space vehicles may be assembled in this building at the same time, protected from salt air and hurricane winds.[9]

Other ways of making statistics more readily understandable include stating very large figures in round numbers (say, "nearly 4,000,000," rather than "3,984,256"), breaking totals down on a per-capita basis, writing figures on the blackboard as you discuss them, pointing to prepared charts or graphs on which the data are presented, handing out mimeographed material summarizing the data you are presenting, and slowing down your rate of delivery. When effectively and honestly used, statistics are invaluable in explanation or proof. You always must be sure, however, to make them understandable.

Testimony

When a speaker cites verbatim the opinions or conclusions of others, he is using *testimony*. Sometimes testimony is used merely to add weight or impressiveness to an idea; at other times it is intended to supply proof for a point.

In the following passage from a speech entitled "National Security," Governor Nelson A. Rockefeller used testimony for the first of these purposes:

> If we are to preserve democracy, our political leaders must be candid rather than clever.
>
> They must be responsive to the people—and they must have the courage to give the people the bad news as well as the good.
>
> The American people are not afraid.
>
> They want to know the facts.
>
> The Scripps-Howard newspapers have a slogan that puts it very well:

---

[9] "The U.S. Space Program," address at the annual dinner meeting of the Pittsburgh Post, The Society of American Military Engineers, April 2, 1963. Text supplied by National Aeronautics and Space Administration.

"Give light, and the people will find their own way."

This is the great privilege and right of which you as members of the press are the guardians for the American people.

It is our mutual obligation to the people and to our free, democratic society, to make certain that the light shines clearly for all to see.[10]

All testimony should meet the twin tests of authoritativeness and audience acceptability. When used to prove a statement, rather than merely to add weight or to clarify, testimony also should satisfy, in so far as possible, four more specific criteria:

1. The training and experience of the person quoted should qualify him as an authority. He should be an expert in the field to which his testimony relates.

2. Whenever possible, the statement of the authority should be based on first-hand knowledge.

3. The judgment expressed must not be unduly influenced by personal interest. The authority must not be prejudiced.

4. Your hearers must recognize that the man quoted actually is an authority. They must respect his opinion.

The following passage from a student speech on water fluoridation employs testimony as proof. Observe that the speaker, Neal Luker, chose as his authority a presumably unbiased expert in a position to know the facts at first hand, and that he was careful to state the authority's full title for his listeners.

> Summing up experiments too numerous to mention and representing the best current professional opinion on fluoridation is the following statement by Dr. Nicholas Leone, Chief of Medical Investigation for the National Institute of Dental Research: "We know without question or doubt that one part per million fluoride in water supply is absolutely safe, is beneficial, and is not productive of any undesirable systemic effect in man."[11]

When citing testimony, watch particularly the tendency to use big names simply because they are well known. A movie star may be famous for her beauty and appeal, but her opinion on the nutritive value of a breakfast food is less reliable than the opinion of your phy-

---

[10] Presented at annual dinner of New York State Publishers Association, January 29, 1963. Text supplied by Governor Rockefeller.

[11] "Water Fluoridation," presented at the University of Iowa May 13, 1963. Quotation taken from *Water Fluoridation: Facts, Not Myths* by Louis I. Dublin (Public Affairs Pamphlet No. 251), p. 15.

sician. The most reliable testimony always comes from subject matter experts whose qualifications your listeners recognize.

Restatement

Restatement is reiteration of an idea in different words. Therefore, it is to be distinguished from mere repetition, in which the words remain the same.

Although they provide no real proof, restatement and repetition often have persuasive impact. Advertisers realize this fact and spend millions of dollars annually repeating the same message in magazines, on billboards, and over radio and television. "Let Hertz put you in the driver's seat," "Hallmark cards . . . When you care enough to send the very best," "Zing! What a feeling with a Coke!"—such slogans are repeated until they are familiar to almost everyone.

But while up to a certain point repetition may persuade, beyond that point it becomes monotonous and bores the listener. By varying your words through restatement, you can avoid this danger. Also, restatement is an excellent way to clarify ideas. In a speech entitled "Leadership and the 'Sane Society,' " Dr. Ralph Eubanks of the University of Arkansas used restatement to make clear the kind of leader he thinks is required in modern America. Not satisfied with one restatement, Dr. Eubanks repeated his idea in three different ways:

> We must, among other things, create a new leadership in America. . . . The leader I shall define as one who can help his group conduct well the ancient search for the "good life in the good society." Put another way, a good leader for our times is one who can hold ever before the members of his group a truly human vision of themselves. In a little different terms, he is one who can help his group find their way to honorable, human goals and can teach them how to "care for persons" in the process. In still different terms, he is one who can help us live up to the ancient definition of ourselves as *Homo sapiens,* or Man the Wise.[12]

Explanation, analogy or comparison, illustration, specific instance, statistics, testimony, and restatement—these, then, are the common forms of verbal supporting material. Fill your speeches with them.

---

[12] Keynote address before the Annual Leadership Conference, Arkansas Federation of Business and Professional Women's Clubs, March 24, 1963. *Vital Speeches,* XXIX (May 15, 1963), 479.

Avoid abstract, unsupported statements. Amplify your ideas and make them concrete.

THE USE OF VISUAL SUPPORTING MATERIAL

Thus far we have discussed only the audible materials that you may use to explain or prove a point—what you may *say* about it. Equally important, sometimes even more so, are the visual materials that you may use to *show* what you mean. These visual materials, which include maps, diagrams, charts, pictures, small working models, or even full-scale equipment, supplement the audible forms of support and help to make your ideas clearer and more convincing. If you were explaining how to use a complicated camera, it undoubtedly would help if you held the camera before your listeners, showed them its parts, and demonstrated the adjustments required for different sorts of pictures. Sometimes actual equipment is not available or is too big to bring into the room where the speech is made. A small scale model may then be used. Model airplanes, for example, sometimes are employed in teaching aerodynamics. Maps are helpful in explaining the layout of a city, a state's road system, or a flood-control project. Diagrams are useful in illustrating the components of an organization or mechanism and in explaining their operation. For example, a diagram can show the structure and function of a government agency or the assembly and operation of a machine. Line, bar, and pie graphs may clarify statistical data. Pictures, including lantern slides and films, are especially valuable when describing persons, places, objects, or events.

Always remember four important rules for using visual aids in a talk. First, do not stand between your listeners and what you show them. Many speakers, when they point to a map or diagram, stand directly in front of it. Keep to one side of the visual material, and talk directly to your listeners. Second, use only visual materials that are closely related to the point you are presenting, and refer only to those parts of a chart or model that are relevant. Avoid the temptation to explain all the details shown on the visual aid unless these details are necessary to the development of your idea. Third, be sure your visual material is large enough so that it can be seen easily from all parts of the room. Fourth, present visually only data which are simple enough to be comprehended at a glance; if your listeners must stop to puzzle out what your chart or diagram means, they will not be able to follow

you as you move on to new ideas in your speech. Use few words and large, heavy print; avoid a mass of meandering or crisscross lines; present your materials in vivid colors instead of weak pastels. Put only one idea or one closely related set of ideas on each chart or graphic.

Whereas in explanatory talks visual materials help clarify ideas, in persuasive speeches they may actually help win support for a point by making the facts you present more vivid and impressive.

THE USE OF SUPPORTING MATERIAL TO EXPLAIN

How should you assemble supporting material in a short talk designed to explain a single point? Usually it is best to divide the speech into

Visual aids used by these speakers exemplify materials you may use to support ideas in your speeches. *Opposite page, left to right, top to bottom:* a diagram depicts types of radioactive decay, a column graph presents statistical data, a line graph depicts stages in a manufacturing process, and a bow and arrow are used in a demonstration of archery technics. *Above, clockwise from upper left:* fire extinguishing and fire alarm equipment are used in a briefing of steel plant safety men, a model of crystal structure is used in a television lecture on physics by Dr. Harvey E. White, and a map supplements information presented by a speaker. Evaluate the effectiveness of these visual materials in making ideas clearer or more convincing.

three parts or steps. First, state the point to be explained; second, bring in your supporting material—especially explanations, illustrations, comparisons, and visual devices; third, restate the point explained. In Step 2 the verbal and visual materials may be presented separately or together. That is, you may first tell your listeners and then show them; or you may show them while telling them. In the following one-point talk, the speaker used the first of these methods.

WHAT IS DEMOCRACY?

Statement	I. The essence of democracy is the control of the government by those governed.
Explanation	A. This means the people have authority to:

1. Make the laws under which they live.
2. Select public officials to administer these laws.

Hypothetical illustration

B. Suppose a group of students were to plan a party in the democratic way.
   1. They would get together to discuss it.
   2. They would decide where and when the party would be held.
   3. They would agree how much each student should contribute to the cost.
   4. In case of disagreement, they would reach a compromise or abide by the vote of the majority.
   5. One of them would be selected to collect the money and pay the bills.
   6. They might select another person or a small committee to arrange for the entertainment, etc.
   7. Each student would have some part in deciding how the party would be run.

Comparison with B

C. If, however, one student took it upon himself to decide all these questions — even to dictating the program of entertainment and how much each one should pay for it — the party would not be *democratic*, regardless of how efficiently it might be run.

Comparison of specific instances

D. Compare these actual cases:
   1. In New England, local government is based on town meetings.
      a. All qualified residents are allowed to speak and vote directly on current problems.
      b. Public officials are selected by vote of the citizens.
   2. Indiana cities are governed by representatives of the people.
      a. City ordinances are made by the city council, whose members are elected by the voters.
      b. Administrative officials are elected.
   3. In Norway and Denmark, under German occupation during World War II, city

government was controlled by *gauleiters* or similar officials.

    a. These men were chosen by the Nazi leaders, not by the people they governed.

    b. They enforced Nazi laws and issued orders over which the people of Norway and Denmark were permitted no control.

Diagram   E. This diagram will show why the first two examples just cited are democratic while the third was not. (Arrows show the direction of government control.)

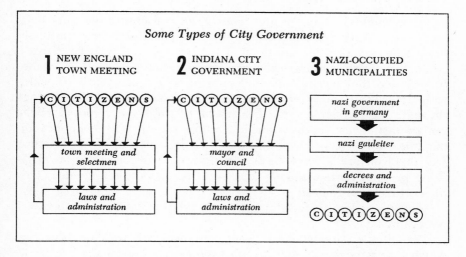

Some Types of City Government

1 NEW ENGLAND TOWN MEETING   **2** INDIANA CITY GOVERNMENT   **3** NAZI-OCCUPIED MUNICIPALITIES

CITIZENS → town meeting and selectmen → laws and administration

CITIZENS → mayor and council → laws and administration

nazi government in germany → nazi gauleiter → decrees and administration → CITIZENS

Restatement   II. Democracy, as Lincoln said of the United States, is government "by the people."

THE USE OF SUPPORTING MATERIAL TO PROVE

There are two common methods of organizing supporting material to prove a point. They may be called the didactic method, and the method of implication.

The didactic method

The didactic method utilizes a pattern like that exemplified in the outline of the one-point expository speech above. In using this method you first state and clarify the proposition you wish to prove, then you present the proof in the form of concrete supporting material, and finally you restate the proposition as an established conclusion. Steps in this pattern may be enumerated as follows:

1. State your point.
2. Make it clear by explanation, comparison, or illustration.
3. Prove it by specific instances, testimony, statistics, or additional factual illustrations.
4. Restate your point as an established conclusion.

The method of implication

The method of implication consists of presenting the facts first, and then stating the conclusion toward which these facts inevitably lead. You do not state the point to be proved until you have made clear the evidence upon which the point rests. This method, sometimes called the "natural" method of argument, more nearly coincides with the way in which we arrive at conclusions when thinking things through for ourselves. For this reason,' though often not so clear nor so easy to use as the didactic method, the method of implication may be more persuasive. Because it avoids making your listeners feel that you are pushing something down their throats, it always is to be preferred when talking to a skeptical or hostile audience. This method includes four steps:

1. Present an analogy or illustration which *implies* the point you wish to make.
2. Offer additional illustrations, instances, statistics, or testimony which point inevitably to this conclusion without actually stating it.
3. Show specifically how these facts lead to the conclusion; use explanation if necessary.
4. Definitely state your point as a conclusion.

Whether you use the didactic method or the method of implication, you will find that the first three forms of support (explanation, comparison, and illustration) are most useful in making an idea clear and vivid, while the next three (specific instances, statistics, and testimony) more often will assist you in proving an idea true or important. Restatement, of course, serves either to clarify or to emphasize. Study the sample speech outline below. Note that the didactic method is used. If the general statement were omitted, however, this outline would illustrate equally well the method of implication.

INSTRUCTION BY TELEVISION

General statement

Hypothetical illustration

Specific instances

Statistics

I. Classroom instruction by television is effective.

   A. Perhaps you have had this experience in one of your classes:

      1. When you entered the room, there was a television set rather than an instructor in front of the class.

      2. On TV you saw the department's best teacher for the course you were taking.

      3. In other rooms other classes were watching the same telecast.

         a. The students in each class could see and hear the lecturer and the teaching materials being used.

         b. The students in each class could obtain individual help when necessary.

      4. You may have learned as much about your subject as you would have learned in a conventional class.

   B. Televised instruction has been used in various subject areas and on various educational levels.

      1. Miami University of Ohio reported that students in TV sections and those in regular classes did equally well in subject matter learning.

      2. The city of Chicago found similar results for high-school physics and algebra.

      3. In Cincinnati, high-school chemistry classes having televised instruction were ahead of other classes.

   C. A special committee headed by Arthur E. Traxler of the Educational Records Bureau and supported by the Fund for the Advancement of Education reported figures that clearly show the effectiveness of televised instruction.

      1. Experiments involving almost 27,000 students were conducted in several cities.

      2. Of 110 comparisons made in this study, 68 — or over 60 per cent — showed the groups instructed by television to have

achieved higher scores than the other groups.

Testimony   D. As the result of studies like these, televised instruction is gaining the approval of educators.
    1. Leslie P. Greenhill, associate director of the Division of Academic Research and Services for Pennsylvania State University, stated in the *National Education Association Journal:*
        "Results of TV research show that when the same teacher teaches in each situation, televised instruction is equivalent in effectiveness to face-to-face instruction."

Analogy   E. Just as training films have assisted in teaching millions of men and women in the armed forces, so television can be useful in the classrooms of our schools.

Restatement   II. Subjects can be effectively taught by television.

The proof of a single point will seldom require as many different forms of support as are used in this sample outline. It is given to show how a number of different forms of support may be combined.

THE USE OF SUPPORTING MATERIAL TO ENTERTAIN

As we pointed out in Chapter 3, when you are giving a speech to entertain, your general purpose is not to explain nor to prove something to your listeners, but to amuse them—to cause them to sit back and enjoy themselves. Although the supporting materials are assembled around a central theme in much the same way as in a speech to inform or persuade, they are chosen not so much to clarify or to add substance as to divert or amuse. Careful explanation and solid proof are less important than lively descriptions and novel facts; statistics give way to humorous anecdotes and tales of your own or someone else's experiences, gossip about unusual people and events, exaggerated descriptions, puns, irony, and unexpected turns of phraseology.

You should not, however, make the speech to entertain a string of unrelated jokes. Let one story or observation lead naturally into the next, and see that all serve to bring out the point around which your talk is built. Underlying your humor should be a central theme—some sentiment of loyalty or appreciation for the group addressed or a serious thought concerning your subject.

A speech to entertain, then, should consist of a series of illustrations, stories, anecdotes, and humorous comments following one another in rapid order and developed around a central idea that has at least some significance or merit. The following is a good way to arrange your material for such a talk:

1. Relate a story or anecdote, present an illustration, or quote appropriate verse.

2. State the essential idea or point of view implied by your opening remarks.

3. Follow with a series of additional stories, anecdotes, or illustrations that amplify or illuminate this central point. Arrange these items in the order of increasing interest or humor.

4. Close with a striking or novel restatement of the central point you have developed.

By organizing your talk in this way, you not only will provide your listeners with entertainment, but you also will help them remember your central idea.

The talk printed below illustrates the four steps we have described. In addition, it shows how a serious thought may be given humorous treatment.

A Case for Optimism

Poem embodying analogy used as opening

I'm sure you have heard the verse that runs:
'Twixt optimist and pessimist
The difference is droll:
The optimist sees the doughnut,
The pessimist, the hole.

Statement

The longer I live, the more convinced I am of the truth of this poem. Life, like a doughnut, may seem full, rich, and enjoyable, or it may seem as empty as the hole of a doughnut. To the pessimist, the optimist seems foolish, but who is foolish—the one who sees the doughnut or the one who sees the hole?

---

[13] Prepared by Douglas Nigh, a student at the University of Iowa, May 1963. Based in part upon material taken from *Friendly Speeches* (Cleveland: National Reference Library).

Somebody else pointed out the difference between an optimist and a pessimist this way: An optimist looks at an oyster and expects a pearl; a pessimist looks at an oyster and expects ptomaine poisoning. Even if the pessimist is right, which I doubt, he probably won't enjoy himself either before or after he proves it. But the optimist is happy because he always is expecting pearls.

Pessimists are easy to recognize. They are the ones who go around asking "What's good about it?" when someone says "Good morning." If they would look around, they would see *something* good, like the merchant did whose store was robbed. The day after the robbery a sympathetic friend asked about the loss. "Lose much?" he wanted to know. "Some," said the merchant, "but then it would have been worse if the robbers had got in the night before. You see, yesterday I just finished marking everything down 20 per cent."

There is another story about a shoemaker who left the gas heater in his shop turned on overnight and upon arriving in the morning struck a match to light it. There was a terrific explosion and the shoemaker was blown out through the door almost to the middle of the street. A passerby who rushed up to help inquired if he were injured. The shoemaker got up slowly and looked back at the shop which by now was burning briskly. "No, I ain't hurt," he said, "but I sure got out just in time, didn't I?"

Some writers have made fun of that kind of outlook. You may recall the fun Voltaire made of optimism in *Candide:* "Optimism," he said, "is a mania for maintaining that all is well when things are going badly." A later writer, James Branch Cabell, quipped: "The optimist proclaims that we live in the best of all possible worlds; the pessimist fears this is true."

These writers, I suppose, couldn't resist the urge to make light of optimists, but I, for one, refuse to take *them* seriously. I like the remark by Keith Preston, literary critic and journalist, "There's

Illustrations

as much bunk among the busters as among the boosters."

Optimism, rather than the cynicism of Voltaire, is the philosophy I like to hear preached. There was a little old lady who complained about the weather. "But, Melissa," said her friend, "awful weather is better than no weather." So quit complaining, I say, and start cheering; there is always something to cheer about. And quit expecting the worst. An optimist cleans his glasses before he eats his grapefruit.

Restatement

Give in to optimism; don't fight it. Remember the doughnut and, as Elbert Hubbard advised:

As you travel on through life, brother,
Whatever be your goal,
Keep your eye upon the doughnut
And not upon the hole.

In this chapter we have discussed the types of supporting material, both verbal and visual, and we have seen how this material may be assembled to clarify or prove the points a speaker wishes to make. We also have seen how to develop an idea in a speech to entertain. Practice using the forms of support by making several one-point speeches. Be sure to state the main point you wish to make in a simple, straightforward manner; choose supporting material that is clear and substantial or light and entertaining; arrange your material so that it develops and emphasizes the point of your speech.

PROBLEMS FOR FURTHER STUDY

1. Select from current issues of the magazine *Vital Speeches*, or from some other suitable source, an informative speech in which you think the forms of verbal supporting material are well used. Select another informative speech in which you think these forms are poorly used.

Prepare a paper explaining and justifying your judgments. Deal with questions such as these: Was the supporting material sufficient in quantity? Did it come from reliable sources? Was it sufficiently varied? Was it suited to the speaker's subject and purpose? Was it adapted to the audience who heard the speech? Was it recent in date, comprehensive in scope, fairly presented?

2. Make the same kind of critical analysis of two speeches designed to

influence belief or action. Again, choose one speech in which the forms of support are well used and one in which they are poorly used.

3. Find a speech in which many statistics are used. Criticize the clarity, accuracy, and fairness with which the figures are presented. If you can, suggest specific ways in which their presentation might have been improved. (Consult the reading list at the end of this chapter for books which discuss accuracy and fairness in the use of statistics.)

4. Listen to a talk in which visual supporting materials are used. (Talks over television and classroom lectures are likely sources.) Comment on the effectiveness with which the visual devices were employed, and suggest how they could have been used more effectively.

5. Read carefully for three days the editorials and signed columns in your local newspaper. To what extent were the forms of supporting material used to substantiate the writers' views? How often were opinions expressed without supporting evidence?

6. Listen to a comedian present a monolog on television. To what extent did the humor appear to depend on the content and organization of his material? To what extent did it seem to depend on his delivery? What do you conclude about the relative importance of content and delivery in gaining humorous effects?

SPEAKING ASSIGNMENTS

1. Organize a one-point informative speech on one of the following subjects or a similar subject. Employ at least three different forms of supporting material.
> The meaning of *pragmatism*
> The principle of stereophonic sound
> How to estimate the height of a building (tree, etc.)
> The rhyme pattern of a sonnet
> "Featherbedding" on the job

2. Organize a one-point persuasive speech on one of the following subjects or a similar subject, using the didactic method. Employ at least three different forms of supporting material.
> You can learn to read faster
> Speed is the principal cause of automobile accidents
> Our foreign aid program has won (or lost) us friends
> State censorship of movies (books) is (is not) desirable
> Driver's license tests are too easy
> Let's adopt the four-day week

3. Organize a one-point persuasive speech on one of the following subjects or a similar subject, using the method of implication. Employ at least three different forms of supporting material.

Stop smoking today

We should have more and larger athletic scholarships

In defense of the closed shop

Higher grading standards are desirable

An argument for agricultural price supports

4. Prepare a four- or five-minute speech to entertain on one of the following topics or on a similar topic of your own choice:

Life in the army (at camp, on the farm)

The art of "reaching" for the check

Seeing our friends at the zoo

Measuring up to a too-good first impression

Counting sheep and other devices

Rediscovering Tom Swift (or any fictional character)

Parkinson's Law works in colleges too

Out of step with the "in" crowd

Love at first sight

SUGGESTIONS FOR FURTHER READING

Russell L. C. Butsch, *How to Read Statistics* (Milwaukee: Bruce Publishing Co., 1946).

Darrell Huff, *How to Lie with Statistics* (New York: The Norton Press, 1954). Explains the tricks and fallacies in statistical proof and how to guard against them.

Rudolf Modley and Dyno Lowenstein, *Pictographs and Graphs: How to Make and Use Them* (New York: Harper & Brothers, 1952).

Harry W. Robbins and Robert T. Oliver, *Developing Ideas into Essays and Speeches* (New York: Longmans, Green and Co., 1943), Chapter 4, "Gathering Primary Materials," and Chapter 5, "Organizing Ideas."

Walter A. Wittich and Charles F. Schuller, *Audio-Visual Materials: Their Nature and Use* (New York: Harper & Brothers, 1953), Chapter 5, "Graphics."

CHAPTER 7

ARRANGING AND OUTLINING

RELATED POINTS

In the previous chapter we examined the kinds of materials from which speeches are built. Moreover, we saw how these materials can be used to explain or to prove a single point. Most speeches, however, contain more than one point, and we are now ready to consider how to put longer speeches together in an orderly manner. We shall discuss how to organize the main points of a speech, how to arrange the subordinate ideas and the supporting materials, and how to state the plan of the entire speech in outline form.

TYPES OF ARRANGEMENT

Always arrange the points in your speech in a systematic sequence so that one idea leads naturally into the next. Not only will such an order make it easier for you to remember what you planned to say, but it also will enable your audience to follow your thoughts more readily. There are several standard patterns for organizing a speech so that each point leads naturally into the next.

Time sequence

One method of organization is to begin at a certain period or date and to move forward chronologically. The climate of Alaska, for example, may be described by considering in order the temperature, precipitation, and wind conditions as they exist in the spring, summer, fall, and winter; the refining of petroleum, by tracing the development of the refining process from the earliest attempts down to the present; or the manufacture of an automobile, by following the process on the assembly line from beginning to end. Here is an example of arrangement in time sequence, which follows the progress of aviation over a period of more than sixty years—from the days of Orville and Wilbur Wright to the present time.

MAN IN FLIGHT

I. In 1903, Orville and Wilbur Wright made the first controlled and sustained flight in a heavier-than-air, power-driven airplane.
II. World War I brought a rapid advance in airplane design and construction.
III. During the 1930's, commercial air travel became popular.
IV. After World War II, jets were introduced.
V. More recently, systems were developed to permit orbital flight.
VI. Now scientists are engaged in perfecting spacecraft for interplanetary flight.

In rare cases, in order to make progress or development seem more striking and vivid, you may wish to move backward from a chosen point in time. Whether you move forward or backward from the beginning date, however, be certain to preserve the actual sequence of events in your discussion. Jumping haphazardly from date to date or from event to event, without regard to how they actually happened, will give an unclear picture and confuse your listeners.

Space sequence

In the space sequence, you arrange your material by moving systematically from east to west, from north to south, from the bottom up, from the center to the outside, etc. For example, the problem of flood control in our nation may be discussed by considering in turn the various geographical areas affected; the plans for a building may be described floor by floor; or the layout for a city park may be explained by proceeding from entrance to exit. The following illustrates a speech arranged by space sequence:

PRINCIPAL AMERICAN DIALECTS

    I. Eastern dialect is heard chiefly in New England.
   II. Southern dialect is heard in the former Confederate States.
 III. General American dialect is common west and north of these two areas.

Cause-effect sequence

In using the cause-effect sequence, you first enumerate certain forces and then point out the results which follow from them, or you first describe conditions or events and then discuss the forces which caused them. For example, you may first recount recent improvements in farming, and then show that these advances have helped to bring about surpluses of agricultural products; or, reversing the order, you may first point to the surpluses, and then explain how improved methods have contributed to this condition.

Using the causal pattern, a speech on the rising cost of living might be arranged in either of the following ways:

THE RISING COST OF LIVING

    I. Wages, transportation costs, and the prices of raw materials have constantly risen since World War II.
   II. These increases have contributed to a rise in the cost of living, as evidenced by the Consumer's Price Index.

THE RISING COST OF LIVING

    I. The Consumer's Price Index has shown a steady increase in the cost of living since World War II.
   II. Higher wages and transportation costs and higher prices for raw materials have contributed to this increase.

Special topical sequence

Certain types of information fall into categories with which the audience already is familiar. It is customary for financial reports to be arranged by assets and liabilities or by income and expenditures, or for talks about our national government to be divided according to its three branches, the executive, the legislative, and the judicial. When such partitions are established by tradition or are specifically suggested by the subject matter to be presented, it is usually well to follow them. A description of qualities or functions, or a series of arguments supporting or opposing a proposition also may be arranged topically. A talk on the Dean of Men's office, for example, might follow this pattern:

FUNCTIONS OF THE DEAN'S OFFICE

    I. It enforces the code of student conduct.
   II. It coordinates extracurricular activities.
 III. It provides individual counseling and advisory services.

Or a speech presenting arguments in favor of a democratic government might employ a special order of this sort:

DEMOCRATIC GOVERNMENT IS BEST

    I. It guarantees freedom to the individual.
   II. It reflects the will of the majority.
 III. It places responsibilities upon citizens as well as office holders.

At times it is wise to let the anticipated responses of your listeners rather than the nature of your subject matter determine the arrangement of the main points of a talk. If you know in advance important questions or objections which are likely to be raised concerning your proposal, you may plan your entire speech to meet these objections. For example, if you are advocating the construction of a new expressway to handle traffic in your community and you know your listeners are likely to ask: "Will it be safe?" "Can the city afford it?" "Will the necessary land be available?" you may plan your speech in this way:

SUPPORT THE PROPOSED EXPRESSWAY

    I. It will reduce accident risks.
   II. It can be financed by municipal bonds.
 III. The necessary land may be purchased from private owners.

Problem-solution sequence

Sometimes you can best organize a speech by dividing it into two major parts: (1) a description of a problem (or related problems) and (2) the presentation of a solution (or solutions) to that problem.

For example, you might first point out some of the technical difficulties involved in sending a man into space, and then explain how these difficulties are being solved. You will find this type of arrangement especially useful when you are discussing a situation which your listeners themselves face or when you are considering future contingencies. You might, for instance, outline to the men of the senior class some of the problems involved in meeting their military obligations and then suggest ways in which these problems can be met, or you might point to the problem that factory workers will face if automation continues to increase and then present suggested solutions to this problem.

In a speech on the control of crime, one speaker employed the problem-solution pattern as follows:

CONTROLLING CRIME

    I. Our crime problem is serious.
       A. The crime rate is increasing.
       B. Major offenses go unsolved.
       C. Juvenile delinquency is rampant.
    II. We must meet this problem in three ways:
       A. We must begin a crime-prevention program.
       B. We must strengthen our police forces.
       C. We must free our court procedures from politics.

As this example shows, one method of arrangement (problem-solution) may be chosen for the main points and another method (special topical) for the subordinate ideas. On no condition, however, should you shift from one order to another in the presentation of the main points themselves, for this would confuse the audience. The following outline illustrates how the space, topical, and time sequences were combined in a classroom talk about Indians:

MAJOR INDIAN TRIBES OF THE WEST

    I. Southwest tribes include. . . .
       A. The Apache tribe. . . .
          1. Its early history. . . .
          2. Its contacts with explorers and settlers. . .
          3. Present conditions. . . .
       B. The Navaho tribe. . . .
          1. etc.

II. Pacific Coast tribes. . . .
    A. etc.
III. Northwest tribes. . . .

Notice that in this outline space sequence is used in the main points, special topical sequence in the subpoints A and B, and time sequence in the sub-subpoints 1, 2, and 3.

PHRASING MAIN POINTS

For reasons of emphasis as well as of clarity, you should word the main points of your speech carefully. While illustrations, explanations, quotations, and the like constitute the bulk of a speech, the main points tie these supporting details together and, therefore, most directly convey the message you wish the audience to accept. Good speakers take particular pains to phrase the main points so that they will be clear and easy to remember. To achieve these results, keep four characteristics of good phrasing in mind: conciseness, vividness, immediacy, and parallelism.

Conciseness

State your main points as briefly as you can without distorting their meaning. A short declarative sentence is easy to grasp; a long and complex statement tends to be vague and confusing. Avoid clumsy modifying phrases and distracting subordinate clauses. State each main point concisely and wait until you present your supporting material to qualify or elaborate it. Say, "Our state taxes are too high, " not "Taxes in this state, with the exception of those on automobiles, motor boats, and trucking lines, are higher than is justified by existing economic conditions." The second statement may express your idea more completely than the first, but it contains nothing that your supporting material could not clarify, and its greater complexity makes it less crisp and emphatic.

Vividness

As a general rule, state the main points of your speech in attention-provoking words and phrases. If they are drab and colorless, they will not stand out from the supporting material which surrounds them, nor will they be easily remembered. Because they are your main points, you should make them the punch lines of your speech. Notice how much more vivid it is to say, "We must cut costs!" than to say, "We must reduce our current operating expenditures." Remember, of course, that vivid phrasing should not be overdone or used to distort the truth. Remember, too, that language suitable at a pep rally or political meeting may be out of place on a more dignified occasion. The presentation of a technical report at a scientific meeting requires accuracy of statement rather than colorful language, while at memorial or dedication services your expression should be quietly impressive rather than dramatic.

Immediacy

Whenever possible, word your main points so that they will appeal directly to the interests and concerns of your listeners. Remember that you are speaking not merely *about* something, but *to* somebody; your main points should have a personal appeal for each member of your audience. Instead of saying, "Chemical research has helped to improve medical treatment," say, "Modern chemistry helps the doctor make you well." Rather than saying, "Air travel is fast," say, "Air travel saves you time."

Parallelism

Whenever possible, use a uniform type of sentence structure and similar phraseology in stating your main points. Since these points represent coordinate units of your speech, word them so they sound that way. Avoid unnecessary shifts from active to passive voice or from questions to assertions. Use prepositions, connectives, and verb forms which permit a similar balance, rhythm, and direction of thought. Avoid this kind of wording for a series of main points:

> I. The amount of your income tax depends on the amount you earn.
> II. You pay sales taxes in proportion to the amount you buy.
> III. Property tax is assessed on the value of what you own.

Instead, phrase the main points like this:

I. The amount of money you earn determines your income tax.

II. The amount of goods you buy determines your sales tax.

III. The amount of goods you own determines your property tax.

Observe that in this series a part of each statement is repeated, while the remainder of the statement is changed from point to point. Such repetition of key words helps the listener remember the major ideas in your talk.

ARRANGING SUBORDINATE IDEAS AND SUPPORTING MATERIAL

With the main points selected, arranged, and phrased, you are ready to organize your subordinate ideas and supporting material in such a way as to give form and substance to your speech.

Subordinating the subordinate ideas

A string-of-beads discussion, in which everything seems to have equal weight — tied together as it usually is by *and-uh, and next, and then, and so* — not only lacks form and obscures meaning, but soon proves tiresome. Because everything receives equal emphasis, nothing seems important. Regardless of how well you have chosen, arranged, and worded the main points, they will not stand out if your lesser ideas are not properly subordinated. Avoid giving subpoints the emphasis due only to main points and avoid listing under main points ideas that are not subordinate to them.

Types of subordinate ideas

Subordinate ideas commonly fall into one of five classes:

Parts of a whole. If a main point concerns an object or a process that has a number of parts or refers to a total composed of many items, these parts or items naturally constitute the subordinate ideas by which that point may be amplified or explained. For example, the grip, shaft, and head are the parts you would discuss in describing the manufacture of a golf club, or the number of television stations in England, Scotland, Ireland, and Wales are the subtotals you would refer to when showing that the number of television stations in the British Isles has increased.

Lists of functions. If a main point suggests the purpose of some mechanism, organization, or procedure, the subordinate ideas may list the specific functions performed. The purpose of a municipal police department, for example, may be made clear by discussing its responsibilities for traffic control, crime detection, safety education, and the like.

Series of causes or results. If a main point states that a cause has several effects, or that an effect results from a number of causes, the various effects or causes may be listed as subordinate ideas. For example, the causes of crop failure may be enumerated as drought, frost, and blight, or its effects as high food prices, deprivation, and possible riots.

Items of logical proof. In a speech designed to influence belief, the subordinate ideas under a main point may consist of a group of separate but related arguments or of the successive steps in a single coordinated line of reasoning. In either case, you should be able to relate the subordinate ideas to the main point by the word *because* (i.e., the main point is true because the subordinate ideas are true). You might support a plea for a new high school in your community with this series of separate but related arguments: "We need a new high school (a) because our present building is too small, (b) because our present building lacks essential laboratory and shop facilities, and (c) because the growth of our city has made it difficult for many students to get to our present building." Or you might contend that we are heading for a recession by using this line of reasoning: "We will have a recession because (a) the recent drop in prices will mean a drop in wages, and (b) a drop in wages will mean a drop in the purchasing power upon which prosperity depends."

Sometimes instead of proceeding from a main point to its subordinate ideas by using the word *because*, you may decide to reverse the process and proceed from the subpoints to a main point by using the word *therefore*. ("Our present high-school building (a) is too small, (b) lacks necessary facilities, and (c) is in a poor location; *therefore* we should build a new school." "(a) The present drop in prices will cause a drop in wages, and (b) a drop in wages will cause a drop in buying power; *therefore* we are going to have a recession.")

Illustrative examples. If a main point consists of a generalized concept or assertion, the subordinate ideas may illustrate it with specific cases or examples. This method is used in both exposition and argument, the examples providing clarification in the first case, and proof in the second. For example, you may explain the theory of reciprocal trade agreements by showing your listeners how such agreements work in actual cases involving specific goods and products, or you may support the contention that fluorine in a community's drinking water helps in the prevention or the reduction of tooth decay by citing the results obtained in certain communities which have added fluorine to their water supply.

While other types of subordinate ideas might be listed, these five — parts of a whole, lists of functions, series of causes or results, items of logical proof, and illustrative examples — are certainly among the most important.

The rules of proper subordination, of course, must govern not only the arrangement of the subordinate ideas themselves but also of the various sorts of supporting materials which fall under them. In long and detailed speeches you may have sub-subpoints which require support. Be careful not to let the process of subordination become too intricate or involved or your listeners will not be able to follow you; but however far you go, keep your subordination consistent and logical.

Coordinating subordinate ideas

If you have analyzed the subject matter of your speech correctly, you will find that each of your main points can be divided into two or more subordinate ideas. These subordinate ideas not only should be encompassed by the main point under which they fall, but they should be coordinate with each other — that is, they should be equal in scope and importance. To list poor teachers, the lack of adequate textbooks, and the loss of a cross-country track meet as the reasons for poor scholarship among the students in a large high school would indicate that your analysis of your subject is in some way faulty, for you are treating as equal three items which obviously are not equal in importance. Either the loss of the cross-country meet is symptomatic of a greater evil — poor coaching, lack of student interest, etc. — and therefore should be placed under this head, or it is irrelevant and should be eliminated from the speech altogether. To treat it as a factor equal to poor teaching and the lack of textbooks is to confuse a less important idea with more important ones and to create an unconvincing if not ludicrous effect.

Arranging subordinate ideas

Subordinate ideas, no less than main points, must be arranged in an orderly and purposeful fashion. Parts of a whole, functions, or causes — even items of proof or illustrative examples — often can be listed according to the patterns already discussed for ordering the main headings. You can put your subordinate ideas in time, space, causal, or topical sequence — whichever pattern seems to best serve the purpose you have in mind. You may want to use one sequence for the items under one main point and a different sequence for those under another, but do not alter the sequence of the subordinate ideas within the same coordinate series or you may confuse your listeners badly. Above all, be sure to employ some systematic order; do not crowd the subordinate ideas in haphazardly just because they are subordinate.

Supporting the subordinate ideas

The importance of supporting material was emphasized in Chapter 6. The general rule should be *Never make a statement in a speech without presenting some facts or reasoning to clarify, illustrate, or prove it.* Too often speakers think that if they divide every main point into two or three subordinate ideas, they have done enough. The fact is, however, that such divisions add only to the skeleton of the speech. They do not supply the supporting material upon which understanding or belief ultimately depends. The real *substance* of any talk lies in statistics, illustrations, comparisons, and testimony. Within reasonable limits, the more of these materials you have, the stronger your speech will be.

We have considered the principles that should govern the arrangement of ideas within a speech and have surveyed several patterns by which the main points may be ordered. Even with a thorough grasp of these principles and patterns, however, few persons can work out all of the details of a speech in their minds. Some orderly method must be followed for setting ideas and facts down on paper. Most speakers find it best to prepare an outline, a particularly effective method because it serves to throw into relief the structure as well as the content of a talk. After noting the requirements of good outline form, we shall indicate how to prepare an outline which sets forth in orderly fashion not only the main points, but the subordinate ideas and the supporting material as well.

REQUIREMENTS OF GOOD OUTLINE FORM

The amount of detail you include in an outline will depend on your subject, on the speaking situation, and on your previous experience in speech composition. But regardless of these factors, any good outline should meet certain basic requirements.

Each unit in the outline should contain but one idea. If two or three ideas are run together in a single point of your outline, their relation to other ideas in the outline will not stand out clearly. Notice the difference between the following examples:

Wrong
I. Our city should conduct a campaign against flies because thousands of them infest the city every year, breeding everywhere and buzzing at every kitchen door, and because they spread disease by carrying germs and contaminating food.

Right
I. Our city should conduct a campaign against flies.
   A. Thousands of flies infest the city year after year.
      1. They breed everywhere.
      2. They buzz at every kitchen door.
   B. Flies spread disease.
      1. They carry germs.
      2. They contaminate food.

Less important ideas in the outline should be subordinate to more important ideas. As you know, a subordinate idea should be a logical subdivision of the larger heading under which it falls and should rank below that heading in scope and importance. Also it should directly support or amplify the statement made in the superior heading.

Wrong
I. Advertising benefits the consumer.
   A. By stimulating sales, advertising makes possible the lower unit costs of mass production.
      1. Sales and special discount prices are announced in advertisements.
   B. It saves him money.
   C. It saves him time.
      1. It acquaints him with a wide range of competing products.
      2. It introduces him to new and improved products and services.

D. The consumer can read about products, rather than having to go to the store to examine them.
  1. It widens his area of choice.
E. He can plan shopping trips more efficiently.

Right
I. Advertising benefits the consumer.
  A. It saves the consumer money.
    1. By informing him of sales and special discount prices, advertising helps the consumer buy economically.
    2. By stimulating sales, advertising makes possible the lower unit costs of mass production.
  B. It saves the consumer time.
    1. He can read about products, rather than having to go to the store to examine them.
    2. He can plan shopping trips more efficiently.
  C. It widens the consumer's area of choice.
    1. It acquaints him with a wide range of competing products.
    2. It introduces him to new and improved products and services.

The logical relationship between units of the outline should be shown by proper indentation. Normally your main points will be the most inclusive as well as the most important statements in your speech. As such, they should be placed nearest the left-hand margin of your outline, with successively less important or less inclusive statements ranged beneath and to the right of them in order of descending scope and importance. Therefore, as the broadest and most central statements lie farthest to the left, the narrowest and least important ones will lie farthest to the right. If a statement is more than one line in length, the second line should be aligned with the first. (For example, see A. 1 in preceding outline.)

A consistent set of symbols should be used throughout the outline. An acceptable set of symbols is exemplified in the outlines printed in this chapter. But whether you use this system or some other, be consistent. Items comparable in importance or scope always should be assigned the same type of symbol.

The four requirements just named apply to any outline you may make. An additional requirement, however, applies to the final draft of a complete, formal outline, such as you will usually prepare for your classroom speeches. *All the main points and subordinate ideas in such an outline should be written out as full sentences.* Putting the outline into sentence form will help to clarify in your mind the meaning of each point and will show its exact relation to the other points in the outline. You will find that a carefully framed statement of each point and a recognition of its place in the overall structure of your speech are invaluable aids in helping you remember what you want to say when it is time to speak.

STEPS IN PREPARING AN OUTLINE

An outline, like the speech it represents, should be developed gradually through a series of stages. While the process of preparing an outline may vary, certain steps should always be included:

1. Select and limit the subject of your speech.
   a. Phrase your general topic.
   b. Consider your purpose and the limiting factors of time, audience, and occasion.
   c. Restate your topic so that it fits these conditions.
2. Develop a rough draft of your outline.
   a. List the main points you expect to cover.
   b. Rearrange these main points into a systematic sequence.
   c. Insert and arrange the subordinate ideas that fall under each main point.
   d. Note the supporting material to be used under each point.
   e. Check whether your rough draft covers your subject and fits your purpose.
   f. If you are dissatisfied, revise your rough draft or start over.
3. Put the outline into final form.
   a. Write out the main points as complete sentences.
      (1) State them concisely, vividly, and, in so far as possible, in parallel phraseology.
      (2) Direct them to the needs and interests of your listeners.
   b. Write out the subordinate ideas as complete sentences.
      (1) Be sure they are subordinate to the point they are intended to develop.
      (2) Be sure they are coordinate to the other items in their series.
   c. Fill in the supporting material in detail.
      (1) Be sure it is pertinent.
      (2) Be sure it is adequate.

d. Recheck the entire outline.
  (1) It should represent good outline form.
  (2) It should adequately cover the subject.
  (3) It should accomplish your purpose.

Now let us see how this process may be followed in a particular situation. We shall apply the principles we have discussed to the selection and limitation of a subject, to the development of a rough draft, and to the development of an outline in final form.

Selecting and limiting the subject

Suppose that you must prepare, as the most important speech of the semester, a fifteen-minute informative talk on a subject in which you are interested. You decide to talk about the Federal Bureau of Investigation because you have already read a good deal about its activities and because you know a special agent of the F.B.I. who can give you information that is not available in the usual printed sources. Your broad topic area is:

THE F.B.I.

In fifteen minutes you will not be able to tell all that you know or can find out about the F.B.I. Therefore, recalling what you learned in Chapter 3, you ask yourself what information will be most interesting and useful to your listeners. After careful consideration, you decide to discuss the history and services of the F.B.I. The history, you think, will be interesting and also will emphasize the achievements of the F.B.I., while the discussion of its services will show how it contributes to law enforcement. Because of the time limit, however, you realize that you must sketch the history briefly and select for discussion only the more important of the F.B.I.'s services. Therefore you limit your topic as follows:

THE F.B.I.
(Limited to a brief review of its history, achievements, and major areas of service.)

Developing the rough draft

In determining the limits of your subject, you have already made a preliminary selection of the main points to be covered in your speech.

Now you set these points down on paper to see how they may be modified and fitted into proper sequence. Your list may look something like the following:

1. Origin and history of the F.B.I.
2. Purpose and functions of the F.B.I.
3. Activities of the F.B.I.
4. Famous cases the F.B.I. has solved

This list covers what you want to say but the order does not please you and at several points the subject matter overlaps. Conceivably, a time sequence could be used for the speech as a whole, and information about the F.B.I.'s activities could be brought in as part of the story of its development; but this would result in a good deal of repetition and also would tend to subordinate certain ideas which you wish to emphasize. After further consideration, therefore, you decide to use a special topical sequence suggested by the nature of the material you wish to cover:

1. Purposes of the F.B.I.
2. Its origin and history
3. Its areas of service

Under this arrangement you find that what you wish to say about the F.B.I.'s major activities can be included in a discussion of its purposes and its famous cases can be included in a discussion of its history. You also decide that recounting its history before you outline some of its services will make for a more natural and logical development of the topic.

With the principal topics, or "heads," of the speech chosen and arranged, your next task will be to phrase these points so that they express more accurately the ideas you wish to convey, and to place under each head the subordinate ideas by which it is explained or supported. This additional development enables you to test the appropriateness of the main points and to see how they "hang together" when the details are added. After inserting and arranging the subordinate ideas, make rough notations under each to indicate what supporting material you may need to illustrate and amplify it. Also make any adjustments that will render the title of your talk more accurate and interesting. This being done, your rough draft may look something like this:

OUR F.B.I.: SERVANT TO THE NATION[1]
(Limited to a brief review of the F.B.I.'s purposes, history, and major areas of service.)

I. F.B.I. is investigative arm of Department of Justice.
  A. Responsibility for gathering evidence in cases involving violations of federal criminal statutes not specifically delegated to other agencies
  B. Charged with protecting internal security of nation
    1. Against espionage
    2. Against sabotage
  C. Assists state and local law-enforcement agencies
    1. Identifies suspected criminals, missing persons, etc.
    2. Provides technical laboratory services
    3. Helps train state and local police officials

II. The history of the F.B.I. is a record of growth and service.
  A. Early history
    1. Founded July 26, 1908, by Attorney General Charles J. Bonaparte
      a. To be a permanent and professional investigative agency
      b. Called Bureau of Investigation
    2. J. Edgar Hoover became director in 1924.
      a. Appointed by Attorney General Harlan Fiske Stone
      b. Reorganized F.B.I. along present lines
      c. Inaugurated policies still in effect
  B. During late 1920's and early 1930's the F.B.I.'s prestige grew rapidly.
    1. Campaign against illegal liquor traffic of Prohibition era brought much favorable publicity.
    2. Congress passed bills increasing its power.
      a. In 1932 the federal kidnaping statute
      b. In 1934 the federal Bank Robbery Act
      c. In 1934 Congress also authorized F.B.I. agents to carry guns and make arrests.
    3. These bills enabled the F.B.I. to increase its effectiveness.
      a. In 1933, the year after the kidnaping bill was passed, all kidnaping cases referred to the F.B.I. were solved.
      b. In 1934 F.B.I. agents ended the careers of three notorious criminals—John Dillinger, Arthur ("Pretty Boy") Floyd, and Lester Gillis (alias "Baby Face" Nelson).

---

[1] Information in this outline was derived from articles on the Federal Bureau of Investigation in *Encyclopaedia Britannica, Encyclopedia Americana,* and *World Book Encyclopedia.*

C. International developments leading up to the United States entry into World War II brought additional responsibilities.
   1. Apprehension of foreign agents
   2. Security of defense plants
   3. Pan-American intelligence force
D. Post-war period
   1. Concern with communist activity
   2. Loyalty checks on employees of Atomic Energy Commission and other federal agencies

III. The F.B.I. provides three principal cooperative services.
  A. The F.B.I. Laboratory provides cost-free scientific crime detection facilities to state and local law-enforcement agencies.
    1. Established November 24, 1932
    2. Has experts in firearms identification, serology, spectrography, metallurgy, explosives, hair and fiber analysis, and handwriting identification
    3. Has large reference collection for identifying tire treads, paint samples, etc.
  B. Identification Division keeps more than 150 million sets of fingerprints on file.
    1. Approximately 23 million of these sets belong to known or suspected criminals.
    2. The remainder, in the Civil Identification Section, are those of members of the armed forces or of other law-abiding citizens.
     a. Used to trace missing persons
     b. Used to identify amnesia and accident victims
    3. International Exchange of Fingerprints since 1932
  C. Instructional activities, in addition to training F.B.I. agents, take several forms.
    1. The F.B.I. National Academy, established in 1935, provides a twelve-week training course for state and local police officials
     a. At Quantico, Virginia
     b. No tuition
    2. At request of local authorities, the F.B.I. cooperates in police training schools.
    3. Annual conferences with state and local agencies provide forums for the discussion of common problems.
    4. Publications
     a. *Law Enforcement Bulletin* provides medium for exchange of ideas on crime prevention and detection.
     b. *Uniform Crime Reports* give statistical analyses of local crime on annual and semiannual basis.

At this point you need to examine your rough draft carefully to be sure (1) that you have included all the points you want to cover, (2) that you have not unbalanced your discussion by expanding unimportant items too greatly or skimping on important ones, (3) that you have followed the principles of systematic arrangement and subordination, and (4) that you have assembled enough supporting material in the form of illustrations, comparisons, and the like. When you are satisfied on these matters, you are ready to recast your outline into final form.

Putting the outline into final form

This phase of your preparation consists mainly of improving your phraseology and of filling in details. Sometimes, however, you also will want to combine and rearrange points in the rough draft, or perhaps to drop certain subordinate ideas. In any event, you will need to restate your main points and subordinate ideas as complete sentences which convey your meaning clearly and exactly, and to see that your outline form meets the requirements listed on pages 149–151.

Usually the work of revision follows the steps suggested on pages 151–152. You begin with your main points, rephrasing them so that they are clear and vivid. Then taking each main point in turn, you restate the subordinate ideas which fall under it, working for proper coordination and subordination. As you do this, you fill in the supporting material in detail, testing it for pertinence and adequacy. After all parts of the outline are completed, you go back and review the whole, checking its form, its coverage of the subject, and its adaptation to your purpose. By now your revision should look something like this:

OUR F.B.I.: SERVANT TO THE NATION
(Limited to a brief review of the F.B.I.'s purposes, history, and services.)

I. The F.B.I. is the permanent investigative arm of the Department of Justice.
  A. It is charged with investigating violations of all federal criminal statutes, except those delegated to other agencies.
    1. It must gather evidence in cases to which the United States is or may become a party.
    2. It must apprehend "public enemies."
  B. The F.B.I. also is charged with protecting the internal security of the United States.

1. It must apprehend foreign espionage agents.
2. It must guard against sabotage and other subversive activities.
C. Another of its purposes is to assist state and local law-enforcement agencies.
    1. It does this by helping identify known or suspected criminals.
    2. It does this by providing technical laboratory services.
    3. It does this by offering training to local police officials.

II. The F.B.I. has a history of service to the nation.
A. The early years of the F.B.I. were marked by decisions important to its development.
    1. In 1908 it was founded by Attorney General Charles J. Bonaparte.
    2. In 1924 J. Edgar Hoover was appointed director by Attorney General Harlan Fiske Stone.
        a. Hoover reorganized the F.B.I. along present lines.
        b. Hoover inaugurated policies which are still in effect.
B. During the late 1920's and early 1930's, the prestige of the F.B.I. grew rapidly.
    1. The F.B.I.'s campaign against the illegal liquor traffic of the Prohibition era aroused favorable publicity.
    2. Congress passed bills increasing its power.
        a. In 1932 Congress passed the federal kidnaping statute.
        b. In 1934 Congress passed the federal Bank Robbery Act.
        c. In 1934 Congress also passed legislation authorizing F.B.I. agents to carry guns and make arrests.
    3. These bills enabled the F.B.I. to increase its effectiveness.
        a. In 1933 all kidnaping cases referred to the F.B.I. were solved.
        b. In 1934 F.B.I. agents ended the careers of three notorious criminals—John Dillinger, Arthur ("Pretty Boy") Floyd, and Lester Gillis (alias "Baby Face" Nelson).
C. International developments leading up to the entry of the United States into World War II brought the F.B.I. additional responsibilities.
    1. It kept watch over the activities of enemy aliens residing in the United States.
    2. It apprehended many foreign espionage agents.
    3. It supervised the security of defense plants.
    4. It was instrumental in developing a Pan-American intelligence force.
D. In the post-war era the F.B.I. turned to important new problems.
    1. It investigated communist activity within the United States.

2. It made detailed loyalty checks on prospective employees of the Atomic Energy Commission and other federal agencies.

III. The F.B.I. provides important cooperative services.
   A. The F.B.I. Laboratory makes available the latest scientific methods of crime detection.
      1. It is staffed by experts in firearms identification, serology, spectrography, metallurgy, explosives, hair and fiber analysis, and handwriting identification.
      2. It maintains large reference collections useful in identifying tire treads, paint samples, etc.
      3. It provides cost-free services to state and local law-enforcement agencies.
   B. The Identification Division is the famous "fingerprint division" of the F.B.I.
      1. It has more than 150 million sets of fingerprints on file.
         a. Approximately 23 million of these are of known or suspected criminals.
         b. The remainder are those of members of the armed forces or of other law-abiding citizens who voluntarily submitted to fingerprinting.
      2. The fingerprints serve various purposes.
         a. Those of known or suspected criminals help in the apprehension of lawbreakers.
         b. Those of law-abiding citizens are used to identify missing persons and accident victims.
   C. Educational services, in addition to training F.B.I. agents, take several forms.
      1. The F.B.I. Academy, established in 1935, provides a twelve-week course for selected police personnel.
      2. The F.B.I. cooperates in police training schools and institutes.
      3. F.B.I. agents participate in annual conferences with state and local police officers.
      4. Two F.B.I. publications dispense information to law-enforcement agencies.
         a. The *Law Enforcement Bulletin* is a general medium for the exchange of ideas.
         b. The *Uniform Crime Reports* give statistical analyses of local crime on an annual and semiannual basis.

In the next chapter we shall consider how to fit a beginning and ending to an outline as here developed. Then in Chapters 9 and 10 we shall consider how to develop outlines especially adapted to informative and persuasive speeches.

A final word of advice is in order here. Arranging and outlining a speech are not simple tasks which can be tossed off in a few moments. Time and effort are required to do the job well. Allow yourself the time and exert the effort; the greater clarity and force of expression which result will more than compensate you. Remember, too, that skill in outlining develops with experience. If you have had little practice in outlining, the task may take you longer than it takes an experienced speaker. As you continue to make outlines, however, your skill and speed will increase. Begin now by carefully outlining every speech you make, in or out of class.

PROBLEMS FOR FURTHER STUDY

1. Indicate the type of arrangement (time, space, etc.) which you think would be most suitable for a speech on each of the following subjects. Be prepared to defend your choice.

The campus parking situation
Facilities of the college library
The fraternity tradition
Why farmers are leaving the farm
Censorship of the press
Preparing for a final examination
Our city government
The development of the modern corporation
Stamp collecting as a hobby
Principles and policies of public taxation

2. Select three of the preceding subjects (or three similar ones) and work out the main points of a speech on each. In phrasing these points, observe the rules given on pages 143–145. (Try to select subjects which in your judgment require different types of arrangement.)

3. Choose one of the following subjects (or a similar subject) and develop it according to three different types of arrangement. Your instructor will tell you whether to confine the development to main points or to include subordinate ideas and supporting material.

The great American novel
Careers in engineering (law, medicine, etc.)
Computers and "thinking machines"
Urban renewal

The theater of the absurd
The "paperback revolution"
Our federal court system
The modern newspaper

4. Following the rules given on pages 149–151, outline two of the speeches in the Appendix. Then, (1) name the pattern of arrangement employed in each speech, (2) discuss the suitability of this pattern to the speaker's subject and purpose and to the occasion on which the speech was delivered, and (3) comment on the consistency with which the chosen pattern was adhered to throughout the talk. (Remember that the subordinate ideas need not always follow the pattern used for the main points, and that the subordinate ideas under one main point may be developed differently from those under another.)

5. Study the final form of the outline on the F.B.I., pages 156–158. What changes, if any, might be made? How might the outline be improved?

6. Try putting the material in the F.B.I. outline into a different pattern of arrangement. What difficulties do you encounter?

7. As you listen to the next group of speeches delivered in class, try to determine the main points and the type of arrangement employed by each speaker. After the speeches have been delivered, see whether the class can agree on (1) the type of arrangement employed, (2) the suitability of this arrangement to the speaker's subject and purpose, and (3) the faithfulness with which the chosen pattern was adhered to.

8. Read at least two speeches from the magazine *Vital Speeches* or some other suitable source. Be prepared to discuss (1) whether in stating his main points the speaker adhered to the criteria of conciseness, vividness, immediacy, and parallelism; and (2) different ways in which the speaker arranged the subordinate ideas under his main points.

SPEAKING ASSIGNMENT

1. Choose one of the subjects listed below (or a similar subject of which your instructor approves). After completing the necessary research, develop a rough outline for a five-minute classroom speech. Then recast the rough outline into final, complete-sentence form. Hand the final draft of your outline to your instructor at least a week before you are scheduled to speak. After your instructor has corrected the outline, revise it according to his directions and return it to him at the time you present your talk.

The decline of the movies
Christmas (or any holiday) in foreign lands
Advances in anesthetics
Playing the stock market
The juke box business
Our crowded colleges
Responsibilities of the college newspaper (radio station)
The future of the laboring man
Cigarettes and your health
The detective story as literature
Practical photography

SUGGESTIONS FOR FURTHER READING

Jacques Barzun and Henry F. Graff, *The Modern Researcher* (New York: Harcourt, Brace and Company, 1957), Chapter 11, "Organizing: Paragraph, Chapter, and Part."

Waldo W. Braden and Mary Louise Gehring, *Speech Practices* (New York: Harper & Brothers, 1958), Chapter 3, "How Speakers Organize Their Speeches."

Laura Crowell, "The Building of the 'Four Freedoms' Speech," *Speech Monographs*, XXII (November 1955), 266–283.

Carl I. Hovland, Irving L. Janis, and Harold H. Kelley, *Communication and Persuasion* (New Haven: Yale University Press, 1953), Chapter 4, "Organization of Persuasive Arguments."

Gilbert S. MacVaugh, "Structural Analysis of the Sermons of Dr. Harry Emerson Fosdick," *Quarterly Journal of Speech*, XVIII (November 1932), 531–546.

Cecil B. Williams and Allan H. Stevenson, *A Research Manual for College Studies and Papers,* 3rd ed. (New York: Harper and Row, 1963), Chapter 5, "Planning and Outlining."

CHAPTER 8

BEGINNING AND ENDING A SPEECH

Every speech, whether long or short, must have a beginning and an end. Too often speakers devote all their time to choosing and arranging the main ideas of a talk and do not plan how to open and close it effectively. Admittedly, the development of the main points deserves the major share of your preparation time and must be worked out before you can sensibly plan how to introduce and conclude your remarks. But it is foolish to leave the introduction and conclusion to the inspiration of the moment. Frequently the inspiration fails to come, and a dull or hesitant beginning and a weak, indefinite ending result. The impact of your speech always will be greater if you plan in advance how to direct your listeners' attention to your subject at the outset and how to tie your ideas together in a firm and vigorous conclusion. In this chapter we shall first discuss the aims of an effective introduction and suggest various ways in which these aims may be achieved; then we shall consider the requirements of a suitable conclusion and review several specific methods by which the conclusion may be developed. Finally, we shall discuss how to integrate the introduction and conclusion with the body of the speech.

BEGINNING THE SPEECH

The attention of the audience must be maintained throughout a speech, but gaining this attention is your principal task at the beginning. Unless people are ready to attend to what you have to say, the most interesting and useful information and the most persuasive appeals will be entirely wasted. Mere attention, however, is not enough; in the first minute or two that you are on the platform, you also must gain the goodwill and respect of your listeners. In many situations your own reputation or the chairman's introduction will help ensure a fair hearing. But when you are confronted by indifference, distrust, or skepticism, you must take steps to change these attitudes. Finally, in addition to gaining attention and winning goodwill, you must lead the thinking of your listeners naturally into the subject with which you are concerned. A good introduction, then, should do three things: (1) it should gain attention; (2) it should secure goodwill and respect for you as a speaker; and (3) it should prepare the audience for the discussion that is to follow.

A number of well-established means for developing the introduction of a speech will help you gain these ends. They include:

1. Referring to the subject or occasion
2. Using a personal reference or greeting
3. Asking a rhetorical question
4. Making a startling statement of fact or opinion
5. Using a quotation
6. Telling a humorous anecdote
7. Using an illustration

Referring to the subject or occasion. If the audience already has a vital interest in the subject you are to discuss, you may need only to state that subject before plunging into your first main point. The very speed and directness of this approach suggest alertness and eagerness to come to grips with your topic. A speaker began a talk to a group of college seniors with these words: "I am going to talk tonight about jobs: how to get them, and how to keep them." Bishop Bryan McEntegart of Brooklyn also referred directly to his subject in opening a talk before the Cathedral Club of that city on January 24, 1963:

> Rarely in history has world-wide attention been concentrated so intensely on such a small section of the globe, as during the deliberations of the recent Vatican Council.
> In the few weeks since my return, I have been asked repeatedly what I thought was the Council's most meaningful contribution

to the betterment of mankind. Tonight I would like to answer this question.[1]

Although such brevity and forthrightness strike exactly the right note on some occasions, do not begin all speeches in this way. To a skeptical audience, a direct beginning may sound immodest and tactless; to an apathetic audience, it may sound dull or uninteresting. When listeners are receptive and friendly, however, reference to the subject often produces a businesslike and forceful opening.

Instead of referring to the subject to be discussed, you may in your introduction refer to the occasion which has brought the audience together. Indeed, in a speech prepared for some special event, ceremony, or anniversary, such a reference is practically obligatory. Here, as in an introduction which refers to the subject, the important rules are: be brief, pointed, and businesslike, and direct the attention of the audience to the topic of your address. These qualities are illustrated in the opening paragraph of a speech delivered by Ambassador Adlai E. Stevenson, United States Representative to the United Nations, at the dedication of the Fordham University Law School Building November 17, 1961:

> For us who have been educated in the law, and who also have something to do with international affairs, the dedication of this splendid new law building carries a simple and forceful moral. It says to us that just as this is a time for building in the life of universities, it is also a time for building in the life of nations.[2]

Using a personal reference or greeting. Under the appropriate circumstances a speaker may begin a talk by referring to his own background or accomplishments. This is particularly true when he occupies a position of prestige or authority. Howard Palfrey Jones, United States Ambassador to Indonesia, used this method to begin a commencement address October 6, 1962, at Fairleigh Dickinson University:

> Since I have spent most of the past eleven years in Asia and all of them in working on the problems of Asia, it may be useful for me, on an occasion of this kind when it is particularly appropriate to look forward,

---

[1] "A Totality of Outlook: Man's Spiritual Purpose," *Vital Speeches*, XXIX (March 1, 1963), 299.

[2] "The American Tradition and Its Implications for International Law." Text supplied by Mr. Stevenson.

to consider with you briefly the importance of Asia to you and to America.[3]

Closely related to the personal reference is the greeting—that sort of introduction in which the speaker expresses his pleasure in appearing before this particular audience. Such an introduction was used by William I. Nichols, editor and publisher of *This Week* magazine, in a speech delivered November 12, 1962, at the annual meeting of the Grocery Manufacturers of America:

> Mr. Chairman and Members of the Grocery Manufacturers of America: It is both a pleasure and a stimulus for me to be here with you today. I say this, because over all these years of working together, so many of you have become my personal friends. We have met often to discuss many ideas in many fields. From these meetings I have never failed to take away new impressions and ideas and, most of all, an awareness of the seriousness, dedication, and enterprise with which the members of the G.M.A. approach their tasks. In every sense of the word, this is a challenging group, and I am proud to have been asked to take a part in your program today.[4]

As long as the personal reference or greeting used in the introduction is modest and sincere, it may establish goodwill as well as gain attention. Effusiveness and hollow compliments, however, should be avoided. Audiences are quick to sense a lack of genuineness on the part of a speaker, and they always react unfavorably toward sentiments that are not sincere. At the other extreme, avoid apologizing. Do not say, "I don't know why the chairman picked me to talk on this subject when others could have done it so much better," or "Unaccustomed as I am to public speaking. . . ." Apologetic beginnings suggest that your speech is not worth listening to. Be cordial, sincere, and modest, but do not apologize.

Asking a rhetorical question. A third way to open a speech is to ask a question or a series of questions which start the audience thinking about your subject. Note this introduction which Dr. Charles Malik, former president of the General Assembly of the United Nations, used in a speech July 6, 1962, before the Virginia State Bar Association. After briefly greeting the audience and announcing his theme, he

---

[3] "Importance of Asia," *Vital Speeches*, XXIX (November 1, 1962), 38.
[4] "Let's Have a Trademark of Freedom," *Vital Speeches*, XXIX (December 15, 1962), 135.

asked four rhetorical questions which stimulated the thinking of his listeners and prepared them for the body of the talk:

> It is a great pleasure, I assure you, to address this distinguished group of American citizens who have dedicated their lives to the determination and realization of justice. One of the eternal truths that has been poignantly brought home to all thinking men in this critical age is that justice is much deeper than mere legal justice between individuals. There is such a thing as "silent injustice" which ravages the lives of men. Is it just that man may be a permanent prey to fear and anxiety and ignorance? Is it just that tyranny remains rampant over whole sections of the globe? Is it just that some people appear to be born unto slavery, so that, so far as we can now see, they will never be free? And above all, is it just that those who know better, those who are blessed with an abundance of mind and means, those whom history has chosen to say the decisive word today, both in utterance and in action, appear to be hesitant, uncertain, complacent, soft, dazed, divided in counsel, paralyzed in will? Justice is much deeper than legal justice: there is the justice of the mind, there is the justice of the spirit, there is the justice of history, and above all there is the justice and righteousness of God.[5]

Employing the same approach more briefly and directly, Dick Montgomery, a student at the University of Iowa, opened a classroom speech on the subject of the trimester plan with two rhetorical questions:

> How would you like to graduate from college in three years? How would you like to be able to get out into the world and begin earning money while gaining valuable experience a year sooner than is now possible? You could do this if Iowa adopted the trimester plan.[6]

Making a startling statement. Sometimes a speech may be opened with a startling statement of fact or opinion. This type of introduction is especially effective before an apathetic audience. A startling series of facts opened a speech which M. Monroe Kimbrel, president of the American Bankers Association, delivered before the National Credit Conference January 21, 1963:

---

[5] "Silent Injustice: A Radical Awakening Is Needed," *Vital Speeches*, XXIX (November 1,1962), 37.
[6] Presented May 1963. Text supplied by Mr. Montgomery and his instructor, Mr. Donovan Ochs.

For 12 of the last 13 years, the United States has experienced a deficit in its balance of international accounts. For at least the last four of these years, it has been widely recognized that these deficits will, if not checked, lead to a breakdown of the international payments system. Upon the strength and viability of this system rest, in turn, the economic security of the United States; the political integrity of developing nations; the prosperity of our Free World allies; and the economic, political, and military unity of the nations of the Western world. These stakes are truly enormous. They are stakes which we cannot afford to lose.[7]

In 1902, Clarence Darrow, the famous trial lawyer, opened a lecture to the prisoners in Cook County Jail, Chicago, with this startling statement of belief or opinion:

> If I looked at jails and crimes and prisoners in the way the ordinary person does, I should not speak on this subject to you. The reason I talk to you on the question of crime, its cause and cure, is because I really do not in the least believe in crime. There is no such thing as a crime as the word is generally understood. I do not believe there is any sort of distinction between the real moral condition of the people in and out of jail. One is just as good as the other.[8]

Using a quotation. If properly chosen and presented, a quotation may be an excellent means of catching the attention of the audience and announcing one's subject. An address by Newton N. Minow, Chairman of the Federal Communications Commission, used this method. Mr. Minow spoke on "Free Enterprise in Space" before the Third National Conference on the Peaceful Uses of Space in Chicago, Illinois, May 8, 1963.

> "Here on the prairies of Illinois and the Middle West, we can see a long way in all directions. We look to east, to west, to north, and south. Our commerce, our ideas, come and go in all directions. Here there are no barriers, no defenses, to ideas and aspirations. We want none; we want no shackles on the mind or the spirit, no rigid patterns of thought, no iron conformity."

---

[7] "Our International Financial Position," *Vital Speeches*, XXIX (March 1, 1963), 303.

[8] *Address to Prisoners in Cook County Jail*, 3rd reprint (Chicago: Charles H. Kerr and Company, 1913). Reprinted in *The Speaker's Resource Book*, ed. Carroll C. Arnold, Douglas Ehninger, and John C. Gerber (Chicago: Scott, Foresman and Company, 1961), p. 137.

Governor Adlai E. Stevenson once spoke those words about Chicago. In those memorable words, Governor Stevenson caught the mood and enthusiasm of this crossroads of America, and I often think of them when I come home. Governor Stevenson's description of Chicago is especially pertinent today when we discuss our new venture into space communications—a venture which requires that all of us see a long way in all directions, with no shackles on the mind or the spirit.[9]

Telling a humorous anecdote. On many occasions you may begin a speech by telling a funny story or relating a humorous experience. But be sure that the story or experience you recount will amuse the audience and that you can tell it well. If your opening falls flat, your speech will be off to a poor start. Also be sure that the anecdote emphasizes the central point of your talk. A joke or story that is unrelated to your subject wastes valuable time and channels the attention of your listeners in the wrong direction. Most important of all, be sure that what you say is in good taste. Not only do doubtful or "off-color" stories violate the accepted rules of social behavior, but they may seriously undermine the respect which the members of the audience have for you.

A humorous anecdote which meets the requirements stated above was used by Janice Caldwell to open a classroom speech entitled "Education by Remote Control":

> A story was told me several months ago by Dr. Jack F. Padgett, my former philosophy professor, and the head of the department at Simpson College. Settling himself on the edge of his desk, he related the tale of a professor at a large state university in our own Middle West, who, busy with his many lecture tours, research projects, and writing activities, went to his department head in extreme consternation. It seemed that the poor professor was just too busy to teach his one class a week. Therefore, he asked for and was granted permission to tape-record all of his lectures.
>
> Toward the end of the term the professor arrived back on the campus and decided to visit his class to see how his plan was working. He walked into the room to find his tape recorder in the middle of the room. . . and twelve little tape recorders around it.
>
> Whether this story is true or not, it does raise an important question—a question which you and I as college students are directly concerned with: Are our professors teachers?[10]

---

[9] Text supplied by Mr. Minow.

[10] Presented at the University of Iowa May 1963. Text supplied by Miss Caldwell and her instructor, Mr. Paul Newman.

Using an illustration. Real-life incidents, stories taken from literature, or hypothetical illustrations may be used to start a speech. The attention of the audience is caught by the incident and is directed toward the main discussion by the point the incident illustrates. Be sure, therefore, that the incident or story has interest of itself and that it is connected to the main idea of your talk. A compelling illustration is more apt to gain attention than any of the other types of introductions we have listed. Here is how Joel L. Swabb, a student at Muskingum College, combined a series of illustrations to begin a speech criticizing the activities of some of the spokesmen for "the far right."

> The time is 3 A.M. The place, the home of a Protestant minister in Phoenix, Arizona. The minister awakens to the ringing of his telephone. He wonders what member of his congregation is in need of his help at this early hour. The voice on the other end of the line is hard and determined, "Are you a communist?"
>
> The time is 11 A.M. A school teacher in Pittsburgh, Pa. sits behind her desk opening the morning mail. She has just received a letter from a friend in New York, a copy of *Time* magazine, and a plain white mailing envelope with no return address. A quick slip of the letter opener and she is greeted with the bright red exclamation, "Communist."
>
> It is now evening. The dinner plates have been removed and the President's light touch speech before the Washington Press Corps is receiving its final ovation. In scanning the audience our eyes come to rest upon one man who is obviously not amused. The ovation dies and a tablemate nudges him with his elbow asking at the same time for his reaction. He replies in a methodical, serious tone of voice. "I regard him as a very dangerous man."
>
> These incidents are typical of the all-encompassing wrath of the arch conservative, the far right, or as Archibald MacLeish put it, "the Irresponsibles." It is not because they deplore softness toward communism that they have derived this title but because, as J. Edgar Hoover stated, "They are merely against communism without being for any positive measures to eliminate the social, political, and economic frictions which the communists are so adroit at exploiting."[11]

These, then, are seven useful means for opening a speech. Sometimes they are used individually; sometimes, as several of the fore-

---

[11] "The Irresponsibles," first-place oration in the Interstate Oratorical Contest, held at Northwestern University, April 1963. Text supplied by Mr. Swabb and his instructor, Professor James Golden.

going examples suggest, two or more means are combined. Always, however, the objectives of your introduction will be the same. In addition to capturing the attention of your listeners, you will want to win their goodwill and respect and lead them naturally into the subject matter of your speech.

ENDING THE SPEECH

The principal function of the ending or conclusion of a speech is to focus the thought of the audience on your central theme and purpose. If you are presenting a one-point speech (see Chapter 6), you will usually restate that point at the end in a manner that makes your meaning clear and forceful. If your speech is more complex, you may bring its most important points together in a condensed and uniform way, or you may spell out the action or belief which these points suggest.

In addition to bringing the substance of the speech into final focus, your conclusion should aim at leaving the audience in the proper mood. If you want your listeners to express vigorous enthusiasm, you should stimulate that feeling in your closing remarks. If you want them to reflect thoughtfully on what you have said, you should encourage a calm, judicious attitude. Therefore, you should decide whether the response you seek requires a mood of serious determination or good-humored levity, of warm sympathy or utter disgust, of thoughtful consideration or vigorous desire for action; then you should plan to end your speech in such a way as to create that mood.

Finally, a good ending should convey a sense of completeness and finality. It annoys an audience to think a speaker has finished, only to hear him ramble on. Therefore, avoid false endings. Tie the threads of thought together so that the pattern of your speech is brought to completion, deliver your concluding sentence with finality — and stop.

Some of the means most frequently used to conclude speeches are:
1. Issuing a challenge or appeal
2. Summarizing
3. Using a quotation
4. Using an illustration
5. Supplying an additional inducement to belief or action
6. Stating a personal intention

Issuing a challenge or appeal. When using this method, the speaker openly appeals for belief or action, or reminds his listeners of their responsibilities in furthering a desirable end. Such an appeal should be vivid and compelling, and should contain within it a suggestion of the principal ideas or arguments presented in the speech. Note how James E. Webb, head of the National Aeronautics and Space Administration, closed a speech to the Department of Elementary School Principals of the National Education Association:

> And, finally, achievement of our goals in space will demand the highest scholastic efforts and intellectual accomplishments in virtually every field of study.
>
> Space is, indeed, a new and challenging frontier, but it is a frontier of the intellect — one which challenges brain, not brawn, with creative intelligence our greatest weapon.
>
> Your elementary schools have a vital role as mankind moves toward the conquest of space.[12]

Summarizing. In a summary conclusion, the speaker reviews the main points of his speech and draws whatever inferences may be implicit in the material he has presented. In a speech to inform, a summary ending is nearly always appropriate since it helps to impress upon the listeners those ideas which you especially want remembered. In a speech to persuade, a summary conclusion provides a final opportunity to reiterate the principal arguments you have presented.

D. Brainerd Holmes, Director of the Office of Manned Space Flight of the National Aeronautics and Space Administration, used this summary to conclude an informative talk before the American Rocket Society:

> Let me conclude, then, by reiterating a few of our basic concepts.
>
> We believe it was necessary to carefully evaluate all feasible mission modes and select the best of these upon which to concentrate our efforts.
>
> We believe that the lunar orbit rendezvous mode is best.
>
> We believe that we must obtain the very best efforts of the very best people we can find, both in Government and industry, if we are to achieve our national goal.

---

[12] Address at Annual Meeting of the Department of Elementary School Principals, National Education Association, Oklahoma City, Oklahoma, April 1, 1963. Text supplied by National Aeronautics and Space Administration.

We believe that our organizational concepts and management techniques must be no less excellent than our technical efforts.

We believe that with constant attention to these concepts, and with the hard work and dedication of the people involved, we will be able to carry out our responsibility to our country to be second to none in man's conquest of space.[13]

An example of a summary conclusion in a persuasive speech is provided by an address which Dr. John T. Caldwell, then president of Alabama College, delivered to the students of that college at the time of the Korean crisis. The purpose of Dr. Caldwell's talk was to urge the students to be calm and to continue their studies.

I hope these remarks prove helpful to you. I could not be more sincere or more earnest. To summarize: Whatever you are studying now, if you will do it with greater purposefulness, unselfishness, diligence, and earnestness, you will be serving and serving with maximum effect this Nation and yourself.

Balance and calm resolution, in contrast to impulsiveness, ill-haste, emotion, and hysteria, in your personal as well as in your cooperative thinking toward decisions, will serve mankind and yourself in this hour as always. Believe me![14]

Using a quotation. A quotation may be used to end a speech if it bears directly on the central idea of the talk or strongly suggests the attitude or action the speaker wishes his listeners to take. U Thant, Secretary-General of the United Nations, used a quotation to such purpose in a speech entitled "Some Major Issues before the United Nations." The speech was delivered March 5, 1963, to the Economic Club of New York City.

What is most needed in these tense times is the will to compromise. In human affairs, no one group is 100 per cent right and another 100 per cent wrong. In international relationships, pure white and pure black are rare. That is why every international agreement represents a compromise of some kind, except where the terms are dictated.

To my knowledge one of the wisest mottoes for every one of us is enshrined in the UNESCO Charter. It says, "Since wars begin in the

---

[13] Address before the American Rocket Society, Cleveland, Ohio, July 17, 1962. Text supplied by National Aeronautics and Space Administration.

[14] "The World Crisis and Your Plans," presented December 12, 1950. Text supplied by Dr. Ralph Eubanks. Dr. Caldwell later became chancellor of North Carolina State College at Raleigh.

minds of men, it is in the minds that the defences of peace have to be constructed."

There is no peace in the world today because there is no peace in the minds of men.[15]

Using an illustration. Just as an illustration which epitomizes your leading ideas may be used to open a speech, so may an illustration of this sort be used at the close. On November 12, 1962, Attorney General Robert F. Kennedy gave a speech to the Linn County Veteran's Council in Albany, Oregon. He closed it in this way:

> The challenge of the future requires not panic but power, not doubt but deeds.
>
> During the Korean War a young American was called out of the ranks by his Chinese captors and they said to him, "What do you think of General George C. Marshall?"
>
> He said, "I think General Marshall is a great American."
>
> The Chinese knocked him to the ground with the butt of a rifle. They picked him up and said, "What do you think of General George C. Marshall now?"
>
> He said, "I think General Marshall is a great American."
>
> This time there was no rifle butt because in their own way they had classified him as brave.
>
> Today, all of us have been called out of the ranks to be questioned and, in the months ahead, we too must give the affirmative answer. I have no doubt that we will.[16]

Supplying an additional inducement to belief or action. Sometimes a speech may be concluded by quickly reviewing the leading ideas presented in the body of the talk and then supplying one or two additional reasons for accepting the belief or taking the action proposed. Observe how these two elements of summary and added inducement are combined in the conclusion of a classroom speech by Linda Mast, urging the use of seat belts in automobiles:

> All in all, you will find that buying seat belts for your car and using them is a worth-while investment. As I have shown, they are a great aid in saving lives and preventing serious injuries; having them in your car may enable you to pay less for insurance; and wearing them

---

[15] *Vital Speeches,* XXIX (April 1, 1963), 364.
[16] Text supplied by the Department of Justice.

will make travel more comfortable and enjoyable. The few arguments which may be raised against seat belts do not outweigh their advantages, but only show how indifferent most people are to their own safety and well-being. Even if you are willing to take chances with your own life, however, you owe this additional security to your family and friends. Install seat belts in your car today![17]

Stating a personal intention. A statement of the speaker's intention to act as his speech recommends is particularly valuable when his prestige with the audience is high. The most famous example of this method of closing a speech, perhaps, is the phrase attributed to Patrick Henry: "As for me, give me liberty or give me death!" This type of conclusion was also used by the British Minister of Science, Viscount Hailsham (Quintin Hogg), in an address in which he urged adherence to democratic ideals despite obstacles existing in the world today.

> For my part and on behalf of my country I pledge myself despite all disappointments and undeterred by criticism and ingratitude to maintain these ideals and pursue the goal which we have set before us.[18]

Whichever of these means you choose—whether you close your speech with a challenge or appeal, or with a summary, quotation, illustration, added inducement, or statement of personal intention—remember that your conclusion should focus the thought of your listeners on the central theme you have developed. In addition, a good conclusion should be consonant with the mood or tenor of your speech and should convey a sense of completeness and finality.

FITTING THE BEGINNING AND END TO THE BODY OF THE SPEECH

In Chapter 7 we considered various patterns for developing the body or substance of a speech and the principles to be followed in outlining this part of your talk. When the introduction and conclusion are added, your completed outline should look something like this:

Introduction

I. _____

---

[17] Presented at the University of Iowa January 15, 1963. Text supplied by Miss Mast and her instructor, Mr. Donovan Ochs.

[18] "The Toast of Democracy," presented January 22, 1963, at the Center for the Study of Democratic Institutions, *Vital Speeches*, XXIX (March 1, 1963), 304.

    A. _____

    B. _____

Body

I. _____

    A. _____

    B. _____

        1. _____

        2., etc. _____

II., etc. _____

Conclusion

I. _____

    A. _____

    B., etc. _____

II. _____

An introduction and conclusion for the speech on the F.B.I. outlined in Chapter 7 (pp. 156–158) might take the following form:

Introduction

I. Recently a group of high-school students were asked to identify ten government agencies from their initials.

    A. Sixty per cent correctly identified the F.C.C. as the Federal Communications Commission.

    B. Seventy-five per cent knew that the I.C.C. was the Interstate Commerce Commission.

    C. One hundred per cent correctly named the F.B.I. as the Federal Bureau of Investigation.

II. These same students were then asked to write a paragraph telling something about the history and activities of the F.B.I.

    A. Only five students were able to say anything about its history.

    B. Less than half could list its principal activities and areas of service.

III. Could we score better than these high-school students?

    A. Do we know why the F.B.I. was founded?

    B. Do we know how it developed?

    C. Do we know all of the ways it serves us?

IV. In the next few minutes I will give you answers to these and similar questions.

    A. My aim is to inform you concerning the F.B.I.'s purposes, history, and services.

B. I also hope to give you a deeper appreciation of the F.B.I.'s importance in your life and mine.

Conclusion

I. Remember, then, that the F.B.I. does more than engage in thrilling gun battles with criminals.
  A. It is a group of highly trained professionals whose investigations are essential to the operation of the Department of Justice.
  B. It has a distinguished record of expanding service to the nation since its founding in 1908.
  C. It provides valuable services to local law-enforcement agencies in the areas of crime detection, identification, and education.

II. Truly, the F.B.I. is the servant of our nation.

PROBLEMS FOR FURTHER STUDY

1. Analyze the introductions and conclusions of fifteen or twenty speeches that you find in recent issues of *Vital Speeches*. Are some types of introductions and conclusions used more frequently than others? Do some types seem to be more common in speeches to inform, and others more common in speeches to persuade? What types of introductions and conclusions are most frequently used in speeches delivered on special occasions — anniversaries, dedications, etc.? Are the types of introductions and conclusions described in this chapter ever combined?

2. Evaluate the introductions and conclusions of the speeches reprinted in the Appendix. How well is each introduction and conclusion adapted to the subject matter and apparent purpose of the speech? Could any of the introductions or conclusions be improved? If so, how?

3. After listening to one of the following types of speeches, evaluate the introduction and the conclusion the speaker used:
  a. A classroom lecture
  b. A church sermon
  c. An address by a visiting lecturer at a student convocation
In making your report, supply sufficient information about the speaker and speaking situation so that a person who was not present could understand why you evaluated the introduction and conclusion as you did.

4. Work out at least two alternative means for beginning and ending a talk to members of your speech class on one of the following subjects:

The R.O.T.C. program	Legislative reapportionment
Career opportunities	The emerging nations
"The Ugly American"	Primitive culture
Pay television	City planning

5. Assume that you are to speak to a non-campus audience of business and professional men on the same subject you chose in Problem 4. Work out a new introduction and conclusion more specifically suited to this audience.

6. Select a subject toward which you think the members of your class are likely to be apathetic. Work out an introduction for a speech that will arouse interest in the subject and secure your listeners' goodwill and respect. Suggested subjects:

 Recent archaeological finds in Egypt
 Needed improvements in county government
 Old-age security
 Migration habits of gamebirds
 Consumption of wheat products in the United States

7. Select a controversial topic likely to arouse strong feeling among members of your speech class. Work out three different conclusions for a speech on this topic, as follows:

 a. One that would leave them in a thoughtful mood
 b. One that would arouse them to enthusiasm and excitement
 c. One that would encourage in them a quiet determination to take some definite course of action

General topic areas from which you might select a subject for this assignment include:

 The abuse of some privilege (excessive cutting of classes, cheating in unproctored examinations, etc.)
 A threat to well-being (air pollution, harmful drugs or cosmetics, etc.)
 Support for a cause (a charity drive, a civic project, civil rights, etc.)

SUGGESTIONS FOR FURTHER READING

Aristotle, *Rhetoric,* 1414b-1415a, "The Proem or Introduction"; 1419b-1420b, "The Epilogue."

Hugh Blair, *Lectures on Rhetoric and Belles Lettres* (London and Edinburgh, 1783), Lecture XXXI, "Conduct of a Discourse in All Its Parts — Introduction, Division, Narration and Explication"; Lecture XXXII, "Conduct of a Discourse — the Argumentative Part, the Pathetic Part, the Peroration." (Blair's *Lectures* were reprinted many times for nearly a hundred years, and many editions are available.)

Wayne Minnick, *The Art of Persuasion* (Boston: Houghton Mifflin Company, 1957), Chapter 3, "Getting and Holding Attention."

Quintilian, *Institutio Oratoria,* iv.i, "The Prooemium or Exordium."

CHAPTER 9

THE SPEECH TO INFORM

An important function of speech is to provide man with a means of transferring knowledge. Through speech one person is able to give others the benefit of his learning and experience. In this chapter we shall discuss how to inform in a clear and interesting fashion.

TYPES OF INFORMATIVE SPEECHES

Informative speeches take many forms. Three forms occur so frequently, however, that they merit special mention: (1) *Reports* — scientific reports, committee reports, executive reports, and the like. Experts who engage in special research announce their findings. Committees carry on inquiries and report the results to the organization of which they are a part. Teachers, representatives of fraternal organizations, and businessmen attend conventions and later report to others the information they have obtained. (2) *Instructions* — class instructions, job instructions, and instructions for special group efforts. Teachers instruct students in ways of preparing assignments and performing experiments. Supervisors tell their subordinates how a task should be performed. Leaders explain to volunteer workers their duties in a fund-raising drive or a cleanup campaign. For convenience, such instructions are often given to a group of persons rather than to individuals, and even when written, may need to be accompanied by oral explanations. (3) *Lectures* — luncheon club lectures, class lectures, and

lectures at meetings, study conferences, and institutes. People often share information and knowledge with groups interested in receiving it. Many informative talks are given each week before businessmen's luncheon clubs and women's study groups. Instructors present lectures daily on every college campus, and visiting speakers lecture before church groups, conventions, and business and professional institutes.

THE PURPOSE OF A SPEECH TO INFORM: TO SECURE UNDERSTANDING

As you will recall from the discussion in Chapter 3, the main purpose of a speech to inform is to ensure the audience's clear understanding of the ideas presented. Hence, you should not view it as an opportunity to parade your knowledge. You should not try to see how much you can get off your chest in a given time; rather, you should try to help others grasp and remember the facts or ideas you present.

But while its primary purpose is to teach, an informative speech need not be dull and dry. Because people absorb information more easily when it interests them, a secondary purpose of such a speech is to make your information interesting to your audience. Be sure, however, that this secondary purpose is really secondary. Too often a speaker rambles from one interesting point to another without specifically relating them to each other or to his central theme. Remember that your principal duty is to make the conclusions of your report clear, to have your instructions understood, or to ensure a proper grasp of the content of your lecture.

ESSENTIAL CHARACTERISTICS OF A SPEECH TO INFORM

Clarity

The first essential of an informative speech is clarity. This is largely achieved through effective organization; therefore, observe the following rules: (1) Confine your speech to three or four main points, and group the remaining facts and ideas under these headings. Do not have too many main points. (2) Clarify the relationship between your main points by observing the principles of coordination set forth in Chapter 7. (3) Keep your talk moving ahead according to a well-developed plan; do not jump back and forth from one point to another.

While clarity is largely achieved through effective organization, it is aided by the wise selection of supporting materials and by the use of certain compositional devices. You learned in Chapter 6 how supporting materials may effectively clarify and illustrate a speaker's ideas. In later sections of this chapter we shall discuss how such devices as initial and final summaries, transitional statements, and definitions also aid clarity.

Concreteness

Concreteness is as important as clarity in a speech to inform. Your speech must be packed with facts — with names and references to actual places, events, and experiences. In presenting facts, however, observe these two rules: (1) Do not multiply details unnecessarily. Present statistics in round numbers, especially if they involve large and complicated sets of figures; outline a general course of historical change or development rather than recount each minute incident; do not labor a story or illustration until the thinking of your listeners is drawn away from the point you wish to emphasize. Facts are indispensable, but excessively detailed facts are confusing. (2) Whenever possible, support your presentation of factual data with charts, diagrams, models, or other visual materials. If the members of your audience can see what you are describing, they usually can take in details more readily.

Association of new ideas with familiar ones

People grasp new facts and ideas more readily when they are able to associate them with things they already know; therefore, in a speech to inform you should always try to connect the unknown with the known. If you are giving instructions or describing a problem, relate your materials to procedures or problems with which your listeners are familiar. A college dean talking to an audience of manufacturers on the problems of higher education presented material under headings of raw material, casting, machining, polishing, and assembling.

CAPTURING AND HOLDING THE LISTENERS' INTEREST

In proportion as an informative talk has the characteristics just described—that is, in proportion as it is clear and concrete and associates new or strange ideas with old and familiar ones—it will tend to be interesting. Often, however, these qualities are not in themselves sufficient to capture the attention of the audience and to hold it at a level which will ensure understanding. Therefore, it is important that the informative speaker know something of the relationship between interest and attention and be acquainted with those types of ideas which help to arouse and maintain interest in an oral discourse.

Interest and attention

Interest and attention are closely related. People not only pay attention to what interests them, but, conversely, what they pay attention to tends to become interesting. Frequently a student begins a required course convinced that it is a waste of time and that he is going to be thoroughly bored. After a while, however, the course begins to interest him and may actually arouse him to the point that he continues for many months or years to investigate the subject matter covered. The important thing in a speech, therefore, is to capture the attention of the audience in the first place and to ensure that the message of the speech will be given a fair hearing. When this is done—if the speaker is skillful and the message worth while—interest may grow as the talk proceeds.

What is attention? Formally defined, it is a focusing upon one element in a given field, with the result that other elements in that field fade, become dim, and for all practical purposes momentarily cease to exist. Consider, as an example, the baseball fan sitting in the bleachers. The home team is one run ahead in the ninth inning and there are two outs; the count is three and two. The pitcher wraps his fingers around the ball, winds up, and a slow curve drifts over the corner of the plate. The umpire bawls, "Strike three; you're out!" Only then does the fan lean back, take a long breath, and notice what has been going on around him: that he has dropped his sack of peanuts or thrown off his hat, that his neighbor has been thumping him on the back, that threatening clouds are gathering on the horizon. While all his faculties were focused on the crucial pitch—while, as we say, he was paying attention to it—he was largely unaware of his immediate surroundings. It is this focusing upon one source of stimuli to the greater or lesser exclusion of others that we call attention.

How can you as a speaker capture the attention of your listeners? How can you get them to focus on what you are saying rather than listen to the knocking radiator, study the hat of the lady in the first row, or worry about tomorrow's date with the dentist? As we pointed out in Chapters 4 and 5, a great deal depends on how you deliver your speech—on the variety and animation in your voice and the vigor and variety of your gestures and bodily movements. Your reputation and prestige also will help secure a degree of attention, and the color and impressiveness of your language or style will contribute. Fundamentally, however, you will capture attention through the types of ideas you present to your hearers. As the experience of many speakers has shown, some types of ideas have greater attention value than do others; people not only are attracted to them in the first place but upon listening to them they also tend to have their interest or concern aroused.

Factors of attention

Those types of ideas which have high attention value are generally known as the factors of attention, and include the following:

1. Activity or movement	4. Familiarity	7. Conflict
2. Reality	5. Novelty	8. Humor
3. Nearness	6. Suspense	9. The vital

These terms, of course, overlap and in an actual speech the qualities they represent often are combined. For purposes of explanation, however, let us consider them separately.

1. *Activity*. If you were at the theater and one actor was standing motionless while another was moving excitedly about the stage, which one would you look at? The moving one, of course. Ideas that move likewise attract attention. Narratives in which something happens or in which there are moments of uncertainty and crisis nearly always have attention value. Similarly, expository talks in which the parts of a machine are made to move or into which some element of suspense or conflict is introduced hold attention.

Your speech as a whole also should move—should, as someone has said, "march" forward. Nothing is so boring as a talk that seems to get nowhere. This is why you are repeatedly advised to make the progress of your speech apparent to your audience by indicating that you are finished with one idea and ready to tackle the next. Do not spend too much time on any one point and do not elaborate the obvious; constantly push forward toward a clearly defined goal.

2. *Reality*. The earliest words a child learns are the names of objects, persons, and acts. This interest in reality persists throughout life. The abstract proposition $2+2=4$ may be important, but it awakens little interest until we know whether it is votes or dollars or noses that are being counted. Instead of talking in abstract terms, mention specific people, events, places, and circumstances. Use pictures, diagrams, and charts; tell what happened to Dr. Smith when he fell out of the boat, or to Mary on the morning she applied for a job as a nurse's aid at City Hospital. Make your descriptions realistic and vivid; use specific references rather than general ones. Instead of saying, "A certain friend of mine . . . ," call him by name. Instead of saying "camp," say what camp or what kind of camp.

3. *Nearness*. A direct reference to an object near at hand, to an incident which has just occurred, to the immediate occasion on which your talk is being made, or to a remark of the preceding speaker will usually get attention. A reference to someone in the group will have the same effect. The next time your listeners' attention wanders while you are speaking, use a hypothetical illustration in which you name one of them as the supposed chief character. The name will wake up that person and everyone near him as well.

4. *Familiarity*. Some things are familiar to us because we commonly meet them in our daily lives. Transistor radios, rain, newspapers, shaving, automobile driving, exams, and a host of other common objects and events are integral parts of our experience. The

mention of such things catches our attention because of their intimate connection with us. We may say, "Ah, that is an old friend," or " . . . an old problem."

On the other hand, we become bored if we see too much of the familiar. The familiar holds attention best when it is connected with something unfamiliar or when some previously unnoticed aspect of it is pointed out. We may listen attentively to new stories about Washington and Lincoln because we know a good deal about them already, but we do not want to hear the same old tales about the cherry tree or the wrestling match repeated endlessly.

5. *Novelty*. A novel event is one that is unexpected or extraordinary. As an old newspaper adage has it, when a dog bites a man, it's an accident; when a man bites a dog, it's news. Perhaps we should marvel that airplanes make countless flights across the oceans every day, but we take this for granted. Uneventful flights are not news; only the crashes become subjects of conversation.

Although listeners will usually pay immediate attention to anything new or unusual, be careful not to discuss things which are so novel that they are entirely unfamiliar. If your listeners do not know what you are talking about, their attention soon will wander. A balanced combination of the new and old, of the novel and familiar, brings best results.

Two special types of novelty are those of size and contrast.

a. *Size*. Extremely large or extremely small objects or amounts attract our attention. In a recent address on the high cost of national defense a speaker remarked, "Considering that it costs more than $5,000 to equip an average soldier for combat, it is disquieting to learn that in a year his equipment will be 60 per cent obsolete."[1] Advertisements of special sales often attempt to attract the readers' attention by displaying in a prominent place the unexpectedly low price of the goods offered. Notice, however, that it is not size alone that attracts attention, but unusual size. Just as prices are not astonishing in ads offering goods at standard rates, so figures are not especially interesting unless out of the ordinary. Reference to an automobile costing three thousand dollars or airplane costing three million would not be striking.

b. *Contrast*. Although attention-arousing in themselves, large and small figures become even more compelling when thrown into contrast with their opposites. In a famous address delivered many years ago at

---

[1] Neal Luker, "Our Defense Policy," a speech presented in a course in advanced public speaking at the University of Iowa, May 1963.

the University of Virginia, the Southern editor Henry Grady declared: "Our great wealth has brought us profit and splendor, but the status itself is a menace. A home that cost three million dollars and a breakfast that cost five thousand are disquieting facts to the millions who live in a hut and dine on a crust. The fact that a man . . . has an income of twenty million dollars falls strangely on the ears of those who hear it as they sit empty-handed with children crying for bread."[2]

6. *Suspense.* A large part of the interest which people have in a mystery story arises from uncertainty about its outcome. If readers were told at once who committed the murder and how and when the deed was done, they might never read the rest of the book. Attendance usually is low at what people think will be a one-sided football game because the result is too nearly certain. The suspense of an evenly matched game, however, draws a crowd. Hold the attention of your listeners by pointing out results which have mysterious or unknown causes or by calling attention to forces which threaten uncertain effects. Introduce suspense into the stories you use to illustrate your points. Mention some valuable information you expect to divulge later on in your talk but which first requires an understanding of what you are now saying. Make full use of the factor of suspense, but remember two things: (a) Do not make the information seem so difficult or mysterious that your listeners lose all hope of arriving at it; and (b) make sure the point, when it finally does come, is important enough to warrant the suspense you have created.

7. *Conflict.* The opposition of forces compels attention. In a sense, conflict is a form of activity, but it is more than that — it is a clash between opposing actions. Fights, election contests, the struggle of man with the adverse elements of nature and disease — because these situations involve conflict, people are interested when you describe them. Similarly, controversial issues are more interesting than uncontroversial ones.

8. *Humor.* Laughter indicates enjoyment, and people pay attention to what they enjoy. In fact, few things hold attention as well as humor judiciously used. Quips and stories provide relaxation from the tensions created by some of the other factors of attention and prepare your listeners to consider the more serious ideas that may follow. Wherever appropriate, introduce humorous anecdotes or allusions to brighten a talk, but observe two requirements for the effective use of humor:

---

[2] From an address before the literary societies of the University of Virginia, June 25, 1889.

(a) *Relevance*—be sure your story or reference bears directly on the point being discussed. (b) *Good taste*—avoid any quip or anecdote which would offend the group before you; do not use jokes about race, religion, or politics which would make your listeners uncomfortable or annoyed.

9. *The vital.* People always pay attention to matters which affect their life, health, reputation, property, or employment. If you can show your listeners that what you are saying concerns them directly, they will consider your discussion vital and usually will listen intently. Pointing out a danger to others also will command the listeners' attention because people tend to identify themselves with others. If the other factors of attention are important, this one is indispensable.

MAIN DIVISIONS OF A SPEECH TO INFORM

A first and governing principle in developing a speech to inform is to lead the thoughts of your listeners rather than force them. Do not develop the points of your speech too rapidly. Do not plunge into your subject until you have prepared your listeners' minds for what you have to say. As steps in this preparation, do two things: (1) gain their *attention;* and (2) show them why they *need* to know about your subject.

Gaining attention

When you are sure that the subject of your speech is of interest to the audience, you may be able to attract attention simply by referring to your theme. When your listeners are indifferent to the subject, however, or are not aware of its importance to them personally, use one of the methods for developing an introduction outlined in Chapter 8.

Showing the listeners why they need to know

Although this may be done briefly, it is exceedingly important. Speakers often fail because they assume that their listeners are waiting to seize the "pearls of knowledge" which their speeches contain. Unfortunately, this is not always the case. You must show your audience that the information you are to present is valuable to them—that it is something they need to know or even to act upon. If you suggest how your information will help them get ahead, save money, or do their work more easily, they will be more ready to listen.

Develop this part of the speech by including these elements:

1. *Statement.* Point out the importance of the subject and the need to be better informed upon it.

2. *Illustration.* Present one or more statements to illustrate the importance of the need.

3. *Reinforcement.* Employ as many additional facts, examples, or quotations as are required to make the need more convincing and impressive.

4. *Pointing.* Show the direct relation of the subject to the interests, well-being, or success of your hearers.

There are times, of course, when the information in your speech is not of a practical or workaday variety. When this is so, you can use the factor of suspense and build your need step on curiosity. Most people have a latent desire to find answers to interesting problems or to understand curious or unusual facts. Take advantage of this desire by setting up a situation that contains mysterious elements and suggesting that you are about to make the mystery clear. A noted chemist, for example, began a speech by telling about an unusual murder case. He made his audience wonder who the guilty man was and then proceeded to show how, through the use of certain chemical tests, the man was identified and convicted.

Satisfying the need to know: presenting the information

Having decided how you will capture the attention of your listeners and how you will arouse their desire to know what you propose to tell them, you are ready to consider ways of presenting the information itself. This presentation will naturally constitute the greatest part of a speech to inform—probably three-fourths to nine-tenths of it—and for this reason requires the most careful development. Review the methods of selecting and arranging the main points of a speech as described in Chapter 7. When you have chosen a pattern—time, space, cause-effect, or special topical—adhere to it consistently.

To facilitate understanding and retention, you may frequently preface your information with a preview or *initial summary* of the points to be covered and conclude it with a *final summary.* And you should always include definitions of any new or specialized terms.

Initial summary. The *initial summary* provides a skeleton around which to group your facts, and indicates the relationship each idea bears to the others. It also helps your listeners to follow your pattern of development—to see clearly where your speech is going. If you are explaining athletic activities on your campus, in an initial summary you might say:

> In my review of athletic activities on our campus, I shall discuss: first, our intercollegiate sports; second, our intramural program; and last, our class work in physical education.

The initial summary should be brief and simple, since a complex statement is difficult to remember and needlessly repetitive. Moreover, the order of points which it announces should be followed exactly in the presentation of the information or the listeners will be confused. Obviously, you need not have an initial summary in every informative talk you deliver, but when appropriate and properly developed, such a preview is useful both to your listeners and to yourself.

Definition of terms. In an informative speech you should define not only all *unfamiliar terms but also any terms that you use in a special sense.* There is no fixed point at which such definitions should be introduced, but when they relate to the entire body of information being presented, they are usually inserted just before or just after the initial summary. When the definitions concern only a part of the information, they are introduced at the relevant point in the discussion.

Detailed information. Following the initial summary, the detailed information of your speech is presented. Explanations, facts, figures, comparisons, and other data should be grouped around each main point in a systematic fashion, and often may be amplified and illustrated by maps, pictures, tables, or diagrams. Follow a consistent pattern in organizing the subordinate ideas that fall under a main point and amplify each idea with an abundance of supporting materials. As you advance from one point to the next, use connective sentences or phrases to emphasize the transition; if you use an initial summary, relate each new point to the plan you announce there. Keep the audience constantly aware of where you are, where you have been, and where you are heading.

How you organize the detailed information in a speech to inform depends in part on whether you are making a report, giving instructions, or delivering a lecture. Suggestions for organizing reports were given in Chapter 1. If you are hazy concerning the recommendations offered there, review pages 8-9.

When the purpose of your speech is to give instructions, it is usually best to divide it according to the various steps or operations to be performed and to consider these in their proper order. In discussing each step you may cover the reason for it, the materials, tools, or special information that are required, and any precautions that should be taken. Many speakers pause after explaining each step in a process to give their listeners an opportunity to ask questions.

The detailed development of an informative lecture depends so much on the subject matter being discussed that no one order can be recommended over others. Sometimes space order, cause-effect, or special topical order is most appropriate. Ask yourself what sequence will best accommodate the particular set of facts or ideas and adhere to that sequence in arranging the main points of the talk.

Final summary. The final summary, coming after the detailed data have been presented, ties the information together and leaves the audience with a unified and coherent picture. This summary usually consists of a restatement of your main points, together with any important conclusions or implications which have grown out of your discussion. Though it is similar to the initial summary in that it states the leading ideas of your speech, the final summary usually is longer and is particularly designed to impress your leading ideas on the listeners' memories. Notice the difference between this final summary and the initial summary on page 188:

> From what I have said, you can readily see that the three main divisions of our athletic program are closely related to one another. The intercollegiate sports stimulate interest in developing superior skills and bring in revenue for financing the rest of the program. Our intramural system extends the facilities for physical recreation to a large part of our student body—three thousand last year. And our physical education classes not only train men to become the coaches of the future, but also build up the physical endurance of the student body as a whole and give corrective work to those who have physical defects. The work of these three divisions, therefore, provides a comprehensive program which is of definite value to the college as a whole.

When you have presented your information and secured an understanding of it, you will have accomplished your purpose. Ordinarily, therefore, your speech will end with a final summary. There are times, however, when you may wish to encourage further study of the subject you have been discussing. In this event, you may suggest how your listeners can learn more by naming one or two specific sources of information or by calling attention to books or instructions which the listeners have. Then, if you wish, you may close quickly with a few sentences of thanks for their attention or, if you are addressing a group of employees or campaign workers, you may express confidence in their ability to carry out the procedures which you have explained.

SAMPLE OUTLINE

The following outline suggests one way to organize materials in a speech designed to inform or instruct:

THE BIRTH OF THE MOVIES[3]

Gaining attention

I. No form of entertainment is more widely popular than the movies.
   A. Throughout the world, people flock to watch movies.
   B. In the United States, despite the inroads of television, movies are still popular.
II. My purpose is to sketch developments which made this form of entertainment possible.

Showing the listeners why they need to know

I. The story of the movies' birth is worth telling.
   A. It forms an interesting chapter in the history of science and invention.
   B. It anticipates the development of an art form.
   C. It shows how far the modern sound and color film has advanced from humble beginnings.
II. As college students who frequent the movies, you should have a special interest in their early history.
   A. This knowledge will enable you to gain a better perspective of the motion picture industry as it exists today.
   B. This knowledge also will deepen your appreciation of the motion picture as an art form.

---

[3] Assembled from material in the *Encyclopaedia Britannica*, *Encyclopedia Americana*, and *Collier's Encyclopedia*.

I. I shall discuss five developments which together are responsible for the movies as we know them today: a new theory of human vision; the beginnings of the science of photography; improved methods and materials for action photography; the devising of projection technics; and the utilization of movies to tell a story.

 A. Explorations into the nature of vision were made by Peter Mark Roget.

  1. Roget's theory, presented before the Royal Society in London in 1824, maintained that "the image of a moving object is retained by the eye for a fraction of a second longer than it actually appears" [*Collier's Encyclopedia*].

  2. Roget developed this theory after observing actions through a Venetian blind.

  3. Roget's theory led to experiments in viewing rapid movement of still images.

  4. Mechanisms based on Roget's theory were limited to the animation of hand-drawn phases of motion.

 B. The development of the science of photography led to attempts to view photographs of subjects in phases of motion.

  1. In 1861 Coleman Sellers patented a machine that mounted posed action photographs on a paddle wheel for viewing.

  2. In 1870 Henry R. Heyl showed a series of action photographs through a "magic lantern" projecting device.

  3. In 1877 two other Americans used a battery of 24 cameras in sequence to photograph a race horse in action.

 C. Better methods and materials for action photography next were developed.

  1. In 1899 George Eastman developed a celluloid film strip.

   a. It was flexible and would not break or buckle.

   b. Its high-speed emulsion permitted photography of continuous action by one camera.

  2. Thomas A. Edison used Eastman's film in his camera, the Kinetograph.

D. Projection technics to permit viewing of the motion pictures were devised.

  1. The earliest and most important of these was Edison's Kinetoscope, a peep-show device, patented in 1891.

   a. The Kinetoscope was first used publicly in penny arcades in 1894.

   b. A customer saw a loop of filmed moving picture lasting about 50 seconds.

  2. Another important projector was Thomas Armat's Vitascope, presented publicly in a New York music hall in 1896.

   a. An entire audience was permitted to see films at the same time.

   b. Some of the films shown were those used in the penny arcades.

E. Movies as we know them were born when they began to tell a story.

  1. In early moving pictures, the story was nonexistent.

   a. Films were bits of vaudeville action or examples of trick shooting.

   b. Some pictures, taken with portable hand-cranked cameras, showed fire engines or trains in motion, or crowds out for a stroll.

  2. By 1899, George Méliès of France began to link brief scenes to form a narrative.

  3. In 1903, Edwin S. Porter produced *The Great Train Robbery.*

   a. It introduced disjunctive editing; events did not follow strict chronological sequence.

   b. It transformed movies into a widely accepted form of entertainment.

   c. It was on the program at the opening of the first moving picture theater—a nickelodeon in Pittsburgh.

(Final summary) II. The history of the birth of the movies is the history of five major developments.

A. Roget supplied the theory of vision.
B. The development of photography spurred other men to apply Roget's theory to the new science.
C. George Eastman and Thomas Edison gave us the film and camera needed for action photography.
D. Projection technics enabled us to see moving pictures on a screen.
E. *The Great Train Robbery* ushered in an era of moving pictures as entertaining narratives.

From the sample outline above, you will observe that the organization of a speech to inform or instruct will have a skeleton outline somewhat like this:[4]

SUBJECT: _____
SPECIFIC PURPOSE: _____

Gaining attention	I. (Opening statement) _____
	A. (Support) _____
	1, 2, etc. (Details) _____
	B. (Support) _____
	II. (Statement of purpose) _____
Showing the listeners why they need to know	I. (Statement of need for information) _____
	A. (Support) _____
	1, 2, etc. (Details) _____
	B. (Support) _____
	1, 2, etc. (Details) _____
	II. (Pointing statement relating to audience) _____
	A, B, etc. (Support) _____
Satisfying the need to know: presenting the information	I. (Statement of subject, including initial summary)
	A. (Statement of first main division of the subject) _____
	1. (Support) _____
	a, b, etc. (Details) _____
	2. (Support) _____
	a, b, etc. (Details) _____

---

[4] Note that the skeleton outline provides for details under supporting statements. Such details, although generally omitted from the streamlined outline on "The Birth of the Movies," are essential to the complete development of your speeches.

B, C, etc. (Statements of other main divisions of subject, supported by subordinate ideas and details)_____

II. (Final summary statement)_____
    A. (First main division of subject summarized)__
    B, C, etc. (Other main divisions of subject summarized) _____

PROBLEMS FOR FURTHER STUDY

1. List at least ten different situations in which informative speeches are called for. To what extent do you think the same principles of content and organization apply in each of these situations, and to what extent must special modifications or adaptations be made? Prepare a paper reporting your conclusions.

2. Make a study of one particular type of informative speaking — the classroom lecture, the expository sermon, the oral report, the informative radio or television talk, etc. After listening to a number of talks of this kind, prepare a paper in which you comment on any special problems of organization or presentation which appear to be present. How were these problems solved in the speeches you studied?

3. Outline an informative speech reprinted in a recent issue of *Vital Speeches* and note compositional devices employed by the speaker. What method is used to gain attention? Does the speaker show the listeners why they need to know the information he is going to present? Is there an initial summary? Would you classify the talk as abstract or concrete? Is time, space, cause-effect, special topical, or some other order followed? What type of conclusion is used?

4. Find two other informative talks in *Vital Speeches,* in a recent issue of *Representative American Speeches* (ed. Lester Thonssen, New York: The H. W. Wilson Company), or some similar source. Compare the methods of organization employed and comment on the suitability of each method to the subject matter being discussed.

5. Analyze the use made of the factors of attention in at least three informative speeches. Are some of the factors used more frequently than others? Which seem to you to be most effective? Can you infer any rules or cautions to be observed when using the factors of attention?

6. Drawing upon your observations as a listener, discuss the role that the speaker's delivery plays in conveying information clearly and interestingly. Can you cite examples where delivery definitely helped or hindered the speaker in these respects?

7. Select a principle of physics, chemistry, biology, or a similar science. How might you relate this principle to concepts familiar to: (a) a farmer, (b) an automobile repairman, (c) a twelve-year-old newsboy, (d) a lawyer? Write out a paragraph making this principle clear to one of the above.

SPEAKING ASSIGNMENT

1. Prepare a speech to inform for presentation in class. Select and narrow your subject from one of the topics suggested below, or from a similar topic. Use whatever visual aids you think will improve your presentation. Follow the rules of organization and development set forth in this chapter.

New wonder drugs
Contemporary American writers (artists, musicians)
Teaching machines and programed learning
The Federal Communications Commission
How to learn through better listening
The use of visual aids in speaking
How television programs are selected
Cosmetics and beauty aids: a big business
Agencies of the United Nations
Alaska: our newest state
The Common Market
Advances in automation

SUGGESTIONS FOR FURTHER READING

John E. Dietrich and Keith Brooks, *Practical Speaking for the Technical Man* (Englewood Cliffs, N. J.: Prentice-Hall, Inc., 1958), Chapter 7, "Make Your Information Clear," and Chapter 8, "Make Your Information Interesting."

L. O. Guthrie, *Factual Communication* (New York: The Macmillan Company, 1948), Chapter 2, "Characteristics of a Factual Message"; Chapter 3, "Making a Factual Talk"; Chapter 4, "Speaking and Writing Problems"; Chapter 5, "Essentials of Understanding."

Roy Ivan Johnson, Marie Schalekamp, and Lloyd A. Garrison, *Communication: Handling Ideas Effectively* (New York: McGraw-Hill Book Company, Inc., 1956), Chapter 10, "Making Reports: Materials and Methods."

David C. Phillips, *Oral Communication in Business* (New York: McGraw-Hill Book Company, Inc., 1955), Chapter 4, "How to Make Oral Communication Interesting."

THE SPEECH TO PERSUADE

A speech to persuade attempts to influence the listeners' beliefs or actions; hence, it supplies arguments and motives for thinking or acting as the speaker recommends.

Belief and action, the goals of a persuasive speech, are closely related. If you wish people to act in a certain way, you first must convince them that such behavior is right, or expedient, or advantageous. Then, if they believe strongly, they will tend to act according to that belief. Most Americans, for example, obey a summons to serve in the armed forces because they believe that such service is part of their responsibility as citizens; the conscientious objector, however, guided by his strong conviction against the taking of human life, rejects the summons.

Some speeches to persuade urge belief in a principle or point of view which, though it could influence future decisions, calls for no immediate action. ("The causes of the American Revolution were primarily economic.") Other persuasive speeches go a step further and openly appeal for action. ("Buy government saving bonds today.") Because of the intimate relationship between belief and action, however, all persuasive talks have the same primary objective — influencing the audience to make some actual choice or decision.

Although the purpose of a persuasive speech is to win belief or action, an unwilling decision is of little value. Beliefs which people are

forced to accept may soon be abandoned; actions done unwillingly are usually done inefficiently and without any sense of reward or accomplishment. To persuade successfully, therefore, you not only must make your listeners believe or do something, but you also must make them *want* to believe or do it. For this reason, two subsidiary purposes of the persuasive speech must be kept in mind: (1) to provide your listeners with motives for believing by appealing to certain of their basic needs or desires and (2) to satisfy their understanding by convincing them that the proposition you recommend will make the satisfaction of these desires possible.

ESSENTIAL CHARACTERISTICS OF A SPEECH TO PERSUADE

Appeals to the interests and desires of the audience

Even though a persuasive speech contains an abundance of facts and demonstrates sound reasoning, it is likely to fail if it does not make a direct appeal to the people who hear it. Therefore, you must relate your proposal to your listeners' interests and desires. In their book *Strategy in Handling People,* the psychologists Webb and Morgan emphasized the importance of this principle. "From a practical standpoint," they wrote, "the first precaution in managing people is to discover what they really want, expecially the exact nature of the most active wants which touch upon us and our plans."[1]

What are these wants and desires that motivate human behavior, and to which of them must our evidence and arguments be addressed? All of them are observable in day-to-day experience. Someone calls me a liar, and I order him out of my room. Someone shows me that the only way I can get a job and provide for my family is to join the union, so I pay my dues and join. I am told that membership in a fraternity will ensure my social prestige on the campus and help me get into activities, so I become interested. My bed is warm and the room cold, so I decide to miss my eight o'clock class, but recalling that I must pass a quiz at nine o'clock or flunk the course, I brave the cold and shiver into my clothes at eight-thirty. In each of these instances, some latent force within me is stirred to action.

Depending upon their point of view, psychologists have called these action tendencies by different names—instincts, emotions, prepotent reflexes, purposive or wish-fulfilling drives, etc. The most common term now is *motives*.

There have been many arguments about the number of motives and the degree to which they are inborn or acquired. With the details of these arguments we are not concerned here. It is more important for us to note the facts agreed upon by all: (1) that in human beings there are certain universal action tendencies which move them in different directions; and (2) these tendencies are set in motion and modified in their direction by pressures put on individuals by their environment.[2]

If, then, you are to persuade successfully, you must associate your message with men's motives. But before you can do this, you must understand what these motives are and how to arouse them.

The primary motives. There are four primary motives—four basic needs, desires, or drives—which influence human beings. Behind nearly every act, belief, or emotion will be found one of the following:

1. Self-preservation and the desire for physical well-being

---

[1] E. T. Webb and J. J. B. Morgan, *Strategy in Handling People* (Chicago: Boulton, Pierce and Co., 1931), p. 73.

[2] It will be noted here and elsewhere in the book that the authors' psychology is frankly eclectic. They are familiar with the theories of present-day psychologists, as well as with the traditional psychology of the nineteenth century. They believe that while no one theory furnishes a complete basis for understanding the psychology of speech, many theories contribute illuminating suggestions. In the present instance, for example, the authors' discussion combines the concept of *purposive* reaction originally advanced by McDougall with the idea of *tensions caused by unclosed patterns* advanced by the Gestaltists.

2. Freedom from external restraint
3. Preservation and increase of self-esteem (ego expansion)
4. Preservation of the human race

Thus, we build a fire to keep from freezing or even from feeling cold (1); we abhor imprisonment and dislike laws that limit what we call our personal liberty (2); we wear attractive clothes, try to excel in our accomplishments, enjoy praise, and dislike appearing in unfavorable circumstances (3); we marry, have children, organize governments, and impose legal penalties for antisocial conduct (4).

Although the four primary motives are always present to some extent, they are not uniformly strong in everyone. One man may care more for his comfort than his freedom; another, more for his family than himself. Experience modifies our desires, and at certain periods in our lives one motive may be stronger than others. Furthermore, we often seek fulfillment of our basic desires in many indirect and complex ways because the conventions of society prevent their direct fulfillment. Through experience and conditioning we acquire a large variety of secondary motives—derivations of the four primary motives as they are related to the concrete objects of our environment. It is to these secondary or derived motives rather than to the primary drives themselves that the speaker usually must direct his motive appeals.

Types of motive appeal. Because secondary or derived motives are indefinite in number and because they vary from person to person, no classification of motive appeals is entirely satisfactory. The list which follows, however, contains most of the specific drives or desires to which speakers appeal. It will be helpful to study this list, and to begin basing the main points of your speeches upon some of the items.

1. Acquisition and saving
2. Adventure
3. Companionship
4. Creating
    a. Organizing
    b. Building
5. Curiosity
6. Destruction
7. Fear
8. Fighting
    a. Anger
    b. Competition

9. Imitation
10. Independence
11. Loyalty
    a. To friends
    b. To family (parental or filial love)
    c. To social groups (school spirit, civic pride)
    d. To nation (patriotism)
12. Personal enjoyment
    a. Of comfort and luxury
    b. Of beauty and order
    c. Of pleasant sensations (tastes, smells, etc.)
    d. Of recreation
    e. Of relief from restraint (sprees, etc.)
13. Power and authority
14. Pride
    a. Reputation
    b. Self-respect
15. Reverence or worship
    a. Of leaders (hero worship)
    b. Of institutions or traditions
    c. Of the Deity
16. Revulsion
17. Sex attraction
18. Sympathy

In practice, of course, appeals to the foregoing motives are not always made singly but are often combined. For example, a speaker may urge students to attend college in order to improve their chances for self-advancement. But what contributes to the desire for self-advancement? Desire for a greater income, for authority over others, and for pride in a higher station in life—all these, acquisition, power, and pride, are combined into the one pattern that is often called "getting ahead." Or to take a common experience: suppose you were going to buy a new coat. What would influence your decision? One factor would be the price—*saving;* another would be comfort and appearance—the *pleasure* to be derived from its beauty or luxury; a third consideration would be style—*imitation*—or individuality of appearance—*independence;* and finally, a combination of these items would make an appeal to *pride.* Some of these appeals might be stronger than others; some might even conflict; but all probably would be present.

Although a variety of appeals may be valuable in a speech, it is important not to dissipate the strength of your argument by too diffuse a scattering. Usually, the better method is to select a few motives which you think will have the strongest attraction for your audience and to concentrate on them, making other appeals incidental. For example, a student who urged his classmates to participate in interclass athletic contests chose the following as the main points of his talk:

Fear	I. Concentrated study without exercise will make your mind stale and will harm your grades.
Companionship	II. Participation in athletics will gain you new friends.
Power and Pride	III. Interclass competition may lead to a place on the varsity teams.
Enjoyment of recreation	IV. The games are a great deal of fun.

In the complete development of his speech, this student also made appeals to imitation by citing examples of varsity athletes who had engaged in interclass sports, stimulated the desire for competition, and suggested that participation would indicate loyalty to the class.

In most cases, too direct or blatant an appeal to the listeners' wishes or desires should be avoided, since instead of winning approval it would tend to create resistance. You should not go before your listeners and say, "I want you to *imitate* Jones, the successful banker," or "If you give to this cause, we will print your name so that your *reputation* as a generous person will be evident to everyone." Rather, you must make your appeal effective by suggesting these rewards through the descriptions and illustrations you use. You must work subtly and by indirection. Moreover, remember that some motives which are privately powerful, such as fear, imitation, personal comfort, or pride, may not be acknowledged in public. Therefore, when appealing to these tendencies, you must word your remarks with special care and perhaps also appeal to motives which will be publicly acknowledged.

Adapting appeals to the audience. In Chapter 3 we discussed the importance of analyzing the audience to determine the types of persons it includes, their fixed beliefs and opinions, and their prevailing attitudes toward the speaker and his purpose. (See pages 44-51.) Nowhere is such analysis more important than in the selection of motive appeals. Choose appeals which are directly adapted to the people you are addressing (appeal to ambition and self-advancement in young men, security in older people, etc.). Work with rather than against the dominant drives of the audience; show your listeners how the judgment or proposal you advance will make them happier, healthier, or more successful. Only in this way will you make them want to believe or act as you suggest.

Sound, logical reasoning

In addition to strong motivation, a successful persuasive speech must contain reasoning which proves that the view or policy you recommend will satisfy one or more of your listeners' basic needs or desires. At times it may also be necessary to prove that these needs or desires actually are threatened. A brief consideration of the three most frequently used forms of reasoning, therefore, is essential.

Reasoning from example. This form of reasoning consists of drawing conclusions about a general class of objects by studying individual members of that class. If a housewife were in doubt about the flavor of the apples in a bushel basket, she would bite into one of them to test it. If the taste pleased her, she would reason that all the apples in the basket had a good flavor. Or perhaps if she were a bit skeptical, she also might test an apple from the bottom of the basket to make sure that all the apples were alike. This sort of reasoning from specific cases to a general conclusion is employed in much of our thinking, whether the point at issue is big or little. Scientific experiments, public opinion polls, and studies of social behavior all depend on reasoning from example. Reasoning of this sort should be tested by asking the following questions:

1. Have enough examples been examined to substantiate the generalization? One robin does not make a spring, nor do two or three examples always prove that a general proposition is incontestably true.

2. Have the examples been fairly chosen? To attempt to prove that Americans oppose federal farm subsidies by citing opinions polled in New York, Chicago, and Los Angeles — all very large metropolitan areas — would be to reason from selected or weighted examples, since the attitudes of urban dwellers on this problem may be quite different from those of farmers or persons living in small towns.

3. Are there any outstanding exceptions to the generalization? One well-known exception may undermine your general conclusion

unless you can show that the exception is the result of unusual or abnormal circumstances.

Reasoning from axiom. In reasoning from axiom, you apply a general rule or principle to a specific situation. For example, it is usually conceded that savings may be effected by purchasing merchandise in large lots. When, therefore, you argue that a grocery chain saves money by buying in large quantities, you merely are applying this general rule to the specific instance of the grocery chain. Reasoning from axiom may be tested as follows:

1. Is the axiom, or rule, true? Many generalizations which are assumed to be true actually are fictions; for example, people once assumed the world was flat. Before applying an axiom, therefore, test its validity. Also, be sure that its validity is recognized by the audience. Unless the principle used as a premise is accepted as true, the conclusion drawn from it will be rejected.

2. Does the axiom apply to the specific situation in question? Too often, good axioms are loosely or incorrectly applied. Thus, you may argue, on the principle mentioned above, that a grocery chain buys goods more cheaply, but you may not argue that the customer always can buy from a chain store at a lower price. The inference extends only to the prices at which the grocery chain buys; not to prices at which its stores sell. In order to establish this second contention, you would require a new premise.

Reasoning from casual relation. When something new or unexpected happens, we look for its causes, or when we see a force in operation, we speculate about its probable effects. A great deal of our reasoning is based upon cause-effect relationship. The crime rate goes up and we lay the blame on war, on bad housing, on public apathy, or on inept police officials. We hear that our star quarterback is hospitalized with a broken ankle and we fear for the outcome of Saturday's game. We reason from known effects to probable causes and from known causes to probable effects. No other form of reasoning, perhaps, is used so much by public speakers; nor is any other form so often misused. To test the soundness of causal reasoning, ask the questions:

1. Has the cause been mistaken for the effect? When two phenomena occur simultaneously, it sometimes is difficult to tell which is cause and which is effect. In a period of prosperity, do higher production costs cause higher prices of raw materials, or do higher prices of raw materials force production costs up?

2. Is the cause powerful enough to produce the alleged effect? A small pebble on the track will not derail a passenger train, but a large boulder will. Be careful not to mistake a pebble for a boulder.

3. Has anything prevented the cause from operating? If a gun were unloaded, pulling the trigger would not make it shoot. Be certain that nothing has prevented the free operation of the cause which you assume has produced the effect.

4. Could any other cause have produced this effect? Four possible causes for an increase in violent crime were listed above—war, bad housing, public apathy, inept police. When assigning causes, try to diagnose the situation correctly; do not put the blame on the wrong cause, or all the blame on a single cause if it should be divided.

5. Does a causal connection actually exist? Sometimes people assume that because two things occur in sequence, they are causally connected. The appearance of a skin rash after you have touched a leafy plant does not necessarily mean that the contact caused the rash. Do not mistake a coincidence for a true cause-effect relationship. You must get adequate proof to establish a causal connection.

Concrete facts and vivid illustrations

In a speech to persuade, as in every type of speech, you should avoid generalities and abstract statements. Use pertinent facts and figures; present an abundance of instances, illustrations, and comparisons. No other single factor is so important in this type of speech as presenting facts, facts, and more facts. Review the forms of support discussed in Chapter 6 and fill your speech with them.

TYPES OF PROPOSITIONS IN SPEECHES TO PERSUADE

Every persuasive speech asserts that in the opinion of the speaker (1) something should or should not be done; (2) something is or is not so; or (3) something is desirable or undesirable. Such judgments or recommendations, when formally expressed in language, are known as propositions.

Propositions of policy

Propositions which recommend or oppose a given course of action are called *propositions of policy*. They are so named because in effect they say that it would be a good idea to accept or reject a proposed policy: "The United States *should increase* the size of its military forces." "Government expenditures for foreign aid *should not be increased*." "The student senate *should have control* over all extracurricular activities."

Establishing propositions of policy

In order to persuade an audience to accept a proposition of policy, a speaker usually must answer four questions affirmatively:

1. *Is there a need for the policy or course of action proposed?* If people are not convinced that a change from the present state of affairs is needed, they will not seriously consider—much less approve—a new policy.

2. *Will the proposed policy or plan work?* If people do not believe that your proposal will correct existing evils or improve conditions, they will reject it.

3. *Will the proposed policy bring greater benefits than disadvantages?* People will not approve a proposal—even though it may correct the present problem—if it promises to bring new and greater evils.

4. *Is the proposed policy better than any other plan or policy?* People usually will not approve a policy if they believe some other course of action is better.

Sometimes your listeners will recognize the need for a new policy or program even before you begin to speak. And occasionally they will recognize that if the proposed policy were practicable—that is, if it could be put into operation, administered, paid for, etc.—it would bring many advantages. Under such circumstances, answers to questions 1 and 3 may be omitted from your speech or merely mentioned in passing. Generally, however, in order to secure belief or action on a policy, you must deal with all four of the questions listed above: (1) show a need for a new policy; (2) show that the particular policy you advocate will work to meet this need; (3) show that it will bring more advantages than disadvantages; and (4) show that it is the best possible course of action to take.

Propositions of fact

When, instead of recommending or opposing a policy, you attempt to persuade your listeners that something is or is not so, you are speaking on a so-called *proposition of fact*. Do not, however, let the name fool you. A proposition of fact is not already accepted as a fact; it is a statement that you are trying to prove a fact. Moreover, not all factual questions should be dealt with in speeches. Often questions of whether or not something is so may be settled best by personal observation, by conducting a controlled experiment, or by looking up the answer in a reliable printed source. It would be absurd for men to argue the question of whether it is raining outside, or whether the fruit in a certain basket is contaminated, or how long it takes to go by train from Seattle to San Francisco. The first of these questions of fact could be settled by glancing out the window, the second by making appropriate chemical tests, and the third by referring to a timetable.

Other questions of fact, however, do not lend themselves to these methods. Is the United States leading other nations in the space race? Is the present government of Eudalia communist-dominated? Is Jones guilty of embezzlement as charged? Because they inquire whether something is or is not so, these questions, too, involve matters of fact. But while observation or experimentation or printed data may help us arrive at a decision concerning them, in the end we must depend upon our own informed judgment—upon reasoning from the best facts available to what appears to be the most accurate or fairest answer. It is on factual questions of this sort that men make speeches, trying to persuade others that their opinions or judgments are correct.

Propositions of value

A statement which asserts that something is desirable or undesirable, or praiseworthy or blameworthy, is a *proposition of value*. This name derives from the fact that such propositions evaluate something and declare its worth. "Progressive education is inferior education," "Modern art is decadent," "John F. Kennedy was one of our great Presidents"—these are propositions of value.

Establishing propositions of fact and value

Whereas in establishing a proposition of policy a speaker usually must answer the four questions listed on page 205, in establishing a proposition of fact or value he will find only the following two questions relevant:

1. *Upon what criteria or standards should a judgment concerning this matter be based?* A standard is essential in judging propositions of fact or value. In saying that today's teenagers are tall, you would have to base your judgment of their heights upon some criterion of "tallness." In presenting the value statement "Our present grading system is undesirable," you would have to show what you conceive a fair grading system to be. Otherwise it would be impossible for your listeners to decide one way or the other concerning your judgment.

When discussing questions of value, you must be sure that the criteria you advance are acceptable to your listeners. Is the worth of a particular institution or practice to be judged by economic or by moral standards? By the standards of the expert or by those of the average citizen? Often it is well to suggest two or three different kinds of criteria which together cover all possible bases for judgment. For example, to determine the quality of a particular college, you might select as criteria the distinction of its faculty, the adequacy of its physical plant, the success of its students in graduate and professional schools, and the reputation it enjoys in its region.

2. *Do the facts and circumstances in question meet the criteria specified?* Just as you would determine whether a product is overpriced or underpriced by comparing it with an established average, so you must judge the worth of a proposition of fact or value by measuring the relevant evidence against standards which have been set up as criteria. What are the standards and practices of our present grading system? Do these standards and practices meet the conditions of "fairness" as you have designated them? Questions concerning criteria or existing conditions are not always easy to answer, and sometimes definitive answers are impossible. In order to establish a proposition of fact or value to the satisfaction of a reasonable listener, however, it is necessary to show that at least a preponderance of the evidence meets the criteria which have been set forth as bases for judgment.

From what has been said about the three types of propositions, you should now be able to see how important it is to know exactly the sort of proposition you are seeking to establish in a given persuasive speech. Is it a proposition of policy, fact, or value? If policy, do all four of the basic questions listed on page 205 need to be covered, or is your audience likely to accept one or more of them without proof from you? If fact or value, which criteria should be used as bases for judgment, and how well are they met by the evidence? Unless there are

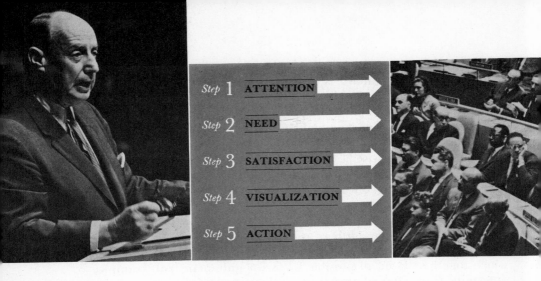

Step 1 ATTENTION

Step 2 NEED

Step 3 SATISFACTION

Step 4 VISUALIZATION

Step 5 ACTION

sound reasons for delay, it is also important to state the proposition early in your speech. If your listeners do not see the precise point they are asked to judge, your strongest arguments and appeals probably will prove useless.

DEVELOPING A PERSUASIVE SPEECH: THE MOTIVATED SEQUENCE

When you have clearly in mind the specific proposition of policy, fact, or value for which you wish to gain acceptance, you are ready to begin gathering material and organizing your persuasive talk. So far as organization is concerned, the most important rule is this: you cannot cram ideas down people's throats, but you must lead their thoughts easily and gradually toward the conclusion you desire. A speech is not something to be planned in isolation, and then brought out and "displayed" before the audience. Rather, it must be planned with a particular audience constantly in mind and must be constructed to conform with the thinking processes of the listeners. To organize a talk otherwise would be as foolish as trying to make a man fit a suit.

How then, one may ask, do people think when confronted with a decision or choice such as a persuasive speech asks them to make? Although individuals always vary to some extent, experience has shown that when thinking carefully most people begin by examining the

When completely developed, the motivated sequence, a speech structure to motivate audience response, consists of five steps. These steps are: attention, need, satisfaction, visualization, and action.

problem or question that calls for a decision. What sort of problem is it? What is its scope, its seriousness? Whom does it affect, and why? Is an immediate decision called for? With these questions at least tentatively answered, attention characteristically moves to searching out a suitable answer or solution. If the question is one of fact or value, does the proffered judgment or evaluation provide a direct and reasonable answer to the specific question raised? If the question is one of policy, would this proposal really solve the problem, and would it do so without introducing new and worse evils? Until they are satisfied on these and similar points, few people will accept a judgment of fact or value or endorse a policy.[3]

As we have said, there is no guarantee that everyone always thinks through problems in this fashion. But much observation and testing has made it apparent that the foregoing pattern is common enough to provide a dependable psychological basis for organizing persuasive appeals. Begin by directing attention to the question to be answered or the problem to be solved; then advance the answer or solution which you believe to be best; third, prove the pertinence and soundness of your position; and finally, ask the audience to believe or act as you recommend. By adhering to this general progression from question or problem to answer or solution, and then on to action, you can develop

---

[3] For a fuller discussion of the problem-solving process, see Chapter 7, "Analysis of Reflective Thinking," in *How We Think* by John Dewey (Boston: D. C. Heath and Company, 1933).

your appeals along the thought lines that most people are accustomed to. Such organization will make your speech easy to follow and will render it more naturally persuasive.

The plan of speech organization which is derived from this analysis of the thinking process may be called the *motivated sequence:* the sequence of ideas which, because it adheres to the steps by which people systematically think their way through problems and make decisions, *motivates* the audience to accept the speaker's proposition.

If this sequence is kept in mind, the method of organizing a persuasive speech becomes comparatively simple. In its complete form the motivated sequence consists of five steps:

1. Getting attention
2. Showing the need: describing the problem
3. Satisfying the need: presenting the solution
4. Visualizing the results
5. Requesting action or approval

For the sake of convenience, we shall henceforth refer to these five steps as (1) *Attention,* (2) *Need,* (3) *Satisfaction,* (4) *Visualization,* and (5) *Action.*

Observe how the foreign correspondent Leland Stowe used the motivated sequence in making an appeal for the relief of hungry children overseas after World War II:

> (1) I pray that I'll never have to do it again. Can there be anything much worse than to put only a peanut between a child and death? I hope you'll never have to do it, and live with the memory of it afterward. If you had heard their voices and seen their eyes, on that January day in the bomb-scarred workers' district of Athens. . . Yet all I had left was a half-pound can of peanuts. As I struggled to open it, dozens of ragged kids held me in a vise of frantically clawing bodies. Scores of mothers, with babes in their arms, pushed and fought to get within arm's reach. They held their babies out toward me. Tiny hands of skin and bone stretched convulsively. I tried to make every peanut count. In their frenzy they nearly swept me off my feet. Nothing but hundreds of hands: begging hands, clutching hands, despairing hands; all of them pitifully little hands. One salted peanut here, and one peanut there. Six peanuts knocked from my fingers, and a savage scramble of emaciated bodies at my feet. Another peanut here, and another peanut there. Hundreds of hands, reaching and pleading; hundreds of eyes with the light of hope flickering out. I stood there helpless, an empty blue can in my hands. . . Yes, I hope it will never happen to you.

(2) Who would say that a child's life is worth less than a movie a week, or a lipstick or a few packs of cigarettes? Yet, in today's world, there are at least 230,000,000 children who must depend upon the aid of private agencies and individuals. From Amiens to Athens, from Cairo to Calcutta and Chungking, millions upon millions of waifs of war still hold death barely at arm's length. Their only hope rests in the private relief agencies which, in turn, depend entirely upon you and me — upon how much we care and what we give.

(3) A world-wide campaign exists as a demonstration that the peoples of the United Nations do care. Our own branch of UNAC is American Overseas Aid — United Nations Appeal for Children, with headquarters at 39 Broadway, New York City. In February, American Overseas Aid makes its appeal to raise $60,000,000 from Americans. That's something to put peanuts forever in their place. Something big enough for every American to want to be in on. Every penny contributed to American Overseas Aid will help bring food, medical care and new life to millions of child war victims.

(4) If we could hear their voices and see their eyes, countless millions of children, now hungry and diseased or soon to die, would run and play and laugh once more. It only depends on how many of us hear and how many see. Look at their reaching, outspread fingers — and (5) send your contribution to American Overseas Aid, 39 Broadway, New York.[4]

Mr. Stowe, you will note, (1) called attention to his subject with a vivid illustration from personal experience, (2) pointed out the need for funds to provide organized relief, (3) explained how American Overseas Aid could meet this need if enough money were contributed, (4) visualized briefly the contrasting results of starvation or relief, and (5) appealed for direct action — contributions from his listeners.

The five steps in the motivated sequence need not be of equal length; nor, for that matter, need they always stand in the same relative proportion. Each situation is unique and will demand adaptations. At times one or more of the steps may even be left out entirely because the previous knowledge or the attitude of the listeners renders them unnecessary. At other times, one of the steps may need to be greatly expanded or otherwise stressed. Recognizing this flexibility of the sequence, let us now consider how each of the main steps may be developed in talks aimed at securing the adoption of various kinds of propositions.

---

[4] Leland Stowe, "Peanuts, Children — and You," *Bluebook Magazine,* LXXXVI (February 1948), 52. Used with permission of Mr. Stowe.

THE MOTIVATED SEQUENCE IN A SPEECH
URGING THE ADOPTION OF A POLICY

Getting attention

Someone has said that too frequently the attitude of a person about to hear someone else give a talk is "Ho-hum!" You must change that attitude at the very beginning if you are going to persuade him to believe or act. The methods for effecting this change were described in Chapter 8. A review of pages 162-170 will remind you how startling statements, illustrations, questions, etc., can be used to overcome the "Ho-hum" attitude and direct wide-awake attention to what you have to say.

Showing the need: describing the problem

With attention caught, you are ready to make clear why the policy you propose is needed. To do this, you must show that a definite problem exists; you must point out what is wrong with things as they are and through facts and figures show just how bad the situation is. For example, "Too few carburetors are being produced in our plant at Littleton, and as a result we have had to shut down our main assembly line at Metropolis three times in the last month."

Normally, this need or problem step requires a four-fold development: (1) *Statement*—a definite, concise statement of the problem; (2) *Illustration*—one or more examples explaining and clarifying the problem; (3) *Ramification*—additional examples, statistical data, testimony, and other forms of support showing the extent and seriousness of the problem; (4) *Pointing*—making clear to the audience how the problem directly affects them. You will not, however, always need to use all four items in the development of the need step. "Statement" and "pointing" should always be present but the inclusion of "illustration" and "ramification" will depend upon the amount of detail required to impress the audience. But whether you use the complete development or only a part of it, the need step is exceedingly important—often the most important in your talk—because here your subject is first definitely related to the needs and desires of your listeners.

Satisfying the need: presenting the solution

The solution or satisfaction step in a speech urging the adoption of a policy has the purpose of getting your listeners to agree that the policy you propose is the correct one. Therefore, it consists of presenting your proposed solution to the problem and proving this solution practicable and desirable. Five items are usually involved in the development of the satisfaction step: (1) *Statement*—stating the attitude, belief, or action you wish the audience to adopt. (2) *Explanation*—making sure that your proposal is understood. (Often diagrams or charts are useful here.) (3) *Theoretical demonstration*—showing by reasoning how the solution you propose meets the need. (4) *Reference to practical experience* —supplying examples to show that the proposal has worked effectively where it has been tried. Use facts, figures, and the testimony of experts to support this contention. (5) *Meeting objections*—forestalling opposition by answering any objections which might be raised against the proposal.

Just as certain items may at times be omitted from the need step, so also may one or more of these phases be left out of the satisfaction step if the situation warrants. Nor must the foregoing order always be followed exactly. Occasionally, objections can best be met by dealing with them as they arise in the minds of the listeners; in other situations the theoretical demonstration and reference to practical experience may be combined. If the satisfaction step is developed properly, however, at its conclusion the audience will say, "Yes, you are right; this is a practicable and desirable solution to the problem you pointed out."

Visualizing the results

The function of the visualization step is to intensify desire. It should picture for the audience how conditions will be in the future (1) if the policy you propose is adopted or (2) if the policy you propose is not adopted. Because it projects the thinking of the audience into the future, it might just as correctly be called the "projection" step.

The projection aimed at in the visualization step may be accomplished in one of three ways: by the *positive* method, the *negative* method, or the method of *contrast*.

The positive method. Under this method you describe conditions as they will be in the future if the solution you propose is carried out. Make such a description vivid and concrete. Select some situation which you are quite sure will arise. Then picture your listeners in that situation actually enjoying the conditions which your proposal will produce.

The negative method. This method describes conditions as they will be in the future if your proposal is not carried out. It pictures for your audience the evils or dangers which will arise from failure to effect your solution to present evils. Select from the need step the most undesirable aspects of the present situation, and show how these conditions will be aggravated if your proposal is rejected.

The method of contrast. This method combines the two preceding ones. The negative approach is used first, showing the disadvantages accruing from failure to adopt your proposal; then the positive approach is used, showing the advantages accruing from its adoption. Thus, the desirable situation is thrown into strong contrast with the undesirable one.

Whichever method you use, remember that the visualization step must stand the test of reality. The conditions you picture must be made vivid. Let your listeners see themselves enjoying the advantages or suffering the evils you describe. The more clearly you can depict the situation, the more strongly the audience will react.

The following is an example of a visualization step developed by the method of contrast. It is taken from a student speech urging the use of fireproof materials in home construction.

> But suppose you do build your home of the usual kindling wood: joists, rafters, and shingles. Some dark night you may awake from your pleasant sleep with the smell of acrid smoke in your nostrils, and the threatening crackle of burning timbers in your ears. You will jump out onto the cold floor and rush to wake up the household. Gathering your children in your arms, you will hurry down the stairs — if they are not already in flames — and out of doors. There you will watch the firemen chop holes in your roof, pour gallons of water over your plaster, your furniture, your piano. You will shiver with cold in spite of the blazing spectacle and the minds of your children will be indelibly impressed with fright. No fire insurance can repay your family for this horror, even though it may pay a small part of the financial loss.
>
> How much better to use safe materials! Then throughout the long winter nights you can dig down under the warmth of your bedclothes to sleep peacefully in the assurance that your house cannot burn, and that any fire which catches in your furnishings can be confined to a small space and put out. No more the fear of flying sparks. Gone the danger to your wife and children. Sleep — quiet, restful, and secure in the knowledge that the "burning horror" has been banished from your home.[5]

---

[5] From a student speech by James Fulton.

Requesting action or approval

The function of the action step in a policy speech is to translate the desire created in the visualization step into overt action. This step commonly takes the form of a challenge or appeal, an inducement, or a statement of personal intention, as described in Chapter 8. A review of pages 170-174, where these endings were discussed, will suggest their appropriateness as methods for developing the action step of a persuasive talk.

Beware, however, of making the action step too long or involved. Someone has given this formula for successful public speaking: "Stand up; speak up; shut up." It is well here to emphasize the final admonition: finish your speech briskly and sit down.

If you develop a persuasive talk in the manner just indicated, your skeleton plan will look something like this:

SUBJECT: _____
SPECIFIC PURPOSE: _____

Attention step
   I. (Opening statement) _____
      A. (Support) _____
        1, 2, etc. (Details) _____
      B. (Support) _____
  II. (Statement or restatement) _____

Need step
   I. (Statement of need) _____
      A. (Support) _____
        1, 2, etc. (Details) _____
      B, C, D, etc. (Support) _____
  II. (Pointing statement—relating need to audience)
      A, B, etc. (Support) _____
 III. (Summary statement) _____

Satisfaction step
   I. (Statement of idea or plan proposed) _____
      A. (Explanation) _____
        1, 2, etc. (Details) _____
      B. (Support) _____
        1. (Details) _____
          a, b, etc. _____
        2, 3, etc. (Details) _____
      C, D, etc. (Support) _____
  II. (Summary statement) _____

Visualization step	I. (Statement of negative projection) _____
	A, B, etc. (Support) _____
	II. (Statement of positive projection) _____
Action step	I. (Request for action or belief) _____
	A, B, etc. (Support or recapitulation) _____
	II. (Restatement or appeal) _____

This plan, of course, is not a rigid model; it merely suggests the general pattern to be followed. The number of main points within each step and the number and order of subordinate or supporting ideas will vary from speech to speech and cannot be determined in advance. Sometimes the restatement will be omitted from the attention step; sometimes, instead of the method of contrast, you will use only a negative or a positive projection in the visualization step; and sometimes other modifications will be in order.

Once the general plan has been determined, however, write out the points of the outline as complete sentences, following the suggestions for phrasing and outline form in Chapter 7 (pp. 143-151). See also that each part of the talk performs the function required of it: that the attention step catches attention; that the need step points out a serious problem, and so on.

An abbreviated outline for a persuasive speech on fire prevention, for example, might take this form:

Fire Prevention at Home

Attention step	I. If you like to live dangerously, try this:
	A. Place a blotter soaked in turpentine in a jar of oxygen.
	B. Immediately the blotter will burst into flames.
	II. If you do not have a jar of oxygen around the house, try this:
	A. Place a well-oiled mop in a storage closet.
	B. In a few days the mop will burst into flames.
Need step	I. Few homes are free from dangerous fire hazards.
	A. Attics contain piles of clothing and combustible paper.
	B. Storage closets contain cleaning compounds, mops, and paint brushes.

	C. Basements often contain dangerous piles of trash.
	D. Garages attached to houses present hazards of spilled fuel.
	II. Your safety probably is threatened by some of these hazards in your own home.
Satisfaction step	I. Protection of your home from fire requires three things:

    A. Removal of all combustible materials from attic, closets, basement, and garage.

    B. Storage of oil mops, paint brushes, and cleaning compounds in fireproof containers.

    C. Checking regularly to see that trash does not accumulate.

  II. Home clean-up programs show practical results.

    A. Campaigns in Evansville kept insurance rates in a "Class 1" bracket.

    B. A campaign in Fort Wayne helped reduce the number of fires.

Visualization step   I. You will enjoy the results of such a program.

    A. You will have neat and attractive surroundings.

    B. Your home will be safe from fire.

Action step   I. Begin your own clean-up campaign now.

THE MOTIVATED SEQUENCE IN A SPEECH OPPOSING A POLICY

As you have just seen, a speech urging the adoption of a policy should (1) secure the attention of the audience: (2) show that there is a need for some action; (3) present a solution that will satisfy the need; (4) visualize the advantages of believing or behaving as the speaker proposes; and (5) request the action or approval indicated.

The speaker who opposes a policy ("The administration should not take cars away from freshmen") also must begin by catching attention. Beyond this point, however, he will proceed by denying any or all of the contentions in steps 2, 3, and 4 above. Thus, he may argue:

(a) There is no need for a change; things are perfectly all right as they are.

(b) The proposed policy does not provide a practicable solution to the alleged problem; it would not remove the evil or deficiency.

(c) Instead of bringing benefits or advantages, the proposed policy would actually introduce new and worse evils; it would be costly, unfair, dangerous to our liberties, difficult to administer, etc.

Sometimes all three of these contentions will be used in a speech urging the rejection of a proposed policy. At other times, not all of them will apply and the speech will be planned accordingly. If, however, any one contention can be proved beyond reasonable doubt, a discriminating listener will reject a proposal, since obviously he will not want to adopt a policy that is unneeded or impracticable or one that may introduce new problems and evils. Proof beyond reasonable doubt on all three contentions constitutes the strongest possible case against a recommended change.

Here is part of an outline of a speech in which a proposed action is opposed on the ground that it is unneeded, impracticable, and undesirable. (In order to make the major contentions stand out more clearly, the attention step and detailed supporting material have been omitted.)

The Proposed Turnpike

Not needed I. The turnpike from Ashton to Waterton proposed by the Governor's Committee on Highways is not needed.
  A. The existing highway connecting the two cities is only ten years old and is in excellent condition.
  B. Automobile traffic between Ashton and Waterton, instead of increasing, has actually decreased 6 per cent during the last decade.

Impracticable II. Even if the proposed turnpike were needed, its construction now would be impracticable.
  A. State funds for road construction are at an all-time low.
  B. Borrowing for road construction is costly and difficult in the present bond market.

Undesirable III. Finally, even if such a turnpike were both needed and practicable, its construction would be undesirable.
  A. A serious hardship would be imposed on owners of motels, filling stations, restaurants, and other businesses along the present highway.
  B. Ashton State Park would be ruined.

THE MOTIVATED SEQUENCE IN SPEECHES
ON PROPOSITIONS OF FACT

How should persuasive speeches on factual questions be organized and developed? Here, as in policy speeches, the motivated sequence furnishes the basic pattern, needing only to be adapted to meet the special requirements imposed by the subject matter.

1. *Getting attention:* Secure the attention and interest of the audience.

2. *Showing the need:* State clearly the question that is to be decided and show your listeners why a decision is needed. Do this by pointing out (a) why the question concerns them personally or (b) why it concerns the community, state, nation, or world of which they are a part.

3. *Satisfying the need:* (a) Set forth the criteria upon which an intelligent answer to the question should rest. (b) Advance what you believe to be the correct answer and offer evidence and argument to show that it meets the criteria.[6]

4. *Visualizing the results:* Picture the advantages of accepting the answer you recommend or the disadvantages of rejecting it.

5. *Requesting action or approval:* Appeal for the acceptance of your proposed answer (and, when appropriate, for a determination to adhere to it).

These steps are illustrated in the following outline.

OUR STUDENT GOVERNMENT

Attention step

I. State University has one of the oldest and most widely imitated systems of student government in the entire nation.
   A. It was founded in 1883, when student government was almost entirely unknown.
   B. It has given many of our state and national leaders their first practical administrative experience.
   C. It has served as a model for other colleges and universities.

---

[6] Sometimes a proposition of fact involves a term or set of terms which the audience may not immediately understand. In such cases, divide the satisfaction step in this way: First define the crucial term or terms, and second show how the pertinent facts or circumstances fall within the definition established. For example, if a lawyer wished to prove that a certain person is mentally incompetent, he would first make clear the legal definition of *mental incompetence* and then demonstrate how the person's behavior justified placing him within this category.

(Statement of question)	II. Has our student government, once a free and powerful institution, become a tool of the dean of men and the university administration?
Need step	I. This is a question of vital importance to each of us. A. The prestige of the university is at stake. B. Our freedom as students to govern ourselves and conduct our own affairs is endangered.
Satisfaction step (Criteria)	I. To answer this question, we should ask: A. Is our student government free to manage student affairs? B. Is our student government powerful enough to exercise effective leadership?
(Answer to questions raised on criteria)	II. The answer to both questions is *No*. A. The dean of men and other administrative officers of the university have taken over the management of student affairs. 1. All actions of the Student Senate must have administration approval.

(Supporting arguments and evidence)	2. The financial affairs of student organizations are controlled by the university treasurer's office.
	    a. Budgets must be approved.
	    b. Accounts must be audited.
	  3. The election of class officers is conducted under the supervision of the dean.
	B. These actions have made it impossible for student government to exercise effective leadership.
	  1. It cannot determine new policies.
	  2. It cannot carry out present policies effectively.

Visualization step	I. Unless we are all aware of these encroachments upon our traditional rights, the abuses will continue. A. Self-government in dormitories and fraternities will be endangered. B. Student government may even be abolished.
Action step	I. Recognize the seriousness of the situation. II. Resolve that student government once again will be a strong and vital force on this campus.

If your purpose is to argue against a proposition of fact (in this case to defend the administration against charges of infringing upon student rights and privileges), you may proceed along similar lines. But in the satisfaction step, after setting up appropriate criteria, you should advance a negative statement ("The dean of men and other administrative officers have not taken over the management of student affairs," etc.). Then you should offer evidence and argument to justify your stand.

THE MOTIVATED SEQUENCE IN A SPEECH
ON A PROPOSITION OF VALUE

When speaking on a proposition of value with a view to persuading your listeners that they should agree with your estimate of a man, practice, institution, or theory, you may adapt the basic pattern of the motivated sequence, as follows:

1. *Getting attention:* Capture the attention and interest of the audience.

2. *Showing the need:* Make clear that an estimate concerning the worth of the man, practice, or institution is needed. Do this by showing (a) why an estimate is important to your listeners personally, or (b) why it is important to the community, state, nation, or world of which they are a part.

3. *Satisfying the need:* (a) Set forth the criteria upon which an intelligent estimate should be based. (b) Advance what you believe to be the correct estimate and show how it meets the criteria specified.

4. *Visualizing the results:* Picture the advantages that will accrue from agreeing with the estimate you advance or the evils that will result from failing to endorse it.

5. *Requesting action or approval:* Appeal for the acceptance of the proposed estimate and for a determination to retain it.

Each of these steps is present in the following speech outline.

THE VALUES OF INTERCOLLEGIATE DEBATE

Attention step
    I. In recent years intercollegiate debate has come under strong attack from many quarters.
      A. Philosophers and social scientists have charged that debate is a poor way to get at the truth of a disputable matter.

B. Educators have charged that debate develops habits of contentiousness and dogmatism rather than of objectivity.

Need step
(Evaluation necessary)

I. How we evaluate debate is important to each of us for at least two reasons:
   A. As students we are' concerned because we help support the debate program on this campus through our activity fee.
   B. As citizens we are concerned because the method of decision-making employed in intercollegiate debate is essentially the same as that employed in the courtroom and in the legislative assembly.

Satisfaction step
(Criteria)

I. Like any extracurricular activity, debate can be evaluated according to two important criteria:
   A. Does it develop abilities and traits of mind which will aid the student in his course work?
   B. Does it develop abilities and traits of mind which will be of value in later life?

(Evaluation provided)

II. The experience of many years has shown that debate is valuable.
   A. Debate helps the student do better work in his courses.
      1. It teaches him to study a subject thoroughly and systematically.
      2. It teaches him to analyze complex ideas quickly and logically.
      3. It teaches him to speak and write clearly and convincingly.
   B. Training in debate is of value in later life.
      1. It establishes habits of courtesy and fair play.
      2. It instills self-confidence and poise.

Visualization step

I. Picture the serious student of debate in the classroom and in his post-college career.
   A. As a student, he will know how to study, analyze, and present material.
   B. As a business or professional man, he will be better able to meet arguments and to express his views in a fair and effective manner.

Action or
approval step

I. Remember these facts whenever you hear the value of intercollegiate debate questioned.
   A. The contribution debate training makes to business or professional success has been affirmed by many prominent men and women who were debaters in college.
   B. We should encourage and support this worth-while activity in every way we can.

A speech that is intended to show that an institution or practice has no value (for instance, a speech proposing that debate training is useless or undesirable) may be developed according to a similar pattern. But in the satisfaction step, instead of showing that the practice or institution in question meets the criteria you outlined, you will show that it fails to meet them. Then in the visualization step, you will show how the practice or institution is useless or actually harmful.

PROBLEMS FOR FURTHER STUDY

1. Supposing your speech class to be the audience, select a specific purpose for a persuasive speech calling for a response of overt action. Then prepare a five-sentence outline of a speech to secure that response — one sentence for each step in the motivated sequence. In writing these sentences, follow the rules for stating the main heads of a talk as described in Chapter 7, pages 143-145.

2. Expand the five-sentence outline prepared for Problem 1 into a full-sentence outline for a five-minute speech by adding appropriate subordinate ideas and supporting details. What proportion of the finished outline is devoted to each of the steps in the motivated sequence? Defend this distribution.

3. Using the motivated sequence as a pattern, construct an outline for a speech urging support or rejection of a proposed reform in college life or administration, in civic affairs, or on the state or national scene. Prepare three different visualization steps for this speech — one using the positive method, one the negative method, and one the method of contrast. Also prepare three different action steps — one using inducement, one using a statement of personal intention, etc. (See pp. 170-174 of Chapter 8). Which type of visualization step and which action step appears most effective for this particular speech?

4. Find in *Vital Speeches* or elsewhere three printed speeches, one dealing with a proposition of policy, one with a proposition of fact, and

one with a proposition of value. Outline each of these speeches carefully. How do they compare with the patterns of development recommended on pages 212-223?

5. List four questions of fact which cannot be settled by observation, experimentation, or direct recourse to data, and which therefore would make suitable subjects for persuasive speeches.

6. In your estimation, which of the following methods, if used singly, would be more likely to result in full and lasting persuasion: (a) making your listeners want to believe your proposal by using motive appeals, or (b) convincing them of the logic of your proposal by presenting facts and reasoning?

7. Study several newspaper editorials or magazine articles to discover the forms of reasoning employed. Find cases of reasoning from example, from axiom, and from causal relation. In each case apply the appropriate tests to determine the validity of the reasoning.

8. In your opinion, which motive appeals are best adapted to persuading an audience of young persons? Of older persons? Of men? Of women? Name some motive appeals that may be combined to strengthen a persuasive appeal. Name some combinations that might produce a negative rather than a positive response. Defend your answers.

9. Clip ten advertisements from popular magazines and list the motive appeals used in each. Evaluate the appeals in terms of their appropriateness to the audience to be persuaded and to the products to be sold.

10. Assuming your speech class to be the audience, list the motive appeals which you think would best support each of the following propositions. Which motive appeals would be most effective if you were opposing these propositions?

Fraternities and sororities should be abolished
Books and magazines should be censored to protect public morals
The United States should disarm unilaterally

11. Identify the motive appeals used by each speaker in the next round of persuasive speeches in class. Did the speaker choose his appeals wisely? Did he at any time use conflicting appeals or otherwise detract from the persuasive power of his speech?

SPEAKING ASSIGNMENTS

1. Conduct a class discussion on the ethics of persuasion. Consider questions such as these: What methods and appeals may legitimately be

used in effecting persuasion? What methods and appeals should always be avoided? Are there any circumstances in which a man not only has the right, but the obligation to undertake to persuade others by any means at his disposal? (See the books and articles in the Suggestions for Further Reading below for discussions of these and similar problems.)

2. Present in class a five-minute speech supporting or attacking one of the following propositions or a similar proposition. Build your speech on the pattern furnished by the motivated sequence.

Speed is the principal cause of accidents

There is life on Mars

Football is becoming our national sport

A liberal education is to be preferred to professional or technical training

Unions harm rather than benefit the working man

Television is indeed a "vast wasteland"

The sale of cigarettes should be controlled by law

Intercollegiate athletics should be abolished

R.O.T.C. training should be made voluntary

SUGGESTIONS FOR FURTHER READING

Winston L. Brembeck and William S. Howell, *Persuasion* (Englewood Cliffs, N. J.: Prentice-Hall, Inc., 1952).

Douglas Ehninger and Wayne Brockriede, *Decision by Debate* (New York: Dodd, Mead & Company, 1963), Chapter 8, "The Unit of Proof and Its Structure," Chapter 9, "Evidence," Chapter 10, "Substantive Proof," and Chapter 13, "The Nature and Sources of Belief."

Franklyn S. Haiman, "A Re-examination of the Ethics of Persuasion," *Central States Speech Journal*, III (March 1952), 4-9.

Carl I. Hovland, Irving L. Janis, and Harold H. Kelley, *Communication and Persuasion* (New Haven: Yale University Press, 1953).

Wayne C. Minnick, *The Art of Persuasion* (Boston: Houghton Mifflin Company, 1957).

Robert T. Oliver, *The Psychology of Persuasive Speech*, 2nd ed. (New York: Longmans, Green and Co., 1957).

Karl R. Wallace, "An Ethical Basis of Communication," *Speech Teacher*, IV (January 1955), 1-9.

CHAPTER 11

SPEECHES FOR SPECIAL OCCASIONS

Chapters 9 and 10 gave directions for preparing and presenting the two kinds of speeches you most often will be called upon to make: those for information and those for persuasion. Occasions sometimes arise, however, which require special types of speeches. You may have to introduce a visiting speaker or welcome a distinguished guest. You may be asked to announce awards or to pay a tribute to a person or to a group. Or you may be asked to present a goodwill speech on behalf of your business or profession or to present a commencement address at a nearby high school or college. In this chapter we shall consider briefly the special types of speeches required by these situations, as well as some of the duties of a chairman in planning and conducting a meeting.

INTRODUCING SPEAKERS

Speeches of introduction are often given by the chairman. Sometimes, however, they are given by another person who is well acquainted with the featured speaker.

Purpose: creating a desire to hear the speaker

If you are invited to give a speech of introduction, remember that your main object is to create in the listeners a desire to hear the speaker of the day, and that you should subordinate everything else to this aim. Do not bore the audience with a long recital of the speaker's biography or with a series of anecdotes about your acquaintance with him. Above all, do not air your own views on his subject. You are only the speaker's advance agent; your job is to "sell" him to the audience. Therefore, you must try (1) to arouse curiosity about the speaker or his subject so that it will be easier for him to capture attention, and (2) to motivate the audience to like and respect the speaker so that they will tend to believe what he says or to do what he asks.

Characteristics of content

When presenting a speech of introduction, follow these rules:

Be brief. To say too much is often worse than to say nothing at all. Some critics think the best introductory speech ever made was that of Shailer Mathews for President Woodrow Wilson; he said, "Ladies and gentlemen: the President." The prestige of the person you introduce will not always be great enough for you to be as brief as this, but it is better to err in this direction than to speak too long.

Do not talk about yourself. There may be a great temptation to tell your own views on the subject or to recount anecdotes about your own experiences as a speaker. Avoid such references to yourself because they call attention to you rather than to the speaker.

Tell about the speaker. Who is he? What is his position in business or government? What experiences has he had that qualify him to speak on this subject? Tell who the speaker is and what he knows or what he has done, but do not tell what a good speaker he is. Such comment usually embarrasses a speaker.

Emphasize the importance of the speaker's subject. Point out to the audience the importance of the information the speaker is about to offer. For example, in introducing a speaker who is going to talk about the oil industry, you might say, "All of us drive automobiles in which we use the products made from petroleum. A knowledge of the way these products are manufactured and marketed is, therefore, certain to be valuable to our understanding and to our pocketbooks. . . ."

Stress the appropriateness of the subject or of the speaker. If your club is considering the construction of a new golf course, a speech on types of grass may be appropriate. If your organization or firm is marking an anniversary, a founder may appropriately be one of the speakers.

Reference to such facts is obviously in order and serves to relate the speaker more closely to the audience.

Use humor if it suits the occasion. Nothing serves better to put the audience at ease and to create a friendly feeling than congenial laughter. Take care, however, that the humor is in good taste and does not ridicule the speaker. Do not lessen his prestige or run the risk of offending him.

Usually the better known and more respected the speaker is, the shorter your introduction can be; the less familiar he is, the more you will need to arouse interest in his subject and to build up his prestige.

COURTESY TALKS: WELCOMES, RESPONSES, ACCEPTANCES

Sometimes a speaker must perform public acts of courtesy, either as a personal duty or on behalf of a group or organization.

Typical situations

Courtesy talks usually are given to fulfill one of three obligations:

Welcoming visitors. When a distinguished guest is present, someone, usually the presiding officer, is expected to extend him a public greeting.

Responding to a welcome or a greeting. When an individual is so welcomed, he expresses his appreciation of that greeting.

Accepting awards. When an individual is presented an award for some special accomplishment, he is expected to express his appreciation of the honor. Sometimes the award is made to an organization rather than to an individual, in which case someone is selected to respond for the group.

Purpose: expressing sentiment and creating good feeling

The speech of courtesy has a double purpose. The speaker not only attempts to express a sentiment of gratitude or hospitality, but also to create good feeling in the audience. Usually the success of such a speech depends upon satisfying one's listeners that the appropriate thing has been said. Just as courtesies of private life put people at ease, public acts of courtesy create good feeling in the recipient and the audience.

Characteristics of content

The scope and content of a speech of courtesy should be guided by the following principles:

Indicate for whom you are speaking. When you are acting as spokesman for a group, make clear that the greeting or acknowledgment comes from all and not from you alone.

Present complimentary facts about the person or group to which you are extending the courtesy. Emphasize the accomplishments or qualities of the person or group you are greeting or whose gift or welcome you are acknowledging. Do not talk at length about yourself or the group you represent.

Illustrate; do not argue. Present incidents and facts that illustrate the importance of the occasion, but do not be contentious. Avoid areas of disagreement. Do not use a speech of courtesy as an opportunity to air your own views on controversial subjects or to advance your own policies. Rather, express concretely and vividly the thoughts which are already in the minds of your listeners.

SPEECHES OF TRIBUTE: MEMORIALS, FAREWELLS, PRESENTATIONS

A speaker may wish to pay tribute in public to another's personal qualities or achievements. Such occasions range from the awarding of a trophy after an athletic contest to a eulogy at a memorial service. Sometimes tributes are paid to people in a group or class—such as teachers, soldiers, or mothers—rather than to an individual.

Typical situations

The memorial. Services to pay public honor to the dead usually include a speech of tribute. Occasions of this kind may honor a famous person and may be held years after his death—witness the many speeches on Lincoln. More often, however, such occasions honor someone personally known to the audience and recently deceased.

Dedication. Buildings, monuments, placques, etc., frequently are set up for a worthy purpose or to commemorate a person or group of persons. At the dedication it is appropriate to say something about the purpose to be served or the person or persons commemorated.

Farewell. When an executive leaves a company to enter another field or when anyone generally admired leaves the community where he has lived or the office which he has held, public appreciation of his fellowship and his work may be expressed in a speech.

Presentation of awards. Awards are frequently presented to groups or to individuals for outstanding achievements or meritorious service. Their presentation calls for appropriate remarks.

Purpose: securing appreciation

The purpose of a speech of tribute is to secure appreciation of the traits or accomplishments of the person or group to whom tribute is paid. If you cause your audience to realize the essential worth or importance of the person or group, you will have succeeded. But you may go farther than this. You may, by honoring a person, arouse deeper devotion to the cause he represents. Did he give distinguished service to his country? Then strive to enhance the audience's sense of patriotism and service. Was he a friend of boys? Then try to arouse the conviction that boys' work deserves the audience's support. Create a desire in your listeners to emulate the person or persons honored. Make them want to develop the same virtues, to demonstrate a like devotion.

Characteristics of content

Frequently speeches of tribute attempt to itemize all of a person's or a group's accomplishments. Such speeches are boring because in attempting to cover everything they emphasize nothing. Focus your remarks by observing the following principles:

Stress dominant traits. If you are paying tribute to a person, select a few aspects of his personality which are especially likable or praiseworthy, and relate incidents from his life or work which illustrate these qualities.

Mention only outstanding achievements. Pick out a few of the person's or the group's notable accomplishments. Tell about them in detail to show how important they were. Let your speech say, "Here is what this person (or group) has done; see how important it is."

Give special emphasis to the person's or the group's influence. Show the effect the person's behavior or the group's activities have had on others. The importance of many people lies not so much in any traits or material accomplishments as in the influence they have had on associates.

Personal traits, achievements, and influence are not mutually exclusive. Most speeches of tribute probably will include references to all three. But in the interest of unity and maximum impact upon the audience, you will be wise not to mention too many items in any one area. Avoid complicated details and long enumerations. The few things you do tell, relate in an interesting way. Let each event you talk about become a story, living and personal. Only in this way will you lead your audience to admire the person or the group to whom the tribute is paid.

GOODWILL TALKS

Every speech seeks the goodwill of the audience, but the type of speech now to be considered has securing goodwill as its principal aim.

Ostensibly, a goodwill speech is a speech to inform; actually, however, it seeks to deepen the listeners' appreciation of some institution, practice, or profession—to make them more favorably disposed toward it. By skillfully blending facts with indirect arguments and unobtrusive appeals, the speaker attempts to develop a positive attitude toward his subject. In short, the goodwill speech is a mixed or hybrid type: it is an informative speech that has a hidden persuasive purpose.

In recent years goodwill speeches have played an increasingly important role in the public relations programs of many business firms. More than eighteen hundred speeches of this kind were made in a single year by representatives of one large Chicago corporation. But business firms are not alone in this practice; schools, churches, and public institutions also employ goodwill speeches as a means of winning approval and support.

Typical situations

Luncheon club meetings. Meetings of luncheon clubs offer an excellent opportunity for presenting goodwill talks. These meetings are semi-social in nature and practically guarantee good feeling. Members of such groups—prominent men or women from all walks of business or professional life — are interested in civic affairs and in the workings of other people's professions.

Educational programs. Educational programs often are arranged by school authorities, clubs, and religious organizations. At such meetings, speakers are asked to talk about the business or profession they represent and to explain to the young people in the audience the opportunities offered and the training required in this field. By use of illustrations and tactful references, a speaker may secure goodwill for the organization he represents.

Special demonstration programs. Special programs are frequently presented by government agencies, university extension departments, and business organizations. For example, a wholesale food company may send a representative to a meeting of nutritionists to show them the varieties of fish that are available, and to demonstrate new ways of preparing or serving some of the kinds of fish. Although the demonstration speech is primarily informative, the speaker may win goodwill indirectly by showing that his company desires to increase customer satisfaction with its products.

There are many other situations in which goodwill speeches are appropriate, but the three we have discussed are typical.

Purpose: securing goodwill unobtrusively

It is obvious from what has been said that the real and the apparent aims of the goodwill speech differ. So far as the audience is concerned, the purpose may appear to be primarily informative. From the speaker's point of view, however, the purpose also is persuasive. By presenting information, he attempts in a subtle and unobtrusive way to gain support for the profession or organization he represents.

Characteristics of content

In selecting materials for a goodwill speech, keep these suggestions in mind:

Present novel, interesting facts about your subject. Make your listeners feel that you are giving them "inside information." Avoid talking about what they already know; concentrate on new developments and facts that are not generally known about your organization or profession.

Show a definite relationship between your subject and the lives of the members of your audience. Make your listeners see the importance of your organization or profession to their safety, success, and happiness.

Offer some definite service. This may be in the form of an invitation to visit your office or shop, or even the simple offer to answer questions. Leave the impression that you are at your listeners' service.

The suggestions above may need to be modified to suit the subject and the occasion. But never lose sight of one fact: indirectly, you must demonstrate to your listeners that your work is of value to them.

COMMENCEMENT ADDRESSES

A teacher, lawyer, businessman, or minister may be asked to deliver the commencement address at a nearby high school or college.

Purpose: to congratulate and challenge the graduates

The primary purpose of a commencement address is to congratulate the graduates upon their achievement and to challenge or inspire them to meet the obligations and opportunities which lie before them. Its secondary purpose, however, is to convey a message of interest and importance to the parents and friends of the graduates who compose most of the audience.

Because the commencement speaker is, in effect, addressing two different audiences simultaneously, he must select a subject that will be appropriate to both. Moreover, while delivering his talk he must endeavor to maintain contact with both groups.

Characteristics of content

A commencement address should be characterized by sincerity of sentiment, freshness of ideas, and brevity of treatment. If you are called upon to give an address of this kind, observe the following principles:

In congratulating the graduates or challenging them to high achievements, do not mouth empty sentiments or pious preachments. Speak with sincerity and earnestness. Make specific the sort of goals and values to which they should adhere. Relate your advice to the needs and problems of the community or world as they exist at the moment—the need for better housing, for improved understanding between the races, for world peace, and the like. Do not talk in vague, general terms of such values as ambition, integrity, or loyalty. Make your recommendations and appeals concrete and factual. Above all, use restraint in developing and wording your ideas, as well as in delivering them; do not be flowery or oratorical.

Present old values and goals in a new and fresh way. While the tested values of industry, faithfulness, and loyalty may be the ones you recommend, cast your ideas into a fresh form and support them with current examples and illustrations. Avoid hackneyed stories and comparisons.

Keep your remarks relatively brief. Remember that you are not the only person on the commencement program. There probably also will be musical numbers, remarks by school officials, short talks by one or two students, etc. Therefore, check in advance to see how much time you will be allotted and be sure to hold your remarks within this limit. Neither the graduates nor the other members of the audience will be prepared to listen to a long and ponderous address.

ACTING AS CHAIRMAN[1]

The success of a program, whether it is a lecture, a dinner meeting, or a series of speeches at a conference or training clinic, may be largely dependent upon the chairman. A good chairman does not say much; he does not parade himself, yet his presence is felt. His unobtrusive control is reflected in the smooth running of the program.

The chairman's planning must be detailed and thorough. Instead of relying on the inspiration of the moment, prepare as follows:

1. Determine the purpose of the meeting.

2. Acquaint yourself with the program. Know who is going to speak or sing or play; know each speaker's subject or the title of each artist's selection; understand the function of each part of the program.

3. Make a time schedule. Determine how long the program should last; apportion the time among the various speakers or performers and, before the meeting begins, tell each person exactly how much time is at his disposal.

4. Prepare your own remarks. Know what you are going to say in your opening speech and at all subsequent times. You may adapt your

---

[1] The duties of the chairman of a business meeting conducted according to the rules of parliamentary procedure are discussed in Chapter 14.

prepared material to the turn of affairs, but you always must be ready with something.

5. Start the program on time. Be on time yourself and see that the others on the program are prompt also; then keep things moving as nearly on schedule as possible.

If you prepare in this way, the chances for the success of a program are greatly improved.

PROBLEMS FOR FURTHER STUDY

1. Select one of the speeches reprinted in the Appendix, and assume that you are to introduce the speaker to a campus audience. Make an outline of an appropriate speech of introduction.

2. Attend a meeting at which one or more speakers are introduced and analyze the speeches of introduction. How closely did they accord with the principles and suggestions set forth in this chapter? How might they have been improved?

3. Find a printed speech of courtesy—welcome, response, or acceptance. Outline this speech and prepare a written report commenting on its general content and organization.

4. Select as an example of a speech of tribute either Lincoln's *Gettysburg Address* or Pericles' *Funeral Oration*. (Both have been reprinted many times; your instructor will help you locate a good text.) Note the methods which the speaker employed to communicate his message. In what sense was the speech addressed directly to the audience? In what sense was it addressed to all men in all ages?

5. Assume that you are to act as chairman on one or more of the following occasions (or on some similar occasion):
   a. A school assembly celebrating a successful football season
   b. A student government awards banquet
   c. A program meeting of a club to which you belong
   d. A student-faculty mass meeting called to protest a regulation issued by the Dean's office

Plan a suitable program of speeches, entertainment, etc.; allocate the amount of time to be devoted to each item on the program; outline a suitable speech of introduction; prepare publicity releases, arrange for press coverage, etc. Work out a complete plan, such as you might show to a steering committee, a faculty sponsor, or the like.

SPEAKING ASSIGNMENTS

1. Preside for one day during the next round of class speeches. See that the program runs on schedule, maintain a lively atmosphere in the classroom, and introduce each speaker in an appropriate manner.

2. Prepare a three-minute speech suitable for one of the following occasions:
   a. Welcoming a distinguished alumnus to a fraternity banquet
   b. Welcoming newly initiated members into an honorary society
   c. Responding to a speech welcoming your group or delegation to a neighboring campus
   d. Accepting an award for athletic or scholastic achievement
   e. Accepting an office to which you have been elected
   f. Presenting a gift to a faculty member on his retirement

3. Prepare a five-minute speech paying tribute to:
   a. A man important in national or world history
   b. Someone in your home community who, though he never gained fame, contributed in a significant way to the welfare or happiness of many
   c. A group of volunteers who participated in a charity drive
   d. A team of scientists that completed a successful program
   e. A faculty member who has long served as a fraternity or campus activity advisor
   f. The highest ranking student in your class
   g. An outstanding athlete or team which has received state or national recognition
   h. An officer of a student organization who has served long and well
   i. Founders of an organization for civic betterment

4. Prepare for delivery in class a five-minute goodwill speech on behalf of a campus organization to which you belong. (You may substitute a national organization, such as the Boy Scouts or Y.M.C.A., if you wish.) Select new and little-known facts to present; pay particular attention to maintaining interest at a high level; keep your arguments and appeals indirect; show tact and restraint in your speaking manner. Be prepared to answer questions after your talk is completed.

5. Imagine the members of your public speaking class to be an audience gathered at the commencement exercises of a nearby high school or college. Prepare and present a ten-minute commencement address suitable to this audience. Instruct your classmates in advance concerning the audience they are supposed to represent.

SUGGESTIONS FOR FURTHER READING

Giles W. Gray and Waldo W. Braden, *Public Speaking: Principles and Practice,* 2nd ed. (New York: Harper and Row, 1963), Chapter 22, "Other Types of Speeches."

Guy R. Lyle and Kevin Guinagh, *I Am Happy to Present: A Book of Introductions* (New York: H. W. Wilson Company, 1953).

Willard Hayes Yeager, *Effective Speaking for Every Occasion* (Englewood Cliffs, N. J.: Prentice-Hall, Inc., 1940).

CHAPTER 12

BROADCASTING A TALK

The public speaker today needs a general knowledge of broadcasting technics. Any man or woman in business, a profession, or a position of community leadership may be called upon to speak over the local radio or television station. In this chapter, therefore, we shall discuss the principles and procedures to be followed in adapting a speech to the broadcasting situation.

Except for their attempt to reach a larger audience than could be gathered in a single place, broadcast speeches are similar in purpose to other speeches. Speakers who broadcast, like speakers in general, seek to entertain, to inform, and to persuade; they introduce speakers, welcome vistors, debate public issues, pay tribute, and attempt to gain goodwill. Your purpose in talking before a visible audience may also be your purpose when you broadcast.

THE RADIO AND TELEVISION AUDIENCE

The radio and television audience is sometimes called "universal," since anyone who has a receiving set within the power range of the station may be listening. The audience is likely to be composed of persons of both sexes and of all ages, creeds, occupations, interests, and degrees of intelligence. Only the hour of the broadcast, the location of the station, and the special nature of the program are limiting factors. Surveys have shown that women listeners predominate during

the morning and early afternoon hours when husbands are at work and children at school. Children listen mainly in the late afternoon and early evening; men listen during the evenings and on Sundays. At mealtimes the audience for a public speech is likely to be varied but it may be small since many people prefer musical programs or brief announcements (markets, news, weather, etc.) at this time. So far as location is concerned, a metropolitan station tends to draw a larger urban audience, and a station in a smaller city, a larger rural audience. However, the more powerful stations and the networks reach every kind of community. Some stations cater to certain types of listeners and some program series are frankly designed for certain groups. College stations, for example, direct many programs to students and faculty.

An important characteristic of radio and television audiences is that the listeners usually are alone or in small, intimate groups. Although the audience as a whole may be large, the individuals are not gathered in a mass but are scattered about in living rooms, offices, automobiles, and the like. While each individual no doubt is aware that others are listening to the same program, he is primarily aware of his own environment and expects the speaker to talk to him in a conversational manner suited to that environment.

Two further facts need to be remembered: listeners can easily turn off a broadcast at any time, and they are apt to have many distractions. People hesitate to make themselves conspicuous by leaving an audience while a speaker is talking to them, but they feel no hesitation about tuning out a radio or television speech. In addition, listeners to a broadcast speech are likely to be surrounded by distracting noises—the baby's crying, the clatter of dishes, a conversation at the other end of the room, or the roar of traffic. To compete with these distractions, the broadcast speech must have a high degree of interest value.

TYPES OF BROADCAST SPEECHES

Broadcast speeches fall into two principal classes: those made in the studio without an audience present and those before an audience.

Broadcasts without an audience present

When you speak from the studio for the broadcast audience alone, it is like conversing with a friend over a telephone. To develop the conversational rapport called for in this situation, some speakers address the announcer when he is in the same room, or they speak directly to a friend who has come to the studio with them.

Broadcasts with an audience present

Often a speech for a particular occasion or audience (an anniversary banquet, a graduating class, etc.) is of sufficient general interest to warrant broadcasting. On such occasions when you address an audience sitting before you, radio and television listeners are allowed, as it were, to "listen in." Your broadcast audience knows that an actual audience is present and they do not mind your talking in a manner appropriate to formal public speaking rather than to informal conversation. They imaginatively project themselves into your presence and in a sense become part of the crowd at the dinner or in the auditorium. If the broadcast is over radio only, you may help your listeners acquire this feeling by referring to the audience before you or to the occasion which has brought the group together. A ripple of laughter or applause also will help the radio listener feel more a part of the audience. Although you owe primary attention to your immediate audience, do not forget the broadcast audience entirely; even in this situation the content and structure of your speech and, to some extent, your manner of speaking, should be modified for the broadcast audience.

His manuscript carefully marked and held in a notebook, President Lyndon B. Johnson delivers a State of the Union message to a joint session of Congress and, via radio and television, to the nation.

THE MANNER OF SPEAKING FOR RADIO

In presenting a radio talk, remember that your listeners cannot see you and, therefore, that you cannot give them visual cues by means of gestures, facial expression, and bodily movement; nor will you be able to use visual aids in explaining or proving an idea. All meaning must be conveyed by sound alone: attention must be secured and held, thoughts made clear, and action impelled simply by means of the voice.

Using the microphone

Many different types of microphones are used in broadcasting. Some pick up sound equally well from all directions; others pick up sound made directly in front of them with much greater volume than sound made at the side or above or behind. Ask the announcer or the technician in the studio how far from the microphone you should stand or sit, and from what angle you should speak into it. Ask also about the volume level at which you should talk.

The loudness of the sound picked up by most microphones varies inversely in approximate geometric ratio to the distance of the microphone from the source of the sound. To illustrate, if you speak with the same degree of force but move about, the sound picked up by the microphone at a distance of one foot will be four times as loud as at a distance of two feet. Therefore, to avoid fading or increasing the volume too much, always stay at approximately the same distance from the microphone. Especially when you have an actual audience as well as a microphone in front of you, do not move too far away. Hand, lapel, and chest microphones have been developed in order to give the speaker more mobility, but you still may have uneven volume if you turn your head too often or too far from the microphone. In the studio, the temptation to move is not so great; if you are seated or standing comfortably, you are likely to stay still. However, if you are reading your material from a manuscript, be careful not to bob your head because this movement may cause the volume to fluctuate markedly.

Most radio equipment is extremely sensitive, and for this reason sudden increases in volume are apt to produce "blasting," an effect similar to that produced by hitting the keyboard of a piano with a sledge hammer — a crash of sound rather than a clear tone. The engineer in the control room can modulate the volume of your voice, building it up or toning it down, within reason, but he cannot anticipate every sudden change. Therefore, keep your vocal force reasonably even.

Two mistakes amateurs commonly make result in sounds that are intensified by the sensitivity of broadcasting equipment. The first is rattling or rustling papers close to the microphone. Any sound in the studio is amplified over the air; therefore, at its worst, paper rustling may sound like the rapid firing of a gun, the flapping of an awning in an angry wind, or the crushing of an orange crate into kindling. At the very least, it will make your listeners aware that you are reading and thus destroy the illusion of direct communication. The second mistake is tapping the microphone or table. This, too, may be a slight noise in the studio but a loud one over the air. Avoid drumming on the table or thumping it for emphasis; let your gestures be noiseless. If you use a manuscript, choose soft paper, unclip it before you approach the microphone, and lay each sheet aside quietly when you have finished reading it. You will make less noise if you leave your manuscript on the table or speaker's stand rather than hold it in your hand. A note of caution: check the pages of your manuscript before the broadcast to make sure they are in the correct order. No pause seems as long as that which occurs when you turn to page three and find page four.

Because broadcasting equipment amplifies sound and because radio listeners focus their attention entirely upon your voice, the distinctness of your speech and the accuracy of your pronunciation are especially important. Errors and crudities that might pass unnoticed on the platform will be very noticeable over the air. Do not, however, talk so carefully that your speech sounds artificial. To speak overprecisely is almost as bad as to speak indistinctly, for it calls attention to the utterance rather than to the thought. Try to avoid both extremes.

Another point to consider is that the quality of the speaker's voice is changed in transmission. In general, high-pitched voices are less pleasant over the radio, while those of moderately low pitch are sometimes improved in the process of broadcasting. The best way to check the effect of transmission on your voice is to have an audition or to make a recording of the broadcast so you can listen to yourself. The fact that you can talk conversationally before the microphone and do not have to increase vocal force to project to an audience should improve the quality of your voice, since most people have better vocal quality when they speak quietly. Keep the resonating passages open, however. Because of the quietness of the studio and the lack of direct audience response, you may sometimes forget you are communicating and allow your voice to become flat and colorless. In articulation, pay particular attention to the sibilants — sounds such as *s, z,* and *sh.* Some microphones minimize the problem, but the high frequencies of these sounds tend to produce a whistling or hissing when they are given too much emphasis. If you have trouble with sibilants, use sparingly words in which these sounds occur in stressed positions — or better, learn to subdue your production of them.

Compensating for the lack of visual cues

The visual cues a speaker gives his audience add emphasis, convey additional meaning, help hold attention, and fill in gaps left by pauses. When, as in radio speech, the burden is thrown entirely on the voice, variety of vocal expression is more than a valuable asset — it is essential. Refer to Chapter 5 and study again the sections on rate and pitch; practice the exercises given there to develop vocal flexibility. As we have already warned, however, avoid sudden changes in vocal force.

When broadcasting by radio, you should speak at a fairly rapid rate. This does not mean that you have to rush, but it does mean that you cannot allow your speech to drag. Long pauses are especially to be avoided. In a face-to-face speaking situation, you sometimes can emphasize a point by standing silent, holding your listeners' attention by your facial expression and the apparent tension of your body; all this is lost to the radio listener—he gets only silence. In radio speaking, therefore, pauses must be used sparingly and must be of shorter duration. On the platform a speaker may pause to search for the exact word to express his thought; he is thinking it out with his listeners and they see him doing it. On the air such pauses may suggest that the speaker is ill-at-ease and unprepared.

Because groping for words is a major sin in radio broadcasting, most people write out radio speeches word for word and read them from manuscript. This procedure not only ensures their knowing what to say next but also makes it certain that they will finish on time. There is one disadvantage, however: some people cannot write with the informality of oral style, and even when they can, they have difficulty reading aloud in a conversational manner. But this disadvantage can be overcome with practice. Experts almost unanimously advise using a manuscript for a radio speech and learning to read from it naturally.

When preparing for a broadcast speech, then, practice reading your manuscript aloud. Do not read it for the first time as you stand before the microphone. Master or alter difficult sound combinations in advance. Become so familiar with your material that you can ad-lib if you happen to lose your place or misplace a page. Above all, practice reading with a mental image of your listeners before you—make your reading sound like talk. Do not stress unimportant words, such as *the, of,* and *to.* Avoid both a monotone and an artificial inflection.

THE MANNER OF SPEAKING FOR TELEVISION

Unlike radio broadcasting, television broadcasting permits your audience to see you while you talk. Therefore, your appearance, facial expression, and movement help convey your thought just as they do when you are speaking to an audience face to face. In fact, the way the television camera picks up your image, especially in close-ups, and the intimacy with which your audience views your image on the screen make your appearance and movement even more important than when you address listeners face to face.

When speaking on television, therefore, your physical behavior is important. You do not depend on voice alone as you do when speaking on the radio. Neither can you talk as if you were facing an immediate audience only. Your voice and action must conform to limitations imposed by the microphone and the television camera.

Generally, you will find that the suggestions we have given for using the microphone and avoiding distracting noises are pertinent to television as well as to radio broadcasts. In addition to observing them, you must adapt to the distractions of the television studio's dazzling lights and their heat, to the movement of the cameras on their booms or dollies, and to the restriction of your movement within the area upon which the lights and cameras are focused. Yet this adaptation must seem natural. Avoid equally a stunned or disconcerted appearance and a tendency to "play to the gallery."

The technical aspects of television are changing rapidly and facilities at different stations vary considerably. Hence, each time you broadcast you will need special advice from the directors and technicians in order to adapt your presentation to prevailing conditions. For this reason, the following discussion omits detailed instructions and includes only suggestions which are fairly universal in their application.

Adapting vocal delivery for television

While many of the vocal requirements of radio broadcasting apply equally to television broadcasting, important differences should be noted. Since on television the speaker is seen as well as heard, he can talk more slowly and can pause longer for transitions or emphasis. When a program is broadcast over both radio and television, however, pauses should not be too long nor the rate of speaking too slow.

In telecasts, be careful also to maintain a quiet, conversational manner. Especially in intimate studio telecasts, remember that you are conversing with your listeners as a guest in their homes. Vocal variety and emphasis are needed, but too excited a tone, too fast a rate, and too assertive an inflection are likely to be offensive.

Adapting movement and appearance to the television camera

The television camera's lens adjustment and its distance from the speaker determine how much of his body will be shown. Moreover, the camera's position determines the angle from which the speaker is viewed. Usually camera angles and distances are changed during the broadcast to provide variety. Often more than one camera is used, the broadcast pick-up shifting from one to another so that the picture changes from a distant to a close-up view or from a front to an angle shot; or the camera is moved on a boom or dolly so that the angle shifts gradually. If an audience is present, the camera may go from speaker to audience and back again. The director will instruct you ahead of time where you are to stand or sit, and how far you may safely move without getting beyond the focal depth or angle of the camera or outside of the lighted area. If you intend to use visual aids, such as maps and models, be sure they are placed where the camera can reach them.

The effect which televising has upon colors, textures, and patterns requires special attention to make-up and clothing. The bright lights cause the normal reddish color of the lips to fade out and the natural shadows of the face to disappear, so that the face appears flattened. Hence, make-up is necessary to make facial color and contour appear natural. Make-up also must be used to reduce glare (perspiring skin or a bald head may gleam unless toned down with dull paint or panchromatic powder) and to obscure blemishes or stubble (a man's shaven face may appear dirty and unkempt unless basic make-up is applied). Finally, clothes must be chosen for pattern and color to give life to the image without creating bizarre effects.

Adapting movement and appearance to the type of broadcast

In an earlier part of this chapter we discussed the difference between radio broadcasts in the studio without an audience and broadcasts with an audience present. In television, this difference is particularly important. If an audience is present, you will be expected to talk to your listeners, not to the camera. Your posture, movements, and gestures must be adapted to the people before you. Use enough bodily activity to maintain interest, but avoid exaggerated gestures.

The studio telecast with no audience present is more intimate. Here you must think of yourself as talking to your listeners in their living rooms. You may stand while speaking, especially if you have something to point out or to demonstrate. Often, however, you will be seated at a desk or even in a large, comfortable chair. In either case, your movements should be suited to easy, animated conversation. Stand or sit in a relaxed manner. Change your position occasionally and use your hands to emphasize and clarify your statements. At times you may lean forward slightly to emphasize important ideas. The sweep of your gestures, however, should be somewhat restrained; move the hand and forearm in a relatively small arc and avoid declamatory

In a television studio for an appearance on "Vistas" are professors from DePaul University. Representatives of six colleges and universities in the Chicago area appear on the program regularly. In purpose the program is similar to others throughout the country which provide speakers an opportunity to discuss topics in their fields.

mannerisms. Look at the camera but do not stare at it continuously. Look away occasionally at a slight angle and then look back again. Above all, do not rely heavily on a manuscript or notes. If you must read all or part of your speech, you may be able to arrange for the use of a teleprompter. This device puts a copy of your speech, in large type, on or near the camera. Thus, even though you are reading, you can maintain fairly good eye contact with the viewers.

Using visual aids

Television makes possible the use of all sorts of visual aids to illustrate and substantiate the content of a speech. Maps, charts, pictures, models, and even short sequences from motion pictures add variety and life to a presentation. Sometimes large-scale visual aids are placed beside or behind the speaker so that he can point to them as he talks. Frequently, small pictures or miniature models are picked up by a separate camera. When broadcasting with an audience present, you may not be able to employ these devices extensively, but when broadcasting from a studio, you usually can employ them with very good effect. In fact, you may be able to organize your entire talk around a series of visual aids devised to portray your ideas.

PRINCIPLES OF CONTENT AND ORGANIZATION

When planning and organizing a speech which is to be broadcast, observe these rules:

Fit your talk to the exact time limit

Most stations operate on a schedule that is adhered to with only thirty seconds' leeway; if a program runs overtime, it is cut off. Moreover, programs start on schedule; therefore, allow yourself plenty of time to get to the studio and to catch your breath before you begin speaking. Remember, too, that part of the program will be taken by things other than your speech. If you are given a fifteen-minute "spot," you will not have a full fifteen minutes available because announcements and introductory remarks will consume part of the time. Find out how much time is actually yours and what sort of signals will be given to indicate how the time is going. Without realizing it, many people talk faster in a studio than elsewhere, and, therefore, tend to finish ahead of schedule. Prepare for this eventuality by having an additional illustration or story which can be inserted near the end of your speech if you see that you are getting through too early. Prepare also to cut a paragraph or two should this become necessary. "Backtime" your speech by noting on the manuscript or teleprompter copy at what point you have one or two minutes of material remaining. If near the end of the broadcast the clock shows that you have too much or too little time, adjust your remarks accordingly.

Make your appeal as universal as possible

Remember that all sorts of people may be listening. Relate your appeal to the everyday experiences of your listeners and try to interest as many of them as you can.

Use lively, concrete material. Avoid abstract theorizing; listeners can tune you out unless you make your speech come alive with stories, illustrations, and comparisons.

Apply as many factors of attention as possible. In choosing ideas, give special emphasis to the *vital*—use materials related to the impelling needs and desires of many people; to *activity* and *reality*—use materials characterized by movement and concreteness; and to *suspense*—arouse curiosity or expectation that some valuable information will be presented later. (Review the discussion of the factors of interest in Chapter 9, pp. 181-186.)

Avoid profanity and offensive remarks. Profanity or risqué stories are never necessary to a good speaker, and on the air they are absolutely taboo. To protect its license, the station will shut you off if you try to use them. Slurs against any religious, racial, or occupational group also must be avoided. Remember that the air is public property.

Make your speech easy to follow

Listeners who are not present in the room with you need extra aids to understanding in addition to the extra incentives to attending mentioned above.

Use simple (but not childish) wording and sentence structure. Avoid technical terms where common terms will do, but if you must use technical terms, explain them. Also avoid flowery, overelegant terms and long, complex sentences. Do not, however, talk down to the audience.

Use simple speech organization. Complex reasoning has no place in a broadcast talk. Rarely is there time to make such reasoning clear, and because you cannot see your listeners, you cannot tell whether they understand. A few main points, clearly related, should furnish the basic structure of your speech.

Make your transitions clear. When you pass from one idea to another, indicate this fact by a sentence or two or by a distinct change of rate or pitch. In a television broadcast, you can indicate transitions by movement or a gesture, but over the radio your voice and language must do this work. Do not allow your transitions to become stereotyped; vary them and keep them informal. Do not overwork such phrases as "In the first place" and "Second"; they may seem too stilted. You might say instead, "It's too costly, for one thing," "There's no need to labor that point," or "But let's look at something else for a minute."

Give a sense of continuous movement and development. A radio or television speech must never bog down or ramble. Keep your listeners aware that you are getting somewhere, that you have an objective and are moving steadily toward it.

We have presented a few of the principles to keep in mind when you prepare a speech for broadcasting. Observe how they are applied in the televised speech by Richard M. Nixon that is reprinted in the Appendix (pp. 308–312) and in speeches that you hear on radio and television. In this way, you may learn additional rules and cautions for broadcasting a talk effectively.

PROBLEMS FOR FURTHER STUDY

1. Be prepared to answer the following questions in class: Do broadcast speeches differ in purpose from other speeches? What are the special characteristics of radio and television audiences? How do broadcast speeches differ when delivered before a studio audience and without a studio audience? What manner of speaking is recommended for radio broadcasts? What special problems in the speaker-audience relationship are created by television? What principles of speech development are especially important for broadcast speeches?

2. Analyze the speech by Richard M. Nixon that is reprinted in the Appendix, p. 308. Determine its purpose and type. Review the chapter which deals with speeches of this type, and then examine critically the speech's organization and content. Does the speech illustrate principles of adapting organization and content to broadcasting, as set forth in this chapter? Be prepared to quote sections of the speech to support your answer.

3. Listen to some skilled speaker over radio or television and prepare a written report analyzing the factors that contributed to his effectiveness. Comment on speech delivery and on organization and content.

SPEAKING ASSIGNMENTS[1]

1. Acting as an announcer, introduce some famous person to the radio or television audience. Limit your remarks to one minute.

2. Select from the longer speeches reprinted in the Appendix a speech which was not broadcast. Prepare in your own words a revised draft of this speech which will, so far as possible, achieve the same purpose as the original speech, but which is suited in organization and style to radio presentation. Fit your version of the speech into a time limit of five minutes. Back-time the speech so you can modify your closing statements and finish exactly on time. Present the reworked speech to the class as

---

[1] If a loudspeaker system with the microphone in an adjoining room is available, its use will make these exercises more realistic and valuable. If not, a workable substitute consists in having the speaker talk from behind a screen or from the rear of the room so that he will be heard but not seen.

if speaking over the radio. To simulate studio broadcasting, be seated while speaking and do not face your listeners directly.

3. Adapt the speech you prepared for Assignment 2 for a television broadcast. Indicate in marginal notes the visual aids that you might use; consider special adaptations of movement and gesture that would be appropriate. Deliver the speech from manuscript first, attempting to maintain good eye contact with the camera. Then present the speech by reading the manuscript from large cards which someone holds.

4. As an alternative to Assignments 2 and 3, adapt one of your own classroom speeches first to radio and then to television. Write out each version in manuscript form and append a paper analyzing the similarities and differences between the two.

5. Team up with another member of the class and, acting as announcer, introduce him and his speech to the radio or television audience. Be sure you know well in advance whether your partner is doing Assignment 2, 3, or 4 above. Either see the manuscript or ask him about the purpose and content of his talk; be sure to get the exact title.

6. Give a five-minute summary of the day's campus news. Prepare for the broadcast by writing out the news in manuscript form and rehearsing your presentation carefully. Set a clock on the table before you and adjust your presentation so that you close exactly on time.

SUGGESTIONS FOR FURTHER READING

Waldo Abbot and Richard L. Rider, *Handbook of Broadcasting,* 4th ed. (New York: McGraw-Hill Book Company, Inc., 1957).

Samuel L. Becker and H. Clay Harshbarger, *Television: Techniques for Planning and Performances* (New York: Henry Holt and Company, Inc., 1958).

Hadley Cantril and G. W. Allport, *Psychology of Radio* (New York: Harper & Brothers, 1935).

Giraud Chester and Garnet R. Garrison, *Television and Radio,* 3rd ed. (New York: Appleton-Century-Crofts, Inc., 1963).

Edward Stasheff and Rudy Bretz, *The Television Program,* 3rd ed. (New York: Hill and Wang, Inc., 1962).

Max Wylie, *Radio and Television Writing,* rev. ed. (New York: Rinehart & Company, Inc., 1950).

CHAPTER 13

DISCUSSION

In our society many of the operations of business, education, and government are directed by groups of people—committees, boards, and councils. Often a business or professional man must spend so much time in meetings that his success in his job depends largely upon his skill in leading or participating in discussion. What is *discussion?* Although methods vary from group to group, the following is a working definition: Discussion is a cooperative process in which a group of persons exchange and evaluate ideas and information in order to learn more about a subject of interest or solve a problem of mutual concern.

From taking part in discussions in the classroom and in social, church, and campus groups, you undoubtedly have discovered that merely having a group of people talk over a matter does not always produce a magical result. Often an intelligent or experienced individual can grasp a situation or solve a problem more efficiently than a group can. On the other hand, a group judgment is often superior to an individual one: a group is more likely than an individual to take into account all aspects of a question; a group decision is more democratic than an individual decision; and, since people tend to support decisions which they have helped frame, a group decision is more likely to produce permanent and satisfying results.

The efficiency and productivity of a group discussion, as of any cooperative activity, can be increased if the participants plan for the discussion and are familiar with methods of participation and leader-

ship. The purpose of this chapter is to help you gain an understanding of the principles upon which successful discussion rests.

TYPES OF DISCUSSION

The four most common types of discussion are learning discussions, decision-making discussions, panels, and symposiums. In a learning discussion, the participants exchange information and ideas in order to increase their understanding of a subject. In a decision-making discussion, the aim is to arrive at an agreement concerning a future policy or course of action. Panels and symposiums are designed to be held before audiences or to be broadcast. Therefore, they are types of "public discussion."

Learning discussions

Learning discussions are usually informal. A recognized expert may give a speech or lecture in order to introduce the subject to the group, but the participants devote the bulk of the time to an exchange of facts and ideas. Their purpose is to learn from one another.

A common type of learning discussion occurs in the college class-room. Another occurs at conventions, where men and women in the same business or profession discuss their experiences, review recent research, or consider methods of dealing with common problems. In addition, members of women's clubs, religious organizations, and civic groups often conduct learning discussions on matters of mutual interest.

Decision-making discussions

Decision-making discussions take various forms. The president of an organization calls a meeting of the executive committee or board of directors so that the group may hear reports and determine policies. The chairman of a fraternity dance committee calls the members together to discuss plans for the spring prom. The business manager of the student dramatic organization gathers his assistants to discuss the budget for the next play or to work out a ticket-selling campaign. The rules committee of the women's self-government association meets to consider problems of social regulation among women students. All these groups, and countless others, use discussion to make decisions and to evolve policies.

Panel discussions

When a group is too large to engage in an informal learning or decision-making discussion, or when its members are not sufficiently informed to make discussion profitable, four or five individuals, usually seated on a platform, may discuss the topic before the larger group. The individuals in this small group, or panel, are chosen either because they can supply the facts needed for intelligent discussion or because they represent views held by members of the larger group and can, therefore, act as their spokesmen. The members of the panel discuss the subject among themselves, asking questions of one another and agreeing or disagreeing as if they were in a learning or decision-making group. In a public discussion of this type, however, they speak *for* the audience and not merely *before* it.

Symposiums

In symposiums several people—usually three to five—give short speeches, each presenting a different point of view or each treating a different facet of the subject. The symposium is a form of public discussion that is common at large conventions or conferences, where experts are invited to speak on specific aspects of a general topic.

Both the symposium and the panel discussion may be followed by an open forum in which the participants answer questions asked by members of the audience. Various combinations and modifications of the panel and symposium are used, but the essential characteristic of each is that most of the talking is done by a small group of experts or spokesmen while the larger group listens.

Discussions on radio and television

Of all the types of group discussion described above, the panel is broadcast most frequently. Local radio stations present students, civic leaders, and others in panel shows each week; radio and television networks give time to the discussion of current events by groups of government officials or news commentators. Symposiums, although more formal than panel discussions, also are adaptable to broadcasting because the speeches can be carefully timed. Speakers with sharply differing points of view usually present their opinions concisely and without interruption, after which all engage in an informal question-and-answer period.

ESSENTIALS FOR EFFECTIVE DISCUSSION

Essentials for the group

The first essential for profitable discussion is *order*. This does not imply great formality; indeed, formality is often undesirable. It does imply, however, that only one person talk at a time, that the members be courteous, and that an attempt be made to keep the discussion relevant and to help it progress. A second essential is *cooperation*. If one person attempts to monopolize the discussion, it usually will get nowhere. Members of the group must be willing to share the speaking time and to listen to views at variance with their own. Also, instead of criticizing other members, they must try to understand and assist. A third essential, in decision-making discussions particularly, is a *willingness to compromise*. There are times, of course, when compromise is not desirable; but reasonable compromise hurts no one and sometimes is the only way of reaching an agreement. Finally, a discussion group should have a *feeling of accomplishment.* Unless the members believe they are getting somewhere, their interest and enthusiasm will diminish. For this reason, a definite goal should be set and the field for discussion appropriately limited. Moreover, the topic for discussion should be phrased as a question and made as specific and impartial as possible. The topic "The road to peace," for example, is too vague and would probably result in a rambling discussion, but the question "How can the United States help protect the security of the free world?" is more specific and would give the group a more definite goal.

Essentials for the participant

For the discussion participant the most important requirement is a *knowledge of the subject* being considered. If you know what you are talking about, you will be forgiven many faults. A second essential is an *acquaintance with the other members* of the group. The more you know about them, the better will you be able to judge the value of their remarks and to determine the role you must play in order to make the discussion profitable. Equally important is close *attention to the discussion* as it progresses. Unless you listen to what is going on, you will forget what already has been said or lose track of the direction the discussion is taking. As a result, you may make foolish comments, require the restatement of points already settled, or misunderstand the positions taken by other participants. Finally, you should make *meaningful contributions to the discussion.* If you keep quiet, you may learn a good deal, but you will not help anyone else to understand the subject or to solve the problem at hand. Develop the ability to present your ideas—when they are pertinent—clearly and tactfully.

Qualities required of the leader

The fruitfulness of a discussion depends a great deal upon the leader's *capacity for rapid analysis.* He must be alert, quick-witted, and clear thinking—able to see the direction the discussion is taking, to catch significant points even when they are buried in superfluous detail, to perceive the basic issues, to note any common elements in diverse points of view, and to strip controversial points of unnecessary complexity. Moreover, a good discussion leader must be capable of *clear, effective expression.* He must be able to state the results of his analysis clearly and briefly, or to make an essential point stand out before the group just as it does in his own mind.

Another important quality which the leader must have is *impartiality*. He must see that minority views are allowed expression and must phrase his questions and comments fairly. By doing so he can help maintain a spirit of cooperation and conciliation among members of the group who may differ from one another vigorously. Discussion groups are no different from other groups in preferring leaders who are fair. There is no place in discussion for a leader who takes sides in a personal argument or who openly favors some members at the expense of others. If a member's comment contains a reasonable argument and a sarcastic connotation, the leader should focus attention on the reason and ignore the sarcasm.

Finally, a discussion leader should have an *encouraging manner* toward the group members. There are times, especially at the beginning of a discussion, when people are hesitant to speak out. Provocative questions may encourage them to participate, but even more encouraging is a manner which conveys confidence that the group members have important things to say about an important subject.

PREPARING FOR DISCUSSION

General preparation

How should you prepare to participate in a discussion or to lead one? As we have already suggested, two fundamental steps are required: (1) you must investigate the problem to be considered; and (2) you must analyze the group which is to consider it.

Investigation of the subject. Unfortunately, many persons believe they do not need to prepare as carefully for a discussion as for a speech. In a discussion, however, you cannot narrow the subject or determine the purpose for yourself; nor can you control the direction the deliberation will take. Since there are so many eventualities which must be considered, preparing for a discussion often is a greater challenge than preparing for a speech.

Carefully think through each facet of the subject to be discussed. First, review what you already know about it. Go over the information you have acquired and the judgments you have formed, and organize these materials in note or outline form. Approach the subject as though you were going to present a speech *pro* and *con* on each phase of it; you then will be familiar with all of its angles and issues.

Second, gather additional material; supplement what you know by reading widely and whenever possible by observing conditions and consulting experts. Bring your knowledge up to date. Correlate this new information with the ideas and data you had previously.

Third, if the discussion has decision making as its purpose, formulate a tentative point of view on the question. Decide what your position will be. Are you in favor of limiting membership in the club or of increasing its size? Is $60,000 too much to spend for a new clubhouse? Do you believe dues should be paid annually or monthly? Work out your position on the overall question for discussion and on more specific questions that may arise. Also have clearly in mind the evidence and reasoning that support your views. But keep your thinking tentative; be willing to change your mind if additional facts disclosed in the discussion prove you wrong.

Finally, examine the effect your point of view may have upon the other members of the group or upon society. If you do this, you will be better prepared to deal with any objections which may arise. Possibly someone will oppose a solution you support on the ground that it would cause him to lose money or to retract a promise; forethought not only will prepare you for his opposition, but also may suggest to you another, more workable solution. If an audience will be present to hear the discussion and to participate in a question-and-answer period, or if radio and television audiences will hear you, do not forget to take into account their probable knowledge of and attitude toward the subject.

Analysis of the group. Even though you are thoroughly familiar with the subject matter to be discussed, you will be handicapped unless you understand the nature and the objectives of your group. Are the members brought together merely to investigate, or do they have power to make decisions? What resources are at their command? Of what larger unit is the group a part? If you are a member of the student council, for example, you should understand not only the functions of the council but also its relation to the policies and traditions of your college or university. In your analysis, consider also the individuals who compose the group. In this way you will come to know that Mr. X usually exaggerates or has an ax to grind and that his comments, therefore, must be taken with a grain of salt, but that Mr. W is thoughtful and well informed and that his comments will bear serious consideration. Moreover, you will understand something of the social structure of the group — who the natural leaders and followers are and in what relation the members stand to one another. Answer as well as you can the following questions: What is the official position of each member? What are each individual's personal traits? What knowledge does each one have of the questions that will be raised? What attitude will each one have toward the ideas or proposals you intend to introduce?

Special preparation for public discussion

When the discussion is to be held before an audience or is to be broadcast, a preliminary warm-up period or even a practice session may prove helpful. Such a session breaks the ice and often stimulates a more animated and vigorous exchange of ideas. Moreover, such a session enables the leader to explain any special details of procedure. Sometimes these practice discussions are recorded so that the participants may analyze their remarks and improve their presentation. Discussions, however, should never be written out and read from a script, because this tends to rob them of their spontaneity and liveliness. Care also must be taken not to continue preliminary discussions until the participants become stale. Mere rehearsals in which the same things are said in the same way soon become boring and lead to a presentation that sounds cut and dried. Either limit the length and number of practice periods or see that new material or fresh points of view are brought in at each session.

DEVELOPING THE DISCUSSION PLAN

In discussion, much time may be lost by needless repetition and by aimless wandering from point to point. A carefully developed discussion plan will guard against this danger.

Ideally, the entire group should cooperate in framing the plan the discussion is to follow; but if this is impossible, the leader must take the responsibility for formulating it. We shall consider separate plans for learning discussions and decision-making discussions and also give suggestions for panels and symposiums. The plans outlined can be used in most situations, although at times modifications may be required because of peculiarities in the composition of the group or because in a decision-making discussion the problem is already in an advanced stage of consideration when taken up by the group. (See pp. 265–266.) We shall not include a separate plan for radio or television discussion because broadcasting does not affect the logical sequence in which ideas should be considered.

A plan for learning discussions

Sometimes a learning discussion concerns a book or parts of it, or is based upon a study outline or syllabus prepared by an authority in a given field. In such cases the discussion generally should follow the organizational pattern used in this resource. The ideas in the book or outline, however, should be related to the experience of individuals in the group, and an effort should be made to give proper emphasis to the more important facts and principles. Sometimes groups find that prepared outlines are out of date or incomplete; if this is true, the plan should provide for bringing the missing information or points of view into the discussion.

When learning discussions are not based upon a book or outline, the leader or the group must formulate a discussion plan. The first step in this formulation is stating the subject for discussion as a question — usually a question of fact or a question of value. (See pp. 205-206.) Questions of fact, such as "What are the essentials for effective discussion?" or "What is our community doing to combat the increasing crime rate?" seek an addition to or a clarification of knowledge within the group; questions of value, such as "How successful is our community recreation program?" or "Is the United Nations the best means to world peace?" seek judgments, appraisals, or preferences. The following suggestions should help you develop a satisfactory discussion plan for both types of questions.

Introduction. The introduction consists of a statement of the discussion question by the leader, together with one or two examples showing its general importance or its relation to individuals in the group. (Usually the discussion question is framed before the discussion begins. If not, the leader and the members of the group must work it out together.)

Analysis. In this step the group explores the nature and meaning of the question and narrows the scope of the discussion to those phases which seem most important. The following questions may be answered:

1. Into what major topical divisions may this question for discussion conveniently be divided? (See pp. 138-143 for some suggestions.)

2. To which of these phases should the discussion be narrowed?

a. Which phases are of the greatest interest and importance to the group?

b. On which phases are the members of the group already so well informed that detailed discussion would be pointless?

At this point the leader summarizes for the group, listing in a logical sequence the particular aspects of the question that have been chosen for discussion. (Suggestions on pp. 138–143 also apply here.)

Investigation. In the investigative phase of the discussion, the members cover the topics they have chosen in the preceding step. Under *each topic* they may consider the following questions:

1. What terms need definition? How should these terms be defined?

2. What factual material needs to be introduced as background for the discussion (historical, social, geographic, etc.)?

3. What personal experiences of members of the group might illuminate and clarify the discussion?

4. What basic principles or causal relationships can be inferred from consideration of this information and these experiences?

5. Upon which facts or principles is there general agreement and upon which points is information still lacking or conflicting?

Final summary. At the close of the discussion, the leader briefly restates (1) the reasons which have been given for considering the question important and (2) the essential points which have been brought out under each of the main topics. This summary need not be exhaustive; its purpose is merely to review the more important points in a way that will make them remembered and that will make their relationship to each other and to the general subject clearly recognized.

A plan for decision-making discussions

As we stated earlier, the principal function of a decision-making discussion is to consider a problem with the aim of reaching a consensus on what to do and how to do it. If, as in the case of an executive committee, the group meets regularly, the members may not know prior to the meeting what will be discussed. More frequently, however, the members know in advance the problem to be considered. At times a serious difficulty or conflict of interests may be the very reason for calling the group together.

The problems with which decision-making discussions usually deal involve questions of policy. (See p. 204.) Examples of such questions are: "What can be done to increase the number of participants in our activity?" and "How can our company meet the competition from foreign imports?"[1] As you will see in the following suggested procedure, answering such questions also requires answering questions of fact and value.

The steps in the following plan are adapted from John Dewey's analysis of how we think when we are confronted with a problem.[2] Although presented in some detail, this plan is only one of several possible ways of deciding upon a course of action, and, therefore, is intended to be suggestive rather than didactic. Any plan that is developed, however, probably should follow a problem-solution order. Steps in the plan should be stated as a series of questions, as in the following:

Defining the problem. After introductory remarks by the chairman touching on the general purpose of the discussion and its importance, the group should consider:

1. How can the purpose of the discussion be phrased as a question? (Note: Usually the question has been phrased before the discussion begins. If not, it should be phrased at this time.)

2. What terms need defining?

    a. What do the terms in the question mean?

    b. Should definitions be provided at this time of other terms or concepts that will be encountered in the discussion?

Analyzing the problem. This step involves evaluating the problem's scope and importance, discovering its causes, singling out the specific conditions that need correction, and setting up the basic requirements of an effective solution. The following sequence of questions is suggested:

1. What evidence is there that an unsatisfactory situation exists?

---

[1] Not all discussions of this sort deal with problems or policies over which the group has immediate control. For example, a group may discuss "Should we de-emphasize intercollegiate athletics?" or "How can the United States increase its trade with Latin America?" The systematic investigation of these subjects, however, requires substantially the same steps as for matters over which the group does have direct control. The only difference is that instead of asking, "What shall we *do*?" the group, in effect, is asking, "What shall we *recommend* to those in authority?" or "What *would* we do if we ourselves were in positions of authority?"

[2] See Chapter 7, "Analysis of Reflective Thinking," in *How We Think* by John Dewey (Boston: D. C. Heath and Company, 1933).

a. In what ways have members of the group been aware of the problem; how have they been affected by it, or how are they likely to be affected?

b. What other persons or groups does the situation affect, and in what way are they affected?

c. Is the situation likely to improve by itself, or will it become worse if nothing is done about it?

d. Is the problem sufficiently serious to warrant discussion and action at this time? (If not, further discussion is pointless.)

2. What caused this difficulty?

a. Are its causes primarily financial, political, social, or what?

b. To what extent is this difficulty the result of misunderstandings or emotional conflicts between individuals or groups?

3. What specific aspects of the present situation must be corrected? What demands must be met, what desires satisfied?

a. What evils does everyone in the group wish corrected?

b. What additional evils does a majority in the group wish corrected?

c. What desirable elements in the present situation must be retained?

4. In light of the answers to questions 1, 2, and 3 above, by what criteria should any proposed plan or remedy be judged? (See p. 207.)

a. What must the plan do?

b. What must the plan avoid?

c. What restrictions of time, money, etc., must be considered?

5. In addition to the above criteria, what supplementary qualities of a plan are desirable, though not essential?

At this stage the leader summarizes the points agreed upon thus far. Particularly important is a clear statement of the agreements reached on questions 4 and 5, since the requirements here set forth will provide the standards against which proposed remedies are judged. Moreover, a clear understanding and agreement regarding criteria tend to make further discussion more objective and to minimize disagreements based upon personal prejudices.

Suggesting solutions. In this step, every possible solution is presented. The group asks:

1. What are the various ways in which the difficulty could be solved? (If the group is meeting to discuss the merits of a previously proposed plan, it asks: What are the alternatives to the proposed plan?)

a. What is the exact nature of each proposed solution? What cost, actions, or changes does it entail or imply?

b. How may the various solutions best be grouped for initial consideration? (It is helpful to list all solutions, preferably on a blackboard.)

Evaluating the solutions. When members have presented all possible solutions which have occurred to them, they examine and compare these solutions in an attempt to agree on a mutually satisfactory plan. The following questions may be asked:

1. What elements are common to all the proposed solutions, and, therefore, are probably desirable?

2. How do the solutions differ?

3. How do the various solutions meet the criteria set up in phases 4 and 5 of the analysis step? (This may be answered by: (1) considering each plan (or type of plan) separately in the light of the criteria agreed upon; or (2) considering each criterion separately to determine which solution best satisfies it.)

4. Which solutions should be eliminated and which retained for further consideration?

5. Which solution or combination of solutions should finally be approved?

a. Which objectionable features of the approved solution (solutions) should be eliminated or modified?

b. (If a number of solutions are approved: How may the best features of all the approved solutions be combined in a single superior plan?)

As soon as agreement is reached on these matters, the leader sums up the principal features of the accepted plan. In groups which have no authority to act, this statement normally concludes the discussion.

Deciding how to put the approved solution into operation. When a group has the power to put its solution into operation, the following additional questions are pertinent:

1. What persons or committees should be responsible for taking action?

2. When and where should the solution go into effect?

3. What official action, what appropriation of money, etc., is necessary? (Note: If several divergent methods of putting the solution into effect are suggested, the group may need to evaluate these methods briefly in order to decide on the most satisfactory one.)

When these matters have been decided, the chairman briefly re-states the action agreed upon to be sure it is clear and fully acceptable to the group.

Adapting the decision-making plan to the question

The discussion plan suggested above covers the entire process of decision making from an initial analysis of existing conditions to the planning of final action. This entire process, however, is not always required in a discussion. As Harrison S. Elliott points out in his book, *The Process of Group Thinking,* "A group may face a question in any one of five stages: (1) a baffling or confused situation; (2) a problem definitely defined; (3) alternatives specifically suggested; (4) a single definite proposal; (5) ways and means of carrying out a conclusion."[3] How much of the five-step decision-making process needs to be included in the discussion depends, then, upon the stage at which the question comes before the group.

For example, a discussion requiring only the final three steps of the process occurred some years ago on a university campus. These events led up to the discussion: Three student organizations had made plans to produce musical comedies on the campus during the same week. Obviously, three such shows would conflict with one another, yet none of the organizations wanted to give up its plan entirely. All thought that the best solution would be for the three groups to combine their efforts in a joint production, but the differences in membership require-ments, financial policies, and skills required of the participants would make this difficult. Therefore, a preliminary meeting was held in which representatives of the student organizations and representatives of the faculty decided that a joint plan, to be acceptable, must provide for (1) skilled professional direction; (2) opportunity for all students, regardless of organization membership, to try out for roles or to work on the stage crew; (3) equal representation of the three student groups on the managing board; and (4) provision for an adequate financial guarantee.

A second discussion then was scheduled. In preparation for it, the chairman secured from members of the joint committee several definite and detailed proposals. He had copies of these proposals, with

---

[3] (New York: Association Press, 1928), p. 89 ff.

the names of the authors omitted, placed before each member at the beginning of the meeting. In opening the discussion, the chairman recalled the four general requirements listed above and secured their confirmation by the group. From this point on, the discussion focused upon the typewritten proposals. The group found that the three plans had a number of common features; they ironed out the differences; they added some details and dropped others; they found a revised plan to be acceptable and adopted it; and they made provisions to put it into operation. Thus, beginning with the suggestion and evaluation of solutions, this second discussion followed almost exactly the procedure indicated in the preceding section of this chapter. The definition and analysis steps, however, were omitted, since these matters had already been settled before the discussion began. Similar abridgments of the five-step discussion plan can often be made, depending upon the stage at which the question comes before the group.

Planning for panel discussions and symposiums

For a panel discussion before an audience, the plan may follow lines similar to those presented above for learning and decision-making groups. If the purpose is to inform only, the learning plan may be used; if the purpose is to consider a problem or to discuss a course of action, the decision-making plan is more suitable. Any discussion plan that is used, however, should provide for utilizing the specialized information of each of the panel members. Although no participant should limit his remarks to his special field of knowledge, he should at least be given first opportunity to discuss questions relating to that field. Unless this is done, the very purpose of selecting a panel to discuss the question for the audience is likely to be defeated.

If the discussion is a symposium, the plan normally includes a partitioning of the topic among the speakers, a different phase being assigned to each. The number of speakers often determines the divisions of the subject. For example, one person may describe the problem and each of the other speakers may suggest and evaluate a different type of solution; or each speaker may discuss a different aspect of the question, one concentrating on the political aspect, another on the economic aspect, etc. After the speakers present their prepared remarks, the meeting may be opened for questions from the audience, the chairman referring the questions to the various symposium speakers for reply.

Adapting the discussion plan to the occasion

When circumstances indicate that a procedure other than those suggested here would lead to more rapid progress and more fruitful results, do not hesitate to devise a different type of discussion plan. In the beginning, however, you will be wise to follow rather closely the procedures described; once these plans are firmly in mind, adaptations and modifications may be made as the need arises. The discussion leader's or the group's good sense and experience in discussion should provide a reliable guide in making necessary adaptations.

PARTICIPATING IN DISCUSSION

One of the principal differences between a public speech and a discussion is that in a speech one person does all the talking, while in discussion everybody contributes. During the greater part of the time, however, a discussion participant is a listener rather than a speaker. For this reason, he should know how to evaluate the ideas advanced by the others, as well as how and when to advance ideas of his own.

Evaluating contributions

As you learned in Chapter 3, where the principles of good listening were discussed (pp. 53-57), in evaluating a speaker's remarks you should pay close attention to the evidence and reasoning upon which his judgments rest. The same rule applies in discussion. When a participant makes a seemingly important contribution, test it by asking the following questions:

1. Is the speaker expressing an authoritative opinion? Is he qualified by training and experience to speak as an expert on the topic under discussion?

2. Is his statement based on first-hand knowledge? Did he observe the evidence himself, or is he reporting someone else's findings?

3. What are the sources of his facts? Does he explain sufficiently where and how he secured his information? Are his sources of information reliable?

4. Is his opinion unprejudiced, or influenced by personal interest? Does he stand to profit personally from some decision the group may reach?

5. Does he usually state his opinions frankly? Does he reveal all the facts known to him, or is he in the habit of concealing facts unfavorable to his cause?

6. Are the facts or opinions he presents consistent with human experience? Do they sound plausible? Could they reasonably be true?

7. Are the facts or opinions he presents consistent with one another? Are they consistent with the reports made by reputable authorities?

8. What weight will other members of the group give to his opinion? Is his prestige so great that the group will agree with him in the face of conflicting evidence, or is he so little respected that he will not be believed unless someone else supports his opinion?

If you ask questions like these while comments are being offered, you can evaluate their worth more easily and accurately. In addition, you will better be able to estimate the reaction of the group to any contributions you may make.

Making contributions

Although you cannot be a good discussant unless you are a good listener, neither can you be a good discussant if you fail to advance constructive ideas, useful information, and sound judgments. As we pointed out earlier, the best listener in the world, if he *only* listens, contributes little toward understanding or toward solving the problem before the group. When and how, therefore, should you enter into the discussion? How should your contributions be phrased and presented?

There is no simple answer to the question "When should I talk and when should I keep quiet?" For the most part, the suggestions for classroom discussions given in Chapter 1 apply to any discussion in which you participate. (See pages 7-8.) Speak when you are asked a direct question, when you have a worth-while idea to offer, or when you can correct or clarify the remark of another person. More important than any specific rules or cautions, however, is the general reminder that discussion is a cooperative process. You should neither monopolize the conversation nor remain consistently silent. Speak when you believe you can be of definite help to the group, but also give the other members a full and fair opportunity to express their views. Experience has shown that the most interesting and profitable discussions are those in which all members of the group participate about evenly.

When you speak, remember again the cooperative nature of the discussion process. Advance your ideas tentatively and present the evidence and reasoning upon which they rest. Speak to the point and indicate that you understand the particular issue under consideration. Show by your manner as well as your words that you are more interested in helping the group attain its objective than in impressing your ideas on the others: try to accept criticism and treat disagreement objectively; be tactful and courteous; keep your voice and manner calm. Doing these things in the heat of an animated discussion may not always be easy; but if you develop the habit of participating with these suggestions in mind, your comments will be more useful and the discussion more productive.

LEADING DISCUSSION

A discussion leader should have all the skills and attributes of a good discussion participant and other abilities besides. He should know how to get discussion started and keep it stimulated, how to prevent it from wandering, how to draw out silent members and keep overtalkative ones in check, how to bring out the essential facts, how to resolve conflicts, and how to summarize and interpret group progress. No wonder good discussion leaders are rare.

Stimulating discussion

To get the discussion started, the leader may follow the suggestion made on page 260 of briefly stating the question to be discussed and stressing its importance, especially as it relates to the participants. His remarks should be made with vigor and earnestness, suggesting the vital nature of the subject, and should be expressed in concrete terms supported by specific instances; but they should not be so long that they seem to exhaust the subject. They should, moreover, lead into a series of provocative questions designed to pull members of the group into the discussion. If such questions fail to provoke discussion, the leader may call on certain individuals by name, asking them to relate their experiences or to express their opinions. Or he may go to the blackboard and start a list—of various aspects of the subject or causes of the problem, of terms needing definition, of proposed courses of action, of anything which calls for enumeration or classification. Curiously enough, people who hesitate to begin a discussion are often ready to add to a list which has been started.

Still another method is to bring out at the beginning one or more extreme points of view on the question. The leader can state these views himself or, better, can call on members of the group who hold them. Nothing stirs participants into active discussion so quickly as a statement with which they disagree; the danger of this method is that it may start a verbal battle which consumes too much time or stirs up personal animosity. Usually the problem which brought the group together is sufficiently provocative to start the discussion; but if the group lags at the beginning or hits a "dead spot" later in the discussion, the methods described above may prove helpful.

Directing discussion

The tendency of a group to stray from central issues can be greatly diminished if the leader outlines on a blackboard the points that require consideration. When people can see what points need to be taken up and in what order, they are likely to focus their attention on those points and in that order. Unless a participant suggests that an important item has been omitted from the outline and asks that it be included, the leader can direct attention to the prearranged points, one after another, and thus keep the discussion progressing steadily. Using the outline on the blackboard as a skeleton, many leaders fill in the details as they are introduced, thus providing the group with a visual record of its progress. If, in spite of this planning, the discussion takes an irrelevant turn—if someone doubles back to a point already discussed, jumps ahead to a point not yet in order, or introduces a seemingly extraneous idea—the leader usually needs only to draw attention to the matter currently before the group. Of course, he must be sensible and fair in doing this. Sometimes the fault is in the outline, and the member who moves away from it may be making an important contribution.

The leader also should see to it that one or two persons do not monopolize the discussion. Occasionally such persons have much to contribute, but more often they repeat what has already been said or belabor unimportant points. When this occurs, the leader should call on other members of the group, by name if necessary, asking them questions which will lead the discussion forward and away from the overworked point and the overtalkative person. If the time for closing the discussion is drawing near, a statement of that fact may keep talk from wandering or becoming repetitive. Remember that while a discussion leader does not have the right to direct the group to a prearranged conclusion, he does have the duty to guide the discussion and to keep it centered on relevant issues. A good leader is one who can do this with tact and firmness.

Bringing out the facts

If the leader follows the preceding suggestions, the facts needed to solve the problem or cover the subject of the discussion usually will be brought out. If the participants are fair-minded and well informed and the discussion includes all the necessary steps, no special effort beyond that already indicated will be required. Unfortunately, discussions do not always proceed perfectly, and the leader sometimes must see that important facts are not ignored and that opinions are not mistaken for factual evidence.

When the leader believes that something important has been overlooked, he may tactfully inquire, "Has anyone noticed that. . . ," adding the missing fact himself. Or he may say, "Mr. Smith called my attention yesterday to the fact that. . . . Has anyone else noticed this to be true?" It is generally better, however, to ask a participant a question designed to bring out the needed fact. Similarly, if there is a tendency to dwell on one point of view to the exclusion of an equally important one, the leader may call attention to the oversight by suggesting, "Perhaps we should ask Paul to express his view of this. . . ," or "I have heard this other point of view expressed too. . . . What do you think of it, Barbara?"

Although a discussion leader should never directly accuse a member of his group of twisting facts or making unsupported statements, he should not let false statements or doubtful assertions pass unchallenged. Ideally, other members of the group should inquire into a speaker's facts, but if no one else does, the leader may handle the matter tactfully by asking for further details or for the evidence on which the statement is based. For example, he may say, "I wonder if you would tell us, Mike, what has led you to this conclusion?" or "Is that a statement of your own opinion, Mary, or have you observed it to be true in practice?" By skillful questioning, a good discussion leader can ensure attention to all aspects of a question, see that the important facts are carefully considered, and put the group on guard against unsupported assertions. Whenever possible, however, he should draw the necessary facts and ideas from the group; he should never dominate the discussion unduly.

Resolving conflict

One of the most difficult tasks of the leader in decision-making discussion is resolving conflict. Although discussion is a cooperative process, progress toward the understanding or solution of a problem can seldom be made unless conflicting ideas are examined. If everyone immediately agreed with each new opinion as soon as it was advanced, there would be no use in coming together to discuss. On the other hand, irrational or heated conflict, with the undesirable attitudes it engenders, stifles discussion and renders reflective choices and judgments difficult.

Because rational conflict is essential, but emotional or personalized conflict is harmful, the leader must walk a middle path. When conflict is becoming destructive, he must sense this fact and take steps to curb it. In particular, he must be able to distinguish between conflict based upon honest differences in interpretation of facts and conflict based upon irrational desires and prejudices. When conflict centers in the interpretation of facts, a careful retracing of the reasoning upon which the competing interpretations rest may resolve the difference. When the conflict becomes irrational, the leader should encourage participants to introduce the facts and reasoning upon which a rational decision may be based. At times, he may find it best to suggest that the group delay consideration of the disputed point until other, less controversial matters have been settled; or, when the circumstances seem to justify such action, the leader may even suggest that the group adjourn and resume discussion at a later date when the members have had a chance to cool off.

Advice about the handling of conflict must be general and incomplete. It is impossible to foresee and provide against all of the situations in which destructive conflict may arise. Through experience the leader increasingly learns how to handle certain kinds of cases; through imagination and resourcefulness he invents conflict-resolving technics on the spot. But he always must be alert to the possibility of conflict and watchful for its emergence if he is to curb harmful conflict before it gets out of hand.

Summarizing progress

As we have remarked, the leader should note the points upon which most members of the group agree and should restate these points in brief summaries at appropriate times during the course of the discussion. In this way he narrows the discussion to matters not yet covered or agreed to and prepares to secure understanding or agreement on them. Summaries also instill a sense of accomplishment and encourage the group to proceed toward a conclusion.

In addition to making internal summaries, at the close of the discussion the leader should make a final summary reviewing the ground covered—and in a decision-making discussion, emphasizing the points of agreement without overlooking any important minority view. If some matters remain unsettled, he should point them out, especially if there is to be a later meeting. The tone of this final summary should be objective and as positive as possible in stressing the progress or accomplishments of the group.

PROBLEMS FOR FURTHER STUDY

1. List some of the more important ways in which discussion is used in business, government, and education. Is the use of discussion in these fields increasing or decreasing? Why?

2. Distinguish in at least three ways between discussion and conversation. If you are acquainted with the methods and purposes of debate, also distinguish in at least three ways between discussion and debate.

3. Describe the ideal discussion participant and the ideal discussion leader. After participating in a discussion in class or elsewhere, evaluate yourself according to these criteria. What appear to be your strong points? What are your weak ones? Lay out a specific program of improvement for yourself as a discussant.

4. What do you think are the advantages and limitations of discussion as a procedure for solving group problems and arriving at courses of action? What are the advantages and limitations of group discussion as a learning device?

5. Compare and contrast the process of preparing for a discussion with the process of preparing for a speech. Which of the two is more demanding and difficult? Why?

6. Under what conditions is a symposium to be preferred to a panel as a form of public discussion? Why?

7. Listen to a broadcast of a radio or television discussion. What type of discussion was employed? How effectively was this type of discussion adapted to the broadcast medium?

8. Assume that you have been selected to arrange for a panel discussion on your campus. Select a subject that would be of interest to the student body. Indicate whom you would invite as panelists and why. What sort of preliminary or practice discussion, if any, would you plan?

9. Read the discussion reprinted on pages 324–336. What methods did the leader appear to use to get it started, keep it from wandering, etc.? Did any instances of conflict arise? If so, how effectively did the leader handle them?

10. Select a point about halfway through this discussion and prepare a short statement which summarizes the discussion up to this point.

SPEAKING ASSIGNMENT

1. Meet with four or five other persons in your class. Select a leader; choose a question; gather information and prepare a discussion plan; then present a panel discussion before the class. Let other especially designated members of the class comment on the discussion after it is concluded and offer suggestions for improvement. Here listed are some suggested subjects:

    a. *For learning discussions:*

        How effective is our freshman orientation program?

        What benefits does the undergraduate gain from participating in extracurricular activities?

        How well are high-school students prepared for college?

        How do Russian and Chinese communism differ?

        What are the causes of juvenile delinquency?

        Is modern music sense or nonsense?

        How are American cities solving their traffic problems?

        Is the Common Market plan succeeding?

        What do employers expect of the college graduate?

        What makes a novel (play, picture) great?

b. *For decision-making discussions:*

What can be done to increase the effectiveness of student government in our college?

How can our colleges and universities best meet the problem of increased enrollments?

What can be done to attract more young men and women into teaching?

What tax program would best meet the increasing costs of our state government?

How can we increase the safety of air (car) travel?

How can labor and management better understand each other's problems?

How can the quality of television programs be improved?

How can the United States improve its relations with Latin America?

How can we best protect civil liberties?

SUGGESTIONS FOR FURTHER READING

Dean C. Barnlund and Franklyn S. Haiman, *The Dynamics of Discussion* (Boston: Houghton Mifflin Company, 1960).

Warren G. Bennis, Kenneth D. Benne, and Robert Chin, *The Planning of Change; Readings in the Applied Behavioral Sciences* (New York: Holt, Rinehart and Winston, Inc., 1961), Chapter 6, "The Small Group in Stability and Change."

David Braybrooke and Charles E. Lindblom, *A Strategy of Decision; Policy Evaluation As a Social Process* (New York: The Free Press of Glencoe, 1963).

Laura Crowell, *Discussion: Method of Democracy* (Chicago: Scott, Foresman and Company, 1963).

Henry Lee Ewbank and J. Jeffery Auer, *Discussion and Debate*, 2nd ed. (New York: Appleton-Century-Crofts, Inc., 1951).

Halbert E. Gulley, *Discussion, Conference, and Group Process* (New York: Holt, Rinehart and Winston, Inc., 1961).

William S. Howell and Donald K. Smith, *Discussion* (New York: The Macmillan Company, 1956).

James M. McBurney and Kenneth G. Hance, *Discussion in Human Affairs* (New York: Harper & Brothers, 1950).

CHAPTER 14

PARLIAMENTARY PROCEDURE

The formality with which a deliberative body proceeds depends upon the nature, traditions, and purposes of that body. Legislative assemblies follow detailed and somewhat complicated rules, while many informal study groups employ very few, if any, rules. Organizations which have more than ten or twelve members, however, usually find it advisable to transact business according to the principles of parliamentary procedure. The detailed rules of parliamentary procedure may be found in such manuals as *Robert's Rules of Order Revised.*[1] Our purpose here is to present only some of the basic principles—those which are useful even in relatively informal situations.

If you wish to participate properly in meetings of groups which observe the principles of parliamentary procedure, you should know these principles and how to apply them. This is especially true if you must assume the duties of chairman. The various rules or principles will seem clearer and more understandable if you recognize the reasons behind them. They have as their objective the furtherance of the aims of the group, the implementation of the will of the majority, the protection of the rights of minority members, and the efficient expedition of business.

---

[1] (Chicago: Scott, Foresman and Company, 1951).

THE CHAIRMAN

If the president of an organization has already been chosen, he automatically becomes the group's presiding officer. When no such officer has been selected, the first order of business is to elect a chairman from the membership by majority vote.

The most important duties of the chairman are to preserve order and to see that all parties receive a fair hearing. In order to ensure that only one person speak at a time, the chairman must recognize members before they begin their remarks. In addition, he customarily has certain appointive powers, including the naming of committees. In informal groups the chairman may enter the discussion; in more formal bodies, however, he usually presides without voicing his opinions on the subjects considered, and votes only when it is necessary to break a tie.

ORDER OF BUSINESS

Nearly every organization has a regular order of business which it follows at each meeting. But when no such predetermined order exists, a group may use the following plan—or such parts of this plan as fit its purposes:

1. Minutes of the last meeting—to be read, corrected when necessary, and approved
2. Reports of officers and of standing committees
3. Reports of special committees
4. Consideration of unfinished business from the previous meeting as indicated in the minutes
5. Consideration of new items of business
6. Determination of the time and place of the next meeting, unless this is regularly established
7. Adjournment

Sometimes a problem arises which is so important that it is made a special order of business for the next meeting. When this is done, the regular order of that meeting is modified to give this special problem precedence, and all other matters are omitted or postponed. Occasionally it is impossible to predict in advance of a meeting how important some question will be. When a matter requiring immediate attention arises, it may be considered in advance of its regular place in the order of business by the vote of two-thirds of the group.

THE SUBJECT FOR DISCUSSION[2]

Introducing the subject

In some cases the subject or subjects to be discussed at a meeting are settled in advance, as, for example, when a particular report is due and requires action. Usually, however, a matter for consideration is introduced to the group in the form of a main motion. The proper way to state a main motion is: "Mr. Chairman, I move that. . ." In order to prevent the consideration of proposals which interest only one member, the rules customarily require a second person to support the proposal by seconding it. To second a motion, you say, "Mr. Chairman, I second the motion," or "I second the motion."

Until a motion concerning a subject is made and seconded, no one may discuss that subject. After a motion is made and seconded, no other subject may be discussed until the motion has been disposed of. Too much emphasis cannot be placed on this second point, for unless only one matter is considered at a time, the meeting cannot proceed in an orderly way.

Dividing or amending a motion

A motion up for consideration may be modified in two principal ways: by dividing the question and by amending.

Dividing the question. Sometimes a motion contains two or more parts, each of which can stand alone, though all are related to the same subject. It can be divided into questions to be discussed and voted on separately through the motion to divide the question. In making this motion, the member should state specifically the manner in which the motion should be divided. Each part of the divided motion must be sufficiently independent of the others to be carried out if the other parts are not adopted. If a motion contains several parts or resolutions which relate to different subjects, it must be divided upon the request of one member.

Amending the motion. There are times when some part of the motion is undesirable or not clearly stated. The motion then may be changed

---

[2] You will note that in this treatment of "a subject for discussion," attention is focused primarily on the manner of introducing and handling a *main* motion. Other kinds of motions are classified as privileged, subsidiary, and incidental motions. For information about privileged, subsidiary, and incidental motions, see *Robert's Rules of Order Revised,* Part I, Articles III-V, and the table of parliamentary motions on pages 280–281 of this chapter.

by striking out or adding certain words. Such action requires a motion to amend, which must itself be seconded and passed by a majority vote before it can become a part of the original motion. The proper way to propose an amending motion is: "Mr. Chairman, I move that the motion be amended by striking out the words ('six months') and inserting the words ('one year') so that the motion as amended will read ('this organization shall rent an office in the Student Union Building for one year')." The motion to amend may itself be amended or discussed, but it must be voted upon before the main question can be decided. If the motion to amend is adopted, the discussion will return to the original motion *as amended;* if the amending motion fails, the discussion will return to the original motion *as made.*

A motion to amend must meet two requirements. First, it must be germane; that is, it must be on the same subject as the original motion even though it may conflict with the original motion's purpose entirely. Second, the amending motion must embody a real change. Merely to change the original motion from an affirmative to a negative statement is not permissible. Thus, you could not move to insert "not" after "we" in the motion "that we reduce dues by $5.00." You could, however, move to substitute "increase" for "reduce" in the motion. Though conflicting with the purpose of the original motion, such an amendment is germane. The following example indicates a proper use of the motion to amend:

1. Original motion: ". . . that an expenditure of $500 be authorized for repairing the clubhouse roof."
2. Motion to amend: ". . . that the sum of ('$1000') be substituted for ('$500'), and that the words ('and completely re-covering') be inserted after the word ('repairing'), so that the motion as amended will read. . ."
3. Motion as amended: ". . . that an expenditure of $1000 be authorized for repairing and completely re-covering the clubhouse roof."

Discussing the subject

Any member who is recognized by the chairman may discuss a motion which is before the group, but he must limit his remarks to that motion. As soon as the motion has been settled or disposed of, no further discussion on it is in order unless a motion to reconsider or to rescind the decision is made and approved. A motion to reconsider must be

PARLIAMENTARY PROCEDURE FOR HANDLING MOTIONS

Classification of motions	Types of motions and their purposes	Order of handling	Must be seconded	Can be discussed	Can be amended	Vote required[1]	Can be reconsidered
Main motion	(To present a proposal to the assembly)	Cannot be made while any other motion is pending	Yes	Yes	Yes	Majority	Yes
Subsidiary motions[2]	To postpone indefinitely (to kill a motion)	Has precedence over above motion	Yes	Yes	No	Majority	Affirmative vote only
	To amend (to modify a motion)	Has precedence over above motions	Yes	When motion is debatable	Yes, but only once	Majority	Yes
	To refer (a motion) to committee	Has precedence over above motions	Yes	Yes	Yes	Majority	Until committee takes up subject
	To postpone (discussion of a motion) to a certain time	Has precedence over above motions	Yes	Yes	Yes	Majority	Yes
	To limit discussion (of a motion)	Has precedence over above motions	Yes	No	Yes	Two-thirds	Yes
	Previous question (to take a vote on the pending motion)	Has precedence over above motions	Yes	No	No	Two-thirds	No
	To table (to lay a motion aside until later)	Has precedence over above motions	Yes	No	No	Majority	No
Incidental motions[3]	To suspend the rules (to change the order of business temporarily)	Has precedence over a pending motion when its purpose relates to the motion	Yes	No	No	Two-thirds	No
	To close nominations[4]	[4]	Yes	No	Yes	Two-thirds	No
	To request leave to withdraw or modify a motion[5]	Has precedence over motion to which it pertains and other motions applied to it	No	No	No	Majority[5]	Negative vote only
	To rise to a point of order (to enforce the rules)[6]	Has precedence over pending motion out of which it arises	No	No	No	Chair decides[7]	No
	To appeal from the decision of the chair (to reverse chair's ruling)[6]	Is in order only when made immediately after chair announces ruling	Yes	When ruling was on debatable motion	No	Majority or tie[1]	Yes
	To divide the question (to consider a motion by parts)	Has precedence over motion to which it pertains and motion to postpone indefinitely	[8]	No	Yes	Majority[8]	No
	To object to considera-	In order only when a main motion is first introduced	No	No	No	Two-thirds	Negative vote only

Privileged motions	(to take a standing vote)	Has precedence after question has been put	No	No	No	Chair decides	No
	To call for the orders of the day (to keep meeting to order of business)[6,9]	Has precedence over above motions	No	No	No	No vote required	No
	To raise a question of privilege (to point out noise, etc.)[6]	Has precedence over above motions	No	No	No	Chair decides[7]	No
	To recess[10]	Has precedence over above motions	No[10]	No[10]	Yes	Majority	No
	To adjourn[11]	Has precedence over above motions	No[11]	No[11]	No[11]	Majority	No
	To fix the time to which to adjourn (to set next meeting time)[12]	Has precedence over above motions	No[12]	No[12]	Yes	Majority	Yes
Unclassified motions	To take from the table (to bring up tabled motion for consideration)	Cannot be made while another motion is pending	Yes	No	No	Majority	No
	To reconsider (to discuss and reverse vote on previously decided motion)[13]	Can be made while another motion is pending[13]	Yes	When motion is debatable	No	Majority	No
	To rescind (to repeal decision on a motion)[14]	Cannot be made while another motion is pending	Yes	Yes	Yes	Majority or two-thirds[14]	Negative vote only

[1] A tied vote is always lost except on an appeal from the decision of the chair. The vote is taken on the ruling, not the appeal, and a tie sustains the ruling.

[2] Subsidiary motions are applied to a motion before the assembly for the purpose of disposing of it properly.

[3] Incidental motions are incidental to the conduct of business. Most of them arise out of a pending motion and must be decided before the pending motion is decided.

[4] The chair opens nominations with "Nominations are now in order." Nominations may be made by a nominating committee, by a nominating ballot, or from the floor. A member may move to close nominations, or the chair may declare nominations closed if there is no response to his inquiry, "Are there any further nominations?"

[5] When the motion is before the assembly, the mover requests permission to withdraw or modify it, and if there is no objection from anyone, the chair announces that the motion is withdrawn or modified. If anyone objects, the chair puts the request to a vote.

[6] A member may interrupt a speaker to rise to a point of order or of appeal, to call for orders of the day, or to raise a question of privilege.

[7] Chair's ruling stands unless appealed and reversed.

[8] If propositions or resolutions relate to independent subjects, they must be divided on the request of a single member. The request to divide the question may be made when another member has the floor. If they relate to the same subject but each part can stand alone, they may be divided only on a regular motion and vote.

[9] The regular order of business may be changed by a motion to suspend the rules.

[10] The motion to recess is not privileged if made at a time when no other motion is pending. When not privileged, it can be discussed. When privileged, it cannot be discussed, but can be amended as to length of recess.

[11] The motion to adjourn is not privileged if qualified or if adoption would dissolve the assembly. When not privileged, it can be discussed and amended.

[12] The motion to fix the time to which to adjourn is not privileged if no other motion is pending or if the assembly has scheduled another meeting on the same or following day. When not privileged, it can be discussed.

[13] A motion to reconsider may be made only by one who voted on the prevailing side. It must be made during the meeting at which the vote to be reconsidered was taken, or on the succeeding day of the same session. If reconsideration is moved while another motion is pending, discussion on it is delayed until discussion is completed on the pending motion; then it has precedence over all new motions of equal rank.

[14] It is impossible to rescind any action that has been taken as a result of a motion, but the unexecuted part may be rescinded. Adoption of the motion to rescind requires only a majority vote when notice is given at a previous meeting; it requires a two-thirds vote when no notice is given and the motion to rescind is voted on immediately.

presented by someone who voted with the prevailing side but who wishes to change his vote, and a majority must favor reconsideration. A motion to rescind can be made by any member for the purpose of reversing a decision which has not been carried out. When no advance notice is given, the motion to rescind requires a two-thirds vote.

Certain types of motions cannot be discussed at all but must be put to a vote at once. The most important of these are the following:

1. Motions to call for the correct order of business
2. Motions for immediate vote — "previous question"
3. Motions to table — "lay on the table"
4. Motions to adjourn (usually, but not always)

Disposing of motions

Motions are disposed of in three principal ways: (1) by a vote, (2) by a motion to postpone or to table, and (3) by a motion to refer the proposal to a committee.

1. *Vote on the motion.* Usually the vote on a main motion comes about of its own accord; the important points having been discussed, the group is ready to make a decision. When the chairman senses this attitude, he may suggest a vote, and if there is no objection, he may put the question to a vote. At times, however, opinions toward the proposal are sharply divided and discussion continues vigorously even after all the important arguments have been presented. In such situations, a motion to stop the discussion and to take a vote may be necessary. Such a motion is called the "previous question." This motion cannot be discussed; it must be voted on at once, and it must receive a two-thirds vote for adoption. If adopted, it stops discussion on the main motion and requires that a vote on the main motion be taken at once. In less formal groups, this result may be obtained by calling out "Question!" If no one objects, the chairman puts the pending motion to a vote at once.

2. *Motions to postpone and to table.* The motion to postpone to a certain time and the motion to table remove a proposal from discussion for the time being. The motion to postpone indefinitely, however, kills a proposal — stops all discussion on it.

The motion to postpone to a certain time is made by saying, "Mr. Chairman, I move that the question be postponed until. . ." Adoption of this motion by majority vote permits consideration of the proposal at a more convenient or suitable time.

The motion to table is made by saying, "Mr. Chairman, I move that the question be laid on the table." Adoption of this motion by majority vote removes the proposal from consideration until a motion to take it from the table is made and adopted. Thus, tabling often results in ignoring a proposal or forgetting about it.

The motion to postpone indefinitely is made by saying, "Mr. Chairman, I move that the question be postponed indefinitely." Adoption of this motion by majority vote defeats a proposal indirectly; that is, by voting against consideration of a proposal, the organization indicates its attitude toward the proposal without committing itself on it directly. This motion is often used to test the support or opposition a proposal has; adoption prevents discussion of the proposal unless a motion to reconsider the decision to postpone is made and adopted.

3. *Motion to refer to a committee.* A motion to refer a proposal to a committee, if adopted, has the effect of removing the main motion from consideration by the group and passing it on to the committee indicated. Sometimes the motion refers the matter to a standing committee, or names a special committee, or authorizes the chairman to appoint a committee. The motion may refer the proposal to a committee without instructions, or it may include instructions to investigate and report back to the group. Occasionally it authorizes the committee to take final action. Referral to a committee is an efficient means of handling questions which the group cannot consider in detail.

The form for stating a motion to refer to committee varies with its maker's intent. A few of the forms frequently used are: "Mr. Chairman, I move that the question be referred to the —— committee," or "to the —— committee, with instructions to report at —— [a definite time]," or "to the —— committee, with power to act." When a special committee is needed to consider a proposal, provision for creating that committee must be included in the proposal, as follows: "Mr. Chairman, I move that this question be referred to a committee of —— members to be appointed by the chair," or "—— members, namely, Mr. ——, Miss ——, Mrs. ——, [etc.]," the remainder of the motion continuing as indicated above.

ADJOURNMENT

The meeting may be concluded at the close of business by the adoption of a motion to adjourn. This motion may be introduced at any time and requires a majority vote. It may not be discussed and must be voted upon at once—unless adjournment would have the effect of disbanding the group entirely with no provision for reassembling, in which case the motion to adjourn is subject to discussion. Without this safeguard, business might be left unfinished with no provision for ultimate settlement.

When a group wishes to schedule another meeting on the same or on the following day and has made no provision for such a meeting, a motion to fix the time to which to adjourn must be made and adopted by majority vote. The motion is privileged in these circumstances; that is, it takes precedence over any pending question—it may be introduced and voted upon without discussion while another question is pending.

MODIFYING THE RULES OF ORDER

In small informal groups, not all of the rules listed above may be necessary. As mentioned earlier, parliamentary procedure is designed to expedite the orderly and democratic conduct of business, not to complicate it with unnecessary dogmatism and detail. Larger and more formal groups, on the other hand, usually require more detailed rules than are presented in this chapter. Sometimes the situation calls for the adoption of special rules not listed even in manuals of parliamentary procedure, but fitted to the needs of a particular group. A group may formulate rules to modify and implement the general rules of order discussed in this chapter. Apply the principles of parliamentary procedure as fully as required to preserve order and to expedite business in your group, but only to that degree.

PROBLEMS FOR FURTHER STUDY

1. After consulting *Robert's Rules of Order Revised,* or a similar manual, let different members of the class present oral reports on the following subjects: privileged motions, incidental motions, subsidiary motions, voting, bylaws, and meetings. Provide an opportunity for questions and general class discussion. Use the table of parliamentary motions on pages 280-281 of this chapter as a reference guide.

2. Assume that you are a member of the student council. Phrase four main motions on matters that might come before that body—a proposed change in women's curfew hours, reorganization of the board controlling student publications, programing on the campus TV station, etc.

3. Phrase amendments to each of the motions you prepare for Problem 2. Be sure the amendments are germane and embody a real change.

4. Taking one of the main motions stated for Problem 2, phrase correctly (a) a motion to postpone to a certain time, (b) to table, (c) to refer to a standing committee, and (d) to refer to a special committee.

5. Phrase correctly a motion (a) for the previous question, and (b) to fix the time to which to adjourn.

6. Give an example of a motion that contains more than one part. How should this motion be divided in order to be discussed properly?

SPEAKING ASSIGNMENT

1. Organize the class into a hypothetical meeting of some organization — for example, the student council, the sophomore class, the dramatics club, or the city council — and proceed to conduct business. Be careful to follow correct parliamentary procedure in the order of business and discussion of motions.

SUGGESTIONS FOR FURTHER READING

J. Jeffery Auer, *Essentials of Parliamentary Procedure,* 3rd ed. (New York: Appleton-Century-Crofts, Inc., 1959).

John W. Grey and Richard G. Rea, *Parliamentary Procedure: A Programed Introduction* (Chicago: Scott, Foresman and Company, 1963).

Henry M. Robert, *Robert's Rules of Order Revised* (Chicago: Scott, Foresman and Company, 1951).

SPEECH TO INFORM

Guy Suits (photo, left) vice-president and director of research of the General Electric Company, delivered a talk on "Polymers, Crystals and Plasmas" at the International Symposium on Science, Industry and Education in Oklahoma City, Oklahoma, June 17, 1957.

The speech is recommended for study because it illustrates many of the principles of informative speaking discussed in Chapter 9. Of course, advancements in science since the speech was given would necessitate various changes in content if the speech were given today. For more recent information on the subjects discussed by Dr. Suits, you should refer to such scientific journals as Scientific American.

Dr. Suits, who was born in Oshkosh, Wisconsin, in 1905, was graduated from the University of Wisconsin in 1927 and received an Sc.D. degree at the Swiss Federal Institute of Technology at Zurich in 1929. He holds honorary degrees from several American universities. He joined the General Electric Company in 1930, and in 1945 became vice-president and director of research.

The speaker provided the following answers to our questions.

What training have you had as a speaker? *"Several years ago I took a General Electric course in Effective Presentation. Following that I was active for some time in a luncheon club, the purpose of which was to give members opportunity to practice and improve their public speaking skills."*

How do you prepare your speeches? *"When I am asked to give a formal speech, I prepare a general outline of the argument I wish to present and list the material I plan to use as supporting evidence. This outline is carefully reviewed with a member of our Public Information section, who then checks out the details and prepares a first draft. This draft, and often several later versions, I carefully edit and revise, adding items and rewording sentences or paragraphs, until a final draft can be written. Even this is read and re-read carefully many times before the speech is given."*

Do you read from a manuscript or speak extemporaneously? *"In any formal speech I usually read from a manuscript although I may add extemporaneous notes as the occasion arises, making them suitable for the audience or the occasion."*

What is your philosophy of effective speaking? *"The key to effective speaking is found in the relationship between the speaker and his audience. First, the speech itself must be appropriate to the audience not only in subject matter, but also in the vocabulary used and in the illustrations that are used as supporting evidence for the argument. If the speaker then addresses himself to his audience with a straightforward simplicity and sincerity, without distracting mannerisms of speech or gesture, he will reach his audience effectively."*

What advice might you give to the college student with respect to improving himself as a speaker in preparation for a professional career?

"Whenever an occasion arises, and whenever you have something meaningful to say to a group, take that opportunity. Only by constant practice in speaking, can you reach the point where you are at ease before an audience, and only then are you in a position to devote all of your attention to the marshaling of your thoughts and to the best expression of them. When through experience you add an awareness of the mood and response of your audience and are able to react to it, then you are truly an effective speaker."

Do you regard the ability to speak well as essential to success in a career such as yours? *"The scientist who works in the field of basic research must be able to communicate his ideas, not only to other scientists, but also to the business men and engineers whose acceptance and development of his ideas are essential if those ideas are to be translated into the most useful forms for industry and the general public. Speaking well is an integral part of such communication."*

Would you care to comment on developments since you gave your speech in 1957? *"Polymer research has made extraordinary advances in the past seven years. . . . The diamond business also has flourished. . . . The fusion research commented on in the 1957 talk has continued with gratifying results, although the objective of economic power from the fusion process remains many years away."**

As you read the speech, note that the attention step (paragraph 1) consists of an illustration which arouses interest in the subject and leads directly into the statement of the speaker's central idea (paragraph 8): ". . . it is highly profitable to apply our newest knowledge to the study of the oldest elements. . . ."

The brief need step emphasizes (paragraph 10) the importance of oxygen, carbon, and hydrogen "to industry . . . especially to the electrical industry," and suggests why the audience should know something about scientific developments in areas where these common elements are key elements.

In the satisfaction step, which presents the detailed information and comprises the remainder of the talk, the speech follows a special topical sequence. Each of the major topics covered in this step, though related to the others, stands out clearly as a separate item of consideration. Therefore, one knows at all times what topic is being discussed and how far the speaker has progressed in his discussion of the subject. By limiting himself to three major topics, Dr. Suits held the speech to a manageable length and enabled each topic to be developed fully.

The conclusion of the talk consists of an informal summary stressing the third major topic combined with a reference to the "young friend" mentioned in the attention step. By thus referring to the illustration with which he began, Dr. Suits gave his discussion unity and completeness.

As might be expected in a speech dealing with so technical a subject, explanation was the principal form of support used by the speaker to develop his ideas. But comparison, example, and quotation also were employed when needed, and many specific instances were cited.

The interest value of the speech is enhanced by the easy, colloquial style, an occasional anecdote or startling fact, and predictions concerning thermonuclear reaction. It should be noted that Dr. Suits often developed a topic by moving from simpler to more complex material or by connecting the unknown with the known. (See, for example, paragraphs 11–16 and 34–35.) Both of these technics are especially useful when attempting to make a difficult idea clear to an audience.

---

*Letter to the editors, February 10, 1964.

POLYMERS, CRYSTALS AND PLASMAS*
Guy Suits

Attention step
developed by means
of an illustration
Recently I became engaged in a conversation about my favorite subject—research in science—with a young friend who was particularly impressed with some new information he had just picked up at school concerning the existence of "more than a hundred" chemical elements./1

"If I were going to become a scientist," he asked, "which elements would be the best ones to study? I don't suppose I'd have time for all of them." /2

Since my young friend is only ten years old, he will have a good deal of time to further his research, but as an immediate answer to his question I mentioned five elements and suggested that these five might be especially interesting to study. /3

After a brief session with his junior encyclopedia, my friend returned, and his disappointment was apparent. My stock as a scientific advisor 'had obviously dropped several points. /4

"I looked up a list of all the elements, and gee, some of them were just discovered last year and the year before. But it says all of the ones *you* told me about were 'known to the ancients.'" /5

In an effort to salvage my reputation, I explained that it was true that the elements I had mentioned had been discovered long ago. "But," I said, "they are also very common, very cheap, and very plentiful and because of that they are the ones to which we can add the most value by research. Almost anything we can do to them makes them more valuable." /6

By way of emphasis, I told him that there was a billion dollars worth of silicon right in his back yard, and that some of our scientists had actually made diamonds out of peanut butter, and by then his eyes were fairly popping. Just plain old iron, all by itself, I assured him, has turned out to be the strongest metal of all, and even the strongest metals may not be as useful for tomorrow's world as some materials made out of new combinations of those wonderfully common elements: oxygen, hydrogen, and carbon. And one member of this simple trio, hydrogen, may contain the ultimate answer to our need for safe and inexpensive energy. /7

Central idea
of speech stated
We are at a place in the cycle of scientific progress where it is highly profitable to apply our newest knowledge to the study of the oldest elements—some so old that they were "known to the ancients." /8

Need step
points out importance
of areas to be discussed
Today I intend to focus on three areas of science where exciting progress is being made, areas where the key elements are the simple ones I have mentioned. Sometimes they appear in combination and sometimes very much alone. These are not the only areas of great scientific progress by any means, and I would not belittle the importance of studying elements with fancier names than oxygen, carbon, and hydrogen—that's an important and exciting frontier too. /9

But these fields which I will discuss are particularly interesting and important to industry—and especially to the electrical industry, and they appear so complex that there is every chance that there will still be opportunities in them even when my ten-year-old friend is weighing the approximately 500 job offers he can expect after finishing his graduate studies in science in 1970. /10

*Text furnished by the speaker and used with permission.

Polymers

Satisfaction step
presentation of
detailed information

First major topic intro-
duced with anecdote

Explanation

First, let us consider polymers, because they touch upon human experience so many times each day, and have so much to do with our future. I trust the term "polymer" does not bother you as much as it did a business associate of mine who is better known for his managerial skill than for his technical prowess. Recently, he called me to say, "Why didn't you tell me that this conference on polymers you had at the laboratory last week was all about plastics—I would have come." /11

Perhaps the toothbrush is the first place, each day, where we contact a polymer, although of course we may have slept on one the night before. The toothbrush handle, and probably the bristles too, are made from polymers, as are all plastics. There was a time, about two or maybe three decades ago, when critical users thought that polymers were not much good for anything but toothbrush handles. To be sure, these early polymers had some deficiencies, particularly in strength. Most anything you could make from them would fall apart in your hands, or under foot, and if you wanted to make something really strong you had to use a metal or an alloy. This difference in strength between polymers, as synthetic chemical solids, and metals, as refined natural solids, includes a basic difference in structure. /12

Comparison

If you take any metallic material, polish it and etch the surface, you can readily see the characteristic crystalline structure, generally made up of many small crystals packed together in random array. Consider one crystal in this aggregate; its atoms are arranged in regular layers and rows, much like the eggs in an egg crate. /13

Comparison

If, on the other hand, we could look at a polymer in the same atomic detail it would look vastly different from the highly-ordered metal crystal. Typical polymer molecules are long chains of carbon atoms, strung out like beads on a string. Numerous chemical adornments—invariably including hydrogen and frequently our old friend oxygen—are attached to this string of beads to form side chains that impart much of the chemical and physical character to the polymer. An aggregate of such polymer molecules, if we could see it under a super microscope, might look something like the arrangement of fibres in a sheet of cotton batting—a tangle of long-chain molecules, running in every direction. This classical structural characteristic of polymers is principally accountable for the poor strength of these materials. The molecules themselves are strong. But the aggregate is not, since the individual molecules run in random directions with very little co-ordination between them. We may tie the molecules together, with chemical cross-links, and improve the strength. Another and more successful way would be to make them more crystalline, by lining up the long molecules, or portions of them. Then they would gain strength from their structural regularity, somewhat analogous to the manner in which a woven fabric gains strength in comparison to our cotton batting. /14

Preceding explanation
summarized and im-
portance of develop-
ments pointed out

With this word of introduction, the new look in polymers is very simply explained; they are becoming more crystalline—that is, more highly ordered—and hence stronger. The newest and strongest polymers are a remarkable improvement over the older ones. /15

The new progress—partly in Ziegler process polyethylene, partly in Montecatini polypropylene, partly in numerous developments in this country in new silicones and polycarbonates—is in aggregate a very significant step forward. There is no doubt that polymers have come a long way from the old toothbrush handles. /16

These new high-strength polymers have led the chemists to make some exciting extrapolations into the future, where they see progressively higher strength and better high-temperature performance. This certainly should result in much wider use for polymers in years to come. /17

No doubt polymers will replace *metals* in many applications. In fact, they are doing it now. Most of them aren't yet as strong as most metals in common use, but many metals in use are stronger than they need to be to do the job at hand. /18

Example

To tell the truth, in our research laboratory, we have a friendly fight on right now between the chemists and metallurgists. The chemists say that in another ten or fifteen years or so our company will be using more polymers than metals in our products. That obviously depends to quite an extent on whether it's measured in pounds, cubic feet, or dollars, but the fact that there is room for an argument is in itself significant and indicates clearly that polymers are getting into the running as structural materials. /19

First topic con-
cluded by reference to
opening story

Need I add that the building blocks of these new polymer materials, carbon, oxygen, hydrogen and silicon, are the ones my young friend said were originally discovered a long time ago. /20

Crystals

Transition to second
major topic

Just as polymers are getting better by becoming more crystalline, the metals are improving too through the development of more perfect structure in their crystals. The striking development of so-called "perfect" crystals of the common metals is now well known. We have measured in our laboratory the tensile strength of a perfect crystal of pure iron and found it to be nearly two million pounds per square inch —vastly stronger than any metal or alloy in common use. This important progress is sure to have a practical impact on technology, but just exactly where is not yet certain. Here is another case of value added by science and technology—it's the same old iron "known to the ancients" —merely rearranged atomically. /21

Example

Another important class of crystalline solids, the semiconductors, have become famous for perfection in purity. The rapidly growing new semiconductor industry is presently based on the two elements germanium and silicon, refined by special processes to a total impurity of only one part per billion. When a new development like this comes about, people interested in minerals start looking for a good ore supply for the new industry, and people interested in speculating start looking for stock in the company that finds the new mineral. In the case of germanium, it was soon found that the principal source was the flues of zinc refineries, where it collects as a minor impurity and is available as a by-product. More recently, primary germanium ores from Africa have become available. /22

When methods were worked out for refining *silicon* to semiconductor grade, a few years ago, some prospecting for ore took place in speculative quarters, but not for long, for the basic supply of silicon ore is excellent; in fact, we've far too much of it. Practically all of the rocks and sand and dirt on earth, with minor exceptions, are full of silicon, which is the most abundant solid on our earth. Thus nearly everyone who owns real estate has extensive mineral rights to silicon, which of course isn't worth much until it's refined to semiconductor-grade material, when its value goes up to as much as one thousand dollars a pound. This value has been added by research and processing and is a striking illustration of making something of great value out of something of almost no value, by the application of modern technology. /23

Hypothetical illustra-
tion with surprise twist
Now let's look into that billion dollars worth of silicon that my small friend and you have in your back yards. First we'll have to dig the silicon ore. The most convenient might be an open pit or surface mine which will of course ruin the lawn and flower beds and will be pretty unsightly. The neighbors might object to having a mess like that on your street, and they might worry about the kids falling in the excavation, and there's probably a local ordinance against mining in your neighborhood, and a lot of other things. But let's overlook all of these practical matters, and see what the silicon might be worth, potentially. /24

If the lot is 100 feet wide and extends back 100 feet from the street, and we excavate to a depth of 100 feet, we would have approximately one million cubic feet of low-grade silicon ore, commonly known as dirt, sand and stone. If this were high-grade ore, it might yield, after processing, about 25 pounds of silicon per cubic foot, but to be conservative we'll plan on only one pound, to allow for some waste and inefficiency. However, that still yields one million pounds of silicon which is *potentially* worth *one billion dollars!* But wait! Don't spend the money—there will be a small processing charge; in fact, the processing cost will be very nearly one billion dollars. This theoretical mining operation, right at home, points up the tremendous ability of modern technology to add value and utility, to supply human needs and wants, and to create wealth from common sources; in short, to perform modern alchemy. /25

Example
Super-pressure research—which a couple of years ago resulted in a process for making diamonds—and more recently, that still more glamorous and valuable substance, borazon, is another prime example of value added by science and technology. It's no secret that diamond, whether made by nature *or* in the laboratory, was transformed from carbon, which in comparison to diamond has almost no value. Even a 49-cent jar of peanut butter has a healthy content of carbon. Since scientists, like everybody else, can't resist having some fun with their work now and then, one of ours recently tried to make diamonds out of peanut butter. He succeeded, but I hasten to add that it's not quite as simple as it sounds. Also, peanut butter, in comparison with some other carbonaceous compounds, just isn't a very good material to start with— at least not good enough to justify further investigation into the relative merits of creamy style versus crunchy style. /26

Plasmas: Stellar Temperatures and Fusion

Third main topic
introduced
As far back as anyone can remember in the arts and sciences, the attainment of high temperatures has been important. High and ever higher temperature continues to be a primary objective of modern scientific research in many fields, with significant technological progress dependent upon the results. Scientific news these days seems dominated by items about high-temperature alloys, high-temperature vacuum tubes and electronic circuits, high-temperature semiconductors, high-

temperature strength in polymers, and—if you will excuse the expression—many other similar hot topics. Nowhere is this goal of high temperature more enticing and exciting than in the study of high-temperature gas plasmas. And nowhere are we talking about such high temperatures, since here techniques are emerging for heating gases to millions of degrees—temperatures that are known to exist in the stars but which have until recently not been available in the laboratory. /27

Explanation

The primary objective of these techniques is to bring under control the process of the hydrogen bomb so that it can be peacefully employed for the production of energy. This process—called a thermonuclear reaction—works by fusing together light atoms to form heavier atoms, with a resultant release of energy. The fusion process is not only the basic process of the hydrogen bomb, but is also the accepted explanation of the prodigious energy production of the sun. The first public discussion of the possibility that the thermonuclear process might be controlled and used for energy production was made by an Indian scientist, Dr. H. J. Bhabha, at the Geneva Conferences on the Peaceful Uses of Atomic Energy in 1955. /28

Subsequently, in April of 1956, the Russian scientist Kurchatov, speaking at the British Atomic Energy Establishment at Harwell, described experiments with stellar temperatures with controlled fusion as an objective. In July 1956, some U.S. work sponsored by the AEC was revealed in a paper by Dr. Richard Post of the University of California Radiation Laboratory. /29

From all of these sources there is now developing the outline, or at least a shadow, of future scientific discoveries potentially of great significance. Because many important scientific events in the past, for example, the nuclear chain reaction, have cast a prophetic shadow in advance of their arrival, there is a strong temptation to jump to the conclusion that the controlled thermonuclear reaction is practically here, or just around the corner. If that is the case, the announcement has not come to my attention. In any event, there is a little too much optimism in some quarters about fusion power, and one would be well advised to relax a bit and thoughtfully consider the nature of the discovery we contemplate will be made, and its possible consequences. And—most important—we should consider how long it will take for this proposed discovery to be felt at home. In this particular scientific challenge, the goal is so immense that there is a correspondingly great need to clearly delineate the difference between hope and accomplishment, for thus far research on a controlled fusion reaction has been much more productive of hope than of power. I am thoroughly convinced, however, that in the longer term these hopes cannot be denied and that eventually a reluctant nature must be made to yield a controlled thermonuclear reaction for energy generation. But vast harm can be done by a myopic view of fusion, and in the appraisal of this not-impossible technological event there is a clear need for perspective and balance. /30

Comparison used as basis for prediction

For perspective, let us review the chronology of the fission, or atom-splitting, process, on which all present atomic power plans are being based. The process was discovered in 1938 and subsequently underwent intensive development in the atomic bomb project. The first appreciable consideration of the possible application of fission to power production dates from 1942, when Fermi's group actually accomplished a chain reaction. Extensive efforts and corresponding expenditures have been made since then to bring this older process of the atomic age to the start of practical use. The *start* of practical use will be approximately 1960. I am overlooking several earlier small-scale pilot power plants and also the important fact that the large-scale plants which will then be in production will at best show only marginal economy. Thus it will have taken approximately eighteen years to bring fission, as a technically feasible new energy process, from Fermi's laboratory to a position where power from Commonwealth Edison's Dresden station may begin to help light that historic room under the University of Chicago stadium. /31

Now, let's look at the timetable for the hydrogen process. Since a technically feasible (not necessarily economically feasible) *fusion* process has not been announced, it is safe to assume that we are not yet at the starting point corresponding to 1942 in the fission process. Furthermore, it is a fact of technological life that a very long time is required to develop technically complex, large-scale power machinery, and the development of fusion, *after a successful process is in hand,* will be subject to this reality. /32

My own view is that: (1) five additional years of research will be required to make possible a realistic appraisal of the fusion process, (2) in ten years we may be at the point of technical feasibility, and (3) pilot-plant production of fusion power will not begin for twenty years. Competitive economic power production lies beyond that. In this picture there is a clear role for power production by fission in the near future, and power by fusion for the longer term. Fission power is technically feasible today, will rapidly become competitive with older energy sources, and is supported by a fifteen-year investment in specialized technology as a firm foundation for growth. The final phasing-in of fusion power, if it eventually becomes feasible, will be greatly facilitated by the accumulated atomic power experience of the utility industry, which by that time will add up to at least two, and perhaps three decades. /33

Transition

Explanation

It is now appropriate to turn from the possible *chronology* of fusion to the *science* of fusion as it looks in the laboratory. To the researcher in the physical sciences, it would be hard to find a more fascinating and challenging problem than fusion. To bring stellar temperatures into the laboratory for study is a dream that, until recently, few astrophysicists would have had the courage to express. Yet the work already reported gives considerable substance to this dream. Perhaps the most important single concept so far is that of magnetic containment. At first sight it would appear to be impossible to contain a gas at a temperature of many millions of degrees, since all known materials melt and vaporize at very much lower temperatures. But stellar gas is a very special gas indeed, so much so that it has been referred to as a "fourth form of matter," to be considered along with conventional gases, liquids and solids. /34

At room temperatures, common gases are electrically insulating— that is, they prevent the passage of appreciable electric current. As the temperature of a gas is raised, it becomes progressively a better electrical conductor because the gas atoms ionize and become electrical in character. This in itself is not new because an ionized gas as a conductor of electricity has long been an article of commerce. Ionized gas fills fluorescent lamps and generates the ultraviolet radiation which causes their phosphors to give off light. Ionized gas is the basis for a wide variety of electron tubes which are important in radio, TV, communication, industrial and military equipment. Finally, ionized gas plays a fundamental. role in the interruption of circuits carrying electric current. In the large electric circuit breakers employed in power systems the ionized gas, or arc, is generally controlled by a magnetic field, and this fact is the clue to stellar temperatures. A gas at a temperature of a million degrees is an electrical gas. It is fully ionized—that is, each gas atom is an electrical charge carrier. This fully ionized or electrical gas is a good conductor of electricity (at ten million degrees its conductivity would be comparable to copper). It also can be controlled with a magnetic field. In this fact lies the hope of bringing stellar temperatures into the laboratory, and eventually of achieving a successful fusion reaction. The idea is to make a "magnetic container" that will hold a bit of cosmic plasma so that it never touches the walls; just how to do this still stumps the experts, and how to fill the container is another sticky problem to be worked out. And to make it more difficult, it isn't a million degrees, but 100 million degrees that we must have eventually. But we have a foot in the door, and in response to what will eventually become an overwhelming need, nature must, if at all possible, be made to yield a successful answer to this effort. /35

In spite of the reservations I have mentioned about the length of time it may take to realize the goal of practical power from fusion, at our research laboratory we are convinced that the ultimate importance of safe and inexpensive power from hydrogen makes it essential for us to study the problem right now. We have established at the General Electric Research Laboratory in Schenectady a substantial research program to study the fusion process. It would be presumptuous for me to compare the magnitude of our effort with that of the AEC's famous Project Sherwood, but we *do* expect to focus the traditional skills of the electrical industry on this primarily electrical problem. We believe it is important for both industry and government to be engaged in studying matters of such great importance to our future. Our work on fusion has been going on for over a year and is expanding. We do not yet have any results to announce publicly and—frankly—have no expectations of building fusion pilot plants in the near future. /36

Use of quotation

As Dr. Henry Hurwitz, who is heading up our fusion program, has put it, "The processes for generating and containing a thermonuclear plasma employ magnetic fields, electric discharge phenomena, power circuit design, and current-handling methods. Fusion technology, as now conceived, thus employs the most basic technical skills of the electrical industry and it is inevitable that the industry can contribute heavily to this important development." /37

Informal summary that stresses third major topic combined with reference to opening illustration

My ten-year-old friend may not have to look very far down the list of elements on the periodic table to find something to concentrate on. The very first on the list, and supposedly the "simplest," is hydrogen. Right now I'd be willing to bet that—if he wants to become an expert on hydrogen—when my young friend is looking over those 500 job offers in 1970 he'll find that one of them is from us. /38

Speeches to Inform for Collateral Study

1. Karl Brandt, "The Population Dilemma," *Vital Speeches*, XXIX (August 1, 1963), 629–631.

2. Karl T. Compton, "The State of Science," *The Age of Danger*, ed. Harold F. Harding (New York: Random House, 1952), pp. 294–312.

3. Paul D. Kilburn, "Contamination of the Environment," *Vital Speeches*, XXIX (May 15, 1963), 475–478.

4. Willy Ley, "The Conquest of Space," *Representative American Speeches: 1960–1961*, ed. Lester Thonssen (New York: H. W. Wilson Company, 1961), pp. 115–130.

5. Samuel Shenberg, "An Experiment in Industry-Education," *Vital Speeches*, XXX (November 15, 1963), 90–93.

SPEECH TO PERSUADE

The following speech, "The Case for Balance," illustrates many qualities of a good persuasive talk. It was given by Thomas J. Watson, Jr. (photo, left) at the dinner session of the forty-sixth annual meeting of the American Council on Education, Washington, D.C., October 3, 1963.

The American Council on Education is an organization for coordinating activities designed to improve education in the United States and throughout the world. It consists of more than 1000 cooperating organizations and institutions.

The speaker, chairman of the board of International Business Machines Corporation, was born in Dayton, Ohio, in 1914, and was graduated from Brown University in 1937. Since then, except for five years as a pilot in the Air Force during World War II, he has been associated with IBM, which his father formerly served as president and board chairman. He was president of the company from 1952 to 1961, when he became chairman of the board. In addition to his position with IBM, Mr. Watson sits on the boards of numerous corporations, educational institutions, and welfare agencies.

Note that the subject and purpose of his speech were well adapted to the interests of the educators who formed his audience. Moreover, Mr. Watson's position with IBM, which employs "as many able [scientists and engineers as it] . . . can find" (paragraph 13), made his plea for increased attention to the humanities in contemporary education all the more impressive.

As marginal annotations indicate, the speech follows closely the steps in the motivated sequence. After a brief attention step in which the speaker greeted his audience, he plunged immediately into a consideration of the problem.

Because the purpose of the speech is to present a "case" for the humanities by showing why they should be given proper emphasis, the need step is unusually long, occupying, in fact, more than three-fourths of the entire talk. It sets forth two major ideas or contentions: (1 – paragraph 14) the humanities are not receiving proper emphasis; (2 – paragraph 25) the humanities are more important today than ever before. The first of these contentions is developed in a cause-effect sequence and is supported by explanation and statistics; the second is supported principally by explanation and by an illustration which draws authority from the speaker's position as a manufacturer of business machines and computers. The two contentions are related so as to form a coherent argument.

In the brief satisfaction step, Mr. Watson's proposal of a National Foundation for the Humanities and Arts is bolstered by his remark that legislation to create such a Foundation already has been introduced into Congress and is favored by many educators.

The visualization and action steps are combined. A direct appeal to the audience precedes the visualization step, which is developed by the negative method and which predicts the evils that will accrue if the humanities continue to be neglected. The concluding remarks consist of a confident assertion that the problem will be met and the evils corrected.

Throughout the talk, the speaker's contentions are supported by a variety of factual material, and ideas are presented in a lively, informal style. Major points frequently are tied together by rhetorical questions and internal summaries.

THE CASE FOR BALANCE*
Thomas J. Watson, Jr.

Attention step
Personal greeting combined with compliments to the audience

I can't begin to tell you how delighted I am to be here tonight. When I was invited to speak to you, I accepted at once because I knew the distinction of this group and because by associating with outstanding educators, I have always been able to learn something myself. /1

Need step
Speaker identifies himself as associated with IBM
First point under need developed by cause-effect sequence, supported by explanation

I have a great faith in education. Along with an affirmation of that faith tonight, I want to express a concern about the current course of education—a concern which has come to me both as a citizen and as a representative of an industry which is involved in some of the rapid changes now taking place in our twentieth century world. /2

That concern had its origin just six years ago tomorrow. It was the day that the Soviet Union put Sputnik I in orbit. Do you remember the thoughts which flooded in on us that day? Thoughts of embarrassment —dismay—concern. /3

To be sure, there were lots of ways of explaining away the Russians' lead and many of us wanted to do that. We could say that they had captured outstanding German rocket scientists in World War II; that for years after the war they had been working on rockets of great thrust while we had done little or nothing; that they could not make atomic bombs compact enough to go into small missiles and therefore had to build powerful engines which were also convenient for putting space vehicles into orbit. /4

We could even try to say that satellites were just stunts, that Sputnik was a silly hunk of iron. But try as we would to whistle in the dark, Americans finally had to reach the conclusion that the Russians had outdistanced us at least temporarily in the exploration of space, a pursuit which in our century might well become as important as the exploration of the oceans had been in the time of Columbus and Magellan. /5

Rhetorical question used in transition from cause to effect

So what happened? You know the answer well. /6

As Sputnik circled the earth, a great change began to take place in our country. We began a large national effort to scrutinize our resources, to see where we were falling short, to make sure that in the intensifying competition between us and the Soviet Union, we would not end up in second place. /7

---

*Text furnished by the speaker and used with permission.

That effort has given the world another example of the greatness and the power of the democratic system of the United States of America — another historic example of how this great cumbersome country of ours, when confronted with a serious problem, pulls itself together, makes decisions, and takes vigorous steps toward correction. /8

We reorganized the Department of Defense, cut down interservice rivalry, and strengthened the control of the President and the Secretary of Defense over military operations and research on missiles and rockets. /9

We established a new National Aeronautics and Space Administration and through it have already produced weather probes, Telstar and intercontinental television, and the flights of the astronauts. /10

Closer to your own professional area, we wrote into law a National Defense Education Act designed to improve the teaching of science, mathematics and foreign languages. The Act also encouraged promising students to enter careers in science and engineering. /11

Under this Act and through the leadership of such organizations as your own and the National Science Foundation, a massive effort has been under way to drive forward in the teaching of science, mathematics, and engineering from first grade through college. /12

I need not further detail these extensive and exciting advances. You know them well — you helped bring them about. And let me add that I should be the last person to deplore them. As you might suspect, we in the IBM Company tend to have a good opinion of computers. We make and sell as many as we can, here and overseas. Scientists and engineers are vital to our success. We employ as many able ones as we can find. Our livelihood depends on their explorations. /13

But having said this, I want to also say that these events of the past six years have had an impact on education which should concern us all — educators, businessmen and citizens. You know this impact well: It has thrown the sciences and the humanities badly out of balance. /14

In the blazing light of man-made comets, the continuing need for an appropriate balance between science and the humanities has been blotted out. /15.

When a balance existed there was rough equality of opportunity in technical and humanist careers in universities and in the business world. Students are very practical and impressionable young people. Most good undergraduates tend to aim in the direction of greatest opportunity in and out of the university. Today a youngster in high school or college can see a striking contrast between the rewards in science and those in the humanities and arts. /16

One recent survey shows that in employment outside the academic world, nearly all natural scientists expect to earn $5,000 a year or more immediately upon receiving a Ph.D. In contrast, fewer than one-half the humanists expect to command such a salary. Graduate students in the natural sciences expect, by the age of 45, to be able to earn more than $13,000 a year; the humanists hope for less than three-quarters of that amount. /17

The spread is smaller inside the academic world, but there the humanists, as you know, still have to resign themselves to longer hours of teaching and supervisory work in return for less money. And they can expect few of the fringe benefits which come the way of the scientist

Effect on humanities stated, narrowing problem to specific areas

Ramification of first point under need stated and supported by explanation and statistics

—Federal stipends for summer research, Federal post-doctoral fellowships, and even corporate consulting contracts. /18

We live in an increasingly technological world and it is natural that the people who are immediately concerned with bringing this progress about become more important in our scheme of things. However, we cannot afford to let the importance of the technical make us forget the very great importance of proper emphasis on the humanities and arts. /19

My own university received more than one and one-half million dollars from the Federal Government for Engineering last year. By contrast, History got sixteen thousand. /20

In the fiscal year of 1961, of all Federal funds for basic research, the physical and biological sciences got 97 per cent. /21

It is quite natural that the Government has been emphasizing the technical side of education and research in its support programs. Any other course would have been most unwise. We know that the Soviet Union has been emphasizing this side of their education for years with impressive results. To have not responded to their challenge would have been the height of folly. /22

Yet, when we look at the number of new teachers we shall need in this decade, we have to face this inescapable fact: that we are not producing enough Ph.D.'s in English, in foreign languages, in the fine arts; not even enough college graduates trained to teach English in high school. /23

Such evidences of decline in the humanities and arts are not new to you. Sputnik intensified them. And, I believe the time has come to arrest that decline. /24

Second major point under need stated and supported by explanation

There are many traditional reasons for re-emphasizing the humanities—which today are more important than ever. /25

In the first place, a thorough grounding in the humanities is vital training for many phases of leadership—for the preparation of leaders who can wisely manage people as well as efficiently manage machines. This need exists in universities, in public service and in business. /26

Secondly, as our planet continues to shrink, we will more and more have to become citizens of the world. We must acquire a better understanding of the language, history and culture of people of other lands. With present day mass-destruction weapons, this understanding is not just desirable—it's vital. /27

Finally, the greater our skills in the humanities—in literature and the arts—the greater our capacity for a constructive use of leisure time, which is bound to increase as machines lift old burdens from men's shoulders and minds. /28

Transition into principal argument under this point

The argument for the humanities, however, does not end there. /29

To my mind, their most compelling justification is simply this: that without the humanities we cannot adequately solve the most crucial problems we face, either as a society or as a member of the world community. /30

Let's get down to cases. Consider the headlines in any typical metropolitan daily newspaper. What questions lie behind the foremost news stories of these days:

What policy should we follow in South Vietnam?

Specific instances lend emphasis to argument

What should we do about our hundreds of thousands of unemployed teenagers, and about our millions of grown men and

298   Appendix

women who for months have looked for work without finding it? How can we best wage ideological competition with the Communist world?

—Or even one as simple as: Do we now ship grain to the Russians? /31

Point supported by additional explanation

No one of these problems can be solved by the application of scientific knowledge alone. Good answers to these questions require valid assumptions about ethics, about the responsibility of a state to its citizens, about the rights of an individual within the state, about the nature of Buddhism, about the differences between the ideology of the Marxists and the ideology of the free world of the West. /32

American solutions must come from background steeped in the philosophies of Paine, Jefferson, Madison—John Adams, John Marshall, Oliver Wendell Holmes and countless others who have contributed to the wide ranging and free mind of the well-educated American. /33

Speaker's position strengthened by admission that computers cannot solve mankind's problems

Let me add that computers can contribute little to the solutions either. /34

As a manufacturer of computers, I feel both shocked and alarmed whenever I hear the prediction—and I hear it often—that one day "the machines will take over" and give us the answers to everything. /35

A computer is a machine and a machine is a tool—a means to an end—nothing more. To be sure, the tools of today will far outstrip those of the past. We live in an age when machines can do things they have never done before—can, for example, take orders, design manufacturing specifications, set rates of production, give data on purchasing, and order stock for warehouses. /36

Machines can even do a little scholarly work. It is just a beginning, but machines can now begin to do a little useful translation of foreign languages. /37

But whatever we teach computers to do, the machines will still be only a means. /38

Illustration

Let me give you a specific example. Just assume we were using an electronic computer to try to determine what we should do about civil rights in the United States. /39

First we might ask the computer questions like these: Do Negroes have the right to freedom of speech, freedom of assembly? Do they have the right to vote? Do they have the right to go to college? Do they have the right to enter the professions? /40

To each of these questions—the machine would flash back the answer "yes." In fact, if not programmed properly, it might even conclude that we had no civil rights problem at all. /41

But, in fairness, we would then have to ask the machine other questions such as these: Have many Negroes in fact voted in recent elections state by state? Has a reasonable percentage of Negroes actually been able to go to college? Have a disproportionate number dropped out of grade school? Have many reached top managerial and professional jobs? /42

To these questions the machine would have to answer "no." And then go on to inform us that a problem certainly does exist. /43

But, after having identified the problem, the machine could *not* then type out a solution. It could not because the solution to a problem such as this would require the exercise of a value judgment. Until somebody—some human being—inserts a value judgment into the machine, it has no preference whatsoever for racial harmony over racial violence or for brotherhood over bloodshed. It has no conscience. /44

Most important of all, to resolve the fundamental issues we face today, it is not enough to *know* the right. What we need over and above *knowledge* of the right is an inspired will to *do* the right as individuals and as a society. Such inspiration, even in an age of the most advanced thinking machines we can imagine, will continue to be the province of the humanities, of literature, philosophy and the arts. /45

Quotation clarifies and reinforces preceding statement

As Wordsworth wrote, poetry is not just truth, but "truth carried alive into the heart by passion." /46

Central ideas of need step summarized

Satisfaction step—*rhetorical question leads up to speaker's proposal*

The imbalance in American education is evident. /47

The need to restore the humanities and the arts is clear. /48

What specific means should we pursue? /49

Each of you probably has a better and clearer answer to that question than I. You may even think it a presumption that I elect to talk on the subject. I do so with humility, but with the knowledge that while advancing technology has paid my salary in business for 26 years—I have been inspired to work through imagination and ambition gained from the humanities and the arts. /50

So to presume further let me make a few very simple suggestions. /51

As you know, in 1950 the Congress of the United States established the National Science Foundation. /52

Feasibility of proposal indicated by use of analogy

I believe the time has now arrived to establish a National Foundation for the Humanities and Arts, which will accomplish for this area what the National Science Foundation has accomplished for the sciences. As many of you doubtless know, legislation proposing such an institution—within the Department of Health, Education and Welfare—has been introduced in the Congress. Many educators have supported this bill, though some would prefer a different approach such as the creation of an independent agency, like the National Science Foundation itself. /53

I am less concerned with the location of such a foundation than with its early establishment. And I am not arguing that its budget match that of the National Science Foundation. But I am arguing that we do something at once to arrest the decline of the humanities. We cannot afford to let it continue. /54

Visualization and Action steps *are combined*

Action will not come, however, without the biggest single need of all: a fighting case for the humanities. /55

We confront the unfortunate habit of many Americans to consider an idea of Thomas Jefferson as something less real than a missile in its silo, to regard a concept of civil rights as something less real than a computer, to think of the arts as frill, not substance. On this sixth anniversary of the flight of Sputnik, we can be sure of one thing: no second Sputnik will come along to jolt us into action, and do for American education in the humanities what the first Sputnik did for American education in the sciences. /56

Direct appeal to the audience

That job must really be done by you. If you are in general agreement about the problem and if you will attack it as you have other educational problems of the past, the imbalance will soon be corrected. /57

Science and technology give us the tools and make us the machines, but the humanities, above all, dictate the job we will do with those tools and machines, and inspire us to do it. That job has never been defined better than it is in the sentence inscribed in marble around the inside of the memorial to Thomas Jefferson here in Washington: "I have sworn upon the altar of God eternal hostility against every form of tyranny over the mind of man." /58

Quotation clarifies and reinforces preceding appeal

To the extent that we fail to renew our acquaintance with such ideas, we forget what the United States is. /59

Negative method used in development of visualization step

To the extent that we forget the disciplines of humane learning, neglect scholarship in literature, history and philosophy, and diminish our capacity for handling ideas as well as we handle implements, we shall fail to arrive at balanced and intelligent solutions to our toughest current human problems. /60

And to the extent that we cut ourselves off from the inspirational power that is the unique characteristic of the humanities, we shall fail to do the right, even though we know the right. /61

And if we fail in these things as a nation, we fail absolutely. /62

But we shall certainly not fail. /63

Attempt to convert proposal into a definitely fixed attitude or belief and to conclude on a confident note

For each of us in this room tonight knows that we can as a society recall and relive our supreme inheritance from ancient Athens handed down through more than two thousand years of humane learning — that, above all, happiness is not in the possession of property but in the pursuit of wisdom — and in action which accords with virtue. /64

Speeches to Persuade for Collateral Study

1. John H. Fischer, "Educational Problems of Segregation and Desegregation of Public Schools," *Representative American Speeches: 1962–1963,* ed. Lester Thonssen (New York: H. W. Wilson Company, 1963), pp. 111–121.

2. Martin Luther King, "I Have a Dream." Excerpts printed in *The New York Times,* August 29, 1963. Speech printed in pamphlet form by the John Henry and Mary Louisa Dunn Bryant Foundation, Los Angeles 29, California.

3. Robert J. McCracken, "To Have and Not to Hold," *Representative American Speeches: 1959–1960,* ed. Lester Thonssen (New York: H. W. Wilson Company, 1960), pp. 173–180.

4. Robert T. Oliver, "Culture and Communication," *Vital Speeches,* XXIX (September 15, 1963), 721–724.

5. Adlai E. Stevenson, "Trained Intelligence — the Nation's Greatest Weapon," *Vital Speeches,* XXIX (July 15, 1963), 581–584.

GOODWILL SPEECH

The following address, "Television's Role in the American Democracy," was presented by Robert W. Sarnoff, chairman of the board of the National Broadcasting Company, before the Chicago World Trade Conference, Chicago, Illinois, March 5, 1963.

As you know, a goodwill speech is a "cross" between an informative and a persuasive speech, combining elements of both. By increasing the audience's understanding of a person, practice, or institution, or by removing doubts and uncertainties concerning it, the speaker hopes to develop a more tolerant or appreciative attitude which in the future may be translated into active support.

In so far as the audience's present attitude appears to be rooted in a lack of knowledge about the subject, the speaker usually tends to stress the informative aspects of his talk; in so far as it appears to lie in doubts or objections, he tends to make his speech more refutatory and hence persuasive.

Note that this speech leans in the second of these directions. Because television had been under attack from many quarters, the speaker set out to meet those criticisms. His principal method of doing so, however, was to stress television's accomplishments and to explain the problems it faced. By giving his listeners a greater appreciation of these he hoped, as he indicated in paragraph 40, to improve their "understanding of the total dimension of . . . television service—its contribution to the political processes that keep us free, its impact upon the economic forces which keep America strong."

Your study of the speech may be more profitable if you have this information supplied by the speaker. In response to questions about his background as a speaker and his views on speaking, Mr. Sarnoff said:

"I believe public-speaking ability is a great asset in business and helpful in achieving success. At the same time, however, there are many successful men who are not particularly good speakers.

"Although some years ago I received brief instruction in delivery, I have had no formal training in speaking. If I were starting over, I would take speaking and debating in college, because I believe that such training is helpful in teaching how to organize thoughts and how to engage and hold an audience.

"In my own talks I use a manuscript or speak extemporaneously, depending upon the occasion and circumstances. In preparing, I first decide upon a principal subject, then talk it out with one or more of my associates until I am satisfied that the ideas are right. Next I have the material researched and prepare a first draft and follow that with as many drafts as necessary until I am satisfied with the language and the way the subject has been developed. My basic philosophy is that a talk should be short, simple and to the point, so that the audience may leave with the memory of one important thought or idea.

"In my opinion, a college student can best improve himself as a speaker by taking at least one course in public speaking and by practicing as much as possible by seeking opportunities to speak both to large audiences and in small, intimate groups. He should, if possible, listen critically to recordings of his own voice and study accomplished speakers to learn proper use of gestures and voice inflection.

"Finally, I believe the successful business executive has a definite responsibility to assume leadership in affairs outside his company. Business has become so integral a part of community life that no business leader can limit his responsibilities to his office."*

TELEVISION'S ROLE IN THE AMERICAN DEMOCRACY**
Robert W. Sarnoff

It is a high honor to be asked to speak before this knowledgeable audience, and I am grateful for your challenging invitation. /1

In approaching my assignment this evening, I am mindful of the many eminent men of government and industry who have

---

*Letter to the editors, February 13, 1964.
**Text furnished by the speaker and used with permission.

occupied this rostrum in the past. This fills me with a sense of modesty, and brings to mind a remark made by another speaker on a different occasion. That, as you may recall, was when Sir Winston Churchill said of his personal friend and political foe, Clement Attlee: "He is a modest man with much to be modest about." /2

Since your last annual conference, the world has experienced both change and stalemate, and from the vantage point of the West, a normal complement of frustrations. There are fresh Indian graves in the Himalayas. Draining jungle wars continue in Southeast Asia. The Wall still stands in Berlin, and Cuba remains a communist fortress in our hemispheric seas. Even the rupture between the two goliaths of world communism was prompted by *how*—not whether—to bury us. /3

Yet, the past year has also seen resolute strides by those nations with a commitment to freedom. In no section of the earth did we yield peoples or principles to communism, and we recently passed the eyeball test without a blink.* In such critical outposts as Formosa and West Berlin, our posture is stronger, not weaker, than a year ago. In the contest beyond the earth's atmosphere, our astronauts brought us nearer to competitive parity with Russia; and our unmanned satellites, such as Telstar, Tiros and Relay, gave us clear leadership in global space communications. /4

But if I were to single out one event of paramount significance in the last year, it would be the performance of the American economy. Its continued resilience and strength, its ability to weather the worst market collapse in thirty-three years and then resume its forward progress, were more meaningful than any political event. There would be no free Berlins, no pacified Congos, if this powerful machine of individual and competitive enterprise were to falter and to fail. /5

In a recent, eloquent statement President Kennedy said: "We shall be judged more by what we do at home than what we preach abroad. Nothing we could do to help the developing countries would help them half as much as a booming United States economy. And nothing our opponents could do to encourage their own ambitions would encourage them half as much as a lagging United States economy." /6

Free Society—Free Enterprise

It is to the indivisible goal of keeping our economy strong and our society free that I would like to address myself. And I hope it will not be regarded as immodest of me to suggest that the industry I represent—television—plays a role of decisive importance in stimulating economic growth and in reinforcing the strength of our democratic process. /7

Essentially, democracy is a union of two concepts. Television was born of both and supports both. /8

One is the concept of free expression which the late Judge Learned Hand characterized as "brave reliance upon free discussion." Rooted in tradition and sheltered by law, it holds that citizens of a democracy, given free access to knowledge, and freedom to discuss issues and views, can best judge their own interests and best guide their own destiny. /9

The other is the concept of a competitive free enterprise economy as best calculated to meet the needs of the individual and the nation. It has a dual premise: that open competition for public favor spurs the constant improvement of goods and services; and that the encouragement of mass demand sparks mass production, which, in turn, decreases the cost and increases the availability of these goods and services. /10

Both of these principles center on the individual as the master, not the servant, of the state; and both support the conviction that he can best realize his aspirations through ways of his own choosing. The opposite is true of the closed society, where the state is the master, controlling personal expression, political choice and all economic activity. The combat between the two systems is waged at every level—not only as a war of ideas, but as a war of economic strength. /11

Historically, free enterprise and democracy have nourished one another. The revolutions that led to the modern political systems of the West also fostered the rise of mercantile enterprise, the forerunner of the modern competitive free economy. Up to this day,

*Reference is to the Cuban crisis of October 1962. [Editor's note.]

those nations achieving the highest degree of consumer-oriented industrialization have also attained the most effective self-government. /12

Television's role in supporting this economic and political process is often obscured by the pervasive yet intimate nature of the service it offers. Most people have strong and subjective programming likes and dislikes. They might love the Beverly Hillbillies and be bored by the NBC Opera, or vice versa. They might become irritated by a commercial, or by a newscaster's comments on a subject where they have a preconceived judgment. The net effect — and this is perfectly natural — is that their personal preferences tend to eclipse a broader understanding of the medium's catalytic function in our society. I suggest the time is overdue for thoughtful Americans to begin evaluating the total dimension of the television service. /13

Its physical dimension is that of a service meeting so many needs and demands that in the United States in the last dozen years its circulation has grown from $10\frac{1}{2}$ million sets to nearly 59 million. The number of television stations, both commercial and noncommercial, has increased from 107 to 647. And television advertisers have expanded their annual expenditures from \$332 million to $1\frac{3}{4}$ billion. /14

Our technology and programming have also provided substantial impetus to the growth of television abroad, in both the established and the emerging nations. From 1951 through 1961, the last year for which figures are available, the number of sets outside North America grew from 1.2 million to 54 million. At the current rate of growth, the total will probably exceed 74 million by the end of this year. /15

To understand television's economic role, one must first relate it to the nature of our economy. Economic growth, as you who live by trade are well aware, hinges on mounting production and a high level of employment, both stimulated by increased consumption. In a free economy, production expansion depends primarily on rising consumer demand; and in the mature American economy, rising demand requires, in addition to population growth, the continuous stimulation of consumer desires. /16

An Economic Force

The primary stimulant is advertising, and among all forms of advertising, television has unique capabilities that power the American economy. For television is more than an advertising tool; like advertising, it creates demand, but with sight, sound, color and demonstration, it goes further and functions as a direct selling force. Its sales messages reach millions simultaneously, yet with the personal persuasion of one individual speaking to another in his home. With its ability to show not only what a product is but what it does, television has given American industry a powerful means of sustaining traditional consumer demands and developing new ones. It also has speeded and streamlined the distribution process. This is a contribution of particular value to our economy, where distribution cost is so important an element of end-cost to consumers. /17

Television's sales impact has contributed to, and has been accompanied by, a marketing revolution in which the primary selling function has shifted from the dealer to the manufacturer. In the past, the dealer had the responsibility for developing the manufacturer's market. Today the manufacturer helps create the market for the dealer by speaking directly to his customers. He does this not only for consumer purchases but also, in increasing degree, for the sale of those products that are purchased for the ultimate user by someone else, such as plywood and plate glass for the home and aluminum for the automobile. /18

This ability of the manufacturer to engage in mass selling as well as mass production — whether of packaged goods on the shelves of supermarkets or automobiles or home appliances — has given our economy a highly effective means of continuous expansion. /19

It is against this perspective that criticism of an advertiser-supported television system should be considered — criticism which claims that the marketing function of the medium prevents it from properly discharging its program function in serving the audience. To my mind, there is no inconsistency, but a close parallel, between these functions. Both seek to engage the interests of large audiences, and this is a valid goal of a mass medium of entertainment and information, quite apart from its marketing role. Additionally, television recognizes minority interests and in doing so, it also serves the advertisers interested in such specialized audiences. /20

The debate over whether television strikes a proper balance between broad and specialized interests turns on a matter of degree. If there is such a thing as a perfect and ultimate balance, I will not claim that we have reached it. Yet this debate tends to lose sight of an undebatable fact — the basic contribution commercial television makes to the national economy; and the paramount need for national economic strength in preserving the institutions of our free society. /21

The premise of growth in the American economy is consumption — a principle underscored by the President in urging that billions of dollars be released to stimulate spending by private consumers, private investors and corporate enterprises. /22

Is the stimulation of private spending incompatible with meeting our public responsibilities? History argues otherwise, for as our consumption has increased, so has our allocation for essential services: billions of dollars for education, for social security benefits, for public welfare and old-age assistance, for highways and police and fire protection. While consuming more, we have paid the highest taxes in peacetime history, fought a war in Korea, given billions in foreign aid and maintained and strengthened our global defense structure, so vital to the survival of the free world. /23

Personal Desires and Public Obligations

Fortunately, we Americans need not choose between satisfying our personal desires and fulfilling our public obligations. We are spared such a choice by a rare, perhaps unique combination of blessings: our vast natural resources, our unsurpassed technological skill and a free and expanding economy based upon prosperity through consumption. Thus we can accomplish both goals. We can enjoy all the things that make work easier and leisure more fun — and at the same time meet the needs of society and the demands of security. /24

But we can sustain this formula, I believe, only if we maintain a protective and jealous attitude toward those institutions that make it possible. To do so, we must understand the nature of the political and economic forces that shape our environment. This is the function of free media of communications in a free society, anchored in the Jeffersonian conviction that men are inherently capable of making proper judgments when they are properly informed. /25

In this dimension of its service, television — alone of all media — is capable of bringing the sight and sound of great events of our time directly and instantaneously to nearly every man, woman and child in the nation, whether the occasion is a national political convention or the tense drama of a manned space shot. It can and does place viewers in direct contact with the pressure of diplomatic crisis in United Nations debate and the violence of controversy over segregation on the University of Mississippi campus. And beyond showing and describing events as they occur, television has pressed the nation's search for truth through its documentaries and its debates on major public issues, such as social welfare, state legislative processes, our diminishing water resources and legalized gambling. /26

As it has developed, television has properly intensified concentration on its journalistic function. For example, news and information programs account for more than 25 per cent of the total broadcast schedule of the NBC television network, and other networks and independent stations are also devoting increasing air time and creative effort to such presentations. /27

In addition to this concentration on equipping the citizen for more useful participation in society, the medium has forever altered the American political process. It has done so by presenting political candidates directly to the voters, culminating in the Presidential campaign of 1960 and "The Great Debate." /28

The Equal Time Restraint

This unrivalled opportunity to assess the two major candidates took place only after the nation's broadcasters had won a Congressional respite from the equal time law. Ironically, once the 1960 campaign was concluded, they were forced back into the legal strait jacket that makes the debates impractical by requiring equal time on the air for all Presidential candidates, no matter how quixotic their intent or meager their support. /29

I am hopeful that before the 1964 election campaign begins, the Congress will relieve the public and the broadcasters of this restriction. An early start has already been made in this direction. Chairman Harris of the House Interstate and Foreign Commerce Committee has introduced a Resolution for suspension of the equal time restriction to permit the 1964 Presidential and Vice Presidential candidates to meet in face-to-face debate on the air. Yesterday, I testified in Washington in support of this proposal. However, I strongly urged that the Congress go further by eliminating, completely and permanently, the equal time restraint which operates against the free flow of information in the crucial area of political judgment and choice. Given this freedom, and the responsibility broadcasters have already demonstrated in providing full and fair coverage, television could serve the voters at the state and local levels as it has served them nationally. /30

While conceding the immense value of the four confrontations of 1960 in exposing the Presidential candidates to intimate public scrutiny, some thoughtful analysts hold that they were neither "great" nor "debates." They argue that the format—which the candidates themselves helped develop—did not permit sufficient analysis of the issues for the guidance of the voter or, in fact, expose adequately what the issues were. This point of view is far from unanimous and addresses itself to method rather than principle, but I believe it is worthy of serious consideration. /31

Accordingly, in the expectation that the law will again be changed to permit debates between Presidential candidates, we should start now to refine the format of these televised encounters, seeking even more effective ways of assisting the American voter to make an informed choice. /32

A Plan for 1964

As a major step in this direction, the National Broadcasting Company has enlisted the aid of the American Political Science Association, the nation's foremost professional organization devoted to the study of government, politics and public affairs. I am pleased to announce that this distinguished organization has agreed to conduct an independent study, under a grant from NBC, to devise the best possible forms and procedures for televised political debates. /33

The Association has made many significant contributions to more effective government—its most recent, a widely acclaimed orientation course for new members of Congress, an innovation that is likely to become a Washington tradition. /34

It has selected a seven-man study group of distinguished political scientists and communications experts to carry out the project proposed by NBC. The group will be headed by the Association's president, Dr. Carl J. Friedrich, Eaton Professor of the Science of Government at Harvard University.* /35

NBC's only participation in this study will be to underwrite the cost and provide necessary and basic information, including tape or film recordings of the 1960 debates. Whatever recommendations are arrived at will be the group's own, the result of careful, scholarly deliberation. By starting at this early date, the group will be able to present its findings well in advance of the 1964 Presidential campaign. I am confident that its proposals will be a major contribution to our democratic process. /36

Beyond equal time, we face the broader issue of whether any communications medium can effectively serve as an instrument of democracy if its freedom is curtailed. Today, television is fettered in many areas of journalistic enterprise. It cannot go wherever the public goes—into the halls of Congress, into public Committee meetings of the House of Representatives, into most courtrooms. /37

Television does not seek this right in order to make a theater of serious forums, and it recognizes the need for care and restraint. I emphasize, however, that wherever the public can attend, television should also be permitted

---

*The other members of the study group are: Evron M. Kirkpatrick, Executive Director of The American Political Science Association; Harold Lasswell, Professor of Law and Political Science, Yale University; Richard Neustadt, Professor of Government, Columbia University; Peter Odegard, Professor of Political Science, University of California at Berkeley; Elmo Roper, Senior Partner, Elmo Roper and Associates; Gerhart Wiebe, Dean of the School of Public Relations and Communications, Boston University.

to attend, so that it can serve as the eyes and ears of *all* the people. The right to witness public business should not be confined only to those whom the hearing room will hold, when television can bring the public business to everyone. /38

Inseparable Freedoms

Wherever it serves, whether entertaining or informing, television functions best in a climate of freedom. It is paradoxical that in the area of news coverage, where television's need for freedom is recognized by all, restrictions on coverage should be placed through the equal time penalty and the limitations on access. And it is even more paradoxical that among the strongest champions of television's freedom to report information and controversy without restraints are those who urge government restrictions on television entertainment. They would erect a double standard—one for information programs, another for entertainment programs—failing to recognize that freedom is indivisible. Would magazines and newspapers be free if only their news columns were unmolested, if the choice and content of features and fiction were subject to government influence, direct or indirect? But this is all part of that democratic process in which television was conceived. Often we who have the responsibility for guiding this service are accused of excessive sensitivity toward criticism. I assure you we welcome responsible criticism and take it seriously. It would be fatal to television's development if it were to operate in a vacuum of indifference and ignorance. /39

What we seek is understanding of the total dimension of our television service—its contribution to the political processes that keep us free, its impact upon the economic forces which keep America strong. /40

These essential and inseparable functions of political and economic freedom are the source of this nation's vitality and strength. Our capacity to support the arch of democracy both at home and around the world can be limited only if these freedoms are limited. It will grow only as we succeed in keeping them unencumbered. Thank you. /41

Goodwill Speeches for Collateral Study

1. Richard J. Babcock, "The Dynamic Future of Agriculture," *Vital Speeches*, XXVII (February 15, 1961), 269–272.
2. Erwin D. Canham, "The Value of Self-Criticism for Business and Labor," *The Speaker's Resource Book*, ed. Carroll C. Arnold, Douglas Ehninger, and John C. Gerber (Chicago: Scott, Foresman and Company, 1961), pp. 187–193.
3. Henry B. duPont, "The Greatest Invention of Them All," *ibid.*, pp. 193–198.

RADIO-TELEVISION SPEECH

On August 1, 1959, Richard M. Nixon, then Vice-President of the United States, presented the following speech to the Russian people over Moscow Television and a radio network that reached all parts of the Soviet Union. He had gone to Russia to open the American National Exhibition in Moscow on July 24, 1959. During the following week he traveled throughout the Soviet Union and Poland and talked with many leaders of these nations.

Mr. Nixon spoke from a prepared manuscript, with interruptions for translation into Russian. Note that his speech exhibits consistent efforts to win a favorable response—compliments to his listeners, their land, and leaders; emphasis on feelings and goals common to both U.S. and Russian peoples; open admission of divergent views; and reiterated assurances of U.S. peace aims.

I first want to express my appreciation to the government of the USSR for giving me an opportunity to speak to the people of this country by radio and television just as Mr. Kozlov and Mr. Mikoyan spoke to the American people on their visits to my country. /1

I realize that nine days is much too brief a time for a visitor to spend in this great country. But in that period I have had the opportunity of having extended and frank discussions with Mr. Khrushchev and other leaders of your government. I have visited Leningrad, Siberia and the Urals and I have had the privilege of meeting thousands of people in all walks of life. /2

What I would like to do tonight is to answer for the millions of people who are listening to this program some of the questions which were asked me over and over again on this trip so that you may get a true picture of the policies of the American government and people. /3

I should like to begin by answering a question which I often heard: What are my impressions of this country and its people? /4

While my visit was brief I did have a chance in addition to visiting this great capital city of Moscow to see the beauty and culture of Leningrad whose brave people won the admiration of the world for their heroic defense of their city during the war; to savor the inspiring pioneer spirit of Novosibirsk; to witness firsthand the thriving productivity of the factory complex of the Urals. I was greatly impressed by the efficient modern equipment of your factories; your magnificent ballets in Leningrad and Novosibirsk; by the competitive drive for progress which is evident on every side. /5

But most of all I was impressed by your people; after all, the greatest asset of a country is not its forests, its factories or its farms but its people. /6

These are some of the characteristics of the Soviet people which I particularly noted on this trip. /7

First, their capacity for hard work, their vitality, their intense desire to improve their lot, to get ahead, is evident everywhere. /8

There was another feature about the Soviet people which I noted that may surprise you and that is in how many respects you are like us Americans. We are similar in our love of humor—we laugh at the same jokes. The people of your frontier East have much the same spirit of what was our frontier West. We have a common love of sports; the name of Vasily Kuznetsov, your great decathlon champion, is known in the United States as well as in the Soviet Union. We are both a hospitable, friendly people. When we meet each other we tend to like each other personally, as so many of our soldiers who met during the last great war can attest. /9

Above all, the American people and the Soviet people are as one in their desire for peace. And our desire for peace is not because either of us is weak. On the contrary, each of us is strong and respects the strength the other possesses. /10

This means that if we are to have peace it must be a just peace based on mutual respect rather than the peace of surrender or dictation by either side. Putting it bluntly, both of our peoples want peace but both of us also possess great strength and much as we want peace neither of us can or will tolerate being pushed around. /11

That is why I was so surprised at a question that was asked me by a worker on the new scientific center outside of Novosibirsk. My heart went out to him as he told me that he had been wounded in World War II and that his father and mother had been killed by bombs. But then he said, "I don't believe you when you say America is for peace." /12

Nothing he could have said could have astonished or saddened me more. /13

And so to the millions of Soviet people who suffered or lost their loved ones in war, and to all of those in this great country who want peace, I say tonight, if you doubt that the American government and the American people are as dedicated to peace as you are, look

*Text from *The Speaker's Resource Book,* ed. Carroll C. Arnold, Douglas Ehninger, and John C. Gerber (Chicago: Scott, Foresman and Company, 1961), pp. 241–245.

at our record, examine our policies and you can reach only one conclusion — only aggressor nations have anything to fear from the United States of America. /14

We have fought in two World Wars and have demanded and received not an acre of territory or a cent in reparations. We enjoy the highest standard of living of any people in the world's history, and there is nothing whatever that we want from any other people in the world except to live in peace and friendship with them. No leader in the world today could be more dedicated to peace than our President. As his brother, who has honored us by making this visit with us, can tell you, President Eisenhower's whole life is proof of the stark but simple truth — that no one hates war more than one who has seen a lot of it. /15

We know as do you that in this age of nuclear weapons it is impossible for either of our nations to launch an attack which would not bring terrible destruction to itself. /16

In this age any leader who is so insane even to think of starting a war should well heed your proverb — "Do not dig a pit for another; you may fall into it yourself." /17

Why then is there any doubt that the American government and people are just as dedicated to peace as the people of the USSR? I think part of the answer is to be found in another question which was often asked of me on this trip and which Mr. Khrushchev, himself, raised in this manner in his speech on July 28 at Dnepropetrovsk. "If you believe in the peaceful intentions of our country, why do you continue the arms race, why do you construct new military bases around our borders?" /18

In answering this question, let me first point out that these bases are not maintained for purposes of attacking you but for purposes of defending ourselves and our allies. /19

Why did we think it was necessary to set up bases? Let us look at the record. We disarmed rapidly after World War II. Then came a series of events which threatened our friends abroad as well as ourselves. The Berlin blockade and the war in Korea are typical of the actions which led the United States and our allies to rearm so that we could defend ourselves against aggression. /20

We must also remember that these events occurred before the 20th Party Congress changed the line to the one Mr. Khrushchev enunciated again in his speech at Dnepropetrovsk — that Communism will now try to achieve its international objectives by peaceful means rather than by force. I could cite statement after statement made by previous leaders of the USSR which advocated and threatened the use of force against non-Communist countries in order to achieve Communist objectives. /21

A striking illustration of why we maintain bases and strong military forces is the fact that one-fourth of the entire production of the USSR goes into armaments. This, in effect, means that every worker in the Soviet Union works one day out of four for armaments. And we in our country are also bearing a heavy burden of armaments. Think what it could mean to both of our countries if we could lift this burden from the backs of our people. /22

Some may ask, why don't we get rid of the bases since the Soviet government declares today that it has only peaceful intentions? The answer is that whenever the fear and suspicion that caused us and our allies to take measures for collective self-defense are removed, the reason for our maintaining bases will be removed. In other words, the only possible solution of this problem lies in mutual rather than unilateral action leading toward disarmament. /23

Another question which was often asked was — why won't the United States agree to stop the tests of atomic weapons? The answer in a nutshell is that the question is not whether we both should enter into an agreement to stop tests but whether that agreement is one which will make sure that the tests actually are stopped. /24

That is why we say that if both sides honestly want to stop tests, we must first agree to set up inspection procedures in both of our countries which will make certain that the agreement is not violated. We believe this position is the only one that gives assurance of accomplishing the objective of stopping tests rather than just signing an agreement to do so. /25

We are encouraged by the fact that at least in this area we are presently engaged in serious negotiations which have made some progress. I know that I express the sentiments of the people of both of our countries when I say that

I am hopeful that these negotiations will finally end in agreement. /26

Another question that has often been asked me went something like this: "The United States says it is for peace, but what the world wants are deeds not words, and the United States is short on deeds and long on words." /27

Nothing could be further from the truth. It is possible that many of you listening to me are not aware of the positive programs the United States has proposed which were designed to contribute to peace. Let me tell you about just a few of them and what happened to them: /28

We had a monopoly on the atomic bomb when on June 14, 1946, we submitted the Baruch plan for international control of atomic energy. What happened? It was rejected by the USSR. /29

Under Article 43 of the United Nations Charter, provision was made for the establishment of the United Nations Armed Forces to keep the peace. On June 4, 1947, we made the first of many requests that agreement be reached. What happened? All have been rejected by the USSR. /30

At the Summit Conference in Geneva on July 21, 1955, President Eisenhower made his offer of open skies aerial inspection. What happened? It was rejected by the USSR. /31

On May 1, 1958, the United States offered an Arctic aerial inspection plan to protect both nations from surprise attack. What happened? It was rejected by the USSR. /32

I realize that your government has indicated reasons for its rejection of each of these proposals. I do not list these proposals for the purpose of warming over past history but simply to demonstrate the initiative that our government has taken to reduce tensions and to find peaceful solutions for differences between us. /33

I realize that my answers to these questions indicate that there are some very basic differences between us. But let me emphasize at the same time that the very fact that we have not made as much progress as we would like in the past in settling our differences is the strongest reason for us to redouble our efforts to create better understanding between our two countries; to remove fear, suspicion and misconception where they exist, and thereby, to pave the way for discussions and eventual settlement by agreement of some of the basic conflicts between us. /34

We should both frankly recognize that we have some very real differences; that they are not easily settled: But two men who are friends can settle an argument between them without using their fists and two nations who want to be friends can do so without war. /35

I should like to suggest tonight some practical steps which will contribute to the cause of peace to which we are both dedicated. /36

First there are some positive things we can do which will create better understanding between us. /37

We can start by removing the language barrier. Here is one place where you are ahead of us. I was amazed at the number of people I met on this trip who were studying English. What we need are millions of American students who understand Russian and millions of Soviet students who understand English. /38

Both the exchange of persons and the cultural exchange programs should not only be continued but sharply expanded. The more Americans who visit and get to know first-hand the people of the Soviet Union and the more Soviet citizens who do the same in the United States, the better understanding we shall have. /39

I believe also that visits by officials like the ones Mr. Mikoyan and Mr. Kozlov made to the United States and which I have just concluded can provide the means of frank and full discussion of some of our problems and the development of solutions for them. Consequently, we should explore ways of increasing contacts of this type. /40

Most important of all, we need a much freer exchange of information between our two countries so that misconceptions we may have about you and that you have about us may be removed. I was rather surprised that Mr. Khrushchev should raise a question about the failure of the Western press to report adequately one of his recent statements. I would estimate that at least 100 of Mr. Khrushchev's words are printed in our American press for every one word of President Eisenhower's speeches that are printed in the Soviet press. /41

Perhaps this is an area where the cause of better understanding would be served if we had a more equal exchange. Let us agree that all of Mr. Khrushchev's speeches on foreign policy be printed in the United States and that all of President Eisenhower's speeches on foreign policy be printed in the Soviet Union. /42

Why not go further and set up regular radio and television broadcasts by Mr. Khrushchev to the American people in return for President Eisenhower having the same privilege to talk to the Soviet people? /43

Let us put a stop to the jamming of broadcasts so that the Soviet people may hear broadcasts from our country just as the American people can hear forty hours of broadcasts a day from the Soviet Union. And let us have a freer flow of newspapers and magazines so that the Soviet people can buy American newspapers and magazines here just as we Americans purchased over one and one-half million Soviet publications in last year alone. /44

I recognize that freedom of information can be abused and that neither of us is free from blame in this respect. The press, radio, television and other means of communication such as film studios, have a heavy responsibility for maintaining the spirit of truth and for preventing misinformation. In the final analysis the misrepresentation of facts or distortion of the truth defeats itself. Let me give you an example from an experience that occurred to me on this trip. /45

There was a report in *Pravda* to the effect that on the morning after I arrived in Moscow I tried to give money to a poor Soviet citizen, with the hope that American press photographers might take pictures of the incident and send them around the world. There was not a shred of truth to this story. /46

Here is what actually happened. On an early morning visit to the Danilovsky Market, I had talked to scores of people and received a most friendly welcome. As I was about to leave, several of the people asked me for tickets to the American Exhibition. I told them I did not have any with me, but that I would be glad to buy some tickets for those present who wanted to attend the Exhibition. One of the group explained that it was not a question of their not having money for the tickets, but simply a question of their not being able to obtain them. I told him I would be glad to check into the matter and see if I could get tickets for him. /47

These are the simple facts as far as this incident was concerned, and I can only add that all irresponsible reporters should never forget that in the end the truth always catches up with a lie. /48

Through this greater exchange of information between our two peoples we not only learn from each other and improve our way of life but we reduce the suspicion, the mistrust, and fear and misunderstanding and assure the understanding and friendship which will lead to the peace we all want. That is why, to me, the concept of co-existence is completely inadequate and negative. Co-existence implies that the world must be divided into two hostile camps with a wall of hate and fear between. /49

What we need today is not two worlds but one world where different peoples choose the economic and political systems which they want, but where there is free communication among all the peoples living on this earth. /50

Let us expand the concept of open skies. What the world also needs are open cities, open minds and open hearts. /51

Let us have peaceful competition not only in producing the best factories but in producing better lives for our people. /52

Let us cooperate in our exploration of outer space. As a worker told me in Novosibirsk, let us go to the moon together. /53

Let our aim be not victory over other peoples but the victory of all mankind over hunger, want, misery and disease, wherever it exists in the world. /54

I realize that this era of peaceful competition and even cooperation seems like an impossible dream when we consider the present differences we have between us. But the leaders of our countries can help make this dream come true. So far as the leader of our country is concerned, I can assure you that President Eisenhower has no objective to which he is more dedicated. /55

As far as Mr. Khrushchev is concerned, as I am sure you know, we disagree sharply on political and economic philosophy and on many world problems. But these characteristics are evident to anyone who meets him — he is a self-made man who worked his way up from the bottom; he is an articulate spokesman for the economic system in which he believes; he has immense drive; in sum, he is one of those individuals who, whether you agree with him or disagree with him, is a born leader of men. Because he has these unique qualities and because the decisions he makes will affect not only the 200 million people of the USSR but the 3 billion people on this earth, he carries a tremendous responsibility on his shoulders. /56

I would not be so presumptuous as to try to give him advice on how he should fulfill that responsibility. But could I relate something that I noted on the trip I have just completed? In every factory and on hundreds of billboards I saw this slogan, "Let us work for the victory of Communism." /57

If Mr. Khrushchev means by this slogan working for a better life for the people within the Soviet Union this is one thing. If, on the other hand, he means the victory of Communism over the United States and other countries, this is a horse of a different color. For we have our own ideas as to what system is best for us. /58

If he devotes his immense energies and talents to building a better life for the people of his own country, Mr. Khrushchev can go down in history as one of the greatest leaders the Soviet people have ever produced. But if he diverts the resources and talents of his people to the objective of promoting the communization of countries outside the Soviet Union, he will only assure that both he and his people will continue to live in an era of fear, suspicion and tension. /59

. The Geneva conference is a case in point. It would not be proper for me to comment on the specific proposals that are pending before that conference at this time. But agreements between great powers cannot be reached unless they take into account the views and interests of all parties concerned. I was encouraged to note in my conversations with Mr. Khrushchev that he recognizes this fact and agrees that a successful outcome of this conference could be a great step forward in settling some of the problems I have discussed tonight. /60

I have one final thought to add. Mr. Khrushchev predicted that our grandchildren would live under Communism. He reiterated this to me in our talks last Sunday. /61

Let me say that we do not object to his saying this will happen. We only object if he tries to bring it about. /62

And this is my answer to him. I do not say that your grandchildren will live under capitalism. We prefer our system. But the very essence of our belief is that we do not and will not try to impose our system on anybody else. We believe that you and all other peoples on this earth should have the right to choose the kind of economic or political system which best fits your particular problems without any foreign intervention. /63

As I leave your country, I shall never forget an incident that occurred as I was driving through your beautiful Ural mountains. A group of children on the side of the road threw wild flowers into my car and cried in English the words "friendship," "friendship." Mr. Zhukov told me that the first word children who study English are taught is the word "friendship." There could be no more eloquent expression of the attitude of the Soviet people, an attitude which we share in common with you. /64

Finally, may I express on behalf of my wife and I, and all the members of our party, our deep appreciation for the warm friendship and boundless hospitality we have found everywhere we have gone in the Soviet Union. I pledge to you that in the years to come I shall devote my best efforts to the cause of peace with justice for all the peoples of the world. /65

Radio-Television Speeches for Collateral Study

1. Charles DeGaulle, "The Future of France," *Vital Speeches*, XXX (January 15, 1964), 197–198.

2. Lyndon B. Johnson, "Our System of Government," *Vital Speeches*, XXX (December 15, 1963), 131–132.

3. John F. Kennedy, "The Arms Quarantine of Cuba," *Vital Speeches*, XXIX (November 15, 1962), 66–68.

4. Harold Macmillan, "The Common Market," *Vital Speeches,* XXIX (March 15, 1963), 232–233.

5. Pope Paul VI, "The Needs of the World," *Vital Speeches,* XXX (January 15, 1964), 198–200.

SPEECH OF INTRODUCTION

W. H. Auden, lecturing at the University of Iowa on March 13, 1963, on "The Poet and His Poems," was introduced by Professor John C. Gerber, chairman of the Department of English. In his introductory remarks, Professor Gerber combined humorous references to the local scene with serious information concerning Mr. Auden's life and accomplishments. As a result, he created a desire on the part of the audience to hear what the speaker had to say and, at the same time, gave the speaker a warm and sincere welcome.

INTRODUCING W. H. AUDEN*
John C. Gerber

Good evening, ladies and gentlemen. /1

For the Committee on University Lectures I welcome you to another lecture in our 1962–63 series—a lecture to which we have all been looking forward. /2

I think you will agree with me that the arrival of a poet in Iowa City is not necessarily an unusual event. Happily we have come to expect poets to migrate here. We rejoice in the fact that Iowa City probably has more poets per city block than any other city in the country. We have tall poets and short poets, good poets and better poets, bearded poets and even a few clean-shaven ones. And we welcome them all and feel fortunate that they are here. /3

Yet despite our familiarity with poets, the arrival of a particular poet who is on the platform with me is an extraordinary event for us all. And the reason is quite obvious. Mr. W. H. Auden is one of the truly great poets of our time. /4

When Emerson spoke of the poet he meant a man of highest insight; the mode of his writing was incidental. Mr. Auden is a poet in this broad sense, for his work has taken many forms. He has been an editor, a translator, a playwright, a librettist, a critic, and an essayist—and in all of these guises he has shown the same shrewd awareness of the dilemmas of our age. His last book of essays, *The Dyer's Hand and Other Essays,* has been called by Alfred Kazin "the most telling collection of critical essays published in this country for a very long time." Mr. Kazin finds in it "the driving quality of a man who feels compelled to define as sharply as possible . . . the poets' predicament in a fallen world." /5

But it has been in poetry, of course, that Mr. Auden has given us his sharpest and most moving perceptions. Beginning with a volume of poems published in 1930, his influence spread so quickly and so firmly that we still refer to his group as the Auden Circle or the Auden generation. In 1937 with seven books already to his credit Mr. Auden was awarded the King's Gold Medal for the best poetry of the year. /6

His move to America in 1939 was followed by what many consider to be his finest period. At least it was during this period that he wrote many of his most frequently anthologized poems, such as "In Memory of W. B. Yeats," "September 1, 1939," and "Herman Melville." /7

Since the publication of his *Collected Poetry* in 1945, there has been no doubt that Mr. Auden is one of the few major poets of our age. His more recent works, like *The Age of Anxiety* in 1947, *The Shield of Achilles* in 1955,

---

*Text furnished by Professor Gerber and used with permission.

and *Homage to Clio* in 1960, have simply strengthened this view. /8

As any thoughtful man inevitably must, Mr. Auden has tried to face up to the question of what we must do to be saved. His earlier poems suggested that regeneration might come from without, that is, through reform of social and political institutions. In his later poems he has suggested the opposite, namely, that a meaningful change can come only from within. Many feel that this change has greatly enriched Mr. Auden's poetry. One of these is our own Professor McDowell, who in a recent essay wrote that under Christian influence Mr. Auden's vision deepened and his technical resources have grown more ample. /9

Originally an English subject, Mr. Auden is now an American citizen. Naturally we are proud of this fact. But his nationality is really incidental. What is important is that he is one of the great spokesmen for our times and to our times. And it is as such that I now present him to you. He will speak on the subject, "The Poet and His Poems." /10

Mr. Auden, we are glad to have you here. /11

COMMENCEMENT SPEECH

On June 3, 1957, while John F. Kennedy was junior senator from Massachusetts, he delivered the following address at the commencement exercises of Syracuse University. In urging the graduates to enter the field of politics, he marshalled an impressive array of facts, quotations, historical references, and anecdotes. Reminding his listeners of their historical heritage and civic responsibility, Mr. Kennedy presented the profession of politics as an exciting and challenging, as well as an honorable pursuit.

THE PROFESSION OF POLITICS*
John F. Kennedy

Anyone who is interested in the history of the United States Senate always feels a great sense of privilege and responsibility in coming to this state and to this part of the state. For New York has had a long parade of unusually distinguished men who served their nation in the Chamber of the Senate—and one of these of whom I am particularly reminded today was a very distinguished member of the opposite party—Elihu Root. His father was the second principal in the history of the Syracuse Academy—and Root himself was always fond of upstate New York. Perhaps one of the most dramatic moments of his life came in Utica in 1906 when as Secretary of State he agreed to speak for his party in this state. The opposition had imported a gang of hecklers to make his speech impossible. Having secured copies of his address in advance, they had instructions to start interruptions on particular lines—shouting, for example, on the first reference to the late President McKinley, "Let McKinley rest in peace," with the others roaring their approval. Unfortunately for the hecklers, the meeting was packed with Root admirers and Hamilton College students; and the first one who started to interrupt was pushed in the face, and the rest were bodily threatened. Finally, when a great roar arose from the crowd to throw out one heckler, Root raised his right hand to quell the uproar, and in a powerful voice cried out: "No, let him stay—and learn!" /1

I trust that all of you will stay—I can only speculate as to how much you will learn—but I will welcome any heckling at the close of these ceremonies. I hope the example of Elihu Root will be an inspiration to all of those

*From *Vital Speeches*, XXIII (August 15, 1957), 657–659.

whom we honor on this solemn day of Commencement. For them, the pleasures, the values and the friendships of college days are coming to an end—the identical group sitting here this morning will probably never gather again—and the sands of time will gradually erase most of the memories which seem so important today. /2

But what concerns us most on these occasions is not what you graduates leave behind but what you take with you, what you will do with it, what contribution you can make. I am assuming, of course, that you are taking something with you, that you do not look upon this university as Dean Swift regarded Oxford. Oxford, he said, was truly a great seat of learning; for all freshmen who entered were required to bring some learning with them in order to meet the standards of admission—but no senior, when he left the university, ever took any learning away; and thus it steadily accumulated. /3

The high regard in which your education at Syracuse is held is evidenced by the intensive competition which rages between those hoping to benefit from it. Your campus is visited by prospective employers ranging from corporation vice-presidents to professional football coaches. Great newspaper advertisements offer inducements to chemists, engineers, and electronic specialists. High public officials plead for more college graduates to follow scientific pursuits. And many of you will be particularly persuaded by the urgent summons to duty and travel which comes from your local draft board. /4

But in the midst of all these pleas, plans and pressures, few, I dare say, if any, will be urging upon you a career in the field of politics. Some will point out the advantages of civil service positions. Others will talk in high terms of public service, or statesmanship, or community leadership. But few, if any, will urge you to become politicians. /5

Mothers may still want their favorite sons to grow up to be President, but, according to a famous Gallup poll of some years ago, they do not want them to become politicians in the process. They may be statesmen, they may be leaders of their community, they may be distinguished law-makers—but they must never be politicians. Successful politicians, according to Walter Lippmann, are "insecure

and intimidated men," who "advance politically only as they placate, appease, bribe, seduce, bamboozle, or otherwise manage to manipulate" the views and votes of the people who elect them. It was considered a great joke years ago when the humorist Artemus Ward declared: "I am not a politician, and my other habits are good also." And, in more recent times, even the President of the United States, when asked at a news conference early in his first term how he liked "the game of politics," replied with a frown that his questioner was using a derogatory phrase. Being President, he said, is a "very fascinating experience . . . but the word 'politics' . . . I have no great liking for that." /6

Politics, in short, has become one of our most neglected, our most abused and our most ignored professions. It ranks low on the occupational list of a large share of the population; and its chief practitioners are rarely well or favorably known. No education, except finding your way around a smoke-filled room, is considered necessary for political success. "Don't teach my boy poetry," a mother recently wrote the headmaster of Eton; "Don't teach my boy poetry, he's going to stand for Parliament." The worlds of politics and scholarship have indeed drifted apart. /7

Unfortunately, this disdain for the political profession is not only shared but intensified in our academic institutions. To many universities and students we politicians represent nothing but censors, investigators and perpetrators of what has been called the "swinish cult of anti-intellectualism." To others, we are corrupt, selfish, unsavory individuals, manipulating votes and compromising principles for personal and partisan gain. /8

Teachers as well as students, moreover, find it difficult to accept the differences between the laboratory and the legislature. In the former, the goal is truth, pure and simple, without regard to changing currents of public opinion; in the latter, compromises and majorities and procedural customs and rights affect the ultimate decision as to what is right or just or good. And even when they realize the difference, most intellectuals consider their chief function to be that of the critic—and politicians are sensitive to critics (possibly because we have so many of them). "Many intellectuals," Sidney Hook has said, "would rather 'die' than agree with the majority, even on the rare occasions when the majority is right." Of course, the intellectual's attitude is partly defensive—for he has been regarded with so much suspicion and hostility by political figures and their constituents that a recent survey of American intellectuals by a national magazine elicited from one of our foremost literary figures the guarded response, "I ain't no intellectual." /9

But this mutual suspicion was not always the case—and I would ask those of you who look with disdain and disfavor upon the possibilities of a political career to remember that our nation's first great politicians were traditionally our ablest, most respected, most talented leaders, men who moved from one field to another with amazing versatility and vitality. A contemporary described Thomas Jefferson as "A gentleman of 32, who could calculate an eclipse, survey an estate, tie an artery, plan an edifice, try a cause, break a horse, dance a minuet, and play the violin." /10

Daniel Webster could throw thunderbolts at Hayne on the Senate Floor and then stroll a few steps down the corridor and dominate the Supreme Court as the foremost lawyer of his time. John Quincy Adams, after being summarily dismissed from the Senate for a notable display of independence, could become Boylston Professor of Rhetoric and Oratory at Harvard and then become a great Secretary of State. (Those were the happy days when Harvard professors had no difficulty getting Senate confirmation.) /11

This versatility also existed on the frontier. Missouri's first Senator, Thomas Hart Benton, the man whose tavern brawl with Jackson in Tennessee caused him to flee the state, was described with these words in his obituary: "With a readiness that was often surprising, he could quote from a Roman Law or a Greek philosopher, from Virgil's Georgics, The Arabian Nights, Herodotus or Sancho Panza, from the Sacred Carpets, the German reformers or Adam Smith; from Fenelon or Hudibras, from the financial reports of Necca or the doings of the Council of Trent, from the debates on the adoption of the Constitution or intrigues of the kitchen cabinet or from some forgotten speech of a deceased Member of Congress." /12

This link between American scholarship and the American politician remained for more than a century. A little more than one hundred years ago, in the Presidential campaign of 1856, the Republicans sent three brilliant orators around the campaign circuit: William Cullen Bryant, Henry Wadsworth Longfellow and Ralph Waldo Emerson. (Those were the carefree days when the "egg-heads" were all Republicans.) /13

I would urge therefore that each of you, regardless of your chosen occupation, consider entering the field of politics at some stage in your career. It is not necessary that you be famous, that you effect radical changes in the government or that you be acclaimed by the public for your efforts. It is not even necessary that you be successful. I ask only that you offer to the political arena, and to the critical problems of our society which are decided therein, the benefit of the talents which society has helped to develop in you. I ask you to decide, as Goethe put it, whether you will be an anvil—or a hammer. The formal phases of the "anvil" stage are now completed for many of you, though hopefully you will continue to absorb still more in the years ahead. The question now is whether you are to be a hammer—whether you are to give to the world in which you were reared and educated the broadest possible benefits of that education. /14

It is not enough to lend your talents merely to discussing the issues and deploring their solutions. Most scholars, I know, would prefer to confine their attention to the mysteries of pure scholarship or the delights of abstract discourse. But "Would you have counted him a friend of Ancient Greece," as George William Curtis asked a century ago during the Kansas-Nebraska Controversy, "who quietly discussed the theory of patriotism on that Greek summer day through whose hopeless and immortal hours Leonidas and his three hundred stood at Thermopylae for liberty? Was John Milton to conjugate Greek verbs in his library, or talk of the liberty of the ancient Shumanites, when the liberty of Englishmen was imperilled?" No, the duty of the scholar—particularly in a republic such as ours—is to contribute his objective views and his sense of liberty to the affairs of his state and nation. /15

This is a great university, the University of Syracuse. Its establishment and continued functioning, like that of all great universities, has required considerable effort and expenditure. I cannot believe that all of this was undertaken merely to give the school's graduates an economic advantage in the life struggle. "A university," said Professor Woodrow Wilson, "should be an organ of memory for the state for the transmission of its best traditions. Every man sent out from a university should be a man of his nation, as well as a man of his time." And Prince Bismarck was even more specific — one-third of the students of German universities, he once stated, broke down from overwork; another third broke down from dissipation; and the other third ruled Germany. (I leave it to each of you to decide which category you fall in.) /16

But if you are to be among the rulers of our land, from precinct captain to President, if you are willing to enter the abused and neglected profession of politics, then let me tell you — as one who is familiar with the political world — that we stand in serious need of the fruits of your education. We do not need political scholars whose education has been so specialized as to exclude them from participation in current events — men like Lord John Russell, of whom Queen Victoria once remarked that he would be a better man if he knew a third subject — but he was interested in nothing but the Constitution of 1688 and himself. No, what we need are men who can ride easily over broad fields of knowledge and recognize the mutual dependence of our two worlds. /17

I do not say that our political and public life should be turned over to college-trained experts who ignore public opinion. Nor would I adopt from the Belgian Constitution of 1893 the provision giving three votes instead of one

to college graduates (at least not until more Democrats go to college). Nor would I give the University of Syracuse a seat in the Congress as William and Mary was once represented in the Virginia House of Burgesses. /18

But I do urge the application of your talents to the public solution of the great problems of our time — increasing farm foreclosures in the midst of national prosperity — record small business failures at a time of record profits — pockets of chronic unemployment and sweatshop wages amidst the wonders of automation — monopoly, mental illness, race relations, taxation, international trade, and, above all, the knotty complex problems of war and peace, of untangling the strife-ridden, hate-ridden Middle East, of preventing man's destruction of man by nuclear war or, even more awful to contemplate, by disabling through mutations generations yet unborn. /19

No, you do not lack problems or opportunities — you do not lack the ability or the energy; nor, I have tried to say, do you lack the responsibility to act, no matter what you have heard about the profession of politics. Bear in mind, as you leave this university and consider the road ahead, not the sneers of the cynics or the fears of the purists, for whom politics will never be an attraction — but bear in mind instead these words which are inscribed behind the Speaker's desk high on the Chamber Wall of the United States House of Representatives, inscribed for all to see and all to ponder, these words of the most famous statesman my state ever sent to the Halls of Congress, Daniel Webster: "Let us develop the resources of our land, call forth its power, build up its institutions, promote all its great interests and see whether we also in our day and generation may not perform something worthy to be remembered." /20

DEDICATION SPEECH

Brotherhood House, on the northwest corner of Seventh Avenue and Fortieth Street in New York City, provides free office and meeting facilities for 100 voluntary social agencies operating in the metropolitan area. The money for building materials was raised through contributions, and construction services were donated. Governor Nelson A. Rockefeller delivered the following speech at the cornerstone laying which took place September 12, 1962.

REMARKS AT THE CORNERSTONE LAYING OF THE BROTHERHOOD-IN-ACTION BUILDING*
Nelson A. Rockefeller

It is with more than official pleasure that I take part in these cornerstone-laying ceremonies today. For if there are two words in the English language which have, for me, specific and urgent meaning, they are "brotherhood" and "action." /1

Too often, one is used thoughtlessly, the other as a symbol rather than the deed itself. But the vision which inspired the Honorable George J. Beldock in 1945 and which will soon take physical form in the useful and inspiring edifice whose cornerstone is laid today was neither. /2

In today's world of surging, conflicting and threatening interests, a realistic appreciation of human brotherhood and what a true understanding of its strength can contribute is morally comforting and reassuring. /3

Such an understanding may well be the priceless product hammered out in the rooms and meeting places of this Brotherhood Hall, a structure combining the monumental and the functional. /4

This is purposeful action. It is a characteristic of programs which we have initiated and activated during these past four years in New York State. /5

I would especially like to commend the type of action which is proposed here. For it is a practical step to bring about greater mutual understanding among the more than one hundred organizations carrying the banner of brotherhood in this great city. /6

Such voluntary groups have, quite properly, specific objectives, but many share common aims. It is to provide a place where the common aims — not the differences — may be discussed, defined and hardened into effective programs that this Hall is being constructed. /7

Just as the skilled workers are bringing their individual talents to bear on the common objective of erecting this beautiful and useful building, so may the users of it find in their common interest in brotherhood an objective to which they may devote their individual talents. /8

Brotherhood House, with its six stories, all-glass front and tastefully landscaped setting, will provide the physical facilities to encourage the conversations, discussions, debates and informal talks needed. Its large library, meditation and music rooms, auditorium, seminar and conference rooms, radio and TV studio are all tangible aids. /9

But what will make this endeavor shine with the lustre of good deeds accomplished is the spirit of the House. It will be a symbol of brotherhood, to be sure, but much more. Judge Beldock has defined its function as "a vision for all to share; a challenge for all to meet." With these sentiments, I am in complete accord. /10

Today is in fact a beginning. But there is great promise for good in an unfolding, action-packed future. Taking part in these ceremonies is, of course, pleasant. But the real joy will come to me — as to all — when Brotherhood Hall is functioning effectively as a continuing influence for realization of that brotherhood of man under the Fatherhood of God which fulfills our highest traditions and heritage as a people. /11

SPEECH OF TRIBUTE

The following tribute to Eleanor Roosevelt, the widow of Franklin Delano Roosevelt, was delivered by her close friend, Ambassador Adlai E. Stevenson,

*Text furnished by Governor Rockefeller.

at a memorial service in the Cathedral of St. John the Divine in New York City on November 17, 1962. The dignified but moving address is characterized by restrained emotion, simple style, and a tone of sincerity.

EULOGY ON ELEANOR ROOSEVELT*
Adlai E. Stevenson

One week ago this afternoon, in the Rose Garden at Hyde Park, Eleanor Roosevelt came home for the last time. Her journeys are over. The remembrance now begins. /1

In gathering here to honor her, we engage in a self-serving act. It is we who are trying, by this ceremony of tribute, to deny the fact that we have lost her, and, at least, to prolong the farewell, and—possibly—to say some of the things we dared not say in her presence, because she would have turned aside such testimonials with impatience and gently asked us to get on with some of the more serious business of the meeting. /2

A grief, perhaps not equalled since the death of her husband 17 years ago, is the world's best tribute to one of the great figures of our age—a woman whose lucid and luminous faith testified always for sanity in an insane time and for hope in a time of obscure hope—a woman who spoke for the good toward which man aspires in a world which has seen too much of the evil of which man is capable. /3

She lived 78 years, most of the time in tireless activity as if she knew that only a frail fragment of the things that cry out to be done could be done in the lifetime of even the most fortunate. One has the melancholy sense that when she knew death was at hand, she was contemplating not what she achieved, but what she had not quite managed to do. And I know she wanted to go—when there was no more strength to do. /4

Yet, how much she had done—how much still unchronicled! We dare not try to tabulate the lives she salvaged, the battles—known and unrecorded—she fought, the afflicted she comforted, the hovels she brightened, the faces and places, near and far, that were given some new radiance, some sound of music, by her endeavors. What other single human being has touched and transformed the existence of so many others? What better measure is there of the impact of anyone's life? /5

There was no sick soul too wounded to engage her mercy. There was no signal of human distress which she did not view as a personal summons. There was no affront to human dignity from which she fled because the timid cried "danger." And the number of occasions on which her intervention turned despair into victory we may never know! /6

Her life was crowded, restless, fearless, and lonesome. Perhaps she pitied most not those whom she aided in the struggle, but the more fortunate who were preoccupied with themselves and cursed with the self-deceptions of private success. She walked in the slums and ghettos of the world, not on a tour of inspection, nor as a condescending patron, but as one who could not feel complacent while others were hungry, and who could not find contentment while others were in distress. This was not sacrifice; this, for Mrs. Roosevelt, was the only meaningful way of life. /7

These were not conventional missions of mercy. What made this unforgettable woman so extraordinary was not merely her response to suffering; it was her comprehension of the complexity of the human condition. Not long before she died, she wrote that "within all of us there are two sides. One reaches for the stars, the other descends to the level of beasts." It was, I think, this discernment that made her so unfailingly tolerant of friends who faltered, and led her so often to remind the smug and the complacent that "There but for the grace of God. . . ." /8

But we dare not regard her as just a benign incarnation of good works. For she was

---

not only a great woman and a great humanitarian, but a great democrat. I use the word with a small "d"—though it was, of course, equally true that she was a great Democrat with a capital "D." When I say that she was a great small-d democrat, I mean that she had a lively and astute understanding of the nature of the democratic process. She was a master political strategist with a fine sense of humor. And, as she often said, she loved a good fight. /9

She was a realist. Her compassion did not become sentimentality. She understood that progress was a long labor of compromise. She mistrusted absolutism in all its forms—the absolutism of the word and even more the absolutism of the deed. She never supposed that all the problems of life could be cured in a day or a year or a lifetime. Her pungent and salty understanding of human behavior kept her always in intimate contact with reality. I think this was a primary source of her strange strength, because she never thought that the loss of a battle meant the loss of a war, nor did she suppose that a compromise which produced only part of the objective sought was an act of corruption or of treachery. She knew that no formula of words, no combination of deeds, could abolish the troubles of life overnight and usher in the millennium. /10

The miracle, I have tried to suggest, is how much tangible good she really did; how much realism and reason were mingled with her instinctive compassion; how her contempt for the perquisites of power ultimately won her the esteem of so many of the powerful; and how, at her death, there was a universality of grief that transcended all the harsh boundaries of political, racial and religious strife and, for a moment at least, united men in a vision of what their world might be. /11

We do not claim the right to enshrine another mortal, and this least of all would Mrs. Roosevelt have desired. She would have wanted it said, I believe, that she well knew the pressures of pride and vanity, the sting of bitterness and defeat, the gray days of national peril and personal anguish. But she clung to the confident expectation that men could fashion their own tomorrows if they could only learn that yesterday can be neither relived nor revised. /12

Many who have spoken of her in these last few days have used a word to which we all assent, because it speaks a part of what we feel. They have called her "a lady," a "great lady," "the first lady of the world." But the word "lady," though it says much about Eleanor Roosevelt, does not say all. To be incapable of self-concern is not a negative virtue; it is the other side of a coin that has a positive face—the most positive, I think, of all the faces. And to enhance the humanity of others is not a kind of humility; it is a kind of pride—the noblest of all the forms of pride. No man or woman can respect other men and women who does not respect life. And to respect life is to love it. Eleanor Roosevelt loved life—and that, perhaps, is the most meaningful thing that can be said about her, for it says so much beside. /13

It takes courage to love life. Loving it demands imagination and perception and the kind of patience women are more apt to have than men—the bravest and most understanding women. And loving it takes something more beside—it takes a gift for life, a gift for love. /14

Eleanor Roosevelt's childhood was unhappy—miserably unhappy, she sometimes said. But it was Eleanor Roosevelt who also said that "one must never, for whatever reason, turn his back on life." She did not mean that duty should compel us. She meant that life should. "Life," she said, "was meant to be lived." A simple statement. An obvious statement. But a statement that by its obviousness and its simplicity challenges the most intricate of all the philosophies of despair. /15

Many of the admonitions she bequeathed us are neither new thoughts nor novel concepts. Her ideas were, in many respects, old fashioned—as old as the Sermon on the Mount, as the reminder that it is more blessed to give than to receive. In the words of St. Francis that she loved so well: "For it is in the giving that we receive." /16

She imparted to the familiar language—nay, what too many have come to treat as the clichés—of Christianity a new poignancy and vibrance. She did so not by reciting them, but by proving that it is possible to live them. It is this above all that rendered her unique in her century. It was said of her contemptuously at times that she was a do-gooder, a charge leveled with similar derision against another public figure 1,962 years ago. /17

We who are assembled here are of various religious and political faiths, and perhaps different conceptions of man's destiny in the universe. It is not an irreverence, I trust, to say that the immortality Mrs. Roosevelt would have valued most would be found in the deeds and visions her life inspired in others, and in the proof that they would be faithful to the spirit of any tribute conducted in her name. /18

And now one can almost hear Mrs. Roosevelt saying that the speaker has already talked too long. So we must say goodbye. We are always saying farewell in this world — always standing at the edge of loss attempting to retrieve some memory, some human meaning, from the silence — something which was precious and is gone. /19

Often, although we know the absence well enough, we cannot name it or describe it even. What left the world when Lincoln died? Speaker after speaker in those aching days tried to tell his family or his neighbors or his congregation. But no one found the words, not even Whitman. "When lilacs last in the dooryard bloomed" can break the heart, but not with Lincoln's greatness, only with his loss. What the words could never capture was the man himself. His deeds were known; every school child knew them. But it was not his deeds the country mourned: it was the man —

the mastery of life which made the greatness of the man. /20

It is always so. On that April day when Franklin Roosevelt died, it was not a President we wept for. It was a man. In Archibald MacLeish's words:

Fagged out, worn down, sick
With the weight of his own bones,
    the task finished,
The war won, the victory assured,
The glory left behind him for-
    the others,
(And the wheels roll up through
    the night in the sweet land
In the cool air in the spring
    between the lanterns). /21

It is so now. What we have lost in Eleanor Roosevelt is not her life. She lived that out to the full. What we have lost, what we wish to recall for ourselves, to remember, is what she was herself. And who can name it? But she left "a name to shine on the entablatures of truth, forever." /22

We pray that she has found peace, and a glimpse of sunset. But today we weep for ourselves. We are lonelier; someone has gone from one's own life — who was like the certainty of refuge; and someone has gone from the world — who was like the certainty of honor. /23

Speeches of Tribute for Collateral Study

1. Richard Cardinal Cushing, "Eulogy to John F. Kennedy," *Vital Speeches*, XXX (December 1, 1963), 100–101.

2. Robert S. Emrich, "The Greatness of Lincoln," *Representative American Speeches: 1958–1959*, ed. A. Craig Baird (New York: H.W. Wilson Company, 1959), pp. 169–177.

3. Pericles, "Funeral Oration," *The Speaker's Resource Book*, ed. Carroll C. Arnold, Douglas Ehninger, and John C. Gerber (Chicago: Scott, Foresman and Company, 1961), pp. 216–220.

SPEECHES OF PRESENTATION AND ACCEPTANCE*

President Kennedy presented the National Aeronautics and Space Administration's Distinguished Service Medal to Lt. Col. John H. Glenn, Jr., February

*Text of both speeches furnished by the White House Press Secretary.

23, 1962. Three days earlier, Colonel Glenn completed a successful orbital flight, the first to be attempted by an American. The ceremony of presentation took place at Cape Canaveral, Florida—now Cape Kennedy.

PRESENTING THE DISTINGUISHED SERVICE MEDAL
John F. Kennedy

Colonel Glenn, will you step forward. Seventeen years ago today, a group of Marines put the American Flag on Mount Suribachi, so it is very appropriate that today we decorate Colonel Glenn of the United States Marine Corps, and also realize that in the not too distant future a Marine or a Naval man or an Air Force man will put the American Flag on the moon. /1

I present this Citation. The President of the United States takes pleasure in awarding the National Aeronautics and Space Administration's Distinguished Service Medal to Lieutenant Colonel John H. Glenn, Jr., United States Marine Corps, for services set forth in the following: For exceptionally meritorious service to the government of the United States in a duty of great responsibility as the first American astronaut to perform orbital flight. Lieutenant Colonel Glenn's orbital flight on February 20, 1962, made an outstanding contribution to the advancement of human knowledge of space technology and in demonstration of man's capabilities in space flight. /2

His performance was marked by his great professional knowledge, his skill as a test pilot, his unflinching courage, and his extraordinary ability to perform most difficult tasks under conditions of great physical stress and personal danger. His performance in fulfillment of this most dangerous assignment reflects the highest credit upon himself and the United States. /3

Colonel, we appreciate what you have done! /4

We have Mr. and Mrs. Glenn, who launched Colonel Glenn originally—they are right here in the front row—and also Mrs. Glenn and David and Lynn. /5

And we would like to have you say a word to everybody. /6

ACCEPTING THE DISTINGUISHED SERVICE MEDAL
John H. Glenn, Jr.

All right—fine, thank you. Sit down, please—it's hot. /1

I can't express my appreciation adequately, to be here accepting this, when I know how many thousands of people all over the country were involved in helping accomplish what we did last Tuesday—and knowing how, particularly this group here at the Cape, and many of the group here on the platform, our own group of astronauts who were scattered all around the world who performed their functions here at the Cape also—we all acted literally and figuratively as a team. It was a real team effort all the way. /2

We have stressed the team effort in Project Mercury. It goes across the board—I think sort of a cross-cut of Americana, of industry, and military, and Civil Service—government work—contractors. It's almost a cross-cut of American effort in the technical field—I think it wasn't specialized by any one particular group. It was headed up by NASA, of course, but thousands and thousands of people have contributed, certainly as much or more than I have to the Project. /3

I would like to consider that I was sort of a figure-head for the whole big, tremendous effort. And I am very proud of the Medal I have on my lapel here, for all of us—you included—because I think it represents all of our efforts—not just mine. /4

Thank you very much. And thank you, Mr. President. /5

SPEECH OF ACCEPTANCE

The following speech was delivered by U Thant, Secretary General of the United Nations, on November 30, 1962. The speaker had been serving as Acting Secretary General since the death of Dag Hammarskjold a year earlier. His words reveal an understanding of the demands of the position and a dedication to the aims for which the UN was founded.

At the time of this speech, the Cuban crisis of October, 1962, was still fresh in men's memories and the UN was engaged in trying to bring peace to the Congo. In surveying the responsibilities which faced him and the UN as he took office, U Thant referred to these problems.

ACCEPTING THE POST OF SECRETARY GENERAL OF THE UN*
U Thant

Exactly 56 weeks ago today I assumed what was to me an unfamiliar role, as Acting Secretary General of the United Nations. Today the General Assembly has done me the further honor of appointing me to serve out the normal term of five years as Secretary General of the United Nations, beginning with my assumption of the office as Acting Secretary General on 3 November 1961. /1

I am grateful to you, Mr. President, for your gracious words, to the President and members of the Security Council for their unanimous recommendation, and to the General Assembly for my unanimous appointment as Secretary General. I deeply appreciate and value this mark of your confidence in me, which I shall endeavor my utmost to justify and deserve. /2

On this occasion I would recall the words of my distinguished predecessor on his re-election to a second term. He said, and I quote: "Nobody, I think, can accept the position of Secretary General of the United Nations, knowing what it means, except from a sense of duty." /3

He had had over four years experience in that office when he made that statement. My experience has been shorter, but I believe that I do know what that office means, and I accept my extended mandate with humility and out of a sense of duty. /4

I also take this occasion to reaffirm my oath of office, and I solemnly swear to exercise in all loyalty, discretion, and conscience the

functions entrusted to me as Secretary General of the United Nations, to discharge these functions and regulate my conduct with the interests of the United Nations only in view, and not to seek or accept instructions in regard to the performance of my duties from any government or other authority external to the organization. /5

At the same time, I enter upon this fresh period of service to the international community with a due sense of responsibility. When I was questioned on this subject at a press conference just before the present session of the General Assembly began, I stated that my decision to accept the position of Secretary General for a longer term would "be governed primarily by a few considerations, including an early settlement of the Congo problem, the prospect of stability of this world organization as a potent force for peace, the prospect of my playing a humble part in bringing about a more favorable atmosphere for the easing of tensions, and if I may say so, the prospect of my ability to bridge somewhat the gulf between the two giants." /6

If I now accept this extended term, it is because I do believe that I may be able to play a role, however humble, in the easing of tensions and in bridging the gulf between the major powers. In this task, I shall count upon the assistance of my colleagues in the Secretariat, high and low, who have, as always, shown a truly admirable team spirit, marked by ungrudging effort, willing cooperation, un-

---

*From *The New York Times*, December 1, 1962.

flagging devotion to duty and dedication to the high purposes of the Charter. /7

Without their assistance I could not have achieved much during the last year, and I wish to take this opportunity to pay tribute to them. I shall call on them for advice and assistance, as I have done in the past, individually, collectively, or otherwise, as the occasion may demand. /8

I referred a moment ago to the problem of the Congo, a problem which has been with us now for over two years and to which I referred in my acceptance speech of last year. /9

The problem remains unsolved in spite of the best efforts of all concerned. As a consequence, the financial problem of the organization also remains unsolved. Both these problems must, however, be solved, and soon, if the usefulness of the organization for the future is not to be seriously affected, and today I appeal anew to all member governments, who have come to value the usefulness of the organization, to assist in solving these long-standing issues. /10

On the credit side, however, I may perhaps recall that the organization was able to settle one source of tension in South and Southeast Asia, namely the problem of West New Guinea (West Irian). /11

The implementation of the triparte agreement between the Governments of the Netherlands and Indonesia, and the United Nations, which was approved earlier in the current session by the General Assembly, has worked smoothly, and I am sure that we will be able to carry this unique operation to a successful conclusion, with the cooperation and scrupulous observance of the terms of the agreement by the Governments concerned. /12

Again, in the Cuban crisis, which seemed so serious some five weeks ago, I believe we are now over the most dangerous phase, even though complete agreement on all outstanding aspects has not yet been registered. /13

I now look at the years ahead. I would hope that these years would be marked by an improvement in the international climate, and by better understanding of the difficult problems which the world faces today. These problems can be solved only by goodwill and mutual understanding, and by a spirit of "give and take." /14

When the future of mankind itself is at stake, no country or interest-group can afford to take a rigid stand, or claim that its position is the only right one, and that others must take it or leave it. /15

No difficult problem can be solved to the complete satisfaction of all sides. We live in an imperfect world, and have to accept imperfect solutions, which become more acceptable as we learn to live with them and as time passes by. /16

In solving these complex problems, I myself and the Secretariat, of which I am proud to be the chief administrative officer, are at the service not only of all member governments but of "the peoples of the United Nations." /17

Speeches of Acceptance for Collateral Study

1. John F. Kennedy, "Inaugural Address," *The Speaker's Resource Book,* ed. Carroll C. Arnold, Douglas Ehninger, and John C. Gerber (Chicago: Scott, Foresman and Company, 1961), pp. 256–259.

2. William Faulkner, "On Accepting the Nobel Prize," *The Age of Danger,* ed. Harold F. Harding (New York: Random House, 1952), pp. 397–398.

3. Douglas MacArthur, "On Accepting the National Football Foundation's Gold Medal Award," *Footballetter,* II (January 1960), 2–4.

DISCUSSION

The following discussion was televised by the National Broadcasting Company May 19, 1963. It exhibits the lively but orderly exchange of ideas at which informal discussion groups should aim. In some few places, the transcript has been abridged, primarily to meet space requirements.

Eric F. Goldman, Lillian Hellman, Walter Kerr, David Merrick, and Richard Watts, Jr.

Announcer: The Open Mind, free to examine, to question, to disagree. The subject of today's discussion: "Critics and the Theater." The moderator of *The Open Mind* is Eric F. Goldman, Professor of History at Princeton University and author of *Rendezvous with Destiny* and *The Crucial Decade.* Mr. Goldman will introduce the topic and guests for this week in just one minute. /1

Commercial /2

Goldman: Hello, ladies and gentlemen. In preparing for this program I had fun looking up some of the quotes that have come down through history about critics. Coleridge put it simply. He said: "Critics — murderers." Mark Twain said: "The trade of critic, in music, literature and the drama, is the most degraded of all trades." Channing Pollock, the playwright: "The critic is a legless man who teaches running." And our contemporary, John Mason Brown: "To many people, dramatic criticism must seem like an attempt to tattoo soapballs." /3

Nature seems to have created certain natural antagonists in this world, dogs and cats, professors and university administrators, critics and the criticized, particularly critics and men of the theater. And *The Open Mind* today is going to inquire into the state of this ancient tension in the year 1963. /4

Our panel, here to my far left, Mr. Richard Watts, Jr., drama critic of the *New York Post.* /5

Mr. David Merrick, the theatrical producer who in the last nine years has produced twenty-seven plays on Broadway, most of them hits, and who is now represented by *Oliver, Tchin-Tchin, Stop the World,* and *Rattle of a Simple Man.* /6

Miss Lillian Hellman, generally recognized as one of America's leading playwrights, who has given us *The Children's Hour, The Little Foxes, Toys in the Attic,* and the recent adaptation, *My Mother, My Father, and Me.* /7

And Mr. Walter Kerr, drama critic of the *New York Herald Tribune,* author of several

volumes on the theater and, most recently, of the book, *The Decline of Pleasure.* /8

Mr. Tyrone Guthrie, who was to be with us, is ill and unfortunately cannot be here. /9

Mr. Merrick, would you get us going by a comment on what's on the minds of a lot of our audience? You have been quite critical of theater critics. What, in general, is your criticism of the state of drama criticism today? /10

Merrick: I'd like to establish here for your audience that we are judged by a supreme court of the theater, the seven New York daily drama critics. Whether the playwrights, the producers, the directors, the various creative elements that go into a play exist or not, that would be determined by these seven gentlemen. We're fortunate to have two of them here today, so any criticism of the past that I've directed has been largely to certain members of this particular group of seven. As for Mr. Watts, I've never had the slightest disagreement with him. He hasn't liked all of my offerings by any means but I've always felt that he did manage a proper balance and we've always got a fair count upon whatever was presented. /11

Goldman: Mr. Merrick, is there in this something which you think is a general phenomenon or is it simply that you think particular — /12

Merrick: No, I think it is specific in my case. It's not general. I think most of the critics are fine and give a very fair appraisal of whatever they are viewing on an opening night. I disagree with some; one in particular has been Mr. Kerr. And in the case of Mr. Kerr, I regard him as a very fine drama critic, a man who writes wonderfully, so it's not a question of his competence at all. But I think you're just too tough. Now, in looking through the records since he began, and his career as a New York drama critic was almost simultaneous with mine as a producer, I find that Mr. Kerr has liked only one play in nine, in general. I'm not referring to my product at all throughout

*Text furnished by WNBC-TV Public Affairs Department. Reprinted with permission of the producers of *The Open Mind* and of Eric F. Goldman, Lillian Hellman, Walter Kerr, David Merrick, and Richard Watts, Jr.

this discussion. It's the theater in general. Whereas Mr. Watts here, who is not considered an easy drama critic by any means, has liked about one out of five. /13

Goldman: Mr. Kerr, I recall from your book, *Pieces of Eight,* that you thought that the critics were not tough enough. /14

Kerr: They're not as tough as the audience is — that is one of the things you find. I don't know, David, how accurate or exact that one-in-nine is. I've never counted it myself. I wouldn't have supposed it would have been quite that high. What I do find, though, is that of the balance of shows that I like, and write favorably about in a season, I will run into a number of people who go to the theater who have detested those. That is to say, I am more often accused of over-praising than under-praising by the people I meet, by the people who write to me. The audience, I think, is a little tougher than we are, a little more demanding than we are. /15

Merrick: Not actually, because many of the plays that you have hated have turned out to be very big hits. Some of mine, for example — I won't go list them — I've talked to a number of *Herald Tribune* readers — your readers — and they very often say, "Oh, he doesn't like anything so we pay no attention to him." So it goes in the other direction. I know you have written that if a critic is too easy he will have no influence at all; they'll say, "Well, he just likes everything." But it also goes in the other direction. I have heard your readers say that you're just too tough and they pay no attention at all. So, you see, you lose influence that way too. /16

Kerr: Well, then, you shouldn't have given me an award last year for being the most influential critic. /17

Merrick: Do you want to turn back the award? /18

Goldman: Mr. Watts? /19

Watts: I can only go by the letters I receive and it's certainly true that I receive more letters attacking me and attacking me much more violently when I have praised something than when I have panned it. I've had two cases this year and one of the cases is Miss Hellman's play. Another one was a rather different play, *The Lady of the Camellias,* which I was almost alone in liking. And I received the most violent letters about that. /20

Goldman: Louis Kronenberger — I was reading a piece of his when he retired from his post on *Time* magazine as drama critic — said that the whole system is wrong, that in no other field is everything that is produced reviewed. In the book field, for example, the *New York Times* or the *Herald Tribune* goes through books and picks out the most significant ones, whereas he was supposed to go review each one of these things. Under the circumstances, he thought it was remarkable how many of the plays got a half-way decent review at all. /21

Kerr: There are many fewer plays than books produced in a given season. It becomes possible to cover them all. On the other hand, the fact that books are not thoroughly covered has been under attack by Dwight Macdonald recently, as you perhaps know — the business of selecting what book you're going to review, perhaps on the basis of whether or not there's a chance you might like it. As a result, maybe 40 — oh, much more, I guess — 80 per cent of the notices in a book section may come out favorable because of the pre-selection. And, therefore, you don't have exactly a representative cross-section or a critical response, really. /22

Merrick: I've heard frequently, not just from you but from drama critics, that they feel a most important function of theirs is to raise the standards of the theater and to force the taste of the public upward. Is that one of your beliefs? /23

Kerr: No, not one of mine. I think the real function of daily reviewing is to make distinctions. I think in your case, David, for instance — I mean I've often thought about you, you see, you've given me much cause to think about you — and I really seriously thought how honestly you must sit down, let's say, to prepare a musical. Suppose you're doing a new show, not an importation now, and I think that when you do it you say, "Who is the best librettist I can get, who is the best composer, who is the best director, who is the best star?" And then you can go out and get them. And having put this package together, and it really is from a point of view of prestige, reputation, money, a very solid and workable kind of package, I think that once you have done that, you sort of consider that your obligation is fulfilled. In a sense it is. You've done the very best you can in all these areas. And then you think, because you've done the very best you can in all these areas, you have provided the finest that is available, we must like it. But as it happens you've skipped one little step, which is that creative accident that happens. Sometimes these people come together and something wonderful comes out of it. And sometimes, unfortunately, the same talented people come together and it just won't work. It just goes wrong somewhere and the problem is never solved. In your own case, let us say, in something like *Gypsy*, it all came together. You could take some of the same people and just as good people for *Subways Are Not* [sic] *for Sleeping*, and it doesn't come together, you see, in the same way. That is the creative accident. I think our job is to make a distinction between *Gypsy* and *Subways Are Not for Sleeping*. /24

Goldman: I think Miss Hellman here, if I read you correctly, would be a little harsher about this process than even Mr. Kerr is. In an interview in *Fortune*, which I read, you said that the theater today is just a dreadful bore, and that what's wrong is— /25

Hellman: In *Esquire*.— /26

Goldman: *Esquire*, yes, I'm sorry. . . . You say that the theater is so concerned with money that it has to make good guesses about what is wanted, and what is wanted is certainly not bite. And the theater is bad, very bad, so far as you're concerned. Is this true? /27

Hellman: I find myself in disagreement with both David and Walter. At the risk of sounding unpleasantly highbrow, I don't think these are the terms in which criticism should be thought about, whether it's one in nine or one in eight hundred or liking something too much or liking something too little. I just don't think the level of dramatic criticism is very high. I would prefer to see it done in other terms. I would prefer the whole theater in other terms. Less successful or more successful doesn't seem to me to be what one needs to know. It's true that, in a commercial sense, David is right in feeling that the theater is killed by New York critics but they didn't choose to do that. And David himself has been the only one who has tried to break this hold. It was nobody's fault. We all just sat around and waited for things to happen. Nobody advertised plays, nobody

went to trouble about plays and this power given the New York newspapers is not in any sense anybody's fault. I'm sure Mr. Watts doesn't want it and Mr. Kerr doesn't want it; nobody wants it. I don't agree with the terms in most dramatic criticism. I think that one of Mr. Watts's great gifts is that he genuinely enjoys the theater. If that's what David means, I think this is a great gift. I myself did theater reviews for one week for *Time* magazine. I don't know what I did them for, *Time* and I quit at the end of the week. I remember reviewing one play—and deciding this wasn't for me. It's very hard to understand how most people can review the Broadway theater. I don't think criticism should be talked about in these terms. /28

Goldman: It isn't quite clear to me what terms you would like to talk to. /29

Hellman: I think most book reviewing does exactly the same thing. There's a general level of sort of middlebrowism which seems to me to calm the theater and to calm literature in our time. I would prefer to see not a question of attack or praise—much too much is praised on Broadway for my taste, and some condemned without proper recognition of what was attempted or done. I think that what I mean is that the terms of criticism should not be the terms of what is successful. What pleases certainly should be important but no sensible, intelligent writer resents a review which is, in a sense, a bad review as long as it tells him something. I find very seldom that most reviews tell me very much of what was wrong. I've probably not defined what I mean by better criticism very well, have I? /30

Kerr: I wonder one thing, Lillian, perhaps if you aren't asking of the daily reviewer more than he can— /31

Hellman: I am— /32

Mixed voices /33

Kerr: There are levels of criticism, you see. It's really a question of whether it should be called criticism or reviewing. Opinion is expressed, of course. But the first night report is one thing, the weekly report is another, written in the longer perspective. The monthly report takes a still longer perspective. And I don't think, until you finally get around to books, that you're getting real criticism of this most responsible kind. /34

Hellman: I don't think you get much then. I was about to say that's always brought up, that idea—and you're perfectly right—it's a miracle any of you do well in an hour or whatever it is given to you— /35

Kerr: Well, I wasn't trying to cop a plea— /36

Hellman: No, but I don't understand why that doesn't get changed. I never have understood it. It would seem to me that there are two possibilities. There's no need for everybody to know the next morning; they can perfectly well wait twenty-four hours. Of course, the main thing, the main difficulty in theater criticism, is a perfectly practical one. When you review a book, there's the author's name, and the author has written it. In a play, none of you know whose responsibility is what. None of you really, for example, have a right to an opinion about a director. You can't possibly tell what's a good director and a bad director. /37

Goldman: Miss Hellman, running through your remarks and Mr. Merrick's remarks is this assumption that seven men in New York make or break plays. Mr. Kerr, if I remember correctly, denies that the critics really have that power. Mr. Merrick, do I understand you correctly, do you think the critics really make or break them? /38

Merrick: Oh, yes. /39

Mixed voices /40

Merrick: I would say that occasionally, with a musical with a star and a big advance sale, that the show can find its own audience with bad criticism. It's happened to me here and there but, in general, a serious play, the kind of play that Miss Hellman usually writes, will make it or not on the basis of those reviews, and generally on the basis of morning reviews. Now, that's another thing. Unfortunately, it's not even a majority of seven. Many plays have received five raves and two negatives. If the two negatives happen to be in those important morning papers, the project is badly wounded. /41

Goldman: Mr. Merrick, excuse me, I looked up the reviews of some of your plays. Take *Oliver*, which is a great success. Mr. Watts said "an exciting and stunningly beautiful musical play." It's all in that tone. Mr. Kerr is rather dour about the whole business, "ener-

getic but energy of a peculiarly mechanical kind, confusing, colors are bright, action is constant but pace falters, etc., etc." It received very mixed reviews, in general. /42

Mixed voices /43

Merrick: It's a big hit anyway. But that's a musical and we had a big advance. The phenomenon, perhaps, of the season for me, and maybe in my career as a producer, is a musical called *Stop the World—I Want to Get Off.* Mr. Watts here liked it quite a lot; Mr. Kerr liked it not at all. And it's a rather off-beat musical and it's been a hit, quite a solid hit. That did get very mixed reviews— /44

Watts: Again, mostly favorable. /45

Merrick: No, no— /46

Kerr: I'd like to come in here because I think it really disproves David's whole point. I don't think we're strict enough about this. I wouldn't deny that the notices have influence, certainly when they're unanimous. If they're all in favor, it's going to help; if they're all against, it's going to hurt. Certainly. But most shows, maybe 80 per cent of all shows, get a mixture of some kind. And if you really track down that mixture year after year, the box office does not respond in relation, in exact correlation, to the mixture. For instance, you this year have two plays, two shows. You talk about *Stop the World.* You lost four morning papers, although just a moment ago you said that it wasn't even a group of seven, that the great weight was in the morning papers. And although you lost all the morning papers, which you feel are so important, actually the show became a success and ran all season and paid off and is still running— /47

Merrick: I— /48

Kerr: May I go on to one more point? There is another play, the name of which I won't mention, of yours, which got six out of seven favorables and you're having trouble getting it off the ground. Your pattern, you see, turns upside down in both cases, and we won't even talk about— /49

Merrick: I mentioned the *Stop the World* musical as rather a phenomenon in my experience and that was because I managed an advance and in that way you can survive reviews. I did say that a serious play didn't have a chance with poor reviews and that's the kind of play Miss Hellman writes. But Miss Hellman was in an area of discussing drama criticism from the point of view of the writer. A drama critic, it seems to me, particularly in a daily, has an obligation primarily to his reader and to what the reader wants to know. Of this I am certain. It's simply: Is it worth that expensive price that they have to pay? /50

Hellman: Now, forgive me, David. I think that should be done. That's just my point. That should be done by reporters. But such people shouldn't call themselves critics; there simply should be a reporter there to say— /51

Merrick: Well, that's what the public wants, I think, Lillian— /52

Hellman: The critics should deal with merit, not with— /53

Merrick: But the daily readers want to know and that's from— /54

Hellman: Yes, but that's not the— /55

Mixed voices /56

Merrick: Well, I'm not for it. I'm just saying, what they seem to want to know is a kind of consumer's research digest— /57

Hellman: That's right. Exactly. /58

Merrick: Watching their habits on trains, buses, subways, we find that they read the first paragraph and the last paragraph. They just want to know whether they should go to see it, whether it's an entertainment or not. /59

Hellman: They want to go to see a hit. /60

Mixed voices /61

Goldman: I wonder if we couldn't— /62

Mixed voices /63

Kerr: Well, you're employed by a newspaper, you see, and you presumably are writing an opinion for the benefit of the reader. But that doesn't rule out the consideration of merit. You may consider that merit is for the benefit of the reader. /64

Hellman: I don't think anybody does. This is just exactly where we disagree. Nobody's got a right to write for anybody. Just write— /65

Mixed voices /66

Hellman: I don't write for the audience, much as I like to have it. /67

Goldman: Mr. Watts? /68

Watts: All I tried to say is that I like or dislike a play and it's for this reason and for that reason—and hoping, by that, that the reader will judge for himself. I also do a column once a week, expressing my opinions on everything in the world—it may seem impertinent of me but I think it has a value. A reader can check up and see how his prejudices go along with mine and see how much he wants to accept me as his adviser on things. But there is a difficulty in the serious play which may not altogether come off but which has excellent things in it. To try to get that kind of play in the proper proportions is the most difficult job that I face as a reviewer. /69

Hellman: Yes, I'm sure that's true and the result is that the serious play suffers far worse than the musical. /70

Kerr: That's a more important matter. However, I think the essence of it is that it's difficult to move the audience today, for whatever the reason, to a serious play. It's very difficult. /71

Hellman: That was my point. You really have no—I have taught at colleges so much, you have no knowledge how important this is that they don't—I think what David means, and I'm in agreement with him, is that the audience we now have in the theater reads dramatic criticism because it wants to know what's going to be a hit or a failure and only wants to go to hits. But enormous numbers of very intelligent and cultivated people find the theater a great bore now. I'm one of them. /72

Kerr: There's the point—you're the problem. You find the theater a bore— /73

Hellman: Since nobody talks to me on my terms— /74

Mixed voices /75

Hellman: In the theater or criticism nobody says anything to me in my terms. I went to see a famous play this year—it is going to be nameless because I don't talk about writers. I'm not a critic. And I'm in a state of shock by the end of this play. Most literary people have been. In my case—I don't like to use myself as an example, but you both refer to it, so perhaps I can—three reviewers liked the play, among them Mr. Watts. Large numbers of literary people, among them the greatest critic in the world, I suppose—Edmund Wilson— liked it. I find it was liked by literary people and not liked by drama critics. And I said to myself, "Well, it doesn't make Edmund Wilson right and you wrong"; it simply means that I'm bewildered by the terms. It doesn't tell me anything. I'm amazed that two educated men find such difference in a work of art. I know that I'm alone in this point of view here and— /76

Merrick: Back to the serious play. Now we get to an interesting point and it's part of your record too. Certainly the standard of your criticism seems to go down for a musical and go up for a serious attempt. And I wonder about that, since you say it's very difficult to drive an audience into a serious play that is good. I find so often you get to one and chill it with all the reservations when it's the kind of play [that] needs more help from the drama critic than any other play. /77

Kerr: You see now, however, you're asking the reviewer, in a sense, to cheat out of sympathy or out of idealism—that is to say, instead of judging the serious play on its own level, by what it's set out to do, you're saying, "Well, be a little more sympathetic. Put in more adjectives." I think we're adjective happy now. I think the over-writing consists mostly in too many exhilarating "brilliant," "bravos," and so on and so forth. I think that's one of the worse burdens, actually, that the reviewers accept at the present time because of this legend of their supreme court power which I don't believe is anywhere near as influential— /78

Merrick: Oh, it's influential but— /79

Goldman: May I try to close up that one point, just how powerful are the critics, and move on to some other things by asking this: Mr. Merrick, when you speak of the power of the critics, aren't you ignoring the fact that people who are going to a play read something besides the seven particular gentlemen who write in the New York papers? For example, about *Oliver*, among the things that I read was the *Time* magazine review which was rather dim and was a bit like Mr. Kerr's. Don't these things influence— /80

Merrick: Not to the extent that the seven daily critics who are considered the supreme court of the theater do, and somehow it fans out across the nation and is reported by the wire services, radio and television critics— /81

Goldman: You don't think *Time* is more influential than— /82

Merrick: No, *Time* is— /83

Mixed voices /84

Merrick: *Time* is important but, in general, the power lies with the seven dailies. /85

Kerr: I think you're buying a legend there and you're the very man, you know, who's keeping very close tabs now on public response and on commercial response to these things. I'd say that of all the people who come to see a play in the long run, more have read *Time* and nothing but *Time* than have ever read the daily notices to begin with. No one reads seven critics, you see. You say, "Do they read only the seven critics?" Who does? Who reads two or more than two? Furthermore, no one knows generally what the balance was. They don't know whether they were all in favor—they get a sense, they get an opinion, but that impression is very often most inaccurate. The wire services run reviews of their own which are actually more widely circulated than the reports of the New York newspapers— /86

Mixed voices /87

Merrick: They do a first round in the morning on radio and television. They do a roundup of last night's openings. And they base it on the four morning— /88

Kerr: They have to at that time. /89

Merrick: They have to at that time. Also the AP and UP by morning have sent out to all the morning papers in the country their own reviews and little tiny quotes from the others. And if it adds up to three and two or four and three or whatever, then you're on the positive side. But there are two papers that seem to be regarded so highly in what they report that they're reaching millions and millions of readers and listeners throughout the country at that point, and it seems to be the *Times* and the *Herald Tribune*. So before a weekly like *Time* magazine gets near it, which would get into homes maybe two weeks later, it's set around the country to those who are interested in the theater at all as to whether that show was a hit. It's either a hit or a flop before the weeklies get at it. Now *Time* is influential by the nature of its circulation and readership. But I think there's little doubt about the power of the critic. /90

I can give you an example on the positive side and why we must have them. . . . /91
[Refers to *La Plume de ma Tante*, whose success he credits to reviews of critics.]

Kerr: That, of course, is a case where you did get unanimous notices, and I certainly grant you that in the case of unanimity it's going to have an immediate impact on the show. /92

Mixed voices /93

Kerr: That is a very discouraging kind of thing to hear, and to some degree it's always true. But at the same time remember this show had been a great success in France and it had been a great success in London, so it's not the first time anyone laughs. You may just have hit some sort of freak reaction in Philadelphia. You may have been— /94

Mixed voices /95

Merrick: But not until the New York critics said it was funny. /96

Kerr: Yes, but many changes, I understand, were made between the . . . . /97

Mixed voices /98

Merrick: I'd like to get to one important question, though— /99

Goldman: Before you get to that question, may I reintroduce you briefly? . . .

Go ahead, Mr. Merrick, I'm sorry. /100

Merrick: The question is this: You have written, Mr. Kerr—it may have been a year or two ago—that things will get worse before they get better. And we know what you meant by that, and you were going to hold out, no matter what, for just what you thought was high quality, and you weren't going to settle for anything shoddy. Well, here we are with some thirty-two theaters in New York and there's an audience who regards Broadway as a place to be entertained in various ways, from serious plays that Miss Hellman might write, the literate play she might write, to the knock-about musical like *Little Me* which you adored, and hasn't found an audience. /101

Kerr: Oh, it's found some; it hasn't done as well as its producers expected. /102

Merrick: They never do. But are you meaning to say with a statement like that that you prefer the theater be run with ten theaters open— /103

Kerr: No— /104

Merrick: Of high quality. Isn't it really the case of the best that we can find at the moment? Let's say you're right, and I think you are right. I don't think the quality is as high as it could be or has been in the past. And we never know when a wonderful crop of new plays or two or three great playwrights will turn up. In the meantime, the theater is becoming quite bankrupt. And I certainly think the critics are contributing toward that. Isn't your function really—at the end of the year there's a publication that says the "Ten Best Plays of the Year." Well, some of them are pretty painful—maybe two should really be in it. /105

Kerr: As a rule, it's difficult to find ten, yes. However, to answer your question if I can—I think it's a kind of complicated one— but I think it's very closely related to what Miss Hellman was saying. She was talking about how bored she is with the theater. I think that, by and large, the contemporary audience has, for whatever reasons, become quite bored with the theater. I think that is why the reviewers have any influence at all. If they weren't bored, if they really loved it, if they were wild to go, if they had a good time every time they went or were deeply pleased in some way, they would go regardless of the critics, as they did forty years ago in this country. Then, they simply dismissed the criticism of George Cohan in the musical field and of William Gillette in a straight play field. They went anyway. They were loyal. Now, I do think we have come into a serious condition where the audience so distrusts the theater that it demands the report of advance scouts, like the reviewers, to sort of go over the mine field and get blown up first. And then, if you come back and you weren't blown up and you tell them it's all right, it's safe to go to this one, then they'll go. That's the condition we're describing. I don't really think it's that serious, but some of it's there. Now, if one were to lower one's standards, self-consciously or consciously, in order to help the theater financially or to keep them from going bankrupt, all you would be doing would be sending them to more boredom. So I think you would in the end achieve only the objective you are afraid of. /106

Hellman: I think the object is to raise standards, not to lower them. Mr. Merrick has quite proper regard—he's a practical producer with a great deal of money riding—and he's quite right to think that he wants to get as many people in as possible. But I don't honestly think that's your business. I have a totally different point of view, as I said three times now. It's not that one is too harsh. It's that most of you, not all of you, seem to me to have frequently very strange standards. There are standards that I don't think are either one

thing or the other. They aren't lowbrow standards, which they could easily well be. I think
in that case you send a reporter; there's nothing wrong with that. I must say I don't often
think they're very highbrow standards either.
I do agree with David when he says I don't
think you should alter your attitude because
a play is serious. What difference does it make
what the author intends? But there is some
great relaxation that goes on at that musical
show. In my own belief, because very few of
you know anything about music — forgive me
for saying so — and that you go in a more pleasant frame of mind; you know more about
writing than you do about music. Not that I
know very much, but so often you like the
score of a show that most people find terribly
surprising that you do. I think David is right
in that case, you do go — /107

Watts: I think that's very true — one field
in which the critics are closer to their audience
than possibly any other is that we like the same
kind of possibly cheap popular music. This
is — /108

Mixed voices /109

Merrick: Mr. Kerr has made this a kind of
generalization, that I think drama criticism,
in general, is too difficult. That's not true. I,
at the outset of this, said I wholly agreed with
Mr. Watts. I disagree with only two of the
gentlemen writing in the daily papers. They
happen to be on a couple of the most influential papers. Mr. Kerr is one. I say he is too
tough. Now, I want an explanation of why he
is twice as difficult as the other critics. It's
one man's opinion, you see. It's his opinion as
against the other critics and the public and yet
great damage is done to the project and to all
the people who contributed to it. And I find
my opinion is that Mr. Kerr has rather bizarre
tastes in the theater. Some of the things he
adores — and there was at least one of mine that
he adored that I thought was awful — and some
that he dislikes become great popular hits and
deservedly so, and the other critics have liked
them. He is the great dissenter of this supreme
court. And my objection to the current drama
criticism is not that it's all too tough, but some
of them, at least, lack excitement in the way
they write about the theater. It's an inability
to write. Let's get back to the reviews of George
Bernard Shaw. He liked very little but in casti-
gating the play he made it so interesting I think

he sent people to the theater. And Mr. Kerr
can write that way — /110

Mixed voices /111

Watts: Don't you think that when Mr.
Kerr does like something, he certainly — /112

Merrick: Yes, he can. He can — /113

Mixed voices /114

Hellman: Forgive me, I don't like discussing Mr. Kerr. /115

Kerr: It doesn't bother me. /116

Hellman: I have no objections to it as a
matter of taste; I object to it — /117

Mixed voices /118

Kerr: Again, not to cop a plea but you're
confusing, I think, categories. Shaw, I think,
was a weekly critic and that makes quite a bit
of difference. He was also a genius and that
makes a difference too. He also disliked the
importance of being earnest which brings us
back to the peculiarity of the attitudes that
some of us have sometime. /119

Goldman: Gentlemen and Miss Hellman,
our time races away and in talking about the
tension between the theater and the critics I
think we ought to get into one thing, namely,
the statement being made by some serious
critics, or ones who consider themselves serious, that what is wrong with the theater is the
producer, and more particularly they lambast
our guest, Mr. Merrick. I'm talking about a
statement like that of Mr. Brustein in the —
/120

Merrick: Oh, now, wait! We were talking
about drama criticism here. Let's stick to the
subject. We're not talking about producers.
Can we reserve that for another day? /121

Goldman: I think what he's saying is that
criticism in the U.S., as I understand the
article, has to be harsh because of what the
producers are doing. And you — /122

Mixed voices /123

Merrick: About the producers, we're producing the best that is available today. There's
no doubt about that. If anything gets away
from us, then off-Broadway will pick it up.
There might be a stray masterpiece around but
we're certainly producing the best that is
being written, and most of us are passing out
large advances and trying to encourage new
writing and new writers. In every possible
way, there are prizes for playwriting. It is not
coming through; it is just one of those periods.
I don't know why. Would you say, Mr. Kerr,

that we're doing the best that is around— /124

Kerr: David, I think I agree with everything you said there; that is, you're producing all that is available. I don't think there are any real lost masterpieces floating anywhere. I certainly don't. The only thing that I would question is that, while you are doing the best that is available and the best that you can, you mustn't ask a reviewer to say that it's better than that. /125

Merrick: I'm only asking one reviewer to— /126

Mixed voices /127

Merrick: Get in line with the others a little more. /128

Kerr: Well, you see, you have made several broad statements today which I have not actually checked myself and I'm not sure that you have. /129

Merrick: Well, I have. /130

Kerr: I would like to know the facts and figures in black and white. I could tell you this—it's three or four years ago and I may have deteriorated terribly since, but three or four years ago *Variety* did a roundup and it was across the top of the page that Kerr was the most accurate critic; that is to say, that instead of being out of line with all the other reviewers, I was the one, commercially speaking—I don't know if I should be flattered by this—who was most nearly on the button. /131

Goldman: Not with Miss Hellman here. /132

Mixed voices /133

Hellman: Forgive me. I think this is a shocking way to talk about criticism. /134

Kerr: I don't like it either. /135

Hellman: Just shocking. I'm uncertain I would have been on this program if I'd known this was going to be what we thought about criticism. Who gets this or who was the most popular—this is what's the matter with the theater, of course. /136

Watts: I don't think— /137

Hellman: This is exactly why good writers don't like the theater, why they write novels and poetry and do not come into the theater. /138

Kerr: I don't think any present-day reviewer—would you agree with this, Dick?—really conducts that kind of guessing game that

you're talking about, where he tries to anticipate or— /139

Mixed voices /140

Hellman: The fact that we're talking about it must be that they take it seriously. /141

Goldman: Miss Hellman and gentlemen, I want to use the last fifteen minutes on this point that Miss Hellman is making, namely, what in the world should the critic do? I want to find out as quickly as possible before we do that if the table is ready to dismiss the kind of thing that Robert Brustein is saying, namely, that the critic ought to get in there and whale away at the producer—more particularly, Mr. Merrick—because, to quote Brustein, "Merrick discriminates neither against the good nor the bad so long as it makes money." You all know this type of criticism. Now, is this— /142 . . .

Merrick: . . . I would ask the two gentlemen seated here as to whether my motive as a producer, based on the plays I've produced, has been entirely making money. They know the kind of plays I've produced. I will turn that over to them for a moment. /143

Goldman: Mr. Watts? /144

Watts: I disagree heartily with that. /145

Mixed voices /146

Kerr: You know perfectly well, David, that I've admired some of the serious plays that you have produced or brought from abroad. I will say this: I have sometimes questioned your own treatment of them in the advertising campaign. For instance, . . . /147

[Discussion centers upon methods used to promote *Look Back in Anger* and *Taste of Honey,* and the Kerr review of *Taste of Honey.*]

Goldman: Gentlemen, I don't think we're going to be very profitable along that road. /148

Miss Hellman, let's come back to this basic point of our discussion. What should the theater critic in the United States be doing today? Do I understand you correctly when you say that you think that, by and large, the metropolitan critic is essentially telling the reader, "Is this going to be a hit or not? Is it the fashionable thing to go to or not?" And that actually he ought to be pursuing a more British-type criticism, so to speak, in which he would put the play in context— /149

Hellman: No, you are misunderstanding. I don't think there's a reviewer on a paper that really tells people whether it's a hit or a failure, maybe on some that I don't read. That was not my point. My point is that I don't think he has long enough to consider in most cases. The standards are not high enough, high enough in the sense of intelligent enough. That's all I mean, intelligent enough in most cases, not in all cases. I do agree with Mr. Merrick that if you like—we are all faced with that, read books, we all have a nice time reading, so I have a nice time reading comic strips and science fiction and detective stories. I don't take them quite so seriously as I do, say, the bad novel of a good writer. And that's really what I'm saying, that I don't think that is done often enough. I think that's what Mr. Merrick is probably saying. /150

Mr. Merrick and I are saying different things and we're saying different things because we're in a different business. Mr. Merrick is right in worrying about the success or failure. I think I am correct in saying, as much as I'd like to have success, it's not my business. My business is only to write a good play. And I wish for that that the standards were higher than they are. Even sometimes when they're liked, I wished they were. It's the only way I have of learning. And there, I think, my case is almost proved by the fact that we've had this discussion so much on the basis of what the reader thinks and how popular the critic is or how unpopular the critic is or what are the influential newspapers. I don't mean to make fun of commerce. God knows I like money but I don't think those are the terms we should be talking about—that serious critics or serious people in the business should be talking about. /151

Goldman: Mr. Watts? /152

Watts: I would like to defend the idea of having the reviews written quickly on the first night. I think they have a value in that immediate white-hot reaction that the reviewer has. And I don't think that if we had more time that he would have much change. Some of the excitement of the things he likes might go out without improving the reviews. I think that is demonstrated by the openings on Saturday night—Mr. Kerr has strength of character to write his review immediately but I haven't. I take all day Sunday and I don't think the review is any better any way. It's not better written, it's not better thought out. /153

Hellman: That may be— /154

Watts: There's great value in having white-hot reaction. /155

Kerr: I tried it that way too and I find that your enthusiasm diminishes just a little bit, as it always does, as you come away from a thing. It's not quite as hot twenty-four hours later. I would like to say this: I think what you're asking for, Miss Hellman, is criticism, you see. Now, I— /156

Hellman: Yes, I am. /157

Kerr: I have a kind of heretical point of view myself on that which will do me no good at all. My own feeling is that criticism has nothing to do with the supreme court function that you attribute to the critics. I think it's a conversation and discussion with a reader or an audience after they've seen the play. Now, that would be my own personal ideal. /158

Hellman: Well, I'm asking for something else and perhaps it's part of what David's talking about. There is a great deal of difference in a bad review—by that I mean a very critical review—written by somebody who has, in a sense, goodwill. I think there are a number of you who have. One senses this in the review immediately, as one senses most things in writing. There is a great deal to be said for a kind of angry review. I think that's part of what David means. It just comes down to mere journalism and not criticism. /159

I think when I used to review books I made a point of saying that sometimes it was the bad book of a good writer and that, I think, is a very necessary thing to say even when you dislike something. There is, I think, a difference between the musical and a straight play. I didn't like Mr. Williams's play this year, as most other people didn't like it, but I really do believe Mr. Williams is owed the respect of not bringing up his past, necessarily, but of saying this man is a decent writer. /160

Watts: Didn't we say that? /161

Hellman: Some of you did. Some of you did and I think there was a quality of anger. I think it was true in my case very often. I think most people with standards—that's my plea, for standards—that's the only standard one can have. Not to like or dislike something. We like or dislike what each of us likes or dislikes. But there must be some standard of judgment. /162

Kerr: You said something a moment ago which seems to me relevant to something else that David said, which is this business of, oh well, you read detective stories or what have you, but then if you take a serious novel—in effect, you said you judge it on a somewhat different level. Now, for instance, I have never in my life consciously altered a standard because I was going to a musical or going to a serious play, not consciously. But I do think that you're always aware of what it is you're looking at. And you do try to describe it and respond to it in those terms. For instance, you mentioned my liking *Little Me.* Well, yes, I did. But I like it for what it was, which was a series of, I thought, quite amusing parodies of a television kind that I enjoy. /163

Mixed voices /164

Merrick: But if you aim higher, the criticism goes higher. /165

Kerr: Oh, yes, we demand more of him because the writer himself has made a lot of— /166

Watts: I think my point— /167

Mixed voices /168

Hellman: Now, now, that's the point we're disagreeing on. I don't agree with you at all. I don't think the writer's intention has anything to do with those things. Because Mr. Smith aims higher than Mr. Jones doesn't mean you either have to be kind or less kind. /169

Kerr: Don't you think you must first try to understand the play? And what it is saying and— /170

Hellman: Yes, I do. /171

Kerr: And what it is doing. /172

Hellman: But I think one should understand one's prejudices as well. /173

Kerr: Oh, yes. /174

Hellman: I don't happen to like musicals very well. That was one of the reasons I quit the reviewing job I was talking about. If you like them better than you like straight plays, then I really don't think you should be reviewing— /175

Kerr: Oh, but I don't— /176

Hellman: I don't think you do but we're talking about— /177

Mixed voices /178

Goldman: Mr. Merrick? /179

Merrick: I am at the box office and I have to represent whatever you have written and sell tickets or it will fold very rapidly. And I can tell you what your readers want to know is whether it's an entertainment or not. Now, they can be entertained by an allegory, a play in blank verse, a melodrama, a serious play, a tragedy, a musical comedy; they can be entertained in many, many ways. But what they really want to know is, are they going to be bored or entertained? And I'm afraid it does become a kind of a consumer's research report. That's what they want. /180

Mixed voices /181

Hellman: The people with enough money to buy tickets— /182

Mixed voices /183

Merrick: No, in general— /184

Mixed voices /185

Hellman: We have lost the whole intelligent intellectual world in the theater—I know we have. One can tell that by looking at an audience. It's a totally different audience from that of twenty years ago. /186

Merrick: That's absolutely true and perhaps that's because of the inordinately high cost of the theater tickets— /187

Hellman: Perhaps it's— /188

Merrick: There's one thing that you raised, Mr. Goldman, that I'd like to defend here in that piece of Mr. Brustein about producers. Don't you think, Miss Hellman, that regardless of what happens to the play, that you expect your producer to fight for it to the last bloody ditch, no matter what? /189

Hellman: Indeed. /190

Merrick: Isn't that his responsibility? /191

Hellman: Absolutely. /192

Merrick: And if it turns out to be not quite as we all hoped it would, and rightly or wrongly, the criticism didn't turn out all that favorable, isn't it the producer's job to get out there and sell it and fight for it? /193

Hellman: It certainly is. /194

Goldman: Miss Hellman, does that include the kind of thing that Mr. Brustein was criticizing— /195

Hellman: I don't agree with Mr. Brustein. /196

Goldman: And about the methods of selling? /197

Hellman: That hasn't anything to do with the theater. Even if it were true—and I don't think it is true in David's case—it has nothing to do with the theater. What the producer produces has to do with what the writer writes. Both Mr. Kerr and Mr. Merrick are right in that nothing has been passed up that I know of. /198

Goldman: And you don't agree with the criticism of the methods of selling the play? /199

Hellman: Oh, I haven't always agreed with David. They're not my methods particularly but I certainly think plays should be sold. I don't think the method is of any—I'm not interested in the methods. /200

Goldman: We have just a couple of minutes here. All these things have been said about theatrical criticism, some pessimistic, some unhappy, some happy; is anything changing in it? Is the situation going to remain essentially the same? /201

Kerr: I would like to see a change. /202

Goldman: Is there— /203

Kerr: I think the root problem really is that at the present time the theater in itself is not a sufficiently vital and exciting an experience to animate its own audience. You see, in other words, the audience just doesn't think, "Oh, my God, it's so good I've got to go, I want to go, I really want to go." They don't see it that way. /204

Merrick: Can I ask— /205

Kerr: Let me finish this, please. And because they don't behave in that way, suddenly the reviewer becomes so enormously important— /206

Mixed voices /207

Goldman: We only have a minute, Mr. Merrick. /208

Merrick: Well, let's hope that you, for a play that you like inordinately, that you will try to create that excitement for us by not only your original review but by getting after it later. I think that that is something we deserve, when you like it that much. /209

Kerr: I'm talking now about a whole feeling and period and time in the theater. I'm hoping that's going to change. In other words, I'm hoping the theater itself is going to rediscover its own vital nature. I hate to use words like that but there's a kind of animal quality that could come alive in the theater. /210

Merrick: When you said it will get worse before it gets better, I hope— /211

Mixed voices /212

Goldman: I'm afraid on that somewhat quizzical note, we are cut off. I'll be back in just a moment. /213

Discussions for Collateral Study

1. William H. Lawrence, George Herman, Sander Vanocur, and John F. Kennedy, "A Conversation with the President," *Representative American Speeches: 1962–1963,* ed. Lester Thonssen (New York: H. W. Wilson Company, 1963), pp. 145–172.

2. Walter Reuther and Harlow Curtice, "Administered Prices," *The Speaker's Resource Book,* ed. Carroll C. Arnold, Douglas Ehninger, and John C. Gerber (Chicago: Scott, Foresman and Company, 1961), pp. 199–215.

Speaker,
  adaptation of, to audience response, 51
  attitude of audience toward, 48-49
  characteristics of good, 3-6
  suitability of specific purpose to, 44
Speaking,
  mechanics of, 75-80
  methods of, 10-11
Special topical sequence, 140-141
Specific instances, as support, 119-120, 183
Specific purpose,
  attitude of audience toward, 50-51
  formulating the, 12, 43-44
Speech,
  beginning a, 162-170
  as circular response, 27-28
  delivery of a, 16-17, 60-70, 74-94, 241-247
  development of, in children, 25-26
  ending a, 170-174
  as habit, 30-31
  importance of, 2-3
  preparation of a, 11-16
  purpose of a, 40-44
  social function of, 24-27
  sources of knowledge about, 33-36
Speech act, nature of, 27-31
Speech content,
  for broadcasting, 248-249
  for commencements, 233
  for courtesy, 229
  to entertain, 132-133
  for goodwill, 232-233
  to inform, 180-181
  to introduce, 227-228
  to pay tribute, 230-231
  to persuade, 197-204
Speech material (See Sources, Supporting material.)
Speech organization, 126-127, 130, 138-159, 180, 186-194, 208-223, 249
  (Also see Outline samples, Motivated sequence.)
Speeches,
  of acceptance, 228-229
  classroom, 10-17
  to entertain, 132-135
  to explain, 126-129
  for goodwill, 231-233
  to inform, 178-194
  one-point, 112-137
  opposing a policy, 217-218
  to persuade, 196-223

on proposition of fact, 219-221
on proposition of value, 221-223
to prove, 129-132
of response, 228-229
for special occasions, 226-235
of tribute, 229-231
urging adoption of policy, 212-217
of welcome, 228-229
Startling statement,
  to begin a speech, 166-167
  to stimulate discussion, 270
Statement,
  in need step, 187, 212
  in satisfaction step, 213
Statistics, as support, 120-122, 180
Steps of pitch, 88-89
Stevenson, Adlai E., 164
  Eulogy on Eleanor Roosevelt, 318-321
Stilwell, Charles J., 117-118
Stowe, Leland, 210-211
Subject,
  adapting physical behavior to, 69-70
  attitude of audience toward, 49-50
  dividing among panelists, 266
  knowledge of audience concerning, 47
  in parliamentary meeting, 278-283
  referring to, 163-164
  selecting and narrowing, 11-12, 152
Subordinate ideas,
  arranging, 145-148
  coordinating, 147
  subordinating, 145
  supporting, 148
Suits, Guy, Polymers, Crystals and Plasmas, 286-294
Summary,
  in discussion, 261, 263, 273
  final, 171-172, 176, 189, 192-193
  initial, 187-188, 191
Supporting material, 112-135
  arranging, 145-148
  defined, 113
  to entertain, 132-135
  to explain, 126-129
  forms of verbal, 113-125
  need for, 112-113
  to prove, 129-132
  in speech to inform, 180
  visual, 125-126
Suspense, as factor of attention, 185, 248-249
Swabb, Joel L., 169
Swift, Jonathan, 101